If I Could Turn and Meet Myself:
THE LIFE OF ALDEN NOWLAN

Alden Nowlan, 1982-1983. KENT NASON

If I could turn and meet myself

The Life of
ALDEN
NOWLAN

PATRICK TONER

GOOSE LANE

Edited by Laurel Boone.
Cover photo by Kent Nason.
Cover design by Julie Scriver.
Book design by Julie Scriver and Ryan Astle.
Printed in Canada by VISTAinfo.
10 9 8 7 6 5 4 3 2 1

Canadian Cataloguing in Publication Data

Toner, Patrick, 1968-
If I could turn and meet myself: the life of Alden Nowlan

Includes bibliographical references and index.
ISBN 0-86492-265-5

1. Nowlan, Alden, 1933-1983.   2. Authors, Canadian (English)—20th century—
Biography. I. Title.

PS8527.O798Z86 2000   C818'.5409   C00-900157-3
PR9199.3.N6Z86 2000

Published with the financial support of the Canada Council for the Arts, the Government of Canada through the Book Publishing Industry Development Program, the New Brunswick Department of Economic Development, Tourism and Culture, and a grant from the Humanities and Social Sciences Federation of Canada, using funds provided by the Social Sciences and Humanities Research Council of Canada.

Written with the support of the Arts Branch of the New Brunswick Department of Municipalities, Culture and Housing and the Explorations program of the Canada Council.

Goose Lane Editions
469 King Street
Fredericton, New Brunswick
CANADA E3B 1E5

For Ervette Hamilton (1910-1999),
the aunt of this book.

CONTENTS

INTRODUCTION

from **The Kookaburra's Song**

If I could turn and meet myself as
*   I was then,*
gaze into that solemn face, those
*   unblinking eyes,*
I suppose I'd laugh until I cried,
*   then laugh again.*

I never met Alden Nowlan. When he died in 1983, I was fifteen and only dimly aware of his importance. Like many New Brunswickers, I was acquainted with his weekly column in the *Telegraph-Journal*, and knew somehow that he was a poet. Thankfully, the public education system filled some of the gaps in my knowledge.

It is hard to imagine what a meeting between us might have been like, although in the course of studying Nowlan's life and art I have found myself yielding to the temptation. Part of the wonder of his writing is how he can make a reader feel as though the two of them are sitting together in a quiet room having a profound and intimate conversation. But I know from first-hand accounts what such conversations with Nowlan the man were sometimes like: one-sided affairs in which the poet's audience was expected to listen, not to dispute or — especially — to probe.

What would our conversation have been like, then, given the fact that as a biographer I could not have helped but prod this great bear in an attempt to elicit answers? I may have earned a growl for my pains, although Nowlan's friend Leo Ferrari, in a memoir published recently in the *Telegraph-Journal*'s supplement *The New Brunswick Reader*, suggests a more gentle yet equally frustrating result. Ferrari relates an incident in which a student interviewer bent on extracting "the truth" from Nowlan was subjected, not to insults and browbeating, but instead to continual interruptions when the poet lumbered out to the kitchen on some mysterious errand, always returning smelling more strongly of gin. The interviewer, at length reduced to shouting questions at an inert mass nearly passed out in his La-Z-Boy, gave up the exercise. With both passive and active weapons at his disposal against such interlopers, Nowlan doubtless would have proved to be a challenging subject, though not an impossible one. Possessed of probably the most intimate and confessional voice in Canadian letters, he could be gracious and accessible to interviewers who came with the right spirit, provided they came on his terms.

Anne Greer, the first person to conduct serious biographical research on Nowlan for her 1973 MA thesis, was one of those lucky ones who was able to earn his trust. She described to me her fascination with the poet, stemming from the almost archetypal quality of his life and writing. Michael Brian Oliver, another writer who has taken a serious look at how Nowlan's life affected his art, echoes critic Milton Wilson's observation that Nowlan's writing lies in the realm of mythology; they describe his work as "pre-literary." When I interviewed Leo Ferrari for my own 1993 MA thesis on the religious imagery in Nowlan's poetry, he characterized his friend's life as a deliberately created thing, much like one of his own poems or stories, something fashioned as he went along.

Much the same can be said for any of us: we all fashion our lives as we go along, plucking the threads that please us from a formless and tangled ball and weaving them into a fragile pattern that shifts and changes as the ball accumulates random straws, hairs and bits of dust. Nowlan was one of those for whom the process of weaving his life took on a life of its own. He came to believe that the small scrap of fabric he had created could stretch to cover a tangled, chaotic ball growing bigger by the day.

Springing from an impoverished Nova Scotia family that had few possessions and no power, he claimed the one thing he could control: his own story. During his early childhood, he could control little else. Young Alden was abandoned by nearly every adult he depended upon in an environment that offered emotional shelter as meagre as the physical shelter provided by his father's house. Nevertheless, he returned obsessively to this world in his writings. Though he speaks of his imaginative world as a means of escape, he could not pull away from the harsh reality of his youth. He had to return — if only symbolically — to impose his will on the time and place that once held him captive, as he says in his poem "The Boil," "now/ at last/ master/ rather than/ servant/ of the pain."

Dealing with the question of truth in Nowlan's fiction and life is a frustrating exercise, like the poser of the box surrounding the statement "Everything inside this box is a lie" or the M.C. Escher drawing of two hands each sketching the other with a pencil. What does it matter whether Nowlan (or, for that matter, any other writer) is telling the factual truth, the underlying truth or the personal truth in his writings? Are writers not paid to tell lies? Perhaps. But Nowlan's readers accepted that what he was writing was the truth, and, more significantly, he came to share that belief. It is not necessary to go to the indefensible extreme of assuming that the "I" or the "Kevin O'Brien" of his poetry and fiction is the literal Nowlan, that, for instance, he literally did go to the store one day for a loaf of bread and returned with a new life in a different world. What is important is that Nowlan believed that this is what happened. If his oeuvre has an over-arching theme, it is that people must own their own lives, really own them, with all their bread, wine and salt, their tears and laughter. *If I Could Turn and Meet Myself* examines the price Nowlan paid to own his life, and it asks whether sometimes he may have paid too much.

Nowlan's life and art bring three other fundamental issues into sharp focus. One is the need shared by many writers to capture the spirit of the geographical and cultural heritage from which they spring. But does this devotion to a sense of place alienate readers who do not share that cultural and geographic heritage? This question has perennial force in a Canada which, some have claimed, needs a unifying myth to offset disintegrating pressures from the dominating cultures of England, formerly, and now of the United States.

When set beside the many examples of good regional literature, however, the regionalism debate becomes moot. Literature that is parochial or folkloric appeals only to a small audience, especially when those who share the particular geographic and cultural heritage are being exploited to add "local colour" to literature that is otherwise trite or sentimental. In every country, strong regional literature retains consistent appeal to readers from outside the region and even internationally. From there, the stream of debate usually diverges into stale bogs such as the question of what constitutes a region ("Isn't Toronto just as much a region as Cape Breton?") and whether universal truths can be found in literature set in Cape Breton or, say, Spoon River or Desolation Creek. Nowlan got sucked into this debate, but the development of his art and his later interviews and letters show that it preoccupied him less and less as time went on, much to his credit.

A second issue, which he addressed with more enthusiasm and less rationality, was the question of whether an academic or critic could also be a creative writer, or vice versa. Nowlan branded most literary theory and criticism as chicanery or sophistry without recognizing that the same charge can be brought against some literature and against politics, economics, religion or even professional sports. Audiences need various perspectives in order to be informed. Being both a literary writer and a literary critic is admittedly a rare ability, but it is no more of a stretch than being both a poet and a journalist, a feat of which Nowlan considered himself entirely capable.

Related to the critic vs. artist debate is the wider and more fruitful question about how accessible art should be. Should the artist strive for excellence within the field no matter how restricted the audience becomes, or is the artist's responsibility to reach out to encompass as wide an audience as possible, even if the quality of the art *as art* suffers as a result? This question is by no means unique to Nowlan, but his confident answer to it deserves serious consideration. In an artistic field and in a country where the material rewards of playing to the masses were not (and are still not) all that much different from playing to the discerning few, Nowlan still chose the larger public as his audience. What is more, Nowlan's writing displays a confidence in the validity of "ordinary" people's lives that is lacking in the voices of those writers, artists and politicians who claim to speak for the people while in fact speaking at them.

Nowlan believed that what made literature great was not artistic virtuosity or verbal gymnastics but rather its ability to reach people on a personal level. And how could a writer best reach out to people? In an age of televised pablum, in any way he can. Nowlan's writing mattered to the "ordinary reader"; he could tear his audience away from their televisions long enough to think for a bit. But his art suffered as a result, at times becoming somewhat prosaic and sentimental. Moreover, Nowlan did not see himself as someone who could educate his audience's taste, to attract the "ordinary" reader with seeming unsophistication and then turn around and demonstrate the levels of complexity inherent in the printed word. His early poetry shows that he had the ability to do this, but he made a conscious, clear-headed decision to sacrifice praise from the ivory tower so that people who would not normally read poetry and fiction would read his.

As a consequence, it is mostly creative writers rather than academics and critics who have undertaken serious critical commentary on Nowlan's work. Michael Brian Oliver and Robert Gibbs are the foremost of these. Oliver has published two book-length essays on Nowlan's work which, despite their tendency to beat the Maritimer's drum a little too loudly, provide valuable and original insight into Nowlan's work. Gibbs, Nowlan's literary executor, has edited several collections of Nowlan's poetry and prose and has contributed critical essays that show that Nowlan's work can be taken seriously by academics. But few academic writers have taken up Gibbs's challenge. Though there are occasional MA theses and scholarly articles that appear at regular intervals from the early 1970s until today, they are indifferent in quality and lead to a dead end. Janice Kulyk Keefer, in her critical study of Maritime literature, *Under Eastern Eyes*, fulfills what Michael Brian Oliver attempted to do by discussing Nowlan within the overall context of Maritime and Canadian literature, and she does an admirable job of it. But the most profitable approach to gauging the critical reception of Nowlan's works was, for me, to follow the comments of book reviewers throughout Nowlan's career, as they reliably indicate not only Nowlan's status among his contemporaries, but also the critical preoccupations of the time, which had an effect on the way Nowlan and his fellow Canadian writers created literature.

Like any of us, Nowlan never expected that the events of his life would actually happen to him, although in the fullness of time it must have sometimes seemed as if he were pulling the strings. He planned to be a hoary-haired Old Testament prophet, a writer-adventurer like Jack London, and the king of a small country such as Nicaragua. Although it may have been a disassociative tactic on his part, Nowlan maintained to the end that he was a collection of semi-detached and often contradictory selves, some isolated in time and place, others existing side by side to spring into being in certain situations and in the presence of certain other personalities, all with their own multiple selves. In my attempt to discover the "real" Alden Nowlan, I may only have created another Kevin O'Brien, another facet in the prism that refracts the original image of Nowlan, a man no more able to meet himself than I was able to meet him.

Keeping the various persons named Kevin O'Brien straight in my head was a gradual task, dependent on alternating rounds of reading Nowlan's work and the reviews and critiques of it, examining his personal papers and correspondence, and talking to those who knew him. Inevitably, each stage of research elucidated the stages that had come before. I discover new, unexplored facets of Nowlan's character whenever I peruse a letter or a poem that I have not read for a while. Each of the Kevin O'Briens tries to keep the other ones honest.

I have tried to construct this biography as narrative, allowing the reader to accompany Nowlan as he lives his life again in these pages. But *If I Could Turn and Meet Myself* is not really his life, of course; Nowlan is playing another role, acting out another of his selves. As director of the drama, I wanted to step back from time to time and allow characters to speak in their own voices without my intervention. I did not create the unmediated dialogue out of my imagination. In some cases, I blended two or more accounts of the same incident into one scene. In other cases dialogue represents verbatim renderings of interviews or letters. Where appropriate, I indicate the source of these dialogue passages in the chapter endnotes.

Naturally, names change as characters mature: Alden the child becomes Nowlan the man, "Johnnie" grows into "John." Naming Nowlan's cousin and unofficial "sister," a figure of great and continuing influence in his life, presented a different challenge. Sylvia Reese became Sylvia Pride when she married Jim Pride, but she made another transition in the mid-1970s when she changed her name to Rachel Paulson Pride. Nowlan lost touch with her for a time and did not learn of her new name until he re-established contact with her in 1980; even then he continued to refer to her as Sylvia. Recently, Rachel Pride remarried and is now Rachel Sherman. I decided to refer to her in my text as Sylvia, as Nowlan did; in the endnotes she is Rachel Pride, the name under which she is listed in the catalogue of the Nowlan papers at the University of Calgary, although I include her former name in parentheses to link the name in the notes to that in the text.

I am indebted to Apollonia Steele, Jean Moore and the other staff at the Special Collections in the University of Calgary Library for the generous help and assistance they gave to me during the months I spent reading Nowlan's collected papers. I also have Mary Flagg, Linda Baier and the staff of the Archives and Special Collections, Harriet Irving Library, University of New Brunswick, to thank for retrieving the same material for me, time and time again, so that I could take one more (never "one last") look at it. My time at the National Library and the National Archives was made abundantly productive by the assistance of Sarah Montgomery, Wilma MacDonald, Anne Goddard and Linda Hoad. For some collections, researchers need permission from the copyright owners or their estates to photocopy and, in some cases, to examine materials, and so I thank Robert Weaver, Louis Dudek, Elizabeth Brewster, Fred Cogswell and particularly Claudine Nowlan for allowing me to do this.

Many of the people who knew Nowlan were generous with their time in granting interviews to share their memories with me. Without them the reader would feel as if Nowlan were again "holding forth" without any other voices to join in the conversation. In the course of my research for this book, the following people contributed their views, either in short conversations, letters or recorded interviews, to help me form a picture of Nowlan: Harold Aiton, Keith Anthony, Lawrence Anthony, Bruce Armstrong, Lennie Barkhouse, Brian Bartlett, Nancy Bauer, William Bauer, Ronald Best, Tim Bond, Elizabeth Brewster, Harry Bruce, Barry Cameron, Ian Cameron, Dalton Camp, Nicholas Catanoy, Lesley Choyce, Carol Church, Hugh Clark, William H. Clarke, Fred Cogswell, Gregory Cook, Louis Cormier, Ralph Costello, Elsie Cotter, Tom Crowther, John Drew, Louis Dudek, Alden Durling, Leo Ferrari, Nathalie Forrestal, Tom Forrestal, Col. Ian Fraser, Ray Fraser, Sharon Fraser, Anne Greer, John Grube, Ervette Hamilton, Fred Hatfield, Kay Hatfield, Fred Hazel, Ken Homer, Edward D. Ives, Leroy Johnson, Walter Learning, Barry Lord, Owen Lowe, Bernie MacDonald, Roy MacSkimming, Gail (Sanford) Manning, John Metcalf, Jim Morrison, John Mulcahey, Jim Murray, John Newlove, Ethyl Ogilvie, Michael Brian Oliver, Harriet (Nowlan) Ottie, Mary Pacey, Hilda Palmer, Al Pittman, Harold Plummer, Al Purdy, Albert Reese, David Adams Richards, Vera Sanford, Gerald Shaw, Joe Sherman, Rachel Paulson Pride Sherman (Sylvia Reese), Laura (Clark) Slicter, Raymond Souster, Jim Stewart, David Tees, Kent Thompson, Alice (Shaw) Tonning, Yvonne Trainer, Kay Turner, Andrew Wainwright, Marty Walker, Robert Weaver, Jackie Webster, Hilda Woolnought and John Zanes.

Dr. Ian Cameron shared not just his memories of his friend but also gave me a medical perspective on Nowlan's life, as did Dr. David Tees. John Sawicki, of Public Affairs at Conestoga College, set me straight on the difference between the college and nearby Wilfrid Laurier University. Leanne Comerford and Bernie MacDonald provided pharmaceutical information that helped me understand the effect of some of the medication Nowlan took during his life. Dr. Greg Marquis gave me some background information on New Brunswick's nineteenth-century poor laws. I also thank Silver Donald Cameron and the Beaton Institute at the University College of Cape Breton for sending me copies of a recorded interview between Cameron and Nowlan, and to Colleen Hannah for allowing me to see a first draft of the play *Lockhartville*. Fellow travellers Brian Guns, Wendy Scott, Andrew Steeves and Tony Tremblay lent me their views, not just on Nowlan, but also on three of his significant companions, Ray Fraser, David Adams Richards and Fred Cogswell. Eric Swanick, New Brunswick's legislative librarian, provided a wealth of knowledge and support.

Although she declined to be interviewed during the writing of *If I Could Turn and Meet Myself*, Claudine Nowlan was kind enough to allow me access to her late husband's collected papers at the University of Calgary. She and Professor Robert Gibbs have also granted me permission to quote from Nowlan's published and unpublished writings, and for this I thank them.

My last words of acknowledgement are for the more personal support I have received from people such as my editor, Laurel Boone, who supported this project back when it was only an idea. She also helped me to assemble my applications for the Canada Council Explorations Program and the New Brunswick Arts Branch's Documentation Grant program, without which I would not have had the resources to begin my research and to take the project to a point where it would have been difficult to abandon it. The financial support of these institutions, combined with Laurel's careful editorial eye, have allowed me to see writing for what it really is: a lot of hard work. I also thank Susanne Alexander, the publisher, and the staff at Goose Lane Editions for their support, and I especially commend Julie Scriver, the art director, for a wonderful book design. Thanks and apologies to my parents, family and friends — especially Dana and Shauna — who tolerated my absences and learned to stop asking me how the book was going, even though they always carried the wish for its success in their hearts.

Ervette (Reese) Hamilton, Alden Nowlan's aunt, supported my

efforts back when I was still writing my thesis, even before I took on the project of writing Nowlan's biography. She and the family of Dora, her daughter, in a way planted the seed from which this book grew and nourished it with memories, photographs and old letters that would have otherwise been unavailable. As I discovered during the course of my research, Ervette's memory was very reliable. After the manuscript had undergone its second revision and was on its way to publication, I received word from Ervette's granddaughter Cyndi that Ervette was stricken with cancer and was not expected to survive long. Ever the matriarch and touchstone for her fragmented family, Ervette wanted to see what the book she had helped with would say about her family's most famous son. Of course I agreed, and a couple of weeks later Dora, Cyndi and Hugh Boudreau drove me down to Noel, Nova Scotia, for the visit. There, on a hospital bed in her son Winston's parlour, Ervette read through the first two chapters, taking breaks for a nap or to offer some corrections or suggestions to the text. Her mind was as sharp as ever to the end. It is to her memory that this book is dedicated.

A Poem to My Mother

I being twelve and scared, my lantern shook,
shrunk to string my stomach knotted,
breathing the sultry mustiness of hay
and dung in the cowbarn,
and the heifer calving.

Ours was a windy country and its crops
were never frivolous, malicious rocks
kicked at the plough and skinny cattle broke
ditch ice for mud to drink and pigs were axed.

Finding the young bull drowned, his shoulders wedged
into a sunken hogshead in the pasture,
I vomited, my mother, yet the flies
around his dull eyes vanished with the kiss
your fingers sang into my hair all night.

Mother, O gentler Christ, O warmest bed,
hearing the wind at bay your heart was milk;
under the crazy quilting of such love,
needles of adoration knit
bandages for my babied eyes; I slept.

The genial souls lying in Fredericton's Forest Hill Cemetery were probably hoping for a resting place as peaceful and secluded as the town they built. Yet the hands of chance and change have been at work here, transforming the social as well as the physical geography of the provincial capital they called "The Celestial City." Once a secluded spot overlooking Fredericton, the cemetery is now squeezed between new housing developments on one side and a busy highway on the other. The highway cuts Forest Hill off from the campus of the University of New Brunswick, which in the days since many of these people were buried has charged up the hill with the enthusiasm of a college freshman.

The names on Forest Hill's gravestones remind the visitor of Fredericton's genteel academic and bureaucratic heritage. The tycoons and industrialists who once called Fredericton home, including Lord Beaverbrook and Alexander "Boss" Gibson, lie in other graveyards, their monuments the many streets and buildings in the city that bear their names. The denizens of Forest Hill Cemetery left monuments of a different sort: books, laws, academic buildings, land for the University of New Brunswick and a stream of students; here lie members of Parliament, justices of the Supreme Court of Canada and New Brunswick, and some of Canada's most significant writers and professors.

In one spot a visitor will find the Bailey family: Professor Loring Woart Bailey, one of Canada's most distinguished nineteenth-century professors, and his grandson Alfred Goldsworthy Bailey, poet, anthropologist, founder of the literary magazine *The Fiddlehead* and a pioneer in forging a Canadian cultural identity. Farther up the hill rests Bailey's colleague Desmond Pacey, a New Zealander who tirelessly promoted Canadian literature long before most academics even acknowledged that there was such a thing. Across from Pacey, to the left, are the literary Roberts clan: George Goodridge Roberts, rector of Christ Church Parish Church and a canon of the Cathedral; his eldest son, Sir Charles G.D. Roberts, the poet and story-writer known as "the Father of Canadian Literature"; his youngest son, Theodore Goodridge Roberts, a poet, novelist and journalist; and his granddaughter, the poet Dorothy Roberts Leisner. Nearby, a few paces downhill beneath a spreading maple tree, lies George's nephew, Charles and Theodore's even more famous cousin, the poet Bliss Carman.

Butted up against the back side of Carman's grave marker sits a foreign-looking monument, a large Celtic cross marking the grave of an Irishman from Nova Scotia. He is a blue-collar proletarian among the political and cultural elite. No streets are named after him in his native village because there are no streets to be named, just a lone country road, a tiny community hall and St. Stephen's United Church. A grade-four dropout, he is nonetheless better known than any of them as New Brunswick's poet. The inscription on the stone is poetic, too:

"*Rest lightly on him O earth/ He loved you so*," and then, on the back of the stone, "*An nuaillanach mor/ Croi amhain, bealach amhain*": The big Nowlan/ One heart, one way.

"The Big Nowlan" was just one of the identities Alden Nowlan liked to assume. When signing letters to friends and family (and sometimes even to strangers) he preferred the more flowery "Ultan, Prince of Fortara, Duke of Wexford." Other self-invented monikers included "The Creature," "The Old Man," "The Mysterious Naked Man," or, a more simple name for intimate friends, plain "Al."

One such letter was written to a young friend who had won the University of New Brunswick's Bliss Carman prize, an award for promising student poets. "We drove past the cemetery where he's buried the other day," Nowlan wrote, referring to Carman. "Before we leave here I hope to go back and visit the old boy's grave. I'm not sure why. Perhaps simply because I hope somebody will visit mine. Not that it will matter *then* but it's nice to think about *now*. A man's funeral should be held while he's still alive and healthy enough to enjoy it."[1]

When Nowlan was buried, the ghosts of his fellow writers in Forest Hill were treated to a drama that some might have found moving, others sacrilegious. The funeral resembled the parties he hosted on New Year's Eve or in recognition of offbeat anniversaries, such as the poet William Blake's birthday or Irish king Brian Boru's victory at Clontarf. This final party also had its share of controversy; a few of Nowlan's friends found themselves struck from the guest list, once again arbitrarily banished from his company. There was music, love, tears and laughter, and one final drink, Nowlan claiming the lion's share of the booze.

On June 29, 1983, when they put Nowlan in the ground, the weather was sunny, the province having just experienced the first heat wave of the summer. Twelve days before the funeral, New Brunswick had welcomed Prince Charles and his new bride, Diana, on her first official visit to Canada. Richard Hatfield, New Brunswick's premier, had embarrassed himself by giving a rambling toast at the royal couple's banquet in Saint John (to which Nowlan had been invited) that earned Hatfield the scorn of the Fleet Street tabloids. Also in that month, Canada lost another of its great popular artists when Stan Rogers's plane burned on the tarmac at Cincinnati airport.

On the day of the funeral, the tiny chapel in the University of New Brunswick's Old Arts Building overflowed with people and emotion. The premier and a former premier's widow were among the invited, along with fellow poets, artists, journalists, professors and a small group of former students who had shared many late nights at Nowlan's home. One of the latter, Jim Stewart, who was a poet and a musician, played an Irish lament on his tin whistle. Overcome by emotion, Stewart ended the air by breaking the whistle over his knee, never again to sound another note.

Actor and director Walter Learning, Nowlan's friend and artistic collaborator, gave a eulogy that was a testament to the genuine nature of his friendships. "Whenever I left Alden, he always hugged me and said: 'If God loves you half as much as I do, you've got nothing to worry about. Keep the faith.' The Nowlan kept the faith, and if God loves him half as much as we do, he'll have nothing to worry about."[2]

At the grave site, after the coffin was lowered into the earth, Nowlan's son John broke the seal on a bottle of Jameson's Irish whiskey and poured it into a loving cup, a large four-handled vessel. The assembled mourners passed the whiskey around, and each one took a drink as two bagpipers played nearby. The novelist David Adams Richards poured the rest of the whiskey into the grave with the words, "Goodbye, brave fighter. Goodbye, great man." The cup joined the whistle and the identity disks of Nowlan's friend Col. Ian Fraser at the bottom of the grave.

But the ceremony would not be finished until the guests buried their host, first with vials of dirt from Ireland and from the site of the battle of Culloden. Nowlan's widow, Claudine, added a few handfuls of earth from the mound beside the grave. John doffed his jacket, grabbed a shovel from the nearby pile and, with the gravediggers looking on, began to bury Nowlan in earnest. Others joined in, taking turns with an extra shovel or throwing in clods of dirt with their hands, until the hole was at last filled in.[3]

During his time as writer-in-residence at the University of New Brunswick, Nowlan gained national prominence as a journalist, playwright, poet and writer of fiction. He was awarded Canada's highest honours and prizes for his writing. Along the way, he made many friends, earned a few enemies, was awarded two honorary degrees to supplement his grade-school education, met the royal family, and lived in a house he called "Windsor Castle." He decided that one of his friends was the only "rightful monarch" and started a restoration society, and he founded an academic society dedicated to proving that the Earth was flat. To his delight, he was a best man at three weddings.

Across the country, writers and journalists erected monuments of words to praise Nowlan's poetry and to sum up his literary legacy, and most tried to define Nowlan's stature, both as a writer and as a man. The editor of *Poetry Canada Review*, Clifton Whiten, called Nowlan "a Chaucer"[4]; Fraser Sutherland in the *Globe and Mail* lauded him as "the best modern poet the Maritimes has produced."[5] Other writers tried to give physical shape to the immense man with the gravelly voice. The poet Milton Acorn, no physical giant himself, conveyed the impression Nowlan created by their rare meetings: "The least that could be said was that he was taller than Mount Everest, because Everest neither had a mouth nor could write poetry."[6]

Beyond the hyperbole about Nowlan's heroic immensity, one could still hear echoes of the critical debates that had provoked so many academics, writers and "ordinary" readers during Nowlan's lifetime. Praise for Nowlan's art competed against the perception that it was fare for "ordinary people," *for* meaning in some cases "on behalf of" and in other cases "for the consumption of." Irving Layton's eulogy for CBC Radio, in which he admires Nowlan's "need for those rare moments that exalt and transform and that punctuate even the drabbest of lives with points of light"[7] is a good example of the former, in contrast to Ken Adachi's more limited assessment in the *Toronto Star* that Nowlan's "plain-spoken" poems "spoke to ordinary men and women, to the underprivileged in society."[8]

Writers still struggled over Nowlan's differentness. He did not just represent the unsophisticated and the unacademic (the "ordinary"), but — more troubling for some — he had achieved literary success and occasionally greatness without following the path that had been laid out by middle-class Canadian society. Nowlan had the wrong education, spoke with the wrong accent, lived in the wrong part of the country (though it was acceptable to come from the Maritimes), had all the wrong opinions and, what was worse, did not apologize for any of it. Though admired by Eli Mandel, with whom he shared the Governor General's Award for poetry, the Toronto poet still found it necessary in his tribute to try to draw a line between Nowlan and the Maritime tradition he embraced. "Alden Nowlan is dead," Mandel wrote "Young, a Maritimer, poet of small-town Maritime experience, recorder of the ironies, poverty and repression of small-town life; but also of the gifted intelligence that transcends such limitations."[9]

Years later, Nowlan readers might wonder if the poet so admired by the foremost writers during his life has not been neglected in death. In a 1996 article, critic Douglas Fetherling gives voice to the whispered suspicion that Nowlan's once gigantic stature has shrunk since his death. "The upward revision [of Nowlan's reputation] will be needed not so much in New Brunswick, where Nowlan's memory is still revered, but in the rest of the country where he's not so well remembered, and also in the US where, by contrast, there's always been a small but select band of Nowlan admirers."[10] In 1998, David Adams Richards's tone is ironic as he writes of the attention given to "other poets and literary gadflies and self-seeking pronouncers of the prevalent opinion," attention that has been denied to the more unfashionable Nowlan.[11] In death, as in life, Nowlan's work was dismissed by many readers, but even in dismissal his critics had to account for him, to explain him, unable simply to ignore the rough-hewn bull moose who had wandered past the fences into their neat literary village after everyone had been assured that the gates had been shut.

The threads of neglect and abandonment wove Nowlan's life together in a sometimes tragic, sometimes triumphant tapestry. Although his grave was surrounded by a circle of friends, none of his own relatives came to see their son off into the next life. No written acknowledgement from his family (save one cherished cousin) can be found among the sympathy cards and letters that poured in from well-wishers near and far. This lack of acknowledgement, however, was mutual. If anyone asked, which seldom happened, Nowlan would say that his mother had died when he was very young and that his sister lived in Connecticut. He did, in fact, have a cousin in Connecticut to whom he was close, Sylvia (later Rachel Paulson) Pride. But his biological sister was named Harriet, and she lives in British Columbia. His mother, Grace Reese, is still very much alive in 2000 and lives near the Nova Scotia village where she and her son were born. On the day of his funeral, in fact, Grace was flying from Halifax to Boston on the way to visit relatives in Massachusetts, accompanied by her sister, Nowlan's aunt, Ervette. Harriet's existence was actually no secret to a handful of people close to Nowlan, but the fact that his mother was living was a fact that even Claudine did not discover until years after they had been married.

Friends and family who later learned about Grace were surprised at the woman's longevity, especially given the persona her son cultivated at the University of New Brunswick as the bearded, wise old man. But appearances were thoroughly deceiving. Nowlan was only fifty years old when he died in 1983. Although it is true that the Reeses are a long-living tribe (in 1999 Ervette died at the age of eighty-eight, survived by Grace and her ninety-year-old brother Albert), Grace's age is by no means remarkable. Her birthdate, March 11, 1918, has an important bearing on the direction Nowlan's life would take, since he was born January 25, 1933, when Grace was only fourteen years old. Nowlan's father, Freeman Lawrence Nowlan, was born on November 2, 1904, making him twenty-eight when his first child was born and twice as old as his new wife.

As Nowlan would later explain, "Child brides weren't terribly rare in rural Nova Scotia in those days."[12] But there was something both terrible and rare about young Alden's childhood, rooted as it was in the doomed relationship between the two most tragic figures in his life, Grace and Freeman.

Nowlan once wrote of his mother's family as being "natural brigands and gypsies."[13] The Reese (or Reece) family came from England, and they were listed in the 1871 census as Church of England members, though by the 1881 census Grace's grandfather, John, was listed as Baptist. Her parents, Coleman and Leonora (Sanford) Reese were married in Massachusetts in 1905, where Coleman had migrated as part of the large Canadian community seeking work in industrial New England. There he met Leonora Sanford, a housemaid who was also recently transplanted from Nova Scotia.

But their union was not destined to be a happy one. When the older children were still little, Coleman and Leonora started to split apart. They managed a reconciliation, and the family moved back to Nova Scotia in 1914, where they spent the first few months with Coleman's parents in Bridgetown, Annapolis County, before settling in a village near Windsor called Newport Station, close to where her parents lived. Leonora, or Nora as she was called, started working at Windsor Textiles. Perhaps because of the pressure of moving back home or perhaps because of her unexpected pregnancy with her fifth child, she and Coleman separated again in 1917. Coleman took their children, Sylvester, Albert, Ervette and Bessie, back to Bridgetown. Nora also left Newport Station, but she went in the opposite direction — about twenty miles east of Windsor where the Sanfords came from, right in the middle of Hants County. Nora went to stay with her sister Maggie in a little village called Stanley to await the birth of her last child, a daughter whom she would name Grace. She was forty-eight at the time.

Ervette described Coleman as a "rolling stone."[14] A few weeks after Grace's birth, Coleman rolled into Stanley to propose getting back together. Nora accepted, and together the Reeses rolled around King's and Hants counties: first back to Newport Station, then to Falmouth, Avonport, Gaspereau Mountain, Wolfville and at last to Mosherville, where the marriage again fell apart, this time permanently. Sylvester, by this time a young man, attempted to impose order on the family's nomadic life by acting as a father figure. He doted on Grace almost as if she were his own daughter. Sylvester's parenting style suited his youth and headstrong nature: he was proud, even arrogant, with a reputation as a good fighter, a prized skill in the rough world of farming and forestry from which he made his living. His daughter, Sylvia, remembers him as someone who did not interact with children, "except as a big shot showing off"[15]; Ervette sums him up as "an angel abroad but a devil at home."[16] Sylvester allowed himself to act like a child only when in Grace's company. Eventually, the two shared a love of photography, or rather of annoying relatives by constantly taking snapshots with their new Kodak.

Nora's other son, Albert, was more easygoing. When Sylvester periodically went away to work in other Nova Scotia communities, Albert would assume the mantle of family provider. The stock market crash of 1929 that sent Wall Street investors plummeting out of office windows barely made an impression in Hants County, where people accepted rural poverty as a way of life. Stanley men who did not work on farms could usually find a job at Russell Palmer's sawmill. Albert worked there as a bundler, content to collect his meagre pay of thirty dollars a month. A man five years his senior worked alongside him and became his friend: Freeman Nowlan.

Unlike the Sanfords, the Nowlans were relative newcomers to Hants County. The 1901 census describes Freeman's father, Fred, and his grandfather Charles Nowlin (as the name was spelled) as "lumbermen." At that time they lived in the village of Black River, near Wolfville in King's County. Nowlins had inhabited the Annapolis Valley since the 1820s, when Patrick Nowlin, after a long passage from Ireland, settled there. Family legend has it that Patrick slept in a coil of rope on the deck of the ship, and that the only things he brought with him were a musket, a salt shaker and a few raw potatoes left over from his shipboard food supply. His descendant Alden, who spelled his name

"Nowlan" but pronounced it "NOE-lin" as his ancestors did, liked to add a little extra romance to his origins:

> From old Patrick's loins have come politicians, prostitutes, rum runners, farmhands, village idiots, Baptist ministers, Catholic priests, cavalrymen, draft dodgers, bulldozer operators, fortune tellers, burglars, pulp cutters, coal miners and your humble servant. Also a great host of sad, drunken Irish navvies and innumerable house [wives] with defeated eyes and wistful dreams.[17]

His Nowlins were not substantial landowners or farmers, and Fred, with his wife, Emma, and their daughters, Roxie, Ivy, twins Hazel and Harriet, and their young son, Freeman, followed the long lumber from the settled, rural Annapolis Valley to the wilder reaches of Hants County.

In that time and place, Freeman's and Albert's friendship made them drinking buddies. Albert, an avid sportsman, took Freeman on hunting trips, although his friend's drinking — exceeding even the amounts required to lubricate the rusty gears of male friendship — must have been a source of concern. Albert had already suffered a hunting accident while with another friend, which cost him the little toe of his right foot. They had been "jacking," hunting deer after dusk by dazzling them with a light. While they were carrying a deer out of the woods with their guns under their arms, Albert's friend decided to stop and tie his boot lace. He stuck his loaded gun under Albert's free arm, it slipped, and, as far as they knew in those first few terrifying minutes, it blew off Albert's foot. Fearful of the wardens, his companion left Albert in the woods to fend for himself. Nowlan would write in the poem "Full Circle":

> *No one called anyone his friend,*
> *although they had friends . . .*
> *As it was, they could quarrel,*
> *even hit one another if they were drunk,*
> *and remain friends, never having said it.*
> *Where nothing was sworn there could be no betrayal.*

It was through Albert that Grace met Freeman. The only school in the area sat just across the road from Palmer's mill, next to the bunkhouse where out-of-town mill workers boarded during the week.

All the children, Grace included, knew the mill and the men who worked there. In fact, many of the teenage boys in Palmer's employ were not much older than the school's students. Madge Parker ran the bunkhouse, which doubled as a cookhouse for mill workers. She cooked for the men during the day and helped her husband sell bootleg liquor at night. The bunkhouse drew some of the bolder girls from the school, and keeping them from the mill's precincts posed a constant challenge for teachers. Grace, however, had no trouble finding excuses to visit her brother and the other men during her lunch hour or after school.

Grace also loved to attend the many dances held in church halls around the area. Freeman, if he attended at all, came with his buddies. In 1932, the mill started its season during the last week of April, and the mill workers welcomed the chance to have one last spring binge before settling down to six months of work. It was probably after one of these dances that Freeman and Grace found each other in the fumbling darkness and unwittingly conceived their first child. Nowlan's poem "It's Good to Be Here" portrays a couple fighting with each other when the woman discovers she is "in trouble," the woman proposing abortion, the man rejecting the idea. At last, the man vows:

well, I just guess we'll have to make the best of it.

While I lay curled up,
my heart beating,
in the darkness inside her.

For Freeman, "making the best of it" meant moving Nora, Albert and Grace into the Nowlan house in Stanley.

Freeman's family was just as fractured as Grace's. His parents, Fred and Emma, had separated when their children were still young, leaving to Emma the burden of raising her five children alone. In 1932, Emma's daughter Hazel worked in Windsor as a maid to a well-to-do family. Emma moved into Hazel's small apartment and left the house in Stanley to Freeman and his new family. At various times, Freeman's sister Roxie also lived in the house.

Nowlan tended to romanticize the circumstances that surrounded his birth, and his light-hearted stories reveal an almost painful aversion to the facts. In one account, he jokingly claims that he was born in a farmhouse with a gramophone in the next room playing Wilf Carter records. Another story is more fanciful still:

The best account of my birth is the one I think I gave you in a letter before you came up here: that when my mother started having labour pains my father hooked up the horses to a sleigh and started with her toward the hospital in Windsor, that they were overtaken by a blizzard and had to take shelter in a barn, where I was born . . . in a manger.

In the same letter, he muses about how facts can sometimes get tangled up in the search for truth: "The fact is I think I was born in a farmhouse, near Windsor. But it is frightening to see these things being pinned down. In an insane sort of way it is *restricting* to have to be born in *one* place."[18] According to his Aunt Ervette, there is an element of truth in both stories. She says he was born at home in Stanley with Dr. R.A. McLellan and Nora in attendance. It actually did snow very heavily that night, forcing the family out into the blizzard to shovel a path for the doctor. It is even possible that Wilf Carter records were playing in the other room while Grace suffered through her first labour.

Freeman's house probably had a squalid and chaotic atmosphere, with Freeman and Albert hunting or off on a bender, and with women from different families forced to live under the same roof, eyeing each other suspiciously. The arrangement did not last long. Albert quickly found and fixed up a new house in Mosherville for the Reeses, which Nora jokingly dubbed "The Castle," as she did her other houses. She had had enough of Freeman's drinking.

Nowlan's memories of those years were happy ones. He was soon joined by a little sister, Harriet, born in November of 1935. His first memory was of picking a handful of wildflowers in the yard and rushing back to the house to present them to Grace, the knowledge of carrying something rare and beautiful propelling his little legs. Even so, from his earliest years he exhibited a haunted imagination. At five, he went through a period when he believed that God was going to end the world by dropping clouds on people's heads, and for a while he would only walk about outside on clear days. This may have had something to do with the impression world events made on his young mind. Seeing a newspaper photograph of dead children in an urban wasteland, he asked his father what had killed them. Freeman told his young son that there was a war going on in a place called Spain.

From an early age, literature affected Alden deeply. At nights the children would curl up in Grace's lap while she read aloud from a book of poetry. The sensitive boy found the imagery both horrible and awe-inspiring, and he was enchanted as his mother read:

Morgan, Morgan the Raider,
And Morgan's terrible men,
With Bowie knives and pistols,
Came galloping down the glen.

The book's pictures haunted him with "an overwhelming sense of wonder."[19] One illustration showed a man in a nineteenth-century costume at a desk on which sit test tubes, books and, most mysteriously, a human skull. Another poem told of a young woman who, to prevent her lover from being hanged when curfew tolled, suspended herself from the tongue of the bell. In the picture, she wears a long, flowing dress, and the bell tower stretches to the sky.

Freeman shared a fondness for storytelling, though in a less conventional way than Grace. Nowlan recalled:

> Every night, my father would take down a book that described the adventures of the Rover Boys and relate to me another instalment crammed with headlong chases and breath-taking escapes. Then a time came when my father had to go away to work.
>
> The first evening after my father went away to work, I asked my mother to read to me from *The Rover Boys*. She took down the book, as my father had done, and started to read. But it wasn't the same story. This was dull, dull, dull.
>
> Alas, she was reading what the book really said. My father, to whom reading was not a painless process, had used the book merely as a theatrical prop, while making up a story of his own.
>
> I'm afraid that I expressed my disappointment by throwing myself on the floor and howling.
>
> I have never since reacted quite as strongly to any book.[20]

But if Freeman had trouble with reading, as Nowlan suggests, it did not stop him from reading what he could. His friends recall that he was an avid reader of the *Family Herald*, and that he followed articles about boxing with special interest. And Freeman wrote regularly to his son after Alden moved away from home. When drunk, Freeman sometimes recited Robert W. Service poems such as "The Shooting of Dan McGrew" and "The Cremation of Sam McGee" for any audience at all.

Like other writers, Nowlan felt compelled to understand himself by creating a fictional world based loosely on events and people from his own life. His two most determined efforts to recreate himself through fiction were the novels *The Wanton Troopers*, written in 1962 but not published until 1988, and *Various Persons Named Kevin O'Brien*, published in 1973. The story about Freeman's supposed lack of reading ability shows Nowlan in the process of muddling fiction and fact, perhaps as a way of romanticizing his childhood to please his audience. He may have been thinking more of his fictional versions of Freeman, who read with difficulty, rather than the real Freeman, who, while not literary, could read and write ably. It is because of this tendency to romanticize himself that it is worth comparing what facts are available about his upbringing with the story he tells in his fiction and non-fiction writings. He often describes more than mere facts can provide, and the omissions sometimes speak as eloquently.

Nowlan wrote his first novel, *The Wanton Troopers*, when he was just starting to draw attention in literary circles. Much of the novel focuses on the relationship between Kevin O'Brien, the boy who is the hero of the story, and his mother, Mary. It gives the reader an indication, not necessarily about Alden's actual relationship with his parents, but rather of how he felt about them. The opening scene of the novel celebrates the sensuality that Kevin enjoys as Mary undresses and bathes him:

> She undid buckles and buttons and let his denim shorts slide down his legs. From May to November, he never wore underwear. He stepped out of the ring of cloth around his ankles and into the tub, recoiling as the cold rim touched his back. He leaned forward, away from the ring of cold.
>
> Now, there was the clean, acid smell of soap in his nostrils, the foam and film of soap in his hair, and across his shoulders, and down his back. He closed his eyes and sank into little-boy inertia, every muscle dormant, every cell in his brain passive and inert . . . .
>
> She rubbed a washcloth over his face. He drew back a

little as the soap bit his eyes and nostrils. She put a hand against the back of his head and made him keep still, and he liked the peremptoriness of her gestures. Like the stinging needles from the stove, this mild discomfort accentuated their intimacy, made it more sweet.

He might have been part of her body. She washed him as she washed her own hands. He was, all of him, hers: not the smallest part of him belonged any longer to himself. And in this surrender, there was a pervasive peace, an ecstasy of negation. (p. 8)

This delicious feeling of powerlessness becomes the bitter taste of fear when Kevin is later punished by his grim father, Judd:

If Kevin's relationship with his mother reached its apotheosis when she bathed him and readied him for bed, his relationship with his father attained its epitome through the strap.

Judd took the strap from its peg and sat on a block of straw. Kevin's stomach felt as though it had turned to rock. His mouth was clogged with invisible dust, the moisture on his tongue and throat transferred to his clammy palms.

"All right, Mister Big Breeches, take down yer pants."

Judd tested the strap on his own palm and grunted. Trembling from head to toe, Kevin unbuttoned his short pants and let them slide from his numbed fingers down his quivering legs. No act in life filled him with greater shame than this. This was the ultimate violation, the final degradation. He hated his father and himself; all of his will was channelled into the wish that they both of them would die. (p. 25)

What is striking about *The Wanton Troopers* is how Nowlan tries to make sense of his childhood through sensuality, the uneasy comingling of pleasure and pain. By the novel's end, Mary becomes a source of both physical pleasure and emotional pain for Kevin.

Serious differences soon began to crop up between Grace and Freeman, differences which in part revolved around sensuality. Grace's youth left her ill-prepared for marriage; in her brother Albert's words, she "couldn't hack it."[21] First, there was Freeman's drinking; even a more mature woman would have had trouble dealing with that. Then, they were almost from different generations. Grace felt drawn by the dances — and the young men — she once frequented, and she started to go without Freeman, who thought such things were too foolish for a married couple. Before long, she started to return from the dances in the cars of her new boyfriends. In a scene from *The Wanton Troopers*, Kevin O'Brien comes home from school to find Mary entertaining an old friend named Ernie Masters, who works at a bank in town.

> For a long time, no one said anything. Kevin knew instinctively that Judd would hate this man. Ernie was the type of person whom Judd dismissed as "big feelin' bastards." Kevin watched him contemptuously as he ran his thumb and forefinger up and down the razor-sharp crease of his trousers. (p. 126)

Eventually Freeman could no longer stand the taunts of the villagers over Grace "stepping out" on him, which was no secret. One night, after she came home from a dance, Freeman confronted her, and they fought. Freeman kicked her out, or she left, taking Alden and Harriet with her to live at The Castle.

Life under Nora's roof was probably at times as chaotic as it was when the whole clan lived with Freeman. Grace continued to see boyfriends, one of whom worked for the railroad, another for the nearby airfield. While their mother wandered, the children were raised by the spirited Nora, who liked to "cook for her own sense of amazement."[22] Albert became Alden's playmate, and uncle and nephew spent their time going on outdoor adventures, picking berries and wild mushrooms. Caught by a sudden rain squall on one of their rambles, they took shelter under a lone boxcar on a nearby railway track. It took some effort for Albert to persuade Alden that the car could not crush them without an engine to move it. The two of them sometimes spent warm Sunday afternoons in the outhouse, where they sat with the door open while Albert shot clothespins off the line with his .45 pistol. An incensed Nora would come out of the house and chase them off with a broom, delighting Alden. "He got more of a kick out of Mother scolding me than he did

Alden Nowlan, aged six or seven, with his uncle Sylvester Reese, c. 1939.

If I could turn and meet myself

shooting for it," Albert says.[23] Nora was apparently quite a shot herself, sometimes sitting up at night in the kitchen, rocking in her chair with a .22 rifle across her lap. The family would be wakened periodically by Nora's potshots at any rodent foolhardy enough to poke its nose out of its hole.

Uncle Sylvester lived at the Castle whenever he was not away working on someone's farm. The headstrong young man had matured into a taciturn and domineering adult. He married later than his sisters, choosing a girl who lived close to his sister Ervette in Noel. Once he discovered Ervette's neighbour, Alberta Henniger, his visits to Ervette became more frequent, and the romance blossomed. On some weekends Alberta would stay at Nora's house to be with her boyfriend. One such visit occurred during a period when the couple had, so the Reeses thought, broken off their engagement. Ervette happened to be at her mother's one day when Nora looked out the kitchen window and spied a young woman skipping down the road, suitcase in hand. Mindful of Sylvester's volatility and her family's history of marital discord, she said to Ervette, "Oh, my. I believe that is Alberta Henniger coming down the road, and how I wish she wouldn't come!"[24]

A decade later, Sylvester and Alberta's only child, their daughter Sylvia, became Nowlan's closest confidante and unofficial sister. Reading their correspondence gives a more factual picture of his childhood, one he glosses over in his novels and even in his non-fiction autobiographical writings like "Growing Up in Katpesa Creek." In his fiction and non-fiction, he merges and refashions both characters and events to suit his sense of artistic unity. Although he seemed to believe these self-created versions of events, and encouraged his friends and family to do the same, the reality was somewhat different.

The scene at Nora's house is a case in point. Although Alden spent about four years of his early life there — from the ages of about four to seven — everything in the novels is played out only under Judd O'Brien's roof. Even Nowlan's non-fictional autobiographical pieces make no mention of his change of address. But the correspondence with Sylvia reveals more intriguing mergers, primarily the conflation of Freeman and Sylvester into Judd O'Brien. "I know what you mean about Sylvester," Nowlan wrote years later to Sylvia. "I don't trust my impression of him, at least not completely, because it's based largely on what's filtered through to me from the small boy I once was." After this cautionary note, he went on to say:

When I was a child and we were all living in that little shack in Mosherville (our grandmother, my mother and her boyfriend, my sister, Sylvester, Albert, and me) I was afraid of him, of Sylvester, not because he swatted me, although he did swat me occasionally (I don't mean he beat me, I think he used to smack my bottom with a copy of *The Saturday Evening Post*, something like that); but because he was always insisting that I be *manly* and ridiculing me for being a baby: actually, I think he was rather a bully, but the worst of it was *I couldn't allow myself to resent it*. I think that's what really ties children in knots. If you bully the child and he feels free to hate you — well, that will make things unpleasant for the child, but it won't torment him the way it will if he feels that, because you're a member of the family, he *has* to love you.

Freeman, according to his son's explanation, embodies the more pathetic elements of the Judd O'Brien character:

It's so damn strange about the parent-child relationship — the symbol created from the real outlives the reality. I'm sure that much of my feeling toward authority stems from my instinctive conception of the authority figure. As a small child I feared my father, hated him with so murderous a hatred that I had to choke it back into the subconscious. To my small boy's soul he was Zeus, Thor and Yahweh. When I started working I feared the bosses, yet hungered for their approval. Because each of them was my father, and my father was Yahweh. (Some linguists say the oldest name of God was Pa.) And, of course, the joke on me — a bit of cosmic black humour — was that my father was, and is, a pathetic shell of a man, utterly incapable of coping with life, so like the winos who hang around in front of liquor stores here that I shudder a little whenever I see them . . . .
    I'm a perceptive human being, yet this parent-symbol confuses us so much that I didn't grasp the truth about my father until I was almost thirty years old [about the same time he was writing *The Wanton Troopers*]. The characters in some of my early stories that I thought were based on

my father weren't like my real father at all, they were much more like the symbol I'd created as a small boy. Strong, taciturn, domineering, masculine men, when actually my father is as weak and frightened as I was when I was eight years old. The tragedy of his life has been due not so much to external forces, such as economics, as to his private weakness and fear.[25]

By the time Nowlan wrote his autobiographical novel, *Various Persons Named Kevin O'Brien*, in 1973, the picture of Judd — and of Kevin — had changed, Kevin a tougher and Judd a less menacing figure. In the later novel Judd seems impotent even in the act of punishment:

> None of this is as tangential as it may seem. We return to the past and change it. What was terrible may become merely distasteful, then ridiculous, then humorous. Or the sequence may be reversed.
>
> The boy Kevin is beaten with a strap. The pain is nothing. What rankles is the rout of the will, the orgiastic cession of the last scrap of privacy, the moment of becoming nobody. This is the prototypal sacrament, the boy Isaac lying naked on the altar. . . .
>
> My father is punishing me for murdering him when I was three years old.
>
> Mind you, I need only rephrase it — the naughty boy, Kevin, is being spanked — and it becomes merely distasteful, or ridiculous, or humorous. (p. 49)

It is almost as if Nowlan used his letters to Sylvia as a rough text on which he could draft revisions of his fictional past.

There are other significant differences between *The Wanton Troopers*, the autobiographical novel he wrote in 1962 and never published, and the one he wrote ten years later. For one thing, Grace's character, called Leah in *Various Persons*, all but disappears, as if Nowlan were trying to write her out of his life. In *The Wanton Troopers* there is no surrogate for Harriet, but in *Various Persons* she appears regularly as Stephanie.

At Nora's house, Grace gradually lost touch with her children as she made up for her missing teenage years. Around this time, she started to take up with a man named Collins, whom local people remember as a scruffy fellow with a speech impediment who lived in a cabin in a strip of woods near Clarksville. Albert recalls that Collins distilled excellent moonshine. A letter from Nora to Ervette's son Edgar on the occasion of his sixth birthday reveals the strained bond between Grace and her children.

> Grace is away she wrote me she thought possibly she would be up next Sunday but I don't know. Harriett and Alden are home with the father and Grandmother [Emma]. Alden was down to see me two or three times he came all by himself such a big boy he is getting to be he will start school this fall too. I hope he likes to go and goes every day.[26]

Nora's wish for Alden's scholastic success would not be granted. He did indeed start preschool in September of 1939 and was painfully shy around the other children. Marty Walker, his teacher that year, remembers having difficulty drawing him out of his shell and protecting him from schoolyard bullies. In return for her attentions, Alden developed a strong attachment to her. Some mornings, Walker would ride to the Stanley school on a railway handcar operated by one of her friends. At Mosherville, they occasionally picked Alden up as a passenger. He later admitted, "I didn't mind [school] much the first year, when I was six, partly because I fell in love with the teacher."[27]

The isolation he suffered would only become worse. Nora, who for years had tried to make up for her daughter's maternal deficiencies, was ailing. She was turning seventy, and Hodgkin's disease took a severe toll on her health. In April of 1940 she passed away. For a little while after Nora's death, Grace tried to make a family life with the children and her boyfriend, Collins, but the authorities intervened. Children's Aid would not accept a separated woman taking her children to live with an unmarried man. According to Ervette, Children's Aid took Alden and Harriet away until they could be placed with their father, which did not happen until later that summer, when Freeman convinced Emma to move back to Stanley permanently. Apparently, his plan was to make Emma the primary caregiver, just as Grace had enlisted Nora. Harriet insists that they were not taken away by Children's Aid, and that the transition to Freeman's house took place at Grace's request. Whether or not the authorities were involved, Grace was probably having a difficult time readjusting to full-time motherhood after the four-year period of relative freedom that Nora had afforded her.

The pain of that separation would haunt Alden and Harriet for the rest of their lives, but in different ways that would eventually entrench their separation from each other. If Alden hoped for reconciliation and reunion there is no indication of it from his writings. Instead, he began to withdraw even further into his shell and to form elaborate dreams of escape — from his family, from Stanley, and from himself. In *The Wanton Troopers*, Mary tries to explain to Kevin what she is about to do:

> "It's wonderful to be alive, Scampi. You don't know how wonderful it is until you've been dead. Sometimes I think that I've been dead for years and years. I work in this old house and I'm dead. I don't feel anything. Then I go into the hall and hear the violins and see the people dancing and, all of a sudden, I'm alive again! It's like rising from the dead, Scampi!"
>
> "Gee whiz!"
>
> "Do you know that most people are dead? Did you ever think of that? Lockhartville is full of dead people. The old women cook and clean and scrub and make pickles. And all the time, they're dead. And the men are dead, too. When I get away from Lockhartville, I feel like somebody who's risen from the dead! You don't know what a terrible, wonderful feeling it is, Scamp!" (p. 82)

But Kevin, like his mother, harbours the same dreams:

> Kevin believed that every one of these boys was stronger, tougher, and braver than he. Secretly, he envied their courage and strength, and wanted to be like them. But he consoled himself by the conviction that when they grew up they would be only pulp peelers and mill hands. They would live all their lives in Lockhartville, fenced in forests and rivers, and at last they would die here and be buried in the cemetery behind the Anglican church. But he — ah, he would be a lawyer, a doctor, a member of parliament, and one day he would come back here, wearing a black

suit and a shining white shirt, and then he would spit in their eyes! And, in thinking this, his eyes and mouth took on that insolent, faintly contemptuous look that made them hate him. (p. 15)

Alden, as he grew up, consoled himself with the belief that Grace's motives for abandoning him were ones he could understand.

Grace, as it turned out, did not effect the escape that her son imagines. Instead she changed the circumstances of her life through slow and painful steps. She lived with Collins for a couple of years after her mother's death, but then she left him to live with another man, Ray McLean, in Dartmouth. After her move, she would take the train back to Stanley every month or so to visit Alden and Harriet. Her departures created a scene in the small village, with the two children crying and begging Grace to take them to Dartmouth with her, and with Grace enduring the hostile stares and muttered comments of her former neighbours. Her trips to see her children became less frequent, and soon they stopped altogether. According to Ervette, Grace knew a woman from Cole Harbour who encouraged her to better herself. With her friend's support, Grace left McLean and began to take nurse's training, becoming a Certified Nursing Assistant. By all accounts, she was good at it and finally made her escape. After working in Halifax, she moved to the Yukon in the early 1960s, then to Manitoba in the 1970s, to Vancouver in the late 1970s, and finally retired back in Nova Scotia.

Harriet eventually re-established contact with her mother, but the mutual rejection of Grace and her son was complete. Gail (Sanford) Manning, the daughter of Madge Parker, was a close friend of Harriet. Manning remembers walking along the dusty roads in Stanley with Harriet during those years before Grace's move to Dartmouth. Sometimes Collins's car would pass the girls, with Grace visible in the passenger seat. If she recognized Harriet at all, Grace gave no sign, and Harriet, staring at the back of her mother's head as she disappeared down the road, made no comment on the tragic circumstances that had torn her family apart. It was not until decades had passed that the two mustered the courage to effect a tentative reunion.

It is possible that neither Alden nor Grace knew whether the other was even alive, but this is unlikely as long as each had some contact with Ervette, who acted as anchor and emotional touchstone for her far-flung family. Nowlan corresponded regularly with Ervette and usually dropped in to see her on his rare visits to the Windsor area. Even his cousin Sylvia remembers Grace from the 1950s, when she visited Sylvester and Alberta. Grace, always nicely dressed, sat on the porch while being spied on by Sylvia through one of the windows in the parlour. "I admired Grace in a way," she says. "She got away from the village as I wanted to do. In a sense, she was somewhat elegant." Elegant but, as she remembers, not approachable; friendly but held in as if by a corset, brimming with what Sylvia remembers as an unspoken energy.[28]

Alden's purposeful rejection of his mother immortalized his pain in its pristine state, even as he denied her existence. Reconciliation would have meant dealing with the reality of his mother; in his writing she could remain in an idealized state, the nature of which would be decided by the artist alone. In his poem "Anatomy of Angels" he alludes to the power of making monuments out of struggle, "his bone/ mending he spent some several tedious weeks/ marking the bed they'd shared, with a great stone." He would attempt nothing like a reunion, which would mar the monument he had created of her, his most powerful and beautiful fiction.

Certainly, Grace did not miss the national attention her son received for his writing. She returned to Nova Scotia each year for her summer vacation, and in 1976 she was caring for Arthur Sanford's father, a distant relative who had had a stroke. Arthur also knew Grace through Sylvester, since they both used to deliver the rural mail. Vera Sanford, Arthur's wife, was in the older grades when Alden was just starting school. She remembers that Grace was an excellent nurse at their house, always cheerful and full of funny stories.

A few weeks later, chance brought Grace back to work for the Sanford's next-door neighbour. One night, an interview with Alden Nowlan came on the television. Excited, Vera rushed over to her neighbour's house. "Grace!" she said. "Come quick! There's something on TV about Alden." Grace did come over, reluctantly, and watched the rest of the interview without any comment or expression on her face. Vera, having no idea of the bitterness of the family break-up, started to doubt the wisdom of inviting Grace over to be confronted with her past. But, rising to leave after the interview ended, Grace could not resist showing a mother's pride or, at least, a small claim of ownership. "He gets his creativity from the Sanfords," is all she said.

TWO

On the Stairs

Knuckling his temples on the shadowed stair,
the boy is for the first time aware
how strange it is to be himself, and here.

Hard knot of consciousness behind the eyes,
hot nails against his forehead as he tries
to free a truth so true we've only lies

in which to hint at it: terror, delight
and an unspeakable confusion, light,
darkness, a pebble thrown from a great height.

The Stanley of today seems comfortable and well off, although much of that wealth now comes from jobs in Windsor, Truro and even Halifax. The automobile has changed and, in some ways, saved Stanley and communities like it all over the Maritimes. Were it not for convenient road travel, villages such as these would probably dry up completely as the number of people willing to live off the land dwindled. A paved road runs through Stanley where a dirt road ran before. Most houses still have substantial gardens of tomatoes, potatoes and string beans. In September the community hosts a fall supper and awards bragging rights to the person who has grown the biggest pumpkin. Some families who participate, such as the Anthonys and the Campbells, are descendants of the earliest settlers who received land grants back when the community was still known as Newport-Douglas.

Like many Nova Scotia villages, Stanley is not without its folklore. One local story tells of Arch Campbell, a wild lad who was galloping back to his house one dark night after carousing in a neighbouring village. Drunk, he rode his horse recklessly along the road. The horse's hoof found a hole, Campbell was thrown from his saddle, and he died there on the ground from a broken neck. The legend says that, on dark nights, those foolish enough to travel the lonely road in Stanley can sometimes hear ghostly hoof beats.[1]

Other ghosts haunt Stanley, ghosts of industry and of great events that are now literally dust. The sawmill with its sixty-foot smokestack that once dominated the little village is gone, just an anonymous pile of sawdust long grown over with grass and trees. Driving along the road from Mosherville on Route 236, the visitor will see the mill's former site on the right-hand side across from the airport road, about fifty yards beyond the sign saying "Stanley." The sign will not be hard to find. It is a plain green Department of Transportation sign close to a small, half-burnt house in the middle of a field on the right-hand side of the road. This dilapidated structure was the Nowlan house, where Alden was born and came to live after his grandmother Nora's death.

In better times, the house and its outbuildings were as sound as any other in Stanley. The house had a modest second storey for the bedrooms. These were seldom used after Alden and Harriet moved back, since they were difficult to heat from the stove in the kitchen, which was located in a one-storey addition that jutted out from the building's east wall. There was no refrigeration, no telephone, no electricity and no indoor plumbing when the children lived there. Neglect eventually claimed the property from the outside in. First, the lilac and rose bushes ran wild on the front lawn. Then the outbuildings and small farm implements fell into disuse, and the animals were consumed or sold off as Freeman's agricultural ambitions slackened. He preferred sleeping on a cot in the kitchen, and, when his mother died and his children moved on, he shut off the rest of the house and lived there, as if it were a one-room shack.

Freeman's next-door neighbour, Russell Palmer's mill, was the very heart of Alden's childhood and the economic heart of the village. The mill was Palmer's inheritance from his father, Frank Palmer, who had built the mill to suit his specifications, right down to the doors that were the proper height for him but too short for most of his workers. The rhythm of its pistons and saws pumped what little money there was through the community. During the working day, wood circulated through the mill's system; raw logs from the pile at one end, staves and sawdust at the other. Four times a day the mill whistle blew, and the child at school or the farmer in the field would know when it was time to have lunch or when to stop working.

"Always be sure of your pay, boy," Freeman advised his son, although he had a hard enough time heeding that counsel himself. The mill once produced magnificent lumber; in later years it churned out mostly laths and barrel staves from the ragged trees found in the area. But it did pay regularly and on time. In the winter months the mill shut down, and Freeman and the other men headed off to the forest to cut trees for contractors, who usually paid with little more than a promise until they could sell their wood in the spring. Being sure of your pay was fine, but survival for a labourer in Hants County often meant doing work for any pay, even for an opportunity to keep the winter cold out of the bones.

Russell Palmer's stammer and short stature belied his high public profile as Stanley's only industrialist. He was by most accounts a fair employer. But the hard times were not as hard for the Palmers, who were the first family in the village to own a car. A school trustee, he had a decisive say in, among other things, the selection of which young women would be hired as new teachers for Stanley's school. It looked as though he might have died a bachelor until Hilda Warner came during the war to teach the upper grades. She and Palmer married, and she taught Alden Nowlan.

From the outset Alden took a dim view of the mill and the work that went on there, which he saw as mindless toil. But it was a lifeline for the Nowlan family, and, like a mechanical god, the mill could be both terrifying and beautiful. The passages in *The Wanton Troopers* that describe it are as evocative as poetry:

> When these saws were working at full speed, they ceased to be substantial, metal things and became rings of nebulous, convulsive light. Kevin could remember moments in which he could hardly resist an urge to thrust his hand into one of those luminous rings. There had been times when his desire had become so strong that he felt his stomach contract in fear as he turned away. He wondered if the men who worked in the mill ever felt tempted to throw themselves into these hypnotic whirlpools. In the twenty-five years that his father had worked at the mill, three men had been killed. (p. 12)

As Alden saw it, the mill, like any god, demanded sacrifice by claiming the lives of its devotees.

Freeman was reputed to be a hard-working mill hand and a skilful axe man in the woods, but he was not frugal. He drank a good part of his wage every week, soliciting booze from Madge Parker or sometimes from his boss when Palmer went to town on business. Freeman and the three Anthony brothers, Reg, Russell and Billy, were known in the community as "The Four Musketeers," but Freeman preferred to be called "The Lone Wolf." He would sometimes come home after a bender with no more energy than a rubber chicken, carried by whichever of the musketeers were sober enough to dump him on his doorstep. In general, Stanley residents seemed to like Freeman, but more from pity for his sad circumstances, mixed with amusement at his antics, than from any real respect for him.

For years after Alden and Harriet left home, Freeman's house still served as the gathering place for local boys too young or too poor to get hooch in conventional ways. The Wolf liked to greet his buddies by going into a mock boxing crouch and pretending to want a fight. At other times, he would greet a visitor with a silent politeness that suggested sobriety until he blurted out some drunken comment that made no sense. "Jeez-jeez," was the habitual way he started these sayings: "Jeez-jeez, if you was a duck an' I held yer head under water for ten minutes, I guess you'd come up a dead pigeon."

The Mother Wolf, Emma, really ruled the den. She claimed most of whatever was left of Freeman's paycheque after the liquor was bought and used it to raise the children as she saw fit. From all accounts, Emma was a feisty character whose spirit was undimmed by failing health. When she developed stomach cancer she relieved the pain by holding a wrapped, heated brick against her abdomen, but in healthier times she played the autoharp and sang wild Irish ballads. Alden Durling, Ivy (Nowlan) Durling's son, remembers how she would adjust her jet-black wig to make her bangs hang over her eyes. Then, with dishevelled clothing, she delighted the Durling children by impersonating a witch. "She should have been an actress, there's no doubt about that," Durling says.[2] Emma gave herself some latitude from her strong Baptist faith with her witch act, as well as by step-dancing and nipping from the homebrew Freeman kept out in the barn.

Nowlan leaves other clues to Emma's personality. In a letter to a friend, he recounts the stories she liked to tell about her family, the Atwells. A favourite tale revolved around her father, Martin Atwell, and his success at swindling the town-dwellers of Wolfville by selling them cartloads of wood made to look bigger by the strategic placement of crooked logs in the centre of the load. "Mart Atwell would scratch out a living where a sheep would starve," she liked to say. She also admired her brother Lawson, who was reputed as a man of great strength and fighting prowess, one who could drink a quart of navy rum without showing any effects from it. "That is a nice paradox," her grandson later mused. "As a hard-shell Baptist she disapproved of rum, but as a hardy old peasant woman she respected the masculinity of men who could master it."[3] The portrait of Lawson is a clue as to the qualities Emma admired: toughness, masculinity and fighting skill — all of which could enhance survival in hard times.

Her dreamy grandson Alden, however, was not the rugged type. Confronted by the confusing and painful events surrounding him and his family, he turned to the realm of the imagination. He once explained that he started writing for the same reason some children invent imaginary playmates,[4] a reason that he did not articulate. There was certainly no shortage of children in the area, but Alden was not the sociable type. Some former neighbours insist that they were not even aware that Freeman had a boy living at the house during those early years. Their neighbour Ethyl Ogilvie says, "He was so bashful that he wouldn't go near anybody, hardly, or talk to anybody. He just kept by himself; he would not talk."[5]

In later years, Nowlan took pains to describe the creative mystery that was growing inside his young mind. "Perhaps I should begin this book with a page containing nothing but a question mark," is how he opens the novel *Various Persons Named Kevin O'Brien*:

> As a child, I ached to put the question into words, but never could. Nor can I find the proper words for it now. That child, Kevin O'Brien, would stop whatever else he was doing when he felt the question returning. He would press his chin against his knees, screw his eyes shut and tighten his fists on his temples like the two halves of a vice: doing to his body what I, the man Kevin O'Brien, do to my mind. . . .
>
> But it's a little like this: a dumb aching wonder at how

strange it is to be here inside this body and in this world. It's somewhat as if I had awakened in a stranger's body on another planet. Or, and this may be closer to the truth, it's as though I were dreaming and knew I was dreaming but couldn't remember who I was or where I lived when I was awake. (p. 1)

Nowlan, like Kevin, often spoke of having separate selves who conversed with one another. In his writing there is often a sense of actor and observer. He developed from an early age the ability to watch events in his life with a dispassionate detachment.

For young Alden, "the question" coalesced into fragments of a fantasy world that he refined as time went on. Godlike, he sat alone in his room and populated entire kingdoms while outside the more sociable Harriet played with the neighbourhood children. One fragment of this fantasy is kept among his papers at the University of Calgary in a thick file labelled "Notes on an Imaginary Kingdom." Inside are elaborate maps, brief accounts of battles and treaties, long lists and genealogies of various imaginary royal houses, and pages of designs for flags. The list is typewritten, indicating that he kept up the fantasy well into adulthood. Some kingdoms' names evolved as time went on; "Whitmania" probably reflects his early love of Walt Whitman's poetry, "Cameronia" is probably named after one of two friends he made later in life. There is an elaborate apparatus to this world but no narrative structure, no key as to how this information fits together. It is the only part of his oeuvre not meant to be shared with an audience.

"That's the Reese in him coming out," Emma Nowlan would comment sourly when Alden displayed any outward signs of his rich inner world. And yet their relationship was a close one. In fact, Emma encouraged the very imagination she claimed to despise by doting on him and sheltering him from social activities. Alden quickly learned that any display of illness would be rewarded by Emma's insistence that he stay home from school. She also fostered his new mania for reading anything and everything that came within his reach. Stacks of books collected and pilfered from various places held up the walls of his room, a barrier against the winter draft. His tastes were quirky and eclectic, as much a reflection of the haphazard assortment of books available in Stanley as an indication of his reading tastes. These ranged from Greek classics to comic books, and in his mind there was little to distinguish between them. Emma diverted a small part of Freeman's paycheque towards her grandson's literary pursuits, and Harriet and her friend Gail Sanford would sometimes meet Emma at the train station to help cart back the load of books she picked up in town.

Alden repaid his Baptist grandmother by devoting himself to the Bible. He claimed that by the time he was fourteen he had read it three times, and he often cited the Bible as another inspiration for his writing career. "There was a time when I wanted to be a Prophet ('the words that the Lord God of Abraham and of Isaac and of Jacob spake unto his servant, Alden')," he once wrote.[6] In *The Wanton Troopers*, Kevin, after his encounter with his adulterous mother and Ernie Masters, calls down hellfire like a prophet:

> "O God," he prayed aloud. "O God of Abraham and of Isaac and of Jacob, make me one of Thy mighty ones! Make me one of Thy kings and prophets, O God of Israel. Give me the faith to move mountains and the power to call down fire from heaven on the enemies of the Most High! Give me the staff of Moses and the Sword of David! Oh God, make me like unto David and Isaiah and Jeremiah and Ezekiel and Solomon! Thy servant, Kevin, asks this, O God. Amen." (pp. 129-130)

Through religious imagery, Alden's solitary and creative mind was able to develop another, darker fragment of his fantasy world populated, not by kings, but by supernatural forces.

Alden's fantasy world did admit some residents besides himself. At one time, he trusted his mother enough to allow her entry, and when they lived with Emma, Alden relied on Harriet as his conduit between the external world and his imaginary one. Despite their differences in temperament, the two shared a close link, forged in part by their common trials. In the novel *The Wanton Troopers* Kevin has no sister, but much of *Various Persons Named Kevin O'Brien* is devoted to the bond between brother and sister:

> Kevin and Stephanie. Kev and Stevie. They've heard their names coupled so often and for so long that now it seems the coupling not only represents but helps create something that incorporates both of their public selves. At the same time, by its sheer formality, it causes their private selves to shrink back, so that this Kevin-and-Stephanie is

simultaneously a little more and immeasurably less than Kevin or Stephanie alone.

They are brother and sister. They've been told that brothers and sisters love one another, and they believe it. (p. 20)

Harriet, in contrast to her brother, responded to her problems at home by seeking affirmation in the social world outside the household. Where Alden was an outcast, she had a circle of friends. "We were close then," Harriet explains. "But he never wanted to play outside. My mum would get so mad because he wouldn't play outside. He'd always have his nose in a book."[7]

His writings about "Stephanie" in *Various Persons* suggest that Alden struggled to keep his sister a participant in his imaginary world, a project that was doomed to fail as Harriet became more outgoing and he more withdrawn. The "Stephanie" passages in the novel convey a feeling of mixed sensuality and loss, emotions that echo earlier passages inspired by his mother in *The Wanton Troopers*. One of his early poems, "I Knew the Seasons Ere I Knew the Hours," mirrors an incident he describes in a letter to Sylvia. In the letter, he writes, "My most vivid memory of Sylvester from those years [in the Castle] is his carrying my puppy by its ears, while it whimpered piteously, and threatening to kill it because it had stolen some venison from a carcass which he had hung in the shed behind the house."[8] The poem reads:

I was once six and so damned lonely
I called love Rover, he had two sad ears,
a black-white checkerboard of face, a nose
for venison, he stole my uncle blind,
was caught and shot and buried in the pasture.

In the final stanza he invokes his sister, "Stephanie," to compound the sense of lost love:

For months I sprinkled daisies over him,
sucking my grief like lemons. Stephanie
shredded the daisies when she punished me
for being born her brother and we wrestled,
crushing the grass like lovers, till our mother

whipt us apart. Eventually the flowers
were laid less for my grief than for that struggle.

As in the passage from *The Wanton Troopers* describing Kevin's bath time with his mother, Nowlan imagines an almost incestuous love marred by separation. Kevin is never in control of his sensual experiences. To enjoy them, he must submit to them, must be dominated by the female who has the power to give him pleasure and, eventually, pain. This embryonic conception of sexuality seems to have influenced Nowlan's later relationships with women. In the stories and poems, Stephanie is usually older, bigger or stronger than Kevin; in reality, Harriet was his younger sister.

Alden's love of literature became linked to the forbidden. One of his favourite places to read was the parlour of the neighbouring Nelson farmhouse, which was inhabited by two old brothers and their elderly sister, "Aunt Lide" Nelson. Emma, a friend of the Nelson family, used to take Alden and Harriet there whenever she went out of town for the day or the weekend. "Aunt Lide used to flirt with me in the covertly sensual manner in which, in my experience, many old women flirt with little boys," he recalls. "So much so that I was a little scared of her, without knowing why." Alden spent his time in the dark front parlour of the house, whose rich carpet and antique furniture were protected from the sun by thick velvet curtains. The Nelson parlour had a well-stocked if antiquated library, and Alden pored over almanacs and the 1910 edition of *Appleton's Encyclopedia* while submitting to the old woman's attentions. "The room's darkness got all mixed up in my mind with Aunt Lide's constant patting, stroking and watching."[9]

The secret nature of his imaginary world became linked to a sense of shame. He quickly learned that dreaming was, in the community's eyes, something practised by idiots. At the age of eleven, he added another fragment to his imaginative world: his own body of literary work. These were mostly little poems and detective stories written in a notebook he started keeping for that purpose. But even into his adult years he felt that writing was something akin to masturbation, and he developed a habit of quickly covering his work whenever someone walked into the room where he was writing.

In *The Wanton Troopers*, he presents the reader with a version of his family life that is — as artistic unity dictates — simplified. His later novel *Various Persons Named Kevin O'Brien* more accurately recreates the texture of his extended family relations. Alden Durling claims that

the character of Lorna — the aunt who lives in the O'Brien house —
is based on his mother, Ivy. Given Nowlan's habit of fictional
compression, Lorna could also represent aspects of his aunt Roxie,
whose husband, incidentally, was named Jud Millett. Ivy's children
were, by his account, the only children he played with. He credited his
cousin Harmie with teaching him how to smoke, and he once wrote a
poem about pushing Helen Durling out of a plum tree, giving her a
minor but permanent scar. Alden Durling, his older cousin and
namesake, was a frequent visitor, especially later when he landed a job
at Palmer's mill.

While Aunt Ivy's brood gave young Alden a taste of carefree childhood, the tragic lives of two of his other aunts, Freeman's twin sisters
Harriet and Hazel, haunted him. Harriet, known as Hattie, was a
promising young woman who had just started teaching when she died
in 1931 of leukemia. "She might have made a big difference in his life,"
Albert Reese speculates, "because she was a schoolteacher."[10]

Aunt Hazel never quite recovered from her twin's death and,
according to village rumour, went slightly crazy afterwards. While
Alden and Harriet were still living at the Castle, Hazel became pregnant
by a man who promptly abandoned her. Nevertheless, she insisted on
taking the man's name and so became Hazel Bruce. She gave birth to
a boy, Robert, who apparently developed hydrocephalus, a condition
characterized by an enlarged skull caused by fluid buildup in the cranial
cavity. Albert says that Robert had rickets. Sometimes when Hazel
visited Freeman, his neighbour, Ethyl Ogilvie, would look out her
window and see Hazel sitting in the henhouse, her usual spot, rocking
her frail child in the morning sun. More often than not, Alden sat out
there with them. Robert did not live beyond four or five years of age.
This tragedy superimposed a gothic menace on Alden's grief over the
loss of his mother.

While his sometimes painful relationships with his family were having
their effect on young Alden, larger forces had also been shaping his life
and the lives of everyone he knew. Canada's declaration of war on
Germany on September 10, 1939, wrenched the village of Stanley out
of its traditional existence forever, and the ready availability of cash
accelerated the social revolution. Younger Hants County men who
might have faced a future of drudgery flocked to recruiting offices

After the First Frost

After the first frost,

resting in the cool shadows,
the undisciplined lilac bushes
a green web around her,

old woman in brown stockings,
smelling of wintergreen
a clean burn in my nostrils,
sipping hot milk and ginger,
among the dead lilacs.

Her daughter I knew as a legion of whispers:
how she lay three summers in the hen house,
rocking her simple baby.

And the old woman swept out the hen house with spruce boughs,
and built her a hammock from a crazy quilt,
till the baby's head grew
unnatural and huge, and he died.

And the old woman pried him loose from her arms
and laid him on a board between two chairs,
and clothed him in velvet trousers
and a shirt bleached out of flour bags,

and went out to wait in the shadows,
the tilting branches closing around her.

hoping for a chance to see some overseas adventure before the Allies beat the Hun back to Berlin. Older men and women who had slaved in the hardscrabble woods and on the farms could make more money than they ever had before while doing easier jobs in wartime industry. The Depression was over, and no one who tasted the nectar of materialism could be satisfied with the vinegar of rural poverty.

Stanley found itself in an unfamiliar role as a strategic location on the home front. It happened that, just before the war, the Department of Transportation had chosen Stanley as the home of a small airfield to be used as an emergency landing strip for Eastern Provincial Airways. Surveyors chose a site on the wooded back acres of the Anthonys' farm. Construction began in 1938. Operating the modest facilities meant bringing electricity to the airfield and to the community. In time, most houses became wired; Freeman's household was one of the few that did not.

When the war broke out, the military decided that the new airfield could be improved to make a full-fledged airport and flight training school. Local men and women found well-paying jobs building and maintaining the airport, its pilots and its planes. Alden's Uncle Sylvester landed one of the better jobs as assistant engineer and mechanic, while Alberta worked in the mess hall. Even Freeman found a measure of financial stability as a labourer; his pay swelled to five to six dollars a day.

The excitement generated by the growing war at least partly distracted Alden from the trauma of Nora's death and Grace's abandonment of him. Along with his reading, the romance of war was a balm for his troubled spirit. The skies were filled with the small yellow biplanes that student pilots from all over the world used for training. Alden's elementary teacher Marty Walker remembers a roomful of children running to the windows to get a better look at the first plane to land at the nearby airport. "All right, then," she said as they rushed past her. "Get a good look now if you want to, but this is the last time I will allow it." Before the serious training began, instructors set aside a day to fly any interested local people from Stanley to Windsor and back again. Walker was one of the lucky ones who could afford the two-dollar ticket.[11] Alden, like most young boys, dreamed of becoming a Spitfire pilot.

Army trains rolled through the countryside, the soldiers hanging out the windows to get a last look at the country for which some of them would perish. Their mood, however, was still jubilant, and some boy or girl waving at the troops could be the lucky recipient of a Glengarry or wedge cap. Chocolate was another treat generously bestowed upon the clouds of children wafting around the feet of teenaged airmen. Young American flyers looking for adventure in the days before Pearl Harbor liked to give chocolate to the kids, who would call them the Royal Canadian-Texan Air Force. There were pilots of other nationalities as well, such as Polish and Dutch, and English officers to oversee some of the training. No matter how young some of the pilots were, to a child like Alden they all looked like heroes.

"You have to understand that the Airport was not so much an addition to our community as a partially open doorway into a parallel universe," he explains in the introduction to his narrative poem about the war, *Gardens of the Wind* (1982).[12] Besides instilling a sense of adventure, the war exposed the children to a wider world through a medium more powerful than radio: the silver screen. Movies were shown at the base every Saturday night. One in particular fired the young writer's imagination:

> When I was eleven I saw this movie about Jack London, a very bad movie. But, you know, it showed how he'd come from a background something like the background that I came from — a very poor and hard environment — and then he'd written books and things and, by the time the movie was over, you know, he was a celebrity and a millionaire. . . . When you're poor, you know, when you're a kid what hurts you isn't the lack of material things . . . I suppose that being a prophet and being a writer helped convince me that I mattered.[13]

The village started to grow. An old community hall building was brought into Stanley to serve as a second school for the older students. The roar of the airplanes now competed with the scream of the mill's whistle, and the two frowned at each other across the tiny Kennetcook River. The mill would still be around after the war, but the airport, with its exciting promise of the outside world, had won the villagers' hearts forever.

Meanwhile, Alden's solitary habits and propensity for bouts of sickness were not helping him in school. He liked to compare himself as a child to Mark Twain's Huckleberry Finn, "not, I stress, the Huckleberry Finn of *Saturday Evening Post* covers, the mischievous freckle-faced angel (that was really Tom Sawyer), but the great, sad, funny, loving, dark, frightful book."[14] When he was not truant, he could summon Tom Sawyer's talent for mischief. His favourite school memory is of the day when he brought a box of rifle cartridges to school and put them in the stove in the centre of the classroom. He had almost forgotten about them when they went off, sending the classroom into an uproar.

His guerrilla warfare against the teachers, however, won him few allies among his like-minded classmates. Though no one in Stanley today owns up to teasing or abusing Alden when he was in school, he nevertheless described his childhood as "a pilgrimage through hell."[15] His academic career speaks for itself:

> I probably hold the Canadian record for truancy. . . . The one thing I learned to do was long division and I didn't learn to do that well. Then some of the big boys, who must have been almost as old as the teacher, derived considerable satisfaction from beating me up on an almost daily basis. In retrospect, I don't much blame them: I was a freaky kid, too small to fight, too stubborn to run and too stupid to shut up. But at the time I found their regular thrashings very distracting. Some days I'd convince Old Em that I was sick and stay home to drink ginger tea (her remedy for colds, bellyaches and unclassified miseries) and read, or listen to her tell stories about witches, ghosts, three-masted schooners and the wrongs suffered by Holy Ireland. Other days I'd start off with my books, scribblers and lunchbox and head for the woods.[16]

His mastery of long division was not enough to prevent him from repeating the third grade, and things did not improve after that, when he was sent to the new schoolhouse next door and to a new teacher, Hilda Palmer. While Marty Walker was indulgent and protective of Alden, Palmer had a reputation as a disciplinarian.

Alden did not last long under Palmer's tutelage. He claimed to have dropped out of school after only thirty-seven days in grade five, but records from the school indicate that he may not even have reached that level. The last record of him was for the 1944-1945 year, when he was in grade four, and also notes that he did not pass into grade five. It is possible that Freeman or Emma appealed to the school authorities over the summer and succeeded in getting him promoted, but it is equally possible that Alden, after starting grade four a second time, decided he could better educate himself. He did return to the school building on one occasion after his departure: on a dark evening he crept in and stole a book from the small glassed-in bookcase. He had been admiring it those last few days in school: Thomas Carlyle's *The French Revolution*. He supposed that no one would really miss it, and, after getting it home and eagerly turning to the first page, he discovered just how right he was. The book's pages were still uncut.

The good times brought on by the war would not last in Stanley. By the start of 1945, as the Allies were finishing off Germany and Japan, military personnel began to wind down the training program at the airport. Work started to dry up, and people moved on or went back to toil in the meagre farms and forests of Hants County. Palmer's mill once again lorded unchallenged over the village. At the same time, Alden's hormones were dragging him towards an adulthood he was not prepared to face. While his fiction describes Kevin's early sexual experiences petting with girls at school — in *The Wanton Troopers* the girl is Nancy Harker, Gail Sanford's persona — by all accounts (including hers) Alden's shyness prevented his curiosity about girls from getting beyond the fantasy stage.

"Now you can do a man's job for a man's pay," was how one of Freeman's friends congratulated Alden after he dropped out of school. But the world of men presented something of a mystery for a boy with little in the way of adult role models. Freeman inducted him into the fraternity the only way he knew how: by getting his son stinking drunk. Alden's Christmas gift that year from his father was a small bottle of moonshine, known locally as "whoop-and-drive-'er" because that was the only way in which anyone could drink the concoction. Not knowing any better, he bolted the entire bottle on New Year's Eve and ended up passed out in a ditch beside the road. He later wrote, "When I looked up the stars were whirling all over the sky; at first I thought I was dying, and then I decided this was the end of the world."[17] And, in a way, it was the end of his childhood world.

The man's job and man's pay that were supposed to accompany adulthood were a little harder to find. Not that he tried. Mostly, Alden loafed around the house with his books, his reading tastes becoming more and more indiscriminate. He supplemented the classics of literature with publications advertised on the back pages of the *Family*

Herald. He was amazed that people would offer books, magazines and pamphlets for free. He sent away for all of them, and thus he became an expert on any number of religions and philosophies, from the Mormon Church to Theosophy to the Ascended Masters. There was also Communist literature available for the asking, and Alden's contemporaries could at last put a label on his anti-social habits, one that fit in with the ideology of the time: he was a Communist. It was a label that he came to adopt for himself, perhaps grasping for an identity, something that could explain why he felt so alone. Alden kept a scrapbook that contains some of his earliest journalistic efforts. On one page he kept track of "Letters published" in *Steelworker and Miner*, a Cape Breton labour magazine: "1946-1, 1948-1, 1949-4, 1951-6, 1952- ." Aside from these letters, he also wrote furiously at other, more literary projects: poems, stories, and short plays and novels.

The religious reading, no doubt abetted by Emma's fanaticism about the Bible and his own isolation from his peers, started to have a strange effect on Alden. He built a stone structure in a swampy area near their house, which he called the Nylonian Church Upon the Rock. People walking by the house late at night would see the lamp burning in his window, his voice carrying across the fields, shouting about damnation and fantastic religious visions. "The people in Stanley started to talk about him being crazy," Gail (Sanford) Manning says. "Mother told us not to go over there, but my brother Leyland — he was about Alden's age — went over anyway. He wasn't ranting, you see, he was just reading out loud."[18] But ranting and reading about demons were both considered by local people to be the acts of a madman.

The listlessness of his early adolescence was not entirely Alden's fault. In 1946, during the year following his departure from school, he became seriously ill with something his aunt Ervette and uncle Albert describe as "anemia." Harriet remembers that he had no energy to get up from his bed, that his chest appeared "caved-in," and that he would sometimes vomit and have no interest in food. Whatever the precise medical condition, it seemed that Alden was slowly wasting away. Emma, herself in the last throes of cancer, stubbornly forbade Freeman to summon a doctor for either one of them. The Reese family, meanwhile, was beginning to take a renewed interest in their nephew. Ervette wrote Freeman on behalf of the family, threatening to call a doctor themselves, and maybe to telephone the authorities while they were at it. By the spring of 1947 Emma was too weak to protest, and Freeman bowed to the greater pressure exerted by the Reese family. The two were sent to Payzant Hospital in Windsor, where Emma expired on July 15.

Freeman lost not only his mother, but also his son and daughter. Alden recovered physically, but it soon became apparent to the doctors that his problems were more than physical. He was even more withdrawn than normal in the alien environment of the hospital and inconsolable over the loss of his grandmother. That summer, according to his aunt Ervette, Children's Aid once again intervened in his life, and, on the advice of doctors and with Freeman's consent, Alden was sent to the Nova Scotia Hospital, a psychiatric facility in Dartmouth. Harriet's version of the story has it that Freeman and the doctors sent him there without the intervention of Children's Aid, but in any event Alden again was faced with loss and abandonment by his family. Harriet, meanwhile, moved in with Sylvester, Alberta and their two-and-a-half-year-old daughter Sylvia, not an unusual arrangement in Sylvester's household, for Alberta was a popular aunt who drew many of her nieces to her door.

Situated in a part of Dartmouth known as Mount Hope, the Nova Scotia Hospital overlooked Halifax Harbour and had an excellent view of the city. The ferry from Halifax docked nearby and provided easy access for visitors, staff and those patients allowed to leave hospital grounds. It is likely that Alden would have been one of these patients; he probably received a common treatment known as occupational therapy, which included developing vocational skills in combination with personal and social skills.[19] Ervette remembers that the doctors taught him to play baseball as a way of getting along with the other children.

Harriet suggests that the treatment her brother received was less benign, that "shock therapy" was also part of the program. If this was indeed the case, it was probably not the electroconvulsive treatments so often dramatized in novels and movies. Although doctors at the hospital first employed this procedure as early as 1943, its use did not peak until the early 1960s. As the poem "Living in a Mad House" suggests, Alden more likely received insulin treatments, the drug injected into the bloodstream to induce a temporary coma in order to combat schizophrenia. Between 1945 and the early 1950s, this treatment was given to about ten percent of patients at the Nova Scotia Hospital.[20]

As with his abandonment by his mother, Nowlan preferred to gloss over his months at the Nova Scotia Hospital with a brief, fabricated story. Psychiatric institutions and mental and social outcasts, however, recur in both his poetry and fiction, a hint of how deeply the experience must have affected him. One of his non-fiction versions of events, as he once told a friend, was that "my uncle used to be an occupational therapist at the Nova Scotia Hospital and I've been through the place from top to bottom, including the violent wards."[21] Later, he changed his story to make himself an employee at the hospital, one of a string of jobs he had held in his teens. He may in fact have done work there, not as an employee but as part of the occupational therapy program.

There is no record of a Nova Scotia Hospital employee named Alden Nowlan, but, coincidentally, Grace trained there as a nurse for a brief period. Harriet claims that this period coincided with Alden's stay as a patient, and that Grace tried to visit him only to be turned away by her son. Indeed, one of his later "mental institution" stories, "Mother and Son," depicts a teenaged boy in an institution who is accosted by a delusional woman from one of the other wards who thinks he is her son. The young patient in the story gives in to the charade, only to have the woman snap out of her delusion and viciously turn on him, accusing him of being a liar. But Sylvia (now Rachel), who has maintained a more regular correspondence with Grace and with whom her cousin spoke about his treatment at the hospital, doubts that Grace trained at the Nova Scotia Hospital when Alden was a patient there, and she has not heard the story of Grace's visit from either Grace or Nowlan. Ervette stresses that Alden's experience at the Nova Scotia Hospital was mostly beneficial. "They kind of got him so he could meet people and so on, because he was very shy and didn't think anybody loved him."[22] Sylvia says that the doctors there started to take an interest in this bright young man and supplied books for him to read. For the first time in his life, Alden was not treated as if he were unwanted or abnormal. As he wrote in his poem, "Living in a mad house/ is not very different/ from living anywhere." But it was different from the torment he had known in Stanley. The hospital experience thrust him through the doorway to the outside world that had been opened by the Stanley airport.

In later years, he would write a story, "The Foreigner," about a mental patient who cannot communicate with his peers because he speaks a language known only to himself. The inmates spread rumours about the man's origins, but in the end it turns out he is John Smith from Nova Scotia. "He is a foreigner," the alcoholic priest of the story explains to the other inmates in a speech that could have described Alden's own situation. "The ultimate foreigner. It is quite possible that *from* **Living in a Mad House**

Living in a mad house
is not very different
from living anywhere.

On Saturdays, the kids
on insulin go to
the movies downtown,
six or eight of them,
escorted by an attendant
named MacPhee, . . .
whose mere appearance
in a crowd of children
is enough to create
near-anarchy.

It's less than half a mile
from the gate to the theatre
and so they walk there and back, . . .
having fun with MacPhee
until they stand in the lobby
where, all of a sudden,
they become Those People
from the Asylum.
The word spreads like
a breeze ruffling the grass.

he will learn to speak English. Perhaps he will be released and sent home. But when he goes home, he will be a foreigner, just as he is a foreigner here." The story, originally published in the November 1964 issue of the *Canadian Forum*, was challenged in the following issue in a letter to the editor written by Renald Shoofler, a Montreal poet and psychiatric nursing assistant. "I am writing this in the office of a ward of a mental hospital," he says, "and, although this hospital may not be typical, only our most paranoid patients could possibly conceive it to be anything like the setting of *The Foreigner*."[23]

Nowlan was quick to pen a rejoinder, which appeared in the January issue:

> In your December issue, Renald Shoofler criticizes my story *The Foreigner* rather presumptuously — I say presumptuously not because I believe my work should be immune to criticism, but because his criticism is based on the rather curious grounds that my story doesn't describe conditions as they exist at the mental hospital where he works.
>
> Really, his letter is too silly to warrant a reply. For instance, he says that the existence of a gate at the institution described in my story is a "minor inaccuracy" because his institution has none. In the very next sentence, he tells of visiting another institution that "had a formidable gate."
>
> He says strait jackets were abolished in 1930. Rubbish. I've seen people trussed up in them. He says jokingly that the clearest picture he has of a strait jacket comes from Mr. Nowlan's description of one. Mr. Nowlan's description should be clear. It was written by an eyewitness.
>
> He says he has never seen a guard do anything more strenuous than collect his pay. I can only assume his experience as a nursing assistant has been limited to a front ward inhabited by placid morons, orphaned idiots and drying-out alcoholics. The guards with whom I'm acquainted would laugh in his face if he handed them any of that guff.
>
> He says the fact that the inmates in *The Foreigner* are allowed to eat only with spoons is another "minor inaccuracy." Balderdash. In the back wards of some institutions, they eat with their hands or shove their faces down into

the plate. I have seen inmates in such wards eating their own excrement.

You're damn right the public image of mental hospitals is deplorable. But you don't cure cancer by calling it a rose.

As for that "oh aren't I suave and superior" stuff about Mr. Nowlan seeing *Shock Corridor* and *The Caretakers* and lifting the courtyard scene from *The Enormous Room*, I can assure Mr. Shoofler that Mr. Nowlan has never seen *Shock Corridor*, has never seen *The Caretakers* and has never read *The Enormous Room*.

But Mr. Nowlan has seen and heard and touched and smelt and tasted everything he ever wrote about.[24]

Shoofler's critique had found its mark. Nowlan's efforts to hide the painful feelings of his past struggled with his desire to make his audience believe that his suffering was authentic. Of course, what Shoofler could not have known, and what Nowlan did not tell him, was that the setting of the story was removed not just in space but in time, more than fifteen years in the past, to be precise.

Like the man in the story, Alden, now fifteen, returned to Stanley early in 1948 and found himself even more of a foreigner than before. Once home, the former night-owl began to rise on cold, dark winter mornings to help his father cut trees in the forest for contractors. At last he was doing a man's work for a man's pay, but village society still did not accept him, and he made no effort to bridge the gulf that was growing between him and them. Alden had been through the doorway into the real world, and his plan was not to reconcile himself to the village but to escape it. Writing would provide the means for his salvation, and he started to hone his talent. Having read that no editor would accept a handwritten manuscript, he spent his man's pay on a typewriter from the Eaton's catalogue. When it arrived, he found himself stymied by the contraption. It came with no instruction manual, and he had never seen one used, so he spent the better part of three days trying to figure out how to operate it.

The next year, Russell Palmer hired him on at the mill. Considered too awkward to work on the machines with the other men, Alden became the night watchman for three dollars a day, eighteen dollars a week. The arrangement seemed to work well for everyone. For Alden, it was a good way to get some reading done. Before his shift, he would sometimes go across the road to get a stack of magazines from his former teacher Hilda Palmer. More often than not, he brought his own reading material. He nodded hello to Joe Best, the man who drove Palmer's team of horses and tended the mill's boiler. They were the only two men there at that hour, and they liked to chat and share a jar of rum or homebrew. The teenager then spent most of the rest of the night on a board suspended between two beams above the boiler, reading in the envelope of heat, clambering down every hour or so to check the grounds or desultorily sweep at the mess left by the day crew.

He got along with his fellow workers no better than he got along with the other children when he went to school. In fact, some of them were former classmates. Years later, he wrote to Freeman:

> The only time I'm ever proud of making money is when I think of all those miserable sons of bitches in Stanley. All those filthy little snots who used to work in the mill when I was there, and every little dirty bastard earned more than I did. I wish I could spit in their eyes.
>
> Of course, it was partly my own fault. If I had my life to live over again and was back in the mill and some of those slimy little arseholes were making fun of me, I'd grab the nearest chair and smash it over their empty heads. In the end I'd probably get beaten up, but at least I'd have earned their respect. Since leaving Stanley I've learned to fight back. Nobody pushes me around anymore.[25]

"He wouldn't talk to people or come out in the daytime or anything like that," says Lawrence Anthony, one of the mill workers. "He wouldn't come to work until everybody else was out of the mill. He didn't come while there were any people there. And he'd be gone before they showed up in the morning." Anthony denies Alden's stories of mistreatment:

> Everybody looks at the world through their own glasses, eh? None of us really see things exactly the same. . . . It still had to be mostly in his imagination because he didn't have contact with anybody besides Frank [Anthony] and Joe [Best]. They were more intimately involved with the boiler and would be there earlier in the morning and later at night.

Anthony's friend Owen Lowe, who knew Alden as a child, sums up the village's attitude towards the harsh descriptions of Stanley in his books, poems and essays. "Most people were either amused or outraged at them, I think, depending on who you were. I was kind of amused by them myself, but some people were outraged."[26]

Alden's alienation from society exacerbated — and was in turn fed by — the growing estrangement between him and his erstwhile soul mate, Harriet. She had returned to Freeman's house from Sylvester's and Alberta's home at about the same time as Alden returned from the Nova Scotia Hospital. Her return was not entirely voluntary. "Harriet stole from my mother on a regular basis, and also lied to her," Sylvia claims. Once, when the family was away on a Sunday trip, Harriet broke in to the house through a window, collecting her clothes and stealing some of Alberta's things.[27] Harriet was now fourteen, with a string of boyfriends and such a wild reputation that Madge Parker forbade Gail to hang around with her former chum any more. Alden felt hurt by the dramatically different directions their lives were taking. An unpublished poem, "Boyfriends," written at about the same time as *The Wanton Troopers*, corresponds with the Ernie Masters episode of the novel:

My sister's boyfriends,
dozens of them, she listed their names
on the inside covers of her exercise books,
all had the same
walk from the hips
(we farmboys walked from the shoulder),
the same Cockney eyes, the same
flexible pool players' fingers,
all talked with the slipped
accent, the tight little smile
of nineteen-year-old Haligonian sailors.

My father hated them —
feared them, too, if the truth were known;
they cracked jokes he couldn't understand,
laughed with their throats,
smelled of hair tonic and motor oil:
"wharf rats from the city."

"This damned hole," my sister said,
staring out the kitchen window
at hardwood heath, oat field, sawmill,
all haunted by the ghosts of
seven generations of land-hungry Nowlans.

When the Hot Rod came,
she ran out to meet it, laughing.

Harriet's escape route seemed to evoke a faint disgust or perhaps jealousy in her brother; for him, boyfriends were a threat because they took the women he loved away from him. In *Various Persons Named Kevin O'Brien*, Kevin muses of Stephanie, "Her only capital was her body" (p. 66).

Mixed in with Alden's feelings about Harriet were his unresolved feelings about his own sexuality. But his reputation as a misfit and a Communist scotched any attempts to make contact with the opposite sex. At one point, his frustration nearly lead him to a violent crime. While he was working in Palmer's mill, he and another equally frustrated teen hit upon a desperate idea: they would lie in wait for a girl to walk home from school, then ambush and rape her. One afternoon they hid themselves and waited for their victim to arrive, but the girl did not come that day as she was expected to, and Alden began to get scared. A violent argument ensued, and the two would-be rapists went home. "[It was] mostly the other kid's idea," he explained to a friend. "Later found out he was psychotic. . . . Do you know how you sometimes feel that a certain experience was crucial? If I were making a movie of my life, for example, this is one of the scenes I'd work into it."[28]

Alden found more wholesome pursuits with other teens on his frequent Saturday night trips to Windsor. The attraction for him was twofold. For one thing, a new library in town had become a pivotal place in his life. It offered mostly donated books, musty rejects from the bookshelves of people in Kings and Hants counties that could still interest a literate mind. "What it did contain was the complete works of Shakespeare, Milton, Sir Walter Scott, Dickens, Thackeray, Robert Louis Stevenson, H.G. Wells, Wordsworth, Jack London and Sinclair Lewis."[29] Eleanor Geary, the librarian, was impressed by the young man who took such an interest in literature, and she would let him keep books far past their due date. He did not forget her kindness.

The second attraction of the trips to Windsor was that girls were part of each expedition. Someone in the village had closed in the back of a pickup truck, built in makeshift benches and charged teens fifty cents for a round trip to Windsor. The trip to town always included a movie at the local theatre, where Alden tried to make passes at the girls. "I was so shy in those days!" he wrote to Freeman. "And scared of girls. Once I took Minnie Harvie to the movies in Windsor and spent the whole time trying to get up the nerve to put my arm around her — and never did."[30] On the truck ride back to Stanley, the jumble of bodies cuddled with each other in the cold darkness of the box, while Nowlan cuddled something that was, to him, just as precious. "The memory of those books, pressing hard against my body, is as sensuous as the memory of a sleepy young girl's head against a young boy's shoulder, his lips in her hair."[31]

The literary interests that made him an object of fun among his peers could not be hidden, so Alden tried at least to write in a way that could be understood by his village. Journalism elbowed its way past poetry and fiction to claim a larger share of his time. His papers at the University of Calgary contain one curious example of this type of writing, a mimeographed, one-page, two-sided newsletter called the *Stanley Advertiser*, dated March 21, 1950. Its editor and publisher is listed at the top of the page: Alden Albert Nowlan. The paper contains items of local interest, plus a pompous editorial introducing the new periodical: "We of the *Advertiser* have a duty as citizens we will not shirk," it concludes. "We will — to the best of our ability — represent the people of Eastern Hants County before the world. Freedom of the press is a right which we thank God and thousands of martyrs for."

Other, more controversial journalistic efforts continued to appear in Communist newspapers. One letter Alden saved in his scrapbook is from the *Canadian Tribune* of November 10, 1951. In it, he attacks big-business-owned newspapers and their opposition to socialism:

> Let us not forget that even were the Soviet Union heaven, Stalin the Messiah, and the Soviet people angels, the big business boys, holding fast to their ancient capitalistic privilege of being the best liars on earth, would continue to publish the same type of material. Naturally enough the millionaires would hate anything apt to restrict their opportunities for grabbing. These chaps are not the men who will do the dying in a third world war.

Even his poetic muse was invoked to support the revolution. "A Letter to Tomorrow" appeared in the November 26, 1951, edition of the *Tribune* under one of his pen names, Del Acadie:

Peace is the envelope of hope
Mailed into tomorrow
On the wings of a dove,
Stamped with the sign of brotherhood
and sealed with the labour of the people.

By this time, his "secret identity" was unnecessary; the writing that had cost him the respect of his community had by then cost him his job. Russell Palmer could no longer tolerate having a Communist in his employ, especially one who did shoddy work.

By the summer of 1951, Alden had found a new job on a road crew. Dreaming of the Spitfires he once flew in his mind, he hitchhiked to Halifax one day and tried to enlist in the army so he could fight in Korea. The army rejected him on the basis of poor eyesight. That summer, he also spent a couple of weeks at the home of his great-uncle, a Baptist minister who lived in New Hampshire; it was his first trip outside Nova Scotia. He redoubled his efforts at publication. In the back pages of one little poetry magazine called *Trace* he discovered a list of every other little magazine in North America. Alden methodically worked his way through the list, sending whatever poems he had been working on. One of the poems found a place in an American periodical called *Gruntvig Review*, edited by Glen Coffield, and opening the letter of acceptance changed Alden's life. "When I read that letter," he recalls, "I almost fainted — literally, the darkness rose in clouds around my feet."[32] At the age of eighteen, Alden Nowlan — or "Max Philip Ireland" as he styled himself this time — had his first published poem:

The Mists

The outer chambers of the castle are filled with mist.
Some lackey neglected to seal the great doors,
So the mists enter, reaching even the chamber where
My thanes are feasting.

My thanes drink much of the red, salt wine;
Eat much of the rich, red meat.
They do not feel the mists.

They, my thanes, breathe deeply,
Gasp, die.
One by one they fall from their places at the great table.

But I am safe in my little room,
Deep within the castle, where the mists do not reach.

I can laugh, I do laugh,
I shall die of laughter.

"The Mists" was the first of many poems that he would publish in American literary magazines.

Harriet, meanwhile, was escaping Stanley in a way that paralleled Grace's escape. By the time she was sixteen, she had married a charming and reckless young man named Ron Anthony. According to her brother, she had been engaged to a sailor fighting in the Korean War, but by the time he returned she was already married to Anthony. Due to her tender age, Freeman had to give the marriage his signed consent, which Alden forged; Harriet and Ron soon moved to Halifax.

Alden was making his own way out of Stanley. By the fall of 1951, he had begun writing occasional book reviews for the *Windsor Tribune*. A reporter there, Ken Miller, noticed unusual talent in the writing of a man so young. He took an interest in Alden and encouraged him to write more. Whether it was with Miller's encouragement or whether it was his own idea, in February of 1952 he enrolled in a special school sponsored by the Department of Agriculture, a two-week program called the Kennetcook Folk School that taught rural people about farming methods and how to organize services in their communities. As Nowlan wrote years later in the poem "What Happened When He Went to the Store for Bread," Ken Miller started a chain of peculiar circumstances that allowed Alden to escape to a better life:

Because I went to the store for bread
one afternoon when I was eighteen
and arrived there just in time to meet
and be introduced to a man who had stopped

for a bottle of Coca-Cola (I've forgotten his name),
and because this man invited me to visit
a place where I met another man who gave me
the address of yet another man,
this one in another province,
and because I wrote a letter and got an answer
which took me away from the place where I was born,
I am who I am instead of being somebody else.

The man "in another province" to whom Miller referred the young writer was the editor of a weekly paper in New Brunswick who needed a reporter. If nothing else, Alden's attendance at the Kennetcook Folk School gave him some education with which to pad his résumé; he also invented a high school education and one year's experience on a newspaper to improve it even further.

The ruse worked; he received a letter from the Hartland *Observer* offering him a position to begin in March of 1952. He wasted no time, packing only a few belongings, mostly books, into a small cardboard suitcase. He marched off to the train station one muddy morning and left his native village for good. He also left behind his father, the mill where he was bullied and then fired, and everyone he ever imagined as having slighted him — everyone he knew, for that matter, including Harriet, a circumstance that perplexed her all her life. "I don't know what happened," she says. "Because he kissed me goodbye, bought me a pen set before he left and everything. I don't know what happened."[33] As he left, an expanse of possibility lay ahead, a world where he could reinvent himself as easily as he had done on his résumé, and no one would be wiser.

What he left behind is suggested in "What Happened When He Went to the Store for Bread": "What would I have been if I hadn't left there/ when I did? I would have almost certainly/ gone mad; I think I might have killed somebody." Without doubt, he would at least have been questioned by the RCMP about his articles in the Communist press. He found out later that they had been to Stanley after he left, asking questions about him. His trusted librarian Eleanor Geary told them off in language, as she described it, "from Wapping bordering on Limehouse." But he was now free in a way that few people — even himself — could have imagined even one year earlier.

There was something else Alden did not carry with him on that day — his heavy typewriter. On July 21, 1984, a year after his death, an article appeared in the *Telegraph-Journal* about his former house in Stanley. By this time, it was owned by the Peverill family. One of their most curious possessions was an old rusted typewriter that was lying in a field with grass growing around its keys.

Disguise

This is the amazing thing
that it is so easy
to fool them —
the sane bastards.

I can talk
about weather, eat,
preside at meetings
of the PTA.
They don't know.

Me foreign as a Martian.
With the third eye in my forehead!
But I comb my hair
cleverly so it doesn't show

except a little
sometimes when the wind blows.

Hartland, New Brunswick, was the sort of town where everyone knew everyone else, where a stranger's arrival would be noted and perhaps even discussed at the gas station or the beauty parlour. The gangly young man who got off the bus from Nova Scotia might have attracted mild curiosity in any community, curiosity he tried to deflect as he stood on the steps of the newspaper office on his first chilly morning at work.

The townsfolk remember the blue serge suit most vividly. It had not kept up with his late adolescent growth spurt, being about two inches shorter on the wrists and ankles than his lanky frame required. "Flood pants" is how they described his trousers. By the standards of 1952 rural New Brunswick, he badly needed a haircut. He had a nervous habit of reaching up and brushing his dark, greasy hair away from his eyes, and he did it often, especially when confronted by the stream of curious Hartlanders who nodded hello to him as they walked past on their way to work.

Alden Nowlan was lost, as anyone could tell from the distracted way he knocked the March mud from his shoes as he stood idly on the steps of the Hartland *Observer*. Two men from the paper, Jim Murray and Ralph Lavigne, had picked the young writer up at the bus stop the night before and brought him to the house of Charlie Allen, the editor. Allen was a bit crusty, and his instructions to the new reporter were clear: Nowlan was to report for work the first thing the following morning. Allen did not know that "first thing in the morning" means "as soon as the sun is up" to lumbermen used to squeezing every productive second from the day.

At last, Nowlan was rescued from the front steps of the office by Jabe Clark, the man who designed ads for the *Observer*. Clark came by early, as he usually did, to stoke up the office stove. That morning, he kindled a friendship with the young man who would become like a son to him. "Charlie Allen might say that was the only day during the ten years that I worked for him that I got to work on time!" Nowlan once remarked to Jabe's wife, Laura.[1]

He later wrote, "I've often thought that my arrival in Hartland, New Brunswick, can't have been very different from a raw Highlands youth coming down to the dour but safe Lowlands in the Scotland of, say, 1785."[2] But Windsor, Nova Scotia, the shire town of Hants County, was much larger than Hartland, which had a population of only about a thousand. Nor was it Nowlan's first time away from home. Aside from his stay at the Nova Scotia Hospital, he had spent part of the previous summer with relatives in New Hampshire.

Yet the "raw" part is true enough. For the first time, Nowlan had access to modern conveniences he had only seen in neighbours' or relatives' houses or in the countless movies he digested in the Stanley and Windsor theatres, things such as indoor toilets, refrigeration and hot running water. He told a story about not knowing how to use a telephone when he arrived at the paper; he was so embarrassed that he ran down the street to deliver the message in person rather than admit his ignorance to anyone in the office. Having escaped to the outside world, he also discovered what to do with himself. Although he had attended to his own needs from the time he was a child, this had, up until now, meant little more than boiling water for his tea and putting his pants on before his boots. In Hartland, he had to learn to make himself part of the social world.

He craved acceptance in mainstream society, but he stubbornly resisted meeting its more basic obligations. Hygiene, fashion and nutrition were not so much normal habits as bothersome concessions to civilization. The woman in charge of finishing the lump of Nova Scotian clay was Bertha Shaw, a formidable lady who ran a boarding house on Lower Main Street, across the street from Charlie Allen's house. Mr. Shaw plied a dwindling trade in harness-making in his basement. Bertha — whom everyone including Nowlan called "Mrs. Charlie Shaw" until the day she died — would have perhaps the greatest influence over the young man during those early years in Hartland.

Living in the Shaws' house was less like being a tenant and more like being adopted as their youngest son. The motherless Nowlan quickly made up for lost time by submitting himself to Bertha's determined affection. Along with seeing that he always ate properly, she straightened up his room, tended to his laundry, and supplemented the meagre wardrobe in the slim cardboard suitcase with a few artfully mended hand-me-downs. Nowlan reciprocated by coming home late at night, smoking, drinking, filling his room with books and papers, and committing any other minor sins that might earn him a sour look or a loving scold. He described Bertha Shaw this way: "She admired Queen Victoria, Queen Elizabeth II, Winston Churchill and John Diefenbaker. She disapproved of alcohol, tobacco, Catholicism, movies and bare-legged girls. She was overweight, her laugh was unpleasantly shrill — and I'll always think of her with vast affection."[3] In the Shaws' house, Nowlan learned the unfamiliar role of being a son.

Hartland is appropriately named, since it sits approximately in the centre of the vast potato-growing region of Carleton and Victoria counties, and Mrs. Shaw's tastes and prejudices were not unusual there. That part of the Upper Saint John River valley was staunchly Protestant St. and conservative, both socially and politically. Just as puritanism in

Nova Scotia owed much to the ministrations of the nineteenth-century evangelist Henry Alline, so could Hartland thank itinerant preacher George Whitefield Orser for founding its own homegrown religion: the Primitive Baptist Church, or the Orserites. "It was a Bible Belt town, in the strict sense of the word," is how long-time resident Harold Plummer describes Hartland. "Either politics or the church dominated everything. . . . You had two groups, and some [people] were intertwined with the Baptist Church and the Conservative party. If you weren't one of either group, you weren't there."[4]

Hartlanders spread not only the gospel of the Lord but also the gospel of the Conservative party. Heber Hatfield, owner of Hatfield Industries, a major potato processing facility, sat in the House of Commons as the member for Victoria-Carleton from 1940 to 1952 and became a trusted friend of fellow-MP John Diefenbaker. J.K. Flemming, originally from nearby Debec, lived in Woodstock and Peel during his reign as premier of New Brunswick from 1911 to 1914; his son Hugh John lived in neighbouring Juniper and held the same post from 1952 to 1960. Heber's son Richard became premier in 1970, bringing the total number of premiers from the Hartland area to three. All were Conservatives.

Hartland's weekly newspaper was — and still is — a fixture as solid as the community it serves. Allen bought the paper in 1950 from Heber Hatfield and expanded it from eight to sixteen pages. A true-blue Tory, Allen also served as secretary of the Carleton County branch of the New Brunswick Conservative party, which in the days of Hugh John Flemming was almost like being secretary of the provincial party. Allen could also call himself the Tories' unofficial printer. The Observer kept afloat financially in part because it handled a lot of the job printing for the party and, when the Conservatives were in power, for the provincial government as well.

A glance through old issues of the Observer suggests another stable source of money: the churches. The most interesting examples of religious revenue are the large, elaborate ads for travelling evangelists. The success of these "evangelistic teams" in places like Hartland earned New Brunswick a stop on the sawdust circuit that stretched all the way from the southern United States. The revivals originated mostly in the US and featured choirs, charismatic speakers, healings, and other pageantry limited only by the showman's imagination.

The Observer's other source of religious revenue came from job printing for various congregations. Charlie Allen supposedly had a

Hartland *Observer*, June 19, 1952.

button installed in his office to ensure that this source would not dry up. The button rang a little buzzer in the production office where most of the staff worked. When Allen saw one of the town's ministers coming up the front steps to check on the progress of the church bulletin, he rang the buzzer. The staff knew that that was the signal to break out in a "spontaneous" round of hymn-singing. Naturally, the clergymen were impressed by the piety of the good Christians singing praises to the Lord while they worked at the *Observer* office. Luckily for Allen, the staff were good singers and good sports.

Allen apparently did not share their high spirits. Nowlan, writing years later in his notebook, says, "I'm ambivalent in my feelings towards him. Hatred mixed with affection. He became a father figure for me. I was shamefully eager to win his approval and never did. So part of me hates him."[5] Among Allen's foibles was a terrible tight-fistedness that led him to steam stamps off incoming envelopes to put on outgoing envelopes and to modify the bottle opener on the pop machine in order to save the caps, which he would later examine in case they contained unclaimed prize tokens.

Nowlan arrived in Hartland at a time of change. Just two months earlier, on January 3, 1952, Heber Hatfield had died while still sitting as Hartland's MP. A by-election was called by the Liberal government of Louis St. Laurent for May 26. With few seats in the House of Commons, the Conservatives wanted to make sure that even a safe riding like Victoria-Carleton would remain in their hands. Hatfield's friend John Diefenbaker came to help Gage Montgomery campaign in the by-election. Diefenbaker was especially known to *Observer* readers, since his speech in support of the proposed Bill of Rights had been printed in its entirety in the paper a few weeks before his visit. When Dief arrived at the office, Allen sent the new kid, Al Nowlan, down into the basement among the boxes of junk and decomposing stacks of newspapers to dig the issue out of the "files":

> Diefenbaker insisted on helping me. We sat on broken cardboard boxes overflowing with stock cuts — pictures of Santa Claus, for instance, that we used in every Christmas edition — and searched through stacks of cobwebby newsprint until we found the issue he wanted. He talked — about weekly newspapers and Joe McCarthy and Sir John A. Macdonald and Winston Churchill and Gabriel Dumont, lieutenant to Louis Riel. The man impressed me even more than the legend. It took me a while to admit to myself that I had been a little un-comfortable when he read his own words from the newspaper: at the end of each sentence he had given a little grunt of self-congratulations. Still, I thought that I had been in the presence of a figure who was larger than life. A great man. I still think so today.[6]

Nowlan was not the only one who thought a lot of Diefenbaker. The Hatfield family hosted him at their house for dinner and later received his thank-you note from Ottawa. Fred Hatfield told his wife, "Kay, you put that letter amongst your keepsakes, because that man's going to be Prime Minister of Canada someday." After winning his third bid to lead the Conservative party, Diefenbaker later proved this prediction to be correct. Gage Montgomery, meanwhile, won the by-election handily by 2360 votes.[7]

That was not the only election of 1952. Hugh John Flemming's Tories were set to end the Grits' seventeen-year reign in New Brunswick, and the *Observer* office was practically campaign headquarters for the "Carry On, Hugh John" campaign. On his way in and out of the paper, Flemming often stopped by the desk of the new kid to chat. Everyone who had met the new reporter knew that he was a different sort of chap: shy and rough around the edges but keenly intelligent. When Flemming was accompanied by his wife, Aida, she stayed with Nowlan while Allen and Flemming talked about the campaign. Aida and Nowlan shared a love of animals and nature, and he became good friends with the Flemmings, so much so that the new Premier could tease the young man one day on his way out of the *Observer* office: "I think you're falling in love with my wife." By that point, the awkward young man could manage a grin. Aida would soon be known for founding the Kindness Club, an organization devoted to the humane treatment of animals. Nowlan kept his friendship with the Flemmings for the rest of his life and would later write an annual newspaper column on behalf of the Kindness Club.

Allen used Nowlan mostly as a reporter to cover local news stories. The duties of running a paper and the added weight of political duties that year had increased to the point where the editor could not report on events himself. He could not always write his weekly editorial, either. These tasks fell to the other staff, who handled in-house jobs including writing regular columns, typesetting, printing and layout. Nowlan ended up covering things that took place outside the office, such as car accidents, city council meetings and agricultural fairs. The "high-school education" he flaunted on his résumé also came in handy when he filled in as the paper's proof-reader.

Nowlan fit in to his new surroundings socially as well as professionally. Hartlanders' curiosity about strangers was mostly benign and in many cases downright friendly. Harold Plummer recalls Nowlan's amusement at unidentified old ladies stopping him on the street to chat. "Someone told her I was strange," he would comment to Plummer. "She just wanted to find out for herself how strange I was."

Initially, Nowlan cultivated friendships with avuncular figures and then, as he grew more used to his surroundings, with young men closer to his age. One of these surrogate uncles was Jack Whitehead, an older gentleman close to retiring from his job with the Canadian Pacific Railway. Whitehead also boarded at the Shaws'. At times cantankerous and opinionated, the older man enjoyed a mock-adversarial friendship with the green kid from Nova Scotia. Among Nowlan's papers at the University of Calgary is an old, scratched audio recording of him and Whitehead having a political debate, with Whitehead taking the Liberal part and Nowlan the Conservative. Whitehead, it seems, usually got the better of the young man in such contests.

Nowlan later wrote about Clinton "Jabe" Clark, the man who let him in to the *Observer* office on his first chilly morning at work, "He was even a kind of father figure, or at the very least, an uncle figure to me."[8] Jabe's son Hugh remembers his father's close relationship with the new arrival: "Of course, they were back and forth together. . . . He saw more of Alden than Mother and Dad saw of one another."[9] Clark mostly did layout for the paper, and in his spare time he played office pranks. His favourite trick was to wait until someone, preferably a female, occupied a stall in the office washroom. He would then ignite an old newspaper and throw it over the transom. When there was no paper handy, he would make do with cold water, coins or a handful of linotype slugs.

"Sit still for a second, Dogberry," Jabe once said to the young man who was writing furiously to make a deadline.

"What's that?" Nowlan craned his head to see what the older man was drawing. Jabe finished and presented his masterpiece to Nowlan: a caricature of a skinny kid with glasses, a prominent Adam's apple, and a cigarette dangling from his mouth.

Or they would compete to see who could identify more B movie bit players. "That's Myron Brand," Nowlan muttered. "That guy there in the black hat playing the sidekick."

"Not bad," the master conceded. "But that one there, the one who got shot? That's Fred J. Zimmerman. He played Shirley Temple's uncle in *The Little Colonel*, and he was the barkeeper in that old Rod Cameron movie, *Panhandle Stampede*."

Buss Oliver was another *Observer* character who became a playmate and uncle to Nowlan. Like the Clark family, the Olivers took Nowlan under their wing. One of the first words out of their little daughter Susan's mouth was "Awl." Buss and Alden became office comedians. They invented a routine in which they imitated two rural housewives gossiping over the back fence. Whether people thought they were hilarious or crazy depended on how much they knew and appreciated the nuances of rural New Brunswick life. They were seen so often wandering about together that they earned the nicknames "Mutt and Jeff," after the comic strip characters. On Christmas Eve, when they would start at one end of Main Street and work their way to the other end visiting friends and partaking of Christmas cheer, they were called "Scrooge and Marley."

Nowlan's older male friends in Hartland gave him the camaraderie he lacked in Stanley and, in a sense, allowed him to finish off his childhood before jumping into the more uncertain waters of being an adult. This "education" had a practical as well as an intangible side. Jabe Clark showed him the ins and outs of working at a newspaper, as well as introducing him to the more esoteric joys of B movies. When Nowlan and Buss Oliver were not performing their comedy routines, Buss was instructing him on some of the finer points of fly fishing or taking him and a few other men down to the harness racing track in Woodstock or Fredericton to bet on the horses. For Nowlan, it must have been reminiscent of his childhood adventures with Uncle Albert.

The younger men at the paper, such as Ralph Lavigne or Jim Murray assumed part of the responsibility for Nowlan's twentieth-century education. Murray volunteered to teach him how to drive a car. Nowlan's first car was as shabby as his wardrobe, and he took equal care of it. He bought it for only two or three hundred dollars, within reach of his meagre salary. Whenever he finished drinking a bottle of pop or beer, he threw the empty over his shoulder, and the bottle collection on the floor soon rivalled the car in value. When he jammed on the brakes — which was often — the bottles would all roll forward to the floor under the driver's and passenger's feet. He remedied this by stepping on the gas extra hard when starting off again. Murray tells of other exciting moments on one of their instructional trips to Woodstock and back. On one occasion, Murray, spying the farm where he usually bought his eggs, told his student to pull in to the farmyard. Nowlan made the turn at too great a speed and ended up driving across the lawn, nearly taking the corner off the house. The next obstacle was the world's longest covered bridge, which spans the St. John River at Hartland. This bridge has room for only one lane of traffic. Although there was no opposing traffic that afternoon, Nowlan hugged the right-hand railing just to be extra safe, scraping the entire side of his car.

Jabe Clark inducted Nowlan into more mystical secrets, which the young man, already educated by mail-order literature about such things as astral projection and the Ascended Masters, was ready to receive. Within a couple of months of his arrival, Clark hustled Nowlan into the building next door to the *Observer*, a building owned by Brighton Lodge No. 31 of the Knights of Pythias, or KPs. Other men at the paper and in town tried to draft him into Hartland Lodge No. 46 of the Free and Accepted Masons. Nowlan could hardly refuse. "If there had been a local branch of the Oddfellows I would probably have joined them, too," he wrote. "That is how it was in small towns in the 1950s."[10]

A reader who knows Nowlan only through his poetry might be

surprised to learn that he was an enthusiastic joiner, even by those 1950s small-town standards. The sarcasm of early poems such as "Our Brother Exalted," where the lodge of "the Mystic East/ encompassed by the hall on Fifth and Main" is guarded by "Arab brothers" who are merely "hardware sales[men]" and "grocery clerks," suggests anything but fraternal goodwill on the poet's part. The lodge meeting ends when the lodge's high priest "in arcane ritualistic prose . . . orders closure of the occult tome," whereupon the brethren "play nickel poker and go home." Nowlan, however, took the rituals seriously. Advancement in the Masonic order depended on being able to memorize long speeches verbatim and perform them in front of the brethren. "He was really dedicated, and he was excellent — went through several offices, knew his work and was always prepared," says Harold Plummer, a former Hartland Mason. "They just thought Al was the greatest thing that ever came along."[11]

Even as a young man, Nowlan was sophisticated enough to appreciate how ceremony can be simultaneously ridiculous and beautiful:

> I once heard a roomful of people laugh over a newspaper advertisement calling for "the brethren to assemble in dress aprons" for a funeral. I don't blame them for laughing. To the uninitiated, it evokes a ludicrous mental picture: men in black suits wearing aprons that one imagines as being dainty, white and frilly, with an enormous Alice-in-Wonderland bow at the back. I couldn't join in the laughter, however, because I had attended funerals where there would have been nobody except the minister, the undertaker and the gravedigger if it hadn't been for the Freemasons or the Knights of Pythias . . . men who were alone at the end not because they were misanthropes or derelicts but because they had outlived their friends, or had died far from home. If you belonged to the Knights of Pythias, you were sure of being visited in the hospital, and by people who weren't complete strangers, even if they had never met you before. The best service performed by the lodges lay in lessening the loneliness of the old.[12]

And, in Nowlan's case, they lessened the loneliness of the young. Still bearing the scars of social isolation, he probably had more complicated motives for becoming a KP or Mason than the beauty of ceremony or a desire to help the aged. Nowlan became a consummate joiner of clubs and committees that had little to do with ceremonies or the public weal, from the local Fish and Game Association to the committee for Hartland's first Potato Festival. Hugh Clark explains, "He was very much, not the joiner, but the organizer. Or, at least, give him something and he could make it work, put it together to make an organization work. I think, in Hartland, somebody like that was very much appreciated, and they used him in various organizations. He ended up quite often being secretary of this or treasurer of that."[13] Ultimately, his writing and reportorial skills kept him in demand as someone who could take legible minutes, which, for the price of companionship, he was willing to furnish.

Still, an irony plays in the background of poems like "Our Brother Exalted" that allows Nowlan both to love and to despise his society. The Masons and KPs, when they were not playing nickel poker or drinking beer at the Legion, engaged in the same fantasy play that helped send him to the Nova Scotia Hospital. Only now the most upright members of the town, God-fearing businessmen, sanctioned this fantasy. Nowlan must have felt a little bitter reflecting on this irony. Were the rituals and beliefs of the KPs really so different from those of his own Nylonian Church Upon the Rock, or was it just that the KPs had more members? The Masonic myths were no more elaborate than those of the Whitroccan or Whitmanian empires he continued to invent on paper during idle moments. Only now he saw that myth and ritual could be not agents of alienation, but communal experiences that drew people together. The trick was in earning the social approbation that upheld and, at the same time, neutralized their sacramental nature.

There was another important reason why Nowlan was drawn to older men and their fraternal orders: they were safe. That a young man who had led such a deprived and isolated life could throw himself into the community with such vigour was impressive, but it was also relatively risk-free. Risk for Nowlan was represented by the activity he was consciously or unconsciously omitting from his Hartland life: social contact with people his own age. No doubt he remembered how his peers bullied him in school or in the mill back home. In Hartland, he tended to become friends with the people he met in his daily life: co-workers at the *Observer* or fellow boarders at the Shaws', mostly people over thirty.

Not only were they older, but many of his friends were also married. Female companionship for the shy young man was thereby also risk-free; there was no possibility of exploring his sexual feelings with his friends' wives. The shy young man preferred things this way; he could explore sex more securely in his writings. Meeting younger people would mean sharing their interests, which usually revolved around the pursuit of single, eligible members of the opposite sex. Many of Nowlan's early poems deal with this risky world of women and of young men like himself in pursuit of them, although accounts of people who knew Nowlan in Hartland suggest that such experiences were strictly vicarious for the awkward young man. "He just had no idea how they worked," says Harold Plummer of his friend's relationships with young women.

> He had no idea how to approach them. He didn't approach them. He just had a fear of what the whole thing was about, basically. It was easier to just sort of ignore it. I took him down to a KC [Knights of Columbus] hall or Masonic hall up where the school is [in Woodstock]. They had Saturday night dances. I took Al down there, and he was about three-quarters snapped [drunk]. He was very awkward in terms of dancing, just in awe. I brought this girl over — I don't know who she was, she was about half snapped. I had her dance with Al for a while, and he just cringed. He wouldn't get up, he just wouldn't. We didn't stay a long time, because, you know, usually when you have a few drinks you lose your inhibitions. But that was not his thing, that was a horror show to him. That was panic city. The worst-case scenario would be his being forced to dance with someone Saturday night at the Masonic Hall. If there was anything that wasn't him, that was it.[14]

Nowlan, years later, told a similar story of his romantic exploits:

> When I was younger and reasonably attracted to nymph-ettes I was too self-conscious to know which of them were willing and would have been too shy to do anything about it even if I had known. . . . Years and years ago when I lived in the Holy City of Hartland, New Brunswick (that is its real nickname, used by its more ribald citizens in reference to its many churches), I was one of the chaperones

If I could turn and meet myself

Saturday Night

Every five minutes they turn,
with their tires like sirens,
tusking the dirt up on the creek road,
and drive back through town —

slowing down on Main Street, manoeuvring
between the farmers' cars, hooting
at girls on the pavement who reply
with little hen movements, laughing, waiting.

The boys sport leather jackets and levis,
but that's their underwear,
the car is their real clothing:
at Taylor's Corner they turn again,
their Hollywood mufflers
making sounds furious, derisive, vulgar —
like a bear growling and breaking wind,

and roar through Main Street again.

at a dance sponsored by one of the town's two score organizations, to all of which I belonged. I was, oh, about twenty-five or twenty-six. Afterwards I drove this little girl of about sixteen home and, on a wicked impulse, did a little groping with her by the roadside — small bites on the earlobes sort of thing. After a bit of that the young lady announced, "You'd better cut out that damn foolishness and stick it into me, because I've got to be home by twelve or the old man will murder me." Silly ass that I am, I burst out laughing and then drove her home.[15]

As with his stories about Kevin O'Brien's sexual exploits in Desolation Creek, there is no gossip in Hartland to confirm anything other than the town's general impression that Nowlan was painfully shy around women.

A few women found this awkwardness endearing, however, and Nowlan's involvement with Hartland's many organizations did afford some opportunities to associate with young, single women. Fred Hatfield remembers one time when Nowlan came into the Hatfield Industries office to talk about fishing with the secretary, Ethyl Downey, an avid angler. "Ethyl," said Nowlan, "as the new president of the Hartland Fish and Game Association, I suppose I should learn how to fish."

"I suppose you should, Al."

"So I'm wondering if, the next time you and Hazel go out fishing, you would mind taking me along?"

The next sunny Saturday saw Ethyl and her friend Hazel, a teacher, splashing up the edge of the stream while, far behind, the president strolled along in his own world. When the women went back to find out what had become of their charge, they found him lolling by the stream reading a book. "You know, I don't understand about this fishing thing," Nowlan said. "I'd sooner read. It's beautiful out here."

He also enjoyed an ersatz experience of female companionship by conducting lonely affairs with telephone operators in various corners of North America. Nowlan managed to make friends with one of the operators at the local telephone exchange. Late at night, when drunk or feeling lonely, he would often call her up to chat about nothing. Sometimes the operator offered to connect him to other operators, and so the young poet courted unknown women working the night shift from Newfoundland to Alabama.

He was not the only young man in Hartland who felt himself to be an outsider. There were others who, like him, wanted more out of youth than to "hitchhike to a dance/ in Larchmont or Bennington,/ get drunk as a fiddler's bitch,/ roostering for skirts and fist-fights" on a Saturday night. Harold Plummer also felt unsatisfied by the alternatives of youthful irresponsibility and conservative respectability that the town offered. A recent graduate of Mount Allison University in Sackville, New Brunswick, he met Nowlan through the Freemasons and was impressed with the wit and intelligence of this grade-school dropout. Wayne Tompkins was another university-educated young man who liked to talk with Nowlan and Plummer in a car in someone's field while sharing a bottle of Rancherman's gin. Tompkins was a little too refined and intellectual for Nowlan's tastes, so Nowlan began developing a skill that would repay him with hours of amusement and a few bitter quarrels in later years: intellectual-baiting. His far-reaching knowledge allowed him the luxury of advancing absurd or wildly controversial notions, to the consternation of those who were burdened with too much brain and too little humour.

Religion and traditional morality were also favourite targets, particularly what he came to describe as the puritan mindset. Harold Plummer often found himself an unwitting accomplice in his friend's mocking of mainstream values.

"What will you two be having this evening?" the waitress asked when the two of them stopped into the Dayesta restaurant one evening. Plummer knew that Nowlan was in one of his mischievous moods.

Nowlan intoned, "And, lo, Alden, prophet of the Lord, spake unto his servant. And he said, 'Bring forth a hamburg and an order of french fries, for supper is good unto mine eyes. And let the drink be Coca-Cola that it might slake my thirst in the desert.'"

The waitress turned red but maintained her composure as she wrote. "Hamburg, french fries and a cola. And you, sir?" she said to Plummer.

The Prophet spake again. "Let Harold, beloved servant of Alden, have a hot chicken sandwich and mashed potatoes. Yea, let there be peas and coleslaw in abundance, and let his cup runneth over with coffee. Amen."

"Uh, sure. That will do," Plummer mumbled as he tried to avoid the hostile glances from other tables.

The waitress returned with the food. "I just hope you know, sir, that Reformed Baptists like myself believe that you can go to hell for making fun of the Bible like that."

"Oh, yes, verily," Nowlan replied without a hitch. "He that maketh fun of the Word shall be boiled in oil as the french fry, battered as the onion ring, and shaken as the malted."

"And I don't want a tip, either," the waitress added.

The safe social world Nowlan constructed for himself in Hartland was actually just the thing he needed to escape the deprivations of "Desolation Creek." Meeting women may have been difficult for him during the early 1950s, but he found a fellowship with men that he did not know before. In Hartland he had companions to laugh with, to drink with, to smoke with, and to talk with, sometimes quite intelligently. He had not one family but several: the Shaws, with whom he lived, and the Clarks and Olivers, with whom he watched hockey games and stayed up late at night playing cards and eating tuna sandwiches. Sometimes the Olivers served up bacon and eggs — usually on mornings after visiting the Northland Lounge in nearby Houlton, Maine.

On one long weekend, Nowlan and some friends travelled down to Boston to watch the Red Sox play a triple-header against the Orioles. These were the days of the great Ted Williams, whose home run Nowlan missed that day because he was buying a beer. Equally entertaining were the girls in the burlesque revue they saw after the game in the Old Howard Theater.

> I watched the most erotic dance I've ever seen, done by a girl — she looked to be about my age or a little younger, which is to say between eighteen and twenty-two or twenty-three — who gave her entire performance in street clothes, while surrounded by gyrating thirtyish women in pasties and G-strings. That was so fantastic that there has been the odd moment since when I believed that the girl must be a trick of memory. Surely, the Old Howard would never have dared offer anything so elegantly perverse. But she was real enough. All long legs and whirling skirts and flashing panties. And on the same bill with Blaze Fury, the Human Heat Wave, whose act concluded with her squealing, "Whee!" while riding the stage curtain like a hobby-horse.[16]

Nowlan had a different taste of the wider world from a trip he took to Ottawa in the spring of 1956. There, he sat in the visitors' gallery and watched the shenanigans in the House of Commons during the pipeline debate, when even C.D. Howe looked "arrogant to the point of insanity."[17]

There was one situation in which Nowlan was not shy: meeting other writers. Even shortly after arriving in Hartland, when he still stammered nervously when meeting people on the street, he had the courage to write to an elderly man just down the river in Woodstock who, he had discovered, was a writer. The man's reply began with the words, "My dearest boy . . ." and, before long, Nowlan was sitting in Dr. George Frederick Clarke's drawing room sipping his first sherry. A dentist by trade and a poet, historian, archaeologist and ecologist by inclination, Clarke was the author of several novels and various non-fiction works about New Brunswick life, including *The Magic Road* and *Seven Salmon Rivers and Another*. The young man was fascinated by Clarke's great stories of adventures in the New Brunswick woods, his collection of Malecite arrowheads and his ornate set of duelling pistols, which Clarke test-fired with his left hand in case one should blow up.

Even Hartland could boast its own writer of sorts. Norris Hayward, the son of a circuit court judge, had never, as far as anyone knew, held a regular job. This was not due to laziness but rather to a birth defect that affected his ability to walk. This affliction, however, did not stop him from driving the car his father willed to him, nor did it prevent him from becoming one of Carleton County's Tory stalwarts. For a time, he was press secretary to Fred McCain when he was MP for the riding. He also wrote the occasional little book or magazine article about sport fishing or operating ham radios, his other chief occupations.

The Hayward household became known as the only house in Hartland with its lights on after eleven o'clock at night. It doubled as a gathering place for those too restless to sleep and too eager to discuss great matters beyond what the little town had to offer. Nowlan was one of the regulars who sat up all night with Hayward, eating his wife Wyonita's sandwiches, borrowing some of his many books, listening to the short-wave radio and shooting the bull.

While Nowlan could find intellectual and literary friends around Hartland, he lacked writers who could be literary mentors. Clarke had a great aesthetic appreciation for English literary figures of the eighteenth and nineteenth centuries, but these writers had little to say about the world Alden Nowlan knew. For that matter, Nowlan had found little to write about in the world he knew. "Most of us have to write badly before we can write well," he later explained.[18] He intensified the poetry-writing campaign he had begun in Stanley and appeared in various little magazines, nearly all of them American, with names like *Flame, Different* and *Epos*. His best literary market in those early years was the *Bridge*, which, like the *Gruntvig Review*, was edited by Glen Coffield.

The poems Nowlan produced during his early Hartland years express the legacy of social isolation and religious and mythological reading that he had brought from Stanley. They demonstrate a prodigious knowledge of words but little sensibility of the artistic possibilities of language. This poem is from a 1956 issue of *Flame*:

The Mind is Turkestan and Proud

The mind is Turkestan and proud,
Ambiguous as clouds and slow to shriek.

The mind is morning sick, but bridal fast
To winds that pillage tents in highest Asia.

The mind is pampas and the night,
Lethiferous in jungled gods and cold.

The mind is Arctic sleep and knotted string,
The mind is midnight with the polar sun.

The poetry also shows an effort to describe things without resort to strings of adjectives. "Ormuzd and Ahriman," from a 1954 issue of *Different*, has a balanced and sparing use of adjectives coupled with strong verbs:

We sing the Phoenix
For we fear to die,
And worship the sacred cow,
Or holy lie.

"The Man with the Ring," from a 1955 issue of *The Bridge*, suggests Nowlan's struggle with metaphor and simile:

He wore a ring on his finger,
And his hands were as white
As the teeth of a thousand
Thirsty unicorns let loose
in a sun-lit street.

It also betrays his strenuous attempts at alliteration.

What is most striking about Nowlan's poems of the early 1950s — particularly to those who are familiar with his later works — is their subject matter. Far from exploring his own emotions or the human beauty around him, as much of his later poetry does, he preoccupies himself with a fantastic religious and mythological landscape. Glen Coffield, in that first acceptance letter for "The Mists" in 1951, picks up on what he thinks will become the young poet's major strength. He writes, "i should say that you might have a flare for medieval folk lore or myth or the myths of the northlands, always interpreting modern experiences, a reality of modern experiences, in the language of these myths and with their stories, much as you have in 'the mists.' the earlier you master a method, the more rapid will be your development."[19] This poem from a 1956 issue of *Epos* illustrates the direction this method took over the next few years:

The Final Prophet

Angry, the final prophet rode an ass
through concrete deserts and the neon noons,
berating undomesticated steel
that writhed through robot jungles dead of rust,
lamenting all the hills of saffron death,
undisciplined by the ploughs of vibrant time.

In spangles of the sun, the prophet rode
and meditated on immobile man,
whose navel cord entwined electric wombs
and chained him to embryos born of mind.

Dismayed by time that vanished, not with man,
but with the silence of his tired watch,
the prophet looked upon the vacuum world
and drank his anger in a wormwood laugh.

"The Final Prophet" begins to articulate Nowlan's feelings about himself and his community, albeit obliquely. Beneath the mass of adjectives, the puffed-up metaphors and the fantastic setting lies a leaner and more personal verse such as that in "The Expatriate":

The Expatriate

Though bred of rocks and stiffened lips
He planned his cruel escape,
And longed to loll in lusty lands
Of garlic and the grape.

And yet, beside another sea,
He finds the frost remains
Within his blood to taunt him with
The privacy of chains.

These two poems have a different feel, but the underlying concern of both — a concern common to many artists — is the poet's perceived alienation from society.

As "The Expatriate" suggests, Nowlan's emotions were more complicated than a general sense of separateness from his new community. He also felt that he was carrying something around inside him, something that made true physical escape impossible without its spiritual component. The backwoods community of his birth reclaimed him every summer, when he left the new friends he had made in Hartland and took the train back to Stanley, more from a reluctance to explain to his friends why he did not return home on holiday than a wish to repair family bonds. More often than not, he found Freeman drunk when he arrived at the house, which deteriorated more with every year.

Alden did find a friend in his aunt Alberta and a kindred spirit in his young cousin Sylvia. Although he and Sylvia were separated by eleven years, the two were united in their desire to use their intellects to escape what they saw as a miserable and poverty-ridden existence in Hants County. Their common lot knit the cousins in a spiritual kinship, and they unofficially adopted each other as siblings, which was fitting since they shared the same "father," Sylvester. Years later, Nowlan sent his cousin a hand-drawn map of the community they had escaped. He bitterly rechristened the geographical features of the village to reflect his attitude towards them: the Slough of Despond, the Road to Ruin and his own nickname for Stanley, Desolation Creek.

Sylvia's family, however, could not really be called poor, especially in comparison with the Nowlans. After Sylvester was injured by a propeller at the airfield, he and Alberta built a front porch onto their house in Mosherville that became the local post office. He delivered the mail and she ran the business end of things at the office, but that was as far as their partnership went. "My mom had taken accountant's courses because she expected to leave Sylvester one day and go to town to lead a quality life," Sylvia recalls. "So Mom was determined that I escape, and she had that ambition for Alden, too, the ambition to be academic and educated. Alden and Mom would sit at the table and talk of ambition and their dreams."[20] But Alberta would not see her dreams come to fruition. Always frail, she had nearly succumbed to a blood clot in her brain in 1947, shortly after Harriet had left their house and returned to live with Freeman.

During and after a long and painful recovery, Alberta took blood-thinning agents to prevent a recurrence of clots, but this medication would later prove her undoing. One November day in 1958, as Alberta was negotiating a boarded path to their outhouse, she slipped on an icy patch and fell, rupturing her spleen. She managed to struggle back to the house, where Sylvia found her when she came home from school. Internal bleeding, aided by the blood-thinning agents, was slowly draining her life away. Sylvester took her to the hospital after he came home that night, but it was too late. However, Alberta had already formulated a plan for Sylvia's escape, a plan that Sylvester, whose relationship with his daughter was almost as tenuous as Grace's was with her children, did not oppose. Alberta's sister and brother-in-law, who lived in Waltham, Massachusetts, and had always been close to Sylvia, arranged to adopt her and take her to the United States. In August, 1959, Sylvia crossed the border into a new life one day shy of her fifteenth birthday, a move that would take her out of her beloved cousin Alden's orbit for the next ten years.

On the long train rides back from his Stanley visits, the realization dawned on Nowlan that he had, in fact, escaped nothing by leaving Stanley; his internal ghosts had chased him from Nova Scotia to New Brunswick and haunted him still. Gradually, he turned his literary efforts to a more frank examination of his roots in "Desolation Creek," his family, and the nature of true spiritual liberation.

One of his first (and surely one of his most naked and heart-wrenching) creations tore the scabs off his childhood wounds. It was not a poem at all. Trying his hand at a short story, Nowlan wrote "Hurt," an unflinching portrait of Stevie, a young boy growing up in rural poverty. In spite of Stevie's desperate boast that "when I grow up there ain't nothin' ever gonna hurt me," he lives in a world where he is doomed by his destitution, his alcoholic father, an uncaring school system — and a powerful and sensitive imagination:

> When Stevie cried it was never for the reasons the rest of the kids cried. Miss Grant, who taught school at Hastings Mills the year I was ten, strapped him every time he skipped school and while she was smacking him he bit his lower lip and blinked at the blackboard and after it was over he went back to the desk and spat on his palms and thumbed his nose at her elaborately as she turned her back, so that everyone laughed.
>
> But one noon hour when he had nothing for lunch except a gooey chocolate bar and she offered him some of her sandwiches, he bolted away from her and afterwards I found him in the woodshed, lying face down in the sawdust, his shoulders shaking with sobs.

What really makes "Hurt" hit home is the glimpse the reader has of the essential humanity and sensitivity of the hero, which we know in time will be crushed by his circumstances, however hard he may try to fight back. Still engaged in his own struggle not to let the pain of his past weigh him down, Nowlan made a critical decision not to tell the story from Stevie's point of view. This, he thought, "would have sounded excessively subjective and no doubt it would also have sounded self-pitying."[21] So he created the character of Skip, the narrator, and made the story even more poignant by seeing it through Skip's dispassionate eyes. Nowlan sent "Hurt" to *Queen's Quarterly*, which published it in 1956 and paid him three dollars for the privilege. When George Frederick Clarke read his protégé's story, as he told Nowlan later, it brought tears to his eyes. "Nothing that anyone has ever said to me about my work has meant more to me than that, coming as it did when I was young, lonely, uncertain and unknown," Nowlan wrote.[22]

He also had another writing career of sorts, as a freelance contributor of articles to various magazines. One of the first to accept his submissions was the *Family Herald*, a magazine he had read nearly all his life. Most of his articles dealt with farm topics such as seed dryers and potatoes, but there were some other, more creative pieces. "I Discovered a Mountain" appeared in the July 28, 1955, issue, at around the same time as he must have been working on "Hurt." The similarities to Ernest Buckler's *The Mountain and the Valley*, published three years previously, suggests that the novel might have influenced Nowlan's fiction writing as much as his renewed contact with Stanley did. "I Discovered a Mountain" is a halcyon portrait of childhood radically tailored to suit the *Family Herald* audience:

> Morning came with golden suddenness. The sunbeams danced on the ceiling and flitted gracefully over multi-coloured quilts. The boastful crow of a rooster and the plaintive bellow of a cow came through the window, and in the rooms below me dishes clattered enticingly. A kick of blankets, a swing of legs and splash of cold water on my cheeks, a noisy rush downstairs, and I was eating, like an undernourished wolf. I gulped down huge spoonfuls of hot, creamy oatmeal porridge, relished the flavoursome hard boiled eggs and washed it all down with the morning's milk, while glancing with mild envy at the coffee simmering on the stove which I was not allowed to drink.[23]

Despite the promise of stories like "Hurt," Nowlan lacked the confidence to take the next big step in making his imaginative writing truly public. As he well knew, the *Family Herald* was read widely in rural communities by the same people he worked beside, grew up with and was related to; *Queen's Quarterly* was not.

Therefore he tried to keep his literary and journalistic worlds separate. "He didn't make [his poetry] common knowledge to anybody else for a long while,"[24] says Jim Murray, and other people who lived in Hartland at the time concur. When the two worlds collided, embarrassment and hurt feelings could result, as when Mrs. Shaw, cleaning in the room of her pack-rat tenant, ran across one of the other magazines he wrote for. Along with contributing to the *Family Herald*, Nowlan wrote opinion pieces for magazines including the *Canadian Commentator* and the *Realist*. The magazines were innocuous by most people's standards, cranky at worst, but some of the articles Nowlan wrote, such as "Some Thoughts on Pornography" for the November, 1958, issue of the *Realist*, would have made Mrs. Shaw's puritan blood boil. The cover of an October, 1956, issue of *Progressive World*, depicting a medallion of Rodin's *Thinker* and emblazoned with the words "Published by the United Secularists of America," features the article "Punitive Morality," by Alden A. Nowlan. "She overlooked a lot of Al's life," says Harold Plummer. "But she couldn't tolerate something like that. Something that would include sex or anything that was anti-religious would be very difficult for her."[25] For Nowlan, the price of showing his creative side was to be labelled in ways which were all too familiar. "She was sure for a long time that he was a Communist, because of the types of books he read," says Fred Hatfield. "They would be books she had never even heard tell of. But she was sure he was some kind of a Communist, or Communist spy or something."[26]

Nowlan was indeed learning the craft of becoming a spy of sorts, a keen observer of the people around him; his observations would soon form the raw materials for the new type of poetry fermenting within him. Something started to trouble him in the back of his consciousness as he found himself staring out the office window. His thoughts carried him, with growing insistence, back to his home, his past. Escape was not possible after all; maybe it was not even desirable. The road that had led him away from Stanley and his family was leading him back towards them again, and this time he could not reject but must explore and embrace. Nowlan began to see the world around him through social bifocals. Hartland was giving him the experience of a man who is one with his community, but he could also perceive society through the eyes of an outcast. Stanley gave him the experience of the poor and powerless, but his new-found acquaintances among the local business and political elite allowed him to observe "the Big Man" in action. From his privileged vantage point, he began to spy on the bourgeoisie.

from **The Bull Moose**

Too tired to turn or, perhaps, aware
there was no place left to go, he stood with the cattle.
They, scenting the musk of death, seeing his great head
like the ritual mask of a blood god, moved to the other end
of the field and waited. . . .

And the bull moose let them stroke his tick-ravaged flanks,
let them pry open his jaws with bottles, let a giggling girl
plant a little purple cap
of thistles on his head.

When the wardens came, everyone agreed it was a shame
to shoot anything so shaggy and cuddlesome.
He looked like the kind of pet
women put to bed with their sons.

So they held their fire. But just as the sun dropped in the river
the bull moose gathered his strength
like a scaffolded king, straightened and lifted his horns
so that even the wardens backed away as they raised their rifles.
When he roared, people ran to their cars. All the young men
leaned on their automobile horns as he toppled.

While Nowlan toiled away at the *Observer*, churning out articles on town council meetings when Charlie Allen was looking and scratching out poems when Allen's back was turned, he discovered that there was someone reading his poetry after all. This person did not hail from Eagle Creek, Oregon, or Lake Como, Florida, but lived seventy miles down the road in the provincial capital of Fredericton. At the back of one of those little poetry magazines, where information on contributors was printed, he saw the name of Fred Cogswell, a professor at the University of New Brunswick.

Cherubic, soft-spoken and blessed with a razor-sharp wit, Cogswell was a lumbering and farming lad from Carleton County who had enrolled at UNB after he was discharged from the army at the end of the Second World War. His eyesight had been too poor for admittance to a combat unit, so the Canadian Army put his skills as a woodsman to good use by giving him a desk job with the Canadian Forestry Corps in Scotland. He credited the army for saving him from a career in the civil service. Bureaucracy's loss was literature's gain. At UNB, Cogswell found a like-minded community of writers in the Bliss Carman Society, led by Professor Alfred Bailey. In 1950, he left New Brunswick to pursue graduate studies in Edinburgh, returning two years later to breathe new life into Bailey's literary periodical, the *Fiddlehead*.

Nowlan wrote, "Two crucial events in my life as a writer took place in 1957. I went back to spend a month in my native village, and I met Fred Cogswell."

> Fred Cogswell was more than the first poet I'd ever met; he was the first person I'd ever met who read poetry. He gave me magazines, and books by people like Louis Dudek, Irving Layton and Raymond Souster, through whose work I found my way to people ranging from Catullus to William Carlos Williams. He gave me postage stamps, sent me the names of new magazines; we drank beer together and, most importantly, he listened. My mental film clips of those early meetings show me getting drunker and drunker, talking more and more, while Fred sips from his glass, puffs on his pipe, and listens. I was twenty-four years old and, in one sense, I had never before had anyone to talk with.[1]

Cogswell's version of the story puts their first meeting in 1956.[2] Both men are mistaken, although their "meeting" did indeed change Nowlan's life as a writer. The beginning of their literary friendship may be dated, not by means of their twenty- or thirty-year-old recollections, but rather from their extensive correspondence.

In a literary sense, Nowlan first met Fred Cogswell in the pages of the professor's first collection of poetry, *The Stunted Strong*, published in 1954. By this time the news editor of the *Observer*, Nowlan wrote many of the editorials, which he often used as a forum to discuss literature. As his first letter to Cogswell (dated February 22, 1955) suggests, it was the strength of the poems in *The Stunted Strong* and not the contributors' notes in the backs of little magazines, as he later claimed, that spurred him to write to Cogswell.

> Dear Mr. Cogswell:
> You may be interested in the enclosed clipping taken from the February 17th issue of the *Observer*. As you will note most of this article was devoted to a reprint of a review of your book *The Stunted Strong* published earlier in *The* [Fredericton] *Daily Gleaner*.
>
> I have noticed some of your poems in *Toronto Saturday Night*, *Flame* and *Different*. I have had verses of my own published in the latter publications and have also had poems accepted by *The Bridge, The Gruntvig Review, The New Athenaeum, The Searchlight* and *The Dalhousie Review*.
>
> All of these magazines are of the limited circulation variety — but poetry does not seem destined to gain a large audience, at any rate.
>
> With best wishes,
> Yours sincerely,
> Alden A. Nowlan
> (News Editor of the *Observer*)[3]

Cogswell's reply of April 3, 1955, shows that he, too, had been aware of a little magazine poet living close by:

> Dear Mr. Nowlan:
> Congratulations on a very fine poem in the last issue of *Flame* ["My Father Died of an Excess of Virtue"]. I enjoyed it.

I also reread with interest your poem on the page adjoining mine in *Different* of last Autumn ["Abiosis"]. I liked it too.

Sincerely yours,
Fred Cogswell
Editor[4]

Thus, while Nowlan may have written years later that Cogswell was the first person he could talk with about literature, in fact neither man hastened to make contact even by letter when they first learned of each other in 1954.

From the vantage point of twenty years, it may have seemed to Nowlan that he did write to Cogswell immediately upon discovering that he lived in Fredericton. Indeed, a few months is not a terribly long time to wait to make contact with a stranger, especially when one is a shy and awkward young writer and the stranger is older and more experienced. As his friendship with Dr. George Frederick Clarke shows, though, Nowlan had the capability to break through his shyness in literary situations. He quickly followed Cogswell's reply with another letter on April 25 that contains a clue as to why he overcame his shyness at this point. Having broken the ice with Cogswell, Nowlan did what any other young poet would have done: he started submitting verses for Cogswell to publish in the *Fiddlehead*.

Cogswell in turn gave him the encouragement to continue writing and, just as important, suggested magazines that might be friendly to his work and books by Canadian poets such as Souster and Layton that he might like to read. He also agreed to publish one of the three poems Nowlan sent for the February, 1956, issue of the *Fiddlehead*, unless, as he suggested, Nowlan might have better poems than "None Wept" for consideration. Nowlan responded on November 22, 1955, with no less than seven possible alternatives. Cogswell finally decided on "All Down the Morning," a brutal poem about marital violence. The flood of poetry that Nowlan produced during the late 1950s was matched only by the flood of literary talk that cascades through his letters to Cogswell. He was the first person to whom Nowlan could talk poetry, but this conversation was somewhat one-sided. Cogswell's advice on poetics is indirect: which writers to read, which magazines might publish his work. Nowlan, on the other hand, wrote news items and editorials in the *Observer* promoting Cogswell's work and filled his letters to the professor with his thoughts on life and literature.

Cogswell's direct advice may have been scant in his letters, but the example of his verse was, it seems, the only teacher the younger poet needed. In his letter of January 17, 1958, Nowlan finally took the liberty of calling him "Fred"; on February 18, 1958, he wrote:

> I'm returning your poems. I liked all of them, especially "Lefty." It is the kind of poem that I like to write. I like honesty in any form of literature. I think that when a poem says what you *really* feel in the best way that you can say it, then it is a good poem. Technical deficiencies don't seem half as important as hypocrisy. All of your poems are honest, so I like them.[5]

"Honesty" was Nowlan's way of explaining his abandonment of the mythological world he had been tapping for poetic inspiration and his new commitment to exploring his community, his past and the people in his life. He needed to write about life in the raw, as raw as the feelings he harboured about himself that lay buried under a ton of books about history, mythology and esoteric religions. He was beginning to recognize in his annual visits to Stanley the possibility of creating a mythology based upon his own reality.

Inspired by Cogswell's approach in *The Stunted Strong* and by the new energy he found in Souster's and Layton's verse, Nowlan began to try his hand at a kind of writing that was new to him. The poem Cogswell finally accepted for the February, 1956, issue of the *Fiddlehead*, "All Down the Morning," was a raw poetic counterpart to "Hurt," a vignette of the suffering inflicted on those who stand outside of village mores. In this case the victim is Janice Smith, a passionate and demonstrative young wife in a small community:

> *city-bred and unaware*
> *That love was bordered by the rumpled quilts*
> *And children bred from duty as the soil*
> *Was ploughed to hide the seed and not for joy.*
>
> *So taunted by harsh laughter, half-ashamed,*
> *Enraged with rum and manhood late one night,*
> *And shouting like betrayal, Jim came home*
> *To bruise his knuckles on her shameless face.*

Although Nowlan came from a family where marital discord was common, there is no evidence to suggest that the poem is based on events in his own life. In fact, there are indications that the many "village" poems he was starting to write were as much about Hartland as about Stanley. His trips between the two villages, between his present and his past, gave him the distance he needed to see these places — and himself — in a more objective light. He began to perceive himself as a survivor, or more accurately as an escape artist who kept himself from becoming ensnared in the village mentality. In "All Down the Morning," Nowlan does not simply rail against marital violence; instead, he personalizes the tragedy of Jim and Janice Smith, who are unable to escape, trapped in roles neither of them want.

In his essay "Something to Write About," and in later interviews, Nowlan singles out the Stanley trip he took in October of 1957 as the one where he could finally see "the people and landscape of my native place as entities separate from myself." To be sure, this trip home was longer than usual, about one month. This time he was returning, not to make himself look normal to his Hartland friends, but to gather poetic material, more a sabbatical than a vacation.

Freeman was still slaving at the mill and getting drunk every weekend. Harriet by this time was on her second marriage. After moving to Halifax with Ron Anthony, she had had two daughters, Wendy and Debbie. But that marriage had ended in tragedy. Shortly after Ron and Harriet separated, Ron was killed while riding his motorcycle, reputedly in the act of trying to save a child who was hanging precariously off the side of a moving truck. The child survived. Harriet, stuck with two children and no one to support her, had given them to their paternal grandparents in Windsor. Now she had found a new man, Ross Bugden, and had two more daughters, Carol and Kathy. Nowlan rejected the life Harriet had started to lead as a teenager, and by 1957 he had decided to have as little to do with his sister as possible. There was no room for sentimentality in his new verses.

"Before [the Stanley trip] I'd written mostly what I've since come to call palpitating eternity poems, like most kid-writers attempting cosmic pole vaults when I was scarcely capable of jumping a mud puddle," he would later write of this transformation. "Now I looked around me and tried to write down what I sensed, intuited and thought about it. Aside from one or, perhaps, two even earlier verses, the best poems that I wrote that fall are the oldest that I still take seriously.[6] The effect of this trip can be seen in the new landscape of his poetic world:

his sister calmly setting a table while outside a barn burns, hens pecking a rooster to death, a mouse dying in a hawk's talons, a young bull drowning in a pasture; drunken husbands, beaten wives, cruel or outcast children. The new work resembled nothing else he had done.

Hartland, like Stanley, had its squalid side that served as a constant reminder of just how far the writer had come in a few short years. His membership in the Knights of Pythias gave him a chance to do more than just "play nickel poker and go home" after meetings. The Hartland KPs, like other service clubs, were involved in charitable activities such as the annual Christmas charity drive that put Nowlan into contact with Hartland's poor. The drive was a tradition started by Heber Hatfield during the Depression, when he made up several baskets with candy and apples to give to needy children. Hatfield's election to Parliament in March, 1940, took him away from the community for much of the year, so Ode Clark, Jabe's father, became the new Santa Claus for Hartland's poor. Christmas shoppers on Main Street were hailed by Clark, who stood on top of a barrel soliciting funds for the needy.

The KPs did not forget impoverished adults and initiated a food drive to serve more basic Christmas needs in the community. Clark so cherished these traditions that he was reluctant to invite a writer to come along with him, out of respect for people's privacy. But Nowlan found himself drawn to the denizens of Hartland's "Stovepipe Alley" and the rural ghettos in nearby East Brighton. By the late 1950s, Nowlan's position in the lodge was such that Clark would have found it difficult to put him off any longer.

"Here, I've got a hunk of meat, a bit of flour and a bag of potatoes for you," Clark would announce modestly at the doorway of a shack while unloading more food than the family would likely have seen in a week. The miserable condition of some of the occupants at times frustrated the KPs. When Clark and Nowlan came to announce their gift at one door, they beheld three blanketed lumps on cots arranged around a makeshift stove. "Bring 'er on in, Ode, and set 'er right down here," one of the lumps instructed. "Bring 'er?" Ode replied. "Hell, no! You can get off your arses and come get it yourselves."

At another cabin, Nowlan stuck his head in and asked a couple, "How are you folks fixed for Christmas?"

"Oh, we're all fine. I got eighteen dollars worth of food the other day, so we're all fixed up," the man said.

When Clark and Nowlan stepped over to inspect the cupboard, they found it bare. Checking another shelf, they found at last the couple's intended Christmas feast: eighteen dollars worth of hard candy.

Nowlan, himself no stranger to poverty, was nonetheless taken aback by the destitution he saw during this Christmas visit. In another house, a woman slumped on the oven door cooing to her malnourished infant, "Poor baby, Mummy loves you, yes, Mummy loves you." She proudly displayed the Eaton's catalogue her husband had given her as a Christmas gift. But what struck Nowlan the most on these visits was how middle-class he had become in the years since he left Nova Scotia:

> I know they regarded us as aliens. The children, especially. I could feel their distrust, the strange mixture of admiration and contempt. There was no racial fellowship between us and them . . . but they feel a clannish fellowship with one another. Of course, they cheat, thrash and cuckold one another. But the fellowship remains. They don't reject one another as they rejected us . . . even as they accepted the beef and flour and margarine.[7]

As he had before in Stanley, Nowlan began to feel an almost schizophrenic sense of dislocation, but here he was both emissary of the bourgeois and spokesman for the marginalized and downtrodden, both an insider and an outsider in his community. In his writing he became more keenly observant, but not too detached to show compassion. His poem "To a Thirteen-Year-Old Charged with Murder," published in the Winter 1958-1959 issue of *Yes*, was one of his earliest attempts to express poetically his observations as a journalist. It was based on an actual case in Carleton County in 1957. Nowlan could see himself in the boy:

> *you, whose brief time is told in winters, find*
> *the cup of vinegar whose drops are days*
> *brimming and, when you drink, the pain confined*
>
> *till now in the four granaries of your heart*
> *rushes through all the rafters to become*

something as simply told as this: the limp
bundle of bloody overalls, your numb

fingers around the gun . . .

He wrote to Cogswell on January 10, 1958, "I've padded the poor ole *Observer* with so many editorials about the case and its background that some of my friends say that I'm a frustrated social worker."[8]

Emboldened by Cogswell's praise in a January 8, 1958, letter, in which he called Nowlan "one of the most promising young poets in Canada,"[9] Nowlan, ever the initiator, proposed sending Cogswell enough material for a Fiddlehead Poetry Book, a series of chapbooks Cogswell had recently started publishing. In May, 1958, Nowlan sent Cogswell a collection of sixteen poems, including "All Down the Morning," with the suggested title *The Scotian Lad*. The poems had nothing to do with Nova Scotia, except that the poet was thinking of Nova Scotia when he wrote them. Instead, they wrestled with love and violence, as in "Weakness," where the speaker's father, who "hates weakness worse than hail," resolves to shoot the family's sick horse the next morning, "cursing her for a bad bargain,/ and spreads his coat/ carefully over her sick shoulders." Fiddlehead Poetry Books accepted the manuscript and gave it a different title after one of its poems, *The Rose and the Puritan*. That fall, Nowlan at last could see his own book sitting on pharmacy and bookstore shelves.

His blood up, he had another manuscript ready to go (probably *Wind in a Rocky Country*) almost immediately, and he sent it off to Ryerson Press by the end of 1958. On February 11, 1959, he wrote to Cogswell saying that E. V. Griffith of Hearse Press in Eureka, California, wanted to put out a Nowlan chapbook. Hearse, unfortunately, had mostly older poems that Nowlan no longer liked. Another letter to Cogswell one week later shows that the chapbook, to be called *A Darkness in the Earth*, was still in doubt, with Nowlan sending Griffith newer and better poems to replace those he wanted to forget. Hearse did publish *A Darkness in the Earth* later that year.

To the people of Hartland, who had scratched their heads over Nowlan's infrequent verses in the *Atlantic Advocate*, it was as if he really had become a Martian with a third eye in his forehead. Their Al, it seemed, was a real poet after all, though not one they could always understand. "I find the reaction among my friends was much like the average person's reaction to a talking dog," he wrote to Cogswell. "A sort of wonder and bafflement, mixed with just the vaguest hint of pity and diluted with a little dutiful admiration."[10] Kay Hatfield, standing in the front yard of the Hatfield home next to the *Observer* office, called out to him one morning, "Al, I suppose you don't know you kept me up half the night last night." He blushed down to his collar, speechless at what the young woman might mean. "I didn't get to read your book until quite late," she finally said. Alden Nowlan was not yet a well-known name in New Brunswick, yet he could no longer count on being the anonymous poet, appearing only in obscure magazines in the United States. His poetic world had become the world he could observe around him, and now his audience was of that world, too.

During Cogswell's absence from the University of New Brunswick during the 1959-1960 academic year, Nowlan redoubled his writing efforts. Jay MacPherson's Emblem Books published a beautifully designed hardcover chapbook, *Wind in a Rocky Country*, and Nowlan's first full-length collection, *Under the Ice*, was accepted by Ryerson for publication in 1961. He was ready to make the leap to full-time writing. No sooner did Cogswell return to UNB in September of 1960 than he received a request from Nowlan for a letter of reference. He intended to escape newspaper work by applying for a Category 4-B grant from the Canada Council, worth $2,300. In addition to writing, he planned to use his time to study poets such as Edwin Arlington Robinson and Thomas Hardy and to do a bit of travelling. He wrote on his form, "If this application were accepted, I'd spend at least several months outside the Atlantic Provinces. . . . Certainly I'd spend a month in Montreal, which is the antithesis of anything that I've ever experienced."[11] Nowlan had done his homework for this grant application, securing references from Canadian literary figures including Milton Wilson, F.R. Scott and Desmond Pacey, all of whom had said good things about his work.

Nowlan's head was spinning with plans for his future, his heart heavy with the dissatisfaction and boredom he felt working at the *Observer*. "Every day here is a little worse, a little harder to bear," he told Cogswell. "I loathe self-pity but it takes an effort of the will to keep me from succumbing to the inertia of depression."

> Poverty, isolation, ignorance, an ingrained and almost crippling Puritanism . . . I've wrestled with these things all my life. And while I can still beat them I need time to retreat and re-organize and reinforce. That is why

something like the Canada Council grant is so important to me.

It is all very complex. But the gist of it is that I am a little more frustrated and miserable, a little more irritable, a little more stupid even . . . every day.[12]

Something else was making his life more complex, something signalled by the dedication of *Under the Ice*: "To Claudine for One Reason and To Fred Cogswell for Another." Nowlan had fallen in love.

The "Claudine" of the dedication, Claudine Orser, had deep roots in Hartland, a descendant of Hartland's first European settler, William Orser, a Loyalist who in 1802 was granted land along the banks of the St. John River. William's son, George Whitefield Orser, became a preacher in 1828, when he was only fifteen years old. In 1870 Rev. Orser split his Hartland congregation off from the Free Christian Baptist church, and they became Primitive Baptists, or "Orserites"; among other things they believed that their ministers should not be paid. At its height in the late nineteenth century, the Primitive Baptist church could claim forty-five congregations from Maine to Nova Scotia.

Claudine was born a year earlier than Nowlan in 1932. She had gone to Saint John to study nursing, married a man named Meehan, and in 1954 had a son, Johnnie. The marriage quickly fell apart, and Claudine took Johnnie back to Hartland, where, in the spring of 1957, she managed to find part-time work with the *Observer* as a linotype operator. Nowlan initially noticed Claudine because of her difficulties with trying to use the linotype machine. Her efforts produced unintentionally funny results. According to Nowlan, one of her first attempts was the sentence, "Her many friends sent her all good wishes and a shower of cards." What came out of the machine was "Her manly fiends sent her all gods dishes and a shower of lard." This sent the office into gales of laughter.

Just as Claudine's awkwardness with the linotype attracted Nowlan's attentions, so his social awkwardness endeared him to her. As Harold Plummer describes the situation, Claudine began to take him on as a "project," dragging her bashful co-worker out of his room at the Shaws' boarding house to enjoy what activities the community had to offer. "If she had let go for just a minute, he'd have slid right back," says

Plummer. "He had no intention really of getting married. I mean, the thought was just like you and I thinking of being rocket scientists. It was just not part of his life.[13]

Nowlan's letters to Cogswell mention Claudine only rarely and obliquely. Yet he was compelled to leave clues; his unspoken desire demanded some form of expression. As early as April 27, 1957, he felt an unusual need to apologize for a typo in an *Observer* article about Cogswell's latest book, *The Testament of Cresseid*, explaining, "We are breaking in a new linotype operator here now which means that our typographical error average is even higher than usual."[14] He dropped other hints about his new love, seemingly hoping that Cogswell would ask about her. His September 19, 1960, letter asking Cogswell for a reference includes as one of his reasons for wanting a grant the wish to "look around for a means of maintaining myself, and eventually a family."[15] In later correspondence the references to Claudine become more direct; for instance, in January, 1962, he remarked, "My girl loved Desmond's line about me seeming to have 'inexhaustible reserves of energy,' etc. She's always teasing me about being lazy."[16] And then, still unable to coax an enquiry from Cogswell that would allow him to unburden himself, he finally blurted out his dilemma on May 27, 1962: "A girl here wants to marry me and about half the time I want to marry her. Another complication."[17]

It was a complication that would add richness to his poetry. In *Under the Ice*, amid the vignettes of small-town characters and village life, are a few touching yet unsentimental love poems, the first of Nowlan's oeuvre that seem to speak frankly of the complications of two people sharing their lives, "exploring this, the oldest country. . . for us the journey/ crosses a beach between tides, and ends." Here the speaker addresses himself to women who seem to be more real than in his previous creations, although in poems such as "Looking for Nancy" their actual presence is still ephemeral. He names his female muse either Nancy or Therese. "Terry" was, in fact, a nickname he sometimes used for Claudine; the sense of loss and abandonment in the poems about Nancy suggest that Nowlan may have been thinking about another woman — or women — he knew in the past. At any rate, whether or not he had particular women in mind, the poems express for the first time, and express effectively, the speaker's search for fulfillment and completion in the arms of another.

The reference to Desmond Pacey in Nowlan's January 10, 1962, letter suggests both a growing personal relationship with other Canadian literary figures and the respect that the young man's work earned from them. Pacey, a University of New Brunswick English professor and the dean of Canadian criticism, was one of Nowlan's strongest supporters, overlooking the young man's social ineptitude. Pacey reminisced to the poet Al Purdy, "Alden Nowlan is painfully shy and drinks a lot to cover up. The first time I met him, for breakfast in the Lord Beaverbrook Hotel about fifteen years ago, he drank a whole bottle of rum *before breakfast* so that he would be able to face me. He's wonderful when he's half-sober."[18] Pacey thought he was a wonderful poet, too. In the second edition of his seminal work *Creative Writing in Canada*, published in 1961, Pacey accords high praise to Nowlan:

> Alden Nowlan (born 1933) is the youngest and in many ways the most promising of this group [of New Brunswick poets]. Although he has so far published only two small books of verse — *The Rose and the Puritan* (1958) and *Under the Ice* (1961) — his poems and short stories have appeared in literary magazines all over the North American continent, and he seems to have inexhaustible reserves of energy and imagination. His poems bear the strong imprint of Cogswell's influence, and consist mainly of ironic or compassionate sketches of rural people or incidents. He seems, however, to possess a confidence in the validity of his perceptions that Cogswell is inclined to lack, and he writes of the mingled beauty and horror of rural New Brunswick with a straightforward honesty that shocks and grips the reader. There is nothing of the artificiality of conventional pastoral in this regional poetry; it is direct, sometimes brutal, always authentic. (p. 250)

Other critics were not as generous as Pacey but were nonetheless solid in their support of what nearly all recognized as a major literary talent about to be launched on the Canadian scene. "If Mr. Nowlan ever really fulfils the potentiality of his early work, he should be a dominating (and maybe notorious) figure in Canadian letters of the next few decades,"[19] Milton Wilson predicted in the *University of Toronto Quarterly*. Michael Hornyansky, both in the *Fiddlehead* and in the *Tamarack Review*, praised the power of Nowlan's imagery and the sparse naturalism of his language, "echoing the simplicity of rural talk."[20]

For Nowlan, it was the right kind of attention but for all the wrong reasons. Having found his poetic voice in the people and places around him, he became concerned that his poetry would be written off by the urban literati as merely regional poetry of purely local interest. Alec Lucas, reviewing *Under the Ice* in the Winter 1962 issue of the *Fiddlehead*, writes about some of the poems, "the result is not regional poetry but Dogpatch verse."[21] Yet, taken in context, there is little that is disparaging in the critics' comments about the poems' regional flavour, except as seen through Nowlan's eyes. In the Summer 1961 issue of *Canadian Literature* Miriam Waddington notes, "He writes out of his isolated chip-on-the-shoulder Maritime culture, out of the New Brunswick rivers and woods," but faults the "very gifted and original poet" only because she feels "few of the issues he raises in a poem are ever honestly resolved."[22] Similarly, in the *Waterloo Review* John Robert Colombo, while noting "a certain backwoods ingredient" in *The Rose and the Puritan*, nonetheless remarks that the poems "are of high enough quality to make him a distinctively important poet."[23]

The only critic to comment negatively on Nowlan's rural subject matter was the poet Eli Mandel, writing an otherwise positive review of *Under the Ice* in the *Canadian Forum*. Mandel's comment in fact suggests that Nowlan is not true enough in describing his environment: "But no one, surely, will mistake Nowlan's Faulknerian world of barn-burning, bear-baiting, child whipping, and Saturday-night dances for the actual Maritimes."[24] Douglas Lochhead, reviewing the same book in the *Dalhousie Review*, probably sums up Nowlan's case best: "These are sure poems about people and country. They are as sure, say, as Raymond Souster's are about Toronto. If they are to be called 'regional,' well then Souster is regional, we are all regional."[25] For the young man who began by writing poems for readers all over the United States, the regionalist label was unexpected and annoying, and he worked hard for the rest of his life to overcome it.

However defensive he may have felt against the Toronto and Montreal professors and critics, the feelings do not seem to have been returned — at least as far as can be judged from the actions of Canada's elite literati, who were more than happy to promote and support his work. Nowlan poems were gratefully received and published by mainstream national magazines, such as the *Canadian Forum*, and by new, exciting Canadian little magazines including Al Purdy and Milton

Acorn's *Combustion* and Michael Gnarowski's *Yes*. Toronto poet Raymond Souster in particular had been a source of inspiration for the budding writer. On the strength of *The Rose and the Puritan,* Souster invited Nowlan to take part in his prestigious Contact poetry reading series at the Isaacs Gallery in Toronto on February 20, 1960. Nowlan was to be the lead reader that night in a program of three poets. On the night of the reading, Nowlan, feeling shy and out of sorts in the city, secreted himself in the audience while Souster, who had never met him face-to-face, puzzled over where his star reader might be. Assuming that the poet had been delayed by the inclement winter weather, Souster announced to the audience that they would have to start without Nowlan, who immediately interrupted the proceedings by clearing his throat, rising to his full six-foot-three and announcing that he was the man they were looking for. From that point, the reading went smoothly. The promotional leaflet for the reading shows poet Kenneth McRobbie's well-meaning introduction juxtaposed with Nowlan's defensiveness:

> ALDEN A. NOWLAN is one of the young and less well-known Canadian poets whom it is the policy of these readings to present to the audience. He has lived all his life in small towns and farming communities in the Maritime Provinces. He has been writing poetry seriously for six years and is known to poets outside his home area solely from his contributions to literary magazines. These contributions are recommendation enough. . . . However, Nowlan says he is not overly enthusiastic about the word "regional." He writes: "I don't see why a writer should be described as a regionalist simply because he works with a rural rather than an urban environment."[26]

The label was starting to stick, giving Nowlan another pastime: Toronto-bashing.

Such poems as "A Mug's Game" show Nowlan biting the hand that fed him both literally and figuratively, and they mark the beginning of the ambivalent relationship he would have with much of Canada's literary and academic community, each perceived slight documented by another satiric poem aimed at some writer or academic, usually one from outside the Maritimes. Robert Weaver (most likely "the man from the CBC" in "A Mug's Game") was the first to promote Nowlan's poetry on the national stage. Weaver did indeed work for CBC radio as producer of *Anthology*, a program devoted to the literary arts. He also edited *Tamarack Review* and so was always on the lookout for new talent in Canadian letters.

In March of 1958, before *The Rose and the Puritan* was even thought of, Cogswell put Weaver on to Nowlan by giving him Nowlan's address. As *The Rose and the Puritan* was being assembled, Nowlan sent Weaver a batch of poems for *Anthology*. Weaver wrote to Cogswell on September 9, 1958, "I hope you'll take it as a private comment between editors when I tell you I was rather disappointed by the poems he sent me for *Anthology* . . . reading a large group gave me the impression of too much surface facility and a number of poems that not only seemed simple and direct but in fact turned out on careful reading to be rather trite."[27] Of the twenty-five poems Nowlan sent, Weaver culled seven for the October 28, 1958, national broadcast. Nowlan ended up missing the program entirely, not from a desire to snub Weaver but because he had tried to cure a cold by catching a quick nap after work and over- slept.

Cogswell was working behind the scenes to get Nowlan noticed by other influential writers and editors from outside the Maritimes. Louis Dudek, a poet and the editor of *Delta*, was, after Cogswell, the literary magazine editor who published the greatest number of Nowlan poems. Cogswell wrote to Dudek on January 2, 1957, shortly after he launched *Delta*, suggesting writers for future issues, Nowlan among them. Of Nowlan, Cogswell writes, "As a matter of fact, he'd be a good bet for a volume from Contact Press. I've hesitated to approach him for a Fiddlehead chapbook because I think he deserves better."[28] Nowlan held Dudek in high regard, even keeping an encouraging letter of Dudek's pinned to the wall over the desk in his room. With Dudek, as with Cogswell, Nowlan felt free to stretch his literary muscles in new and unfamiliar directions. Like any artist, he tried on different influences and different personae to find out which ones fit. When writing for Dudek he liked to play at being a Maritime Irving Layton. In his essay "A Defense of Obscenity," published in the Fall 1959 issue of *Delta*, he railed against the "Anglo-Saxon conception of sex which is literally that it is a necessary evil," concluding, "To oppose sickness it's necessary to endorse obscenity, practise lust and promote licentiousness."[29]

A February 16, 1962, letter to Dudek suggests that his libertine pose might have had something to do with the pressures brought about by his deepening relationship with Claudine.

A Mug's Game

At the party that followed the poetry reading,
one girl kept telling me how thrilled she was to meet
someone who hadn't gone to university, and another said
I reminded her so much of whoever it was who played
in Bus Stop she kept expecting Marilyn to walk in,
    and the hostess
extending three bite-size salami sandwiches
and a glass of warm whiskey and ginger ale
smiled at me like L'il Abner's Aunt Bessie
welcoming her nephew to Toronto.

The man from the CBC, who said: "Of course you're staying
at the YMCA" and thought he was humouring me
by acting impressed when he found out I wasn't,

explained: "The purpose of such readings is to give writers
from unlikely places like Hartland, New Brunswick,
the chance to communicate
with others
of their own kind."

I told you I don't have a family. But, really, in my case that can't be answered by a flat "yes" or "no." I have a girl here who has an eight-year-old son, whom I call my illegitimate son, sometimes, although he isn't, really. And she wants to marry me . . . but I don't know. She is a little peasant — I don't say that unkindly but as a statement of fact: here in the Maritimes we have a peasant class, almost in the European sense. I've sprung from it. But I've moved so far, and I keep moving . . . and the girl of whom I speak, no matter how much she loves me, will never really get away from the parish in which her people have lived for two hundred years. I mean that in the spiritual, rather than the geographical sense. Sometimes I think it will work, and sometimes I know that it won't.

And then, after this frank confession, he slips back into his Laytonesque guise:

The thing that dissatisfies me about most poems about sex is that they treat it as though it were something distinct from everything else in the world. But, to me, there is never — except in the act itself — the simplicity of a man making love to a woman. There is always a certain man making love to a certain woman. Deliberately, in the process of fighting the spiritual emasculation of a Baptist boyhood, I've made love to girls I hardly knew. I suppose I was seeking that attitude exemplified by the people in Henry Miller's books who never refer to a woman as anything other than a cunt. As though the sexual organs were disembodied, or as though the body were as soul-less as those rubber dolls supposed to be used by sailors and Japanese soldiers. But it has never worked for me. I can pick a stranger up at a bar or at a dance and by the time we begin to make love I've created her whole life and personality out of a few words and gestures. So she becomes a person, someone toward whom I have certain responsibilities, someone who is involved in me.[30]

Nowlan, like any young writer, found himself lost in dealing with the best literary minds of his country, vaguely resentful at any attempts to pigeonhole him and yet unsure how to present himself in terms this new world would accept. His alternating efforts to please and to parody writers such as Weaver and Dudek demonstrate a lack of confidence in his uneducated, rural background. To be sure, the prevailing intellectual climate of the time, in which writers and critics praised art that promoted a national (meaning "central Canadian") identity at the expense of regional voices from places like New Brunswick, did not help either. But, rather than exercising his own formidable intellect or at least his abundant common sense, Nowlan began to play his own "Mug's Game," assuming a defensive crouch when confronted with literary criticism and striking back with the nearest — though not always the best — weapon.

During this period of rising success and frustration, he began working on a big project that he had started shortly after returning from a 1959 trip to Nova Scotia. Always eager to prove himself not just a poet but a fiction writer as well, he dreamed of writing a novel that would finally encapsulate his feelings about Stanley and his childhood. Beginning on January 1, 1961, Nowlan made and kept a promise to himself to write one page per day until the novel was finished. This novel, which would become *The Wanton Troopers*, proved to be a cathartic experience. "In the past four or five months I've [under]gone an internal change," he wrote to Cogswell on March 21. "It has been a strange movement in the mind and heart, purging and strengthening. As if everything were being cleaned away to make room for something new."[31] That something new was heralded by word from the Canada Council in June that his grant application had been successful. Strangely, his reaction was subdued. "I suspect that, in reality, I'm ashamed of begging for money," was how he would later explain his unenthusiastic acceptance of money for doing something he liked instead of for "real work." "If it weren't for the social workers and the fact that the amounts given out are so pitifully small, I'd prefer to go on relief. I felt guilt rather than elation when the Canada Council granted me $2,300."[32]

A threshold in the Nowlan-Cogswell relationship had yet to be crossed. Finally, after having bought a car, Cogswell accepted a renewed invitation from the poet he had been reading, corresponding with, publishing and promoting for almost seven years. He drove to Hartland to meet Nowlan face to face. Later in life, Nowlan often quoted

Chekhov's line: "We must have great meetings, for great partings are inevitable"; Cogswell's arrival must count as one of Nowlan's great meetings. On the afternoon of Saturday, November 25, 1961, Cogswell landed on the doorstep of the Shaws' boarding house. There stood the respectable professor of English dressed in a tweed jacket and tie — a tie which bore a cartoon image of a semi-nude bubble dancer. Mrs. Shaw was perhaps too overwhelmed by his education and his position in society to be shocked. In the end, it was Nowlan who was more put out by his friend's arrival, nervous, stammering, afraid that the restaurant he had chosen for supper was not up to Cogswell's standards. But gradually he did open up; Cogswell recalls that "even when we talked freely, the conversation was about his lack of confidence with respect to women, reading poetry in public, meeting strangers at a literary gathering."[33] The young man's confidence returned only after supper, as the two shared a bottle of rum in the car parked in a deserted school yard.

Not all literary gatherings were ordeals for Nowlan, who made other unlikely connections through his poetry. One of these resulted from a simple form letter, one of many sent out to newspapers all over Maine and the Maritimes. In 1957 a young scholar from the University of Maine, Edward (Sandy) Ives, was starting research on a biography of the folk poet Larry Gorman. Ives sent his form letter to newspapers in the region asking anyone for information about Gorman, and he received a response from the news editor of the Hartland paper. This was a curious one — no information, just an assurance that the paper would print the letter and the observation that he, the editor, did not think very much of those old woodsmen's ballads.

The name at the bottom, Alden A. Nowlan, held no clues for Ives. Whoever this Nowlan was, Ives thought, he must be squinty, cranky and ink-stained like all those old editors who almost single-handedly print their small-town weekly newspapers. Ives fired off a rebuttal and was "rewarded" with this editor's book of poetry, *The Rose and the Puritan*. He groaned, but he read the book anyway.

> Obviously this was not the sort of thing I had expected at all. It ["Hens"] had all the spareness, the understatement, the balance between laughter and shock that makes for real poetry. Next to it was a poem called "A Letter to my Sister," and once again there was that balance, this time of calm and holocaust — the flaming shingles coming down

like bombs and the sister "adjusting napkins on the table." The last stanza wasn't up to the rest, or at least the last three lines weren't . . . but this was good poetry, no doubt about it. [34]

Ives bought several copies of the chapbook and distributed them among his friends, some of whom did not share Ives's enthusiasm for Nowlan. Others, though, compared him favourably to Edwin Arlington Robinson.

Ives's first meeting with Nowlan did not happen until April 20, 1962, and his image of the wizened old editor was quickly dispelled. Ives was teaching an extension course in Presque Isle, Maine, and had phoned Nowlan to say that he was coming over to Hartland for a visit. Now he was sitting across a Dayesta restaurant table from a strapping, vital poet with a booming laugh. He gave Ives a copy of *Wind in a Rocky Country* as a gift. Ives was particularly taken with the delicious curse-rhyme of "God sour the milk of the knacking wench/ with razor and twine she comes/ to stanchion our blond and bucking bull/ pluck out his lovely plumbs."

Nowlan pointed out the word "dibble" in the last line. "Is that a word?" Ives tilted his head and squinted at it. "I don't really know." "Then I think I invented it."

In November, Ives invited his new friend to do a couple of readings in Presque Isle, one at a teachers' college, the other the next morning in his own class. It was worth seventy-five dollars for Nowlan, plus all the booze he could drink. At the evening session at the teachers' college, he read to an audience of about twenty-five. Afterwards a young man invited Ives and Nowlan to a party that he and some of the rest of the group were having in a house nearby. The two agreed, but Ives said they would be a little late.

"Sorry, Al," he explained as they walked out to their cars. "I didn't know whether I should have accepted that invitation or not. I went to their last party and all they gave me was coffee with whipped cream on it. I think what we should do first is go back to the motel and have a beer."

"Several," the poet replied.

There were no bite-sized salami sandwiches or coffee with whipped cream at this party after all, but enough booze to get both men blessedly drunk. Nowlan did not particularly care for his hosts, all proper crew-cut kids who, in Nowlan's words, "believed that Eisenhower was a

Communist plot."[35] There were guitars — one player was a B-52 pilot from nearby Loring Air Force Base — and college students sweetly singing ditties such as "The Skye Boat Song." All very precious, and just the kind of thing Nowlan loved to deflate. He urged Ives, an ex-Marine, to grab a guitar and start playing some of his folk songs. Ives chose to sing Communist songs from the 1930s with refrains like "And the Soviet Union keeps rolling along," while Nowlan clapped and hooted as some of the people at the party became more and more incensed.

The song that touched Nowlan's sentimental heart the most that night was a woodsman's ballad by Joe Scott, Ives's latest research project. Tears came to Nowlan's eyes. After Ives had finished singing, Nowlan complimented him the best way he knew.

"Sandy," he said, "you sang 'The Maid of the Mountain Brow' exactly the way my poor old father used to sing it when he got drunk every Saturday night. But he'd never finish it, you see; he only knew parts of songs."

On the way back to the motel that night, he sang Freeman's version of the song "Howard Carey" under his breath, the same verse over and over:

My name is Howard Carey, in Grand Falls I was born,
In a cosy little cottage on the banks of the St. John,
Where song birds chant their notes so sweet and rippling waters roar,
Where the ivy vine so thickly twines around the little cottage door.

The two sat up in the darkness of the motel room, finishing off the last of the warm beer and talking long into the night. The next morning, in Ives's class, Nowlan read at the top of his form. Ives remembers a comment Nowlan made during the reading, perhaps a reflection on the good luck that had at last found the young writer over the past few years.

"I don't know many poets who believe in God any more," Nowlan said, "but I don't know any poets who don't believe in angels."

*from **Britain Street***

This is a street at war.
The smallest children
battle with clubs
till the blood comes,
shout "fuck you!"
like a rallying cry . . .

On this street,
even the dogs
would rather fight
than eat.

I have lived here nine months
and in all that time
have never once heard
a gentle word spoken.

I like to tell myself
that is only because
gentle words are whispered
and harsh words shouted.

Fred Cogswell, describing how Nowlan survived on his Canada Council grant, says that he "wrote and starved throughout the year 1961-1962."[1] Nowlan's initial success as a writer had not made Hartland any easier to endure. Harold Plummer remembers a growing frustration in his friend:

> When he left Hartland . . . he was ready to go; he had done everything there was to do. He admitted there was a pint of vodka down in the bottom drawer the last year. He knew that there was boredom and fear. I think he knew he had to go. He obviously wasn't going to write for the *Observer* for the rest of his life. He had to expand his poetry and his writing, and I think there was the same fear he came to Hartland with.[2]

Nowlan later elaborated on these feelings:

> A few years ago, in Hartland, I almost joined the bourgeoisie. . . . I was accepted, too. By the time I was forty I could have controlled the weekly there and been elected mayor without opposition. Even while continuing to write poetry which wouldn't have bothered anyone, because nobody there reads any of the magazines that publish poetry. I even succumbed to most of the bourgeois forms of hypocrisy. Was invited to all the secret parties at which the bourgeois let down their hair. There was a brief period back then, when I was thin and respectable (at one point I bore a startling physical resemblance to King Baudoin of Belgium except that I smiled more often) when women pointed me out to their daughters as an eligible catch; and the wives of most of my bourgeois friends were willing to sleep with me, because I was younger than their husbands and very, very discreet.
> Then, something happened.
> Probably a stirring of the old messianic complex.
> Quite deliberately, I cut myself off from almost all the bourgeois ties.
> In a very subtle way, I forced myself to leave Hartland.
> Because I couldn't trust myself to make the break, unless I was forced into it, I guess.[3]

Curiously, Hartland had become a kind of punching bag for his frustrations in much the same way Stanley did, being alternately too puritan and not puritan enough for him. He would later say that the Biblical text for the Holy City of Hartland should be "Woe unto them that are at ease in Zion."

As early as 1959, Nowlan was sniffing out opportunities that would allow him to make his second escape. One of them was the *Daily Gleaner* and its monthly magazine the *Atlantic Advocate*, both owned by Brigadier Michael Wardell, an British ex-serviceman and friend of Lord Beaverbrook who had come to Fredericton in 1952 to establish the University Press. Wardell was known for the patch over his bad eye and his eccentric manner. Nowlan continued freelancing for magazines in order to stretch his Canada Council money — and to cement his credibility as a journalist. An article on liquor in the *Canadian Commentator* attracted the attention of the managing editor of the *Telegraph-Journal*. A March 18, 1960, letter from Ralph Costello, while admitting "no desire to entice you away from Hartland,"[4] nonetheless made it clear that he was interested in having Nowlan on staff if he wanted a change.

Nowlan did a lot more during his 1961-1962 sabbatical than write and starve. Paradoxically, his involvement with the community reached its zenith even as he searched for the means to escape it. In 1962, for example, he was elected Grand Master of the Brighton Lodge of the Freemasons. To beat boredom and to supplement his grant, he undertook to manage a county-western band, George Shaw and the Green Valley Ranch Boys. In the end, this did not turn out to be a money-making proposition. "George is a pretty fair singer of the blue grass variety, but won't discipline himself," was Nowlan's assessment. "[He] would rather sit in the back seat of a car parked on a woods road, drink rum and coke and play the guitar and sing and daydream about becoming another Hank Williams, rather than really do anything about it."[5] Nowlan booked gigs in small communities around central New Brunswick, but the band never made more out of the trips than the cost of gas, food and liquor.

Other activities were less recreational. Back in 1957, he had been moved by the case of a thirteen-year-old boy charged with murder; now the issues of crime and capital punishment took hold of Nowlan's imagination once again. In April, 1960, a murder took place at the Tobique Indian Reserve near Perth, about one hour's drive from Hartland. A young man, Fred Bernard, was to be hanged on June 21, 1961, for killing William Sappier. Many people felt that the sentence should be commuted to life in prison because Bernard was considered to be mentally handicapped and had been in three mental hospitals.

Perhaps remembering his own experience as a "retardate" and hospital inmate, Nowlan chaired a committee formed to lobby the federal government for a stay of execution. As part of its work, the committee visited Bernard in the Perth jail, where the gallows were being built. Since the jail was not designed for executions, carpenters had to convert a basement closet to suit the task, digging a pit underneath it to allow for a sufficient drop. Nowlan was appalled at the squalor and inhumanity of the whole set-up. Aboriginals, unions and church congregations rallied behind the committee and petitioned the federal cabinet to commute the sentence. Three days before the execution, the justice minister granted the committee's wish. Nowlan later wrote, "I belonged to a dozen or more organizations in Carleton County and, I think, that committee was about the only one that ever accomplished anything."[6]

Crime haunted Nowlan more than any other type of story he covered for the *Observer*, perhaps because he, more than his middle-class neighbours, could appreciate how a perpetrator can be as much a victim as the person who suffers at the hands of a criminal. As someone who as a teen had been institutionalized and who had once planned to commit a rape, Nowlan could identify with his own darker side. The "frustrated social worker" part of his personality reasoned that he must oppose capital punishment because he could not support any system that killed more poor people than rich people. But he could also admit to a darker and more personal reason why he opposed hanging. As he often told people, he was half-afraid that he might one day volunteer to be a hangman himself. At the fringes of his consciousness, he could allow himself to flirt with homicidal and bizarre impulses.

During his year away from the *Observer*, Nowlan cultivated new friendships in Hartland, even as he felt himself draw away from the community. The 1961 provincial by-election in Carleton County allowed him to solidify one such friendship. Buoyed by the success of the Save Fred Bernard Committee, Nowlan turned his energies toward helping elect a promising young Hartlander to the legislature: Richard Bennett Hatfield.

Hatfield was another regular at Norris Hayward's house. He and Nowlan met each other there, and they often sat up nights discussing politics with Hayward while he fiddled with his shortwave radio. The Hatfields, like the Orsers, were a prominent family in Hartland, but for reasons of industry rather than history. Nowlan would later write of them: "It's true that to be a Hatfield in Hartland is to possess certain privileges so intangible that the recipient is seldom fully conscious of being granted them. The most important such privilege consists in being permitted to stand a little apart, to maintain a measure of privacy in so insular a community."[7] Young Richard studied at Dalhousie law school before moving to Ottawa to serve as secretary for Gordon Churchill, Minister of Trade and Commerce in Diefenbaker's government. In 1958 he returned to Hartland to help run the family business, and before long he discovered his real ambition to follow his father into public life.

The two young men, Hatfield and Nowlan, shared many interests: a love of art and literature, a passion for philosophy (political or religious), and a fascination with the world beyond New Brunswick. Nowlan admired Hatfield for the intellect he brought to politics and became a committed supporter. At the 1961 local riding convention to choose the Conservative candidate for the provincial legislature, Nowlan took the podium to give his first and only political speech — against his friend Hatfield. The party executive did not want to have an acclamation, so Lorne Britten, a funeral director, was encouraged to run to make the race look interesting. Nowlan gave a speech introducing Britten and did his best to denigrate Hatfield. "Great fun," Nowlan wrote later, "except I found out too late that the sacrificial sheep [Britten] didn't know he was supposed to be a sacrificial sheep and he was very hurt when he found out, which made me feel like a louse."[8] From then on, Nowlan helped Hatfield only from behind the scenes.

Despite these extracurricular distractions, work on *The Wanton Troopers* became almost obsessive; Nowlan put in long days at his desk in an effort to complete the manuscript and to convince himself that he was not leeching off Canada Council funds. His original plans to use the money for travel were abandoned. Periodically, he sent draft copies of chapters off to Cogswell or took sections from his manuscript and had them published as short stories. Having received national attention as a poet, he would rest on his laurels. To the working-class part of his soul, there was something more honest in good, solid prose than there was in poetry, and he would not consider himself a real working writer until there was a book-length work of fiction with his name on it.

Nowlan's proletarian conscience would not bother him for long. The Canada Council money that he had hoped would last a year lasted only nine months. By the time he met Sandy Ives at the Dayesta restaurant in the spring of 1962, he had been forced to go back to the *Observer* on a part-time basis to stave off a growing list of creditors. He told Cogswell:

> When my money runs out I will have the choice of (1) returning to *The Observer* permanently and ending up as a cynical alcoholic editing copy on the annual meeting of the WCTU and the Altar Guild of the Primitive Baptist Church, living out my years in a boarding house and trying to stay one jump ahead of my creditors or (2) moving to another publication which shall be nameless and earning a slightly higher pittance as a flunky to a pretentious faker who makes my flesh crawl.[9]

By then, Wardell had offered Nowlan the position of managing editor of the *Atlantic Advocate*, the general-interest glossy magazine that had published so many of Nowlan's stories, articles and poems — even more than *Delta* or the *Fiddlehead*. But he bore no love for Wardell, and his dislike only grew later that year when he heard that Wardell, who was a juror for the Canada Council, opposed his application for a renewal of the $2,300 grant. Another application for a Eugene Saxton Memorial Trust grant fell through in March of 1963, despite recommendations from Louis Dudek, Milton Wilson, Irving Layton, Ives and Cogswell.

The year 1962 brought more bad news for Nowlan. *The Wanton Troopers*, over which he had slaved during the past year, was rejected by Ryerson Press. Determined to prove himself as a fiction writer, he sent the manuscript to McClelland and Stewart. Cogswell, once again trying to promote his friend, put a word in to Dudek: "Nowlan is very discouraged since Ryerson turned down his novel and the Canada Council refused to renew his grant. Maybe you could cheer him up."[10] This cheer eventually took the form of a book contract from Raymond Souster at Contact Press, which in 1963 published Nowlan's fifth collection of poetry, *The Things Which Are*. The collection contains what would become his two most-anthologized poems, "The Execution" and "The Bull Moose."

Unlike the chronicle of small-town life that was *Under the Ice*, *The Things Which Are* is a much more personal and pessimistic collection. As in his first chapbook, *The Rose and the Puritan*, violence and cruelty are once again at war with compassion. But it also shows a poet fighting a losing battle against the critics' earlier dismissal of him as a regional poet. *The Things Which Are* suffers from what seems like Nowlan's attempt to gain respect from central Canadian critics by forging a link between regional locality and universal truth. This link is at times tenuous and forced and hurts such poems as "The Bull Moose" and "Salvation," in which the speaker is no longer a spokesman for the villagers but instead takes the stance of a distant and more urbane observer. In "The Bull Moose," everyone — neighbours, children, the elderly, and the game wardens — shares equally in the animal's demise. Everyone except the speaker, that is. In the poems of earlier collections, such as *Under the Ice*, the speaker often has the insight to recognize his own (sometimes willing) participation in the village's persecution of the innocent, as in "Bear," when "at Easter we went out to kill the bear/ who stole the lambs; the dogs encircled her — / our rifles stuttered." In *The Things Which Are* the speaker identifies with the downtrodden and the drunks, celebrates "the terrible dignity/ with which he prolongs/ his descent" when one falls, notes how "a trick/ of hunger or heredity" turns a shack dweller into "one of the lost/ Bourbons or Romanoffs,/ dirty toes protruding/ from the holes in his sneakers." Finally, though, he loses credibility because of his inability to implicate himself as a cause of their misfortune. Instead, the drunks accept the speaker, who can afford to give away the quarters and dimes they need to buy liquor, as their own: "'You know what it's like,' they say./ 'You know what it's like.'"

If *The Things Which Are* was supposed to prove to the urban Canadian critics and readers that Nowlan was something more than a regional bard, they did not applaud his efforts. In fact, Milton Wilson, in his annual review of Canadian poetry for the July 1963 issue of the *University of Toronto Quarterly*, laments that "the world which Nowlan conjures up this time has lost much of its localized richness of substance: there is far less of his characteristic Maritime claustrophobia — indeed, in a number of senses, far less character."[11] Eli Mandel writes, "I find in many of [Nowlan's] poems hysteria rather than poetic energy, the power of a shriek rather than the vitality of a poem." Then, perhaps re-thinking his earlier denial of the veracity of Nowlan's Maritime experience in his review of *Under the Ice,* he continues, "This remark is not meant to suggest that I am taking issue with the actuality of the experiences Nowlan chooses to describe or dramatize. It's by the way to ask whether or not so much blood flows in New Brunswick."[12] Nowlan countered Mandel's review with a satiric poem about critics entitled "The Shriek," suggesting that he felt a continuing frustration with trying to please critics and perhaps implying that he would not try to do so in the future.

The years 1962 and 1963 witnessed the tentative beginnings of an evolution in the Canadian literary landscape as established writers such as Dorothy Livesay, Irving Layton, Raymond Souster and A.J.M. Smith were giving way to the new voices of Leonard Cohen, Al Purdy, Milton Acorn and, later, Margaret Atwood. Contact Press published groundbreaking collections by Acorn (*Jawbreakers*) and Purdy (*Poems for All the Annettes*) within a year of *The Things Which Are*. In 1963 Leonard Cohen followed his first two collections of poetry with his first novel, *The Favourite Game*. Though the influence of central Canada (and its literary boosters such as Margaret Atwood, D.G. Jones and Northrup Frye) would keep alive the myth of a unified Canadian literary voice for the remainder of the 1960s, the vitality of writers from Canada's margins (exemplified by Acorn, Purdy, Nowlan and the West Coast writers of the *TISH* group) were vindicating the strength of Canada's regional experience.

At the beginning of his review of *The Things Which Are*, Mandel recognizes the challenge posed by the new poets:

> Only a short while ago it seemed as if Canadian poetry was about to define itself in a single, coherent shape: professional, accomplished, distinctive. There were rumours that its voice would be prophetic and its sound — to the delight of the critics — unmistakable. Not surprisingly, poetry being what it is, nothing of the sort has happened. Instead, like that famous rider (was he in Leacock's stories?), contemporary poetry has mounted its horse and ridden off in all directions at once.[13]

In the poem "Stoney Ridge Dance Hall," Nowlan's speaker, describing the tough people who have lived on the land for eight generations, defends regionalism more effectively than any literary critic when he says:

This is the only
country they know.
There are men here
who have never heard of Canada.

But Nowlan did not need "sharp spikes/ in [his] orange logging boots" to defend the poetic territory he had staked out. The poems in *The Things Which Are* that do not try to be "universal" are among Nowlan's best. He is most effective in his love poems "Sometimes," "Bird of Prey" and "Canadian Love Song," in which the speaker cannot stand outside and condemn puritanism, but instead must recognize the split in himself between flesh and spirit. Nowlan the man may have felt trapped in Hartland and may have yearned to step outside the community and condemn it, but Nowlan the poet is caught in the tension between the desire and the spiritual inability to escape his society, burdened even during the "Party at Bannon Brook" with the knowledge that "the bobcat is not driven away/ by smoke, and the eagle/ makes reconnaissance from the coast."

What kept Nowlan hanging on in Hartland was love. "I've almost decided to marry a girl here," he wrote to Cogswell in March. "Divorced with a nine-year-old son. Partly because of the boy, there is already a kind of family aspect to our relationship. They both of them need me, and, in many ways, I can only think of myself in relationship to them."[14] Nowlan still only referred to his new family as "the girl" and "the boy" in his letters to Cogswell and Dudek, but little Johnnie was an unexpected pleasure for Nowlan, an anchor that kept him committed to his job and to planning for the future. His childhood did not prepare him for fatherhood, although perhaps his own experience with neglect gave him the empathy to allow Johnnie into his life.

Since so much of his writing during this period was from the point of view of the boy he once was in Stanley, Johnnie became a sort of muse for Nowlan. "Earlier this evening I was out flying a kite with my girlfriend's little boy," he told Cogswell in May. "Doesn't that sound ridiculous: my girlfriend's little boy. Great fun. I didn't give a damn about being a writer or anything else except getting that kite higher up than Johnnie had ever seen a kite go before."[15] No doubt Nowlan saw in Johnnie (finally called by name) the possibility of giving the same happiness he enjoyed as a boy while wandering around with his Uncle Albert, and he may have felt that by being a good husband and father he might somehow heal the wounds inflicted on him by his own family. But none of these psychological theories come through in his writings; the reader sees only a man gladly learning to share his life.

Johnny Five

Nearing the mystery:
how these arduous symbols —
          JOH
              NNY
touch you, the name
that is six labours;

fisting the pencil,
drawing each letter
like a horse or a house —

        fish-hook,
        a mouth laughing,
        chair backward,
        two gates
        and, nobody knows why,
        a swing!

and whenever you see a word
with one of your
letters in it, you yell:
Look! There's part of me!

as if the whole world
were trying to spell Johnny.

In that same letter to Cogswell Nowlan outlined the plan that would take him and his new family out of Hartland at last. He was ready to make his move to one of Wardell's two publications in Fredericton, the *Daily Gleaner*, for which he had been the Hartland correspondent, or the *Atlantic Advocate*, which had been publishing his poems and short stories since he began his writing career. He had also made up his mind about Claudine, whom he would marry just before he left. Financing the move was another problem, since his resistance to returning to full-time work at the *Observer* left him in debt. "I'm going to try to get all my local debts joined into one back-breaking loan through a bank loan," he told Cogswell. "Sometime next week I will grovel before the local Bank Manager. Crawl in on my hands and knees licking the dust at his feet — except there ain't any dust in banks." After the bank approved his loan one morning, Nowlan spent the afternoon placating the Calvinist part of his soul by walking around town paying off his debts. At the end of the day he had fifty dollars in his pocket. Then the wild Irish part of his soul took over. He bought a wedding ring for Claudine, and for himself he purchased six pints of vodka to drain that very evening while he and a friend played chess.

The assumption that he would automatically land a job at the *Gleaner* or the *Advocate* proved to be unfounded. In July, 1963, Wardell wrote to say that he could not offer him anything at that time. Embittered by this turn of events, Nowlan scrambled to find an alternate route out of Hartland. He still preferred the idea of working in Fredericton, either in the publications section of the New Brunswick Tourism Department or as a broadcaster for a local radio station, CFNB. But a letter he had sent to the *Telegraph-Journal* produced an expected, if not entirely welcome, response. They were eager to hire him. He, Claudine and Johnnie would have to live in foggy old Saint John.

Nowlan did not waste any time in moving. Materially speaking, he left Hartland not much richer than he was on that March day in 1952, when he came to town with a cardboard suitcase, six paperbacks, a clean shirt, a package of cigarette makings, and thirty-seven cents. Now he was leaving with a beat-up old car stuffed with books, a typewriter, clothes, a few sticks of furniture . . . and two passengers.

The day before the departure, August 26, 1963, Claudine and Alden were married. They had intended to ask a friend, the Reverend Tom Miles, to perform the service, but he had left for another congregation. So the two of them shocked everybody by being, as Nowlan said, the first and only couple in Carleton County to be married, without witnesses, by a County Court judge. "The judge obviously didn't believe in civil marriage and officiated only because the law required him to do so," Nowlan told Miles. "He was very suspicious of our motives, very dubious about me. It was sort of funny and sort of sad."[16]

Nowlan left with something else of great importance that he did not bring from Stanley: his five collections of poetry.

As when he arrived at the *Observer* eleven years earlier, Nowlan joined the *Telegraph-Journal* staff at a hectic time. The weekend before his arrival on August 27, the paper had moved from the old offices on Canterbury Street to a brand-new building on Crown Street. Writing for the *Telegraph* was nothing new to him. He had been the paper's Hartland correspondent for years and had visited the Canterbury Street office a couple of times. The new building was located at the corner of Crown and Union Streets, in the midst of an enclave that the powerful Irving family, who owned the *Telegraph-Journal*, was building all around the Courtney Bay area of Saint John.

By 1963, K.C. Irving had parlayed a chain of service stations into an oil, forestry and media empire. Working (indirectly) for such a powerful man as K.C. Irving did not faze Nowlan, who had hobnobbed with the Hatfields, Hugh John Flemming and John Diefenbaker in Hartland. "The truth is, there is no Irving Press," he later wrote. "Back when I was night news editor of the *Telegraph-Journal* I often wished that there were."[17] New Brunswick's Irving-owned dailies actually competed with one another, and K.C. Irving never patrolled the halls firing any reporters foolhardy enough to write anything negative about the company. The most jarring thing for Nowlan about the *Telegraph* office was the wildly busy atmosphere and the naked ambition of some of the staff. "Almost everyone here has his nose in the ass of the man above him and his foot on the neck of the man below him," he reported to Cogswell.[18]

Nowlan's major worries upon arriving in Saint John were more immediate than being fired by K.C. Irving. The move was not well planned, which was probably more a function of circumstances than of any laxness on his part. The family endured their first month in Saint John with virtually no money, their Hartland friends being too poor (or the Nowlans too proud) and perhaps too surprised by the wedding to offer much assistance. Nowlan worked only three days at the paper before his first paycheque came through, and the paltry amount barely covered that month's rent. Furthermore, he received a notice from the bank in Hartland to pay $75.18. His loan payments had caught up with him. With nowhere else to turn, he screwed up his courage, stifled his pride, and wrote to Cogswell, asking him for money. His friend gladly loaned him eighty-five dollars. It was enough to pay the bank and have a little left over for food, but it took Nowlan almost two years to repay Cogswell. During one two-day period that month, they had only two cans of sardines and half a box of crackers to sustain them; they literally did not have a cent. It was a long time until the accumulated pay-cheques started to keep pace with their needs.

Saint John in those days was a rough port city. The family lived that first year in a small tenement on Britain Street in the South End, about a twenty-minute walk from the *Telegraph* offices. The fortress-like Armories building stood guard on the other side of nearby Broad Street, and any view they had of the ocean was obstructed by the Atlantic Sugar Refinery. The cheerless surroundings gave Nowlan his first taste of urban reality. As he had done in Hartland, he wrote poems that explored the characters and landscape of his new environment.

In fact, he loved the very toughness and impersonality of the city, despite what poems such as "Britain Street" suggest. His working-class heart was at last with the people he identified with the most: the urban proletariat, more savvy and less nosy than the rustics of Stanley or Hartland. He wrote to Cogswell:

> It is strange that in Hartland where everyone I met said
> "Hello, Al" I was desperately lonely, toward the end. Here,
> where I can walk the streets all day without meeting a
> familiar face, I am not lonely at all. And that isn't due
> altogether to my having my wife and the little boy with
> me. I think if I were living alone I'd feel much the same
> way. The feeling wouldn't last indefinitely, of course — but
> for the moment it is a good feeling. Perhaps I'll try to put
> it into a poem. If so, I'll send you the result. When people
> don't know you they don't try to force you into some pre-
> conceived mould. When I buy a package of cigarettes here
> I am only a hand outstretched containing a quarter, a dime
> and a nickel. Nothing else. Which is all I want when I buy
> a package of cigarettes. It is all right when one's friends
> think they know one intimately — it is terrible when
> strangers act on the same assumption.[19]

Nowlan kept his relationship to the city as impersonal as the city was to him. In later years he would encourage young writers from Saint John to write the great, gritty novel of the port city, but he declined to try it himself since he claimed to know little about the place. That was true enough; work and family kept him occupied most of the daylight hours.

In the midst of the workaday world, Nowlan clung to his lifeline of correspondence with writer friends across Canada. A new acquaintance, the poet Al Purdy, introduced him to the practice of saving his personal papers — even making carbon copies of outgoing mail — so he could one day sell them to some library or rare book collector. Nowlan finally met Irving Layton face to face in Montreal that year under somewhat trying circumstances. Everyone who was alive during that era can remember where they were and what they were doing when they heard that John F. Kennedy had been shot in Dallas. Nowlan was giving a poetry reading to several hundred people at the Museum of Fine Arts. "It was a very strange experience," he wrote. "I felt as if everyone in the world, except that one small group of which I was an unwilling member, was thinking and talking about the murder."[20] Nolwan read for only twenty minutes. He was entertained at Layton's house the next morning, and the two men corresponded regularly. "How is it that you poets from the Maritimes are all such big men?" Layton reportedly asked. "All our little poets are beaten to death before the age of twelve," Nowlan replied.

"What do you think of Gregory Cook's plans for book publishing?" Nowlan asked Cogswell upon returning from Montreal. "I don't want to get very involved in this sort of thing. What time I have I have to give to earning a living and trying to get out of debt, and trying to get back to writing, and trying to cope with the complexities of living."[21] He had met Cook in June, 1963, just as he was planning his escape from Hartland. A young writer and a student at Acadia University, Cook edited the university's literary magazine, *Amethyst*. He wanted to do a special feature on Nowlan, which would include a full-length published interview, Nowlan's first. Cook remembers a feisty but shy man, one who did not explain the presence of the nine-year-old boy who showed up at the *Observer* office at the end of the interview to take Nowlan swimming.

A friendship developed between the two men. An ardent admirer of Nowlan's work, Cook started his own magazine, the *Crier*, in 1964 while working for a Halifax daily. He proposed using his press to put out a collection of Nowlan's short stories. Nowlan, eager to demonstrate that his fiction was a match for his poetry, warmed to Cook's project. Cook promised Nowlan that he could convince Ernest Buckler, the Nova Scotian novelist and a friend of Cook's, to write a favourable introduction. This as much as anything else attracted Nowlan, who thought Buckler's *The Mountain and the Valley* was one of the best novels he had ever read. *The Wanton Troopers* was still languishing somewhere in the bowels of McClelland and Stewart. In a December 18, 1965, letter, Nowlan thanked Cogswell for his editorial assistance on a proof copy of the proposed short fiction book, to be called *The Glass Roses*.[22] He mostly drew upon the fiction he had already published during the time he lived in Hartland, since his job at the *Telegraph* did not afford much opportunity for generating new fiction. Throughout 1965, Cook assembled and edited the collection, for which Buckler wrote a glowing introduction, and Cook even prepared the printing plates for the book. But financial difficulties bogged the press down by the beginning of 1966, and Cook lacked the money to complete the printing and binding. By then, Nowlan would be too distracted by his own affairs to be of much assistance.

Nowlan made another young friend at that time who would come to play a central role in his life. In 1961, a young student from St. Thomas University in Chatham, New Brunswick, was jotting poems in the margins of his notebook during boring Latin or philosophy lectures. This man, Raymond Fraser, had discovered Nowlan's poems in the *Fiddlehead*. Inspired by Cogswell's magazine, he and a friend printed one issue of *Tom-Tom*, St. Thomas University's literary periodical. In the fall of 1961, Fraser wrote to Nowlan and received a friendly and enthusiastic reply. Fraser even paid a visit in person by inducing Cogswell to drive him and a friend, University of New Brunswick student LeRoy Johnson, from Fredericton up to Hartland one autumn afternoon in 1962. Cogswell left the two young men with Nowlan, who talked with them into the evening and prepared what Johnson remembers as the worst scrambled eggs he had ever eaten in his life before driving them back to Fredericton.

Both Fraser and Cook found in Nowlan something more than a mentor who could instruct them in the craft of writing. Actually, Nowlan was less than a decade older: Fraser was born in 1941, Cook in 1942. These young men were the vanguard of the post-war generation, the first to invade universities en masse. But the rural, working-class background of the two men was at odds with the urbanity of academe, even as it manifested itself in Chatham or Wolfville. Fraser says,

> He [Nowlan] probably felt kind of inferior to these people with all this education. . . . I suppose I was interested in writing rather than commenting on writing, and that is one of the differences [between academic and non-academic people]. Also, I wanted to come to my own decisions on everything. I didn't want to quote somebody, what Dr. So-and-so said about all of this stuff. I wanted to figure it out for myself.[23]

Nowlan satisfied Cook and Fraser's need for creative and intelligent discourse, but he still stood outside the world of privileged academics — was even critical of that world — and so validated their working-class identities.

Nowlan's fondness for drinking also fit into the young men's lifestyle, and alcohol became a sort of sacrament that Nowlan could share with them in the same way he shared with some of the young men in Hartland (but could not with his mentor Fred Cogswell). Cook was the first to visit Nowlan in Saint John; Fraser followed in the fall of 1964. Each meeting was no doubt solemnized by getting hammered on wine, which was Fraser's preferred mistress, or gin, which was Nowlan's. Cook and Nowlan made a more sober pair. On Cook's trip to Saint John, he and Nowlan decided to visit Kay Smith, a noted Saint John poet who appeared with Nowlan in Fiddlehead Press's 1963 anthology *Five New Brunswick Poets*. But neither man had met Smith before, so they just assumed that the bewildered old lady who greeted them at the door was the poetess they were seeking. "No magazines, no food either," the woman observed. "What are ya, religious people?" They chatted with her at the doorway about poetry until the real Kay Smith appeared behind her aged mother and invited them in.

Nowlan was self-educated and self-made, and his example probably spurred both Cook and Fraser to reject the tried-and-true paths to respectable success that had been mapped out by society after the war. Fraser left St. Thomas for a year in 1962-1963 to travel around Canada and land himself in trouble with the law; Cook graduated from Acadia but resisted further studies in favour of abortive publishing ventures. Later, in 1967, he would return to Acadia to study for his MA; by that time, Fraser and LeRoy Johnson had moved to Montreal to found their own publishing venture, Poverty Press, with its flagship magazine *Intercourse*.

At the paper, meanwhile, Nowlan suffered the temptations of security and respectability. "I have been adapting to *The Telegraph-Journal* so well that it worries me," he wrote to Fred Cogswell on October 1, 1963.[24] It seems that Ralph Costello had correctly assessed Nowlan's competence three years earlier when he invited him to join the paper. Despite his disorderly appearance, he was an effective and versatile journalist. On October 6, 1963, Nowlan began a two-week stint as provincial editor, filling in for the regular editor when he went away on vacation. These two weeks were nerve-racking enough to convince him that being a reporter was in many ways much better than being an editor. Nevertheless, he was destined to rise in the *Telegraph-Journal* hierarchy. Fred Hazel, the editor, was so impressed by Nowlan's performance that he made him provincial editor for the two nights a week when the regular editor was off duty.

As at the *Observer*, he was sometimes chosen to travel around the province to report on important events, especially when they involved people he already knew. Such was the case one winter night in 1964, when Nowlan found himself navigating a dark, icy road, with Johnnie in the co-pilot's seat, on the way to a meeting protesting the construction of the Mactaquac hydroelectric dam, which would damage the salmon fishery and inundate farms in the upper St. John River valley, many of them first cultivated by Loyalists. Now the descendants of many of these Loyalist pioneers sat mute in the chilly hall, angry but unsure how to fight the New Brunswick Electrical Power Commission.

"I say that you meet them in the manner of your ancestors of the King's American Dragoons," said the final speaker, Nowlan's old friend Dr. George Frederick Clarke. The old man paused for emphasis. "Meet them with your rifles." But the farmers only grinned shyly and avoided each other's eyes, and the reporter had his story.

Still not a steady driver even at the best of times, Nowlan skidded on the deserted roads in search of a phone booth in order to make his deadline. Finding one in a snowdrift by a gas station, he made Johnnie hold a flashlight up to his notes while he dictated a story to the rewrite man off the top of his head. He also had to give him a brief history lesson about the Loyalists and a thumbnail sketch of the gentle doctor who loved the natural environment enough to advocate violence. The next morning, secure at his own kitchen table, a mug of coffee in hand, Nowlan read his story: not great literature, but a good, honest night's work.

Despite his journalistic success, alarm bells were ringing in his head about the direction his literary career was taking. Ever since the year he worked on the Canada Council grant, he was certain that newspapering would always be at war with his real work. In Saint John, that war turned decisively against his writing. Already a nighthawk, he adopted a routine at the *Telegraph* where he worked nights preparing the paper for the next morning. After work, in the wee hours while it was still dark, he and his colleagues sometimes frequented the only place in town where a thirsty man could get a drink: the local bawdy house. Claudine seemed to take these visits in stride. "The more attractive and skilful whores always ended up in Toronto," she once explained to one of Nowlan's friends. "So most of the Saint John ladies of the night were cross-eyed or hump-backed, retarded or sixty years old."[25] After a drink, Nowlan would walk home along Crown Street while it was still dark. He slept, woke up in the early afternoon, wrote, spent time with Claudine and Johnnie, then went back to work in the evening. The routine was starting to make him numb, and he looked for ways to escape. One possibility was particularly intriguing. "Is there any word on the poet-in-residence matter?" he asked Cogswell after that first exhausting two-week stint as provincial editor. "Ever since you mentioned the possibility of this, I've been daydreaming about it. . . . I don't want to work for a newspaper for the rest of my life."[26]

The initiative for the writer-in-residence project had come from Desmond Pacey. Canadian literature was burgeoning in the 1960s, and the University of New Brunswick wanted to be the first to create a semi-academic position for an established Canadian writer. As head of UNB's English department, Pacey sought to entrench Fredericton's reputation as "the poet's corner of Canada." The writer would be free to work on his or her own projects but would also be available for readings and to consult with budding student writers. A similar resident artist program already existed at UNB, and Nowlan yearned for the creative leisure such an arrangement could afford him.

In September of 1964, Pacey formally presented the idea to members of the English department and canvassed three professors for nominations for the post. All three were known to Nowlan. One, the poet Robert Gibbs, had appeared with Nowlan and Kay Smith in *Five New Brunswick Poets*. Another, John Grube, was a professor at UNB's Saint John campus. Fred Cogswell was the third.

Norman Levine and Leonard Cohen were stand-out favourites for Pacey, Gibbs and Cogswell. Gibbs wrote of Cohen, his number one choice: "I understand he's a very good reader and accompanies himself on the guitar. He should appeal to the students."[27] Cogswell seemed more interested in using the post as a way of giving established but impecunious writers a break, as his support of Levine, Nowlan, Buckler and Purdy suggests.

Grube's more arcane choices reflected his wish that the writer-in-residence be someone who would shake up the literary establishment. The person who could best do this shaking-up was, in Grube's opinion, Bert Glay, a Canadian writer known mostly to American pulp-fiction aficionados. Second on Grube's list was an unknown poet named George Whipple. Coming in at number four behind F.R. Scott was an open vote for any French-Canadian writer, although Grube did not shy away from stating his own preference. "In my opinion," he wrote to Pacey, "Paul-Elliot [*sic*] Trudeau writes the best French in this country — although he would not consider himself a writer but an *engagé* intellectual of the Paris type."[28] In the end, Pacey decided to accept Norman Levine for the 1965-1966 year, leaving Trudeau to find another road to fame and fortune.

Nowlan did not take the news of Levine's appointment with Trudeau-like aplomb. After learning of UNB's choice in the pages of the *Atlantic Advocate*, he fired off sarcastic letters to Cogswell and Pacey. "You must tell me all the nasty gossip," he wrote to Cogswell on April 26, 1965. "Is he the illegitimate son of Michael Wardell? Did he serve in the same regiment as Colin Mackay during the Late Unpleasantness? Is he playing D.H. Lawrence to Lady Beaverbrook's portrayal of Lady Ottoline Morrell?"[29] "I can concede that Levine may have been a better choice than Nowlan," he wrote on May 4, 1965, to Pacey. "But I don't feel the arguments advanced in your letter are valid":

> First, he has three children and no job. This is the first time
> I ever heard physical prolificy used as a literary criterion.
> Tolstoi, I believe, had a numerous progeny, but I have never

heard this used to prove his superiority to Dostoievsky who, as far as I can remember, had none. And as far as his having no job is concerned — who stopped him from working? Certainly, with an MA from McGill he could have earned a salary at least twice as large as mine.

Second, he knows English publishers etc. I grant this is a valid argument, at least from a commercial standpoint. If a student writes anything saleable he'll be able to tell him where he'll have a chance to sell it.

Third, he lives in England — in your words, "he has been exiled." But, of course, he hasn't been exiled. He left by choice. Exile implies banishment. He did not have to leave. He could have stayed in Canada and worked and written whenever he could find the time and energy — in which case he wouldn't have qualified for endorsement by the University of New Brunswick.

None of these arguments has any relevance whatever to literature. He may well be a "sad young man" and I have no doubt the $5,000 will cheer him up. What has that got to do with art or literature or anything else?

It may well be that a grant of this type coming to me at this time would have meant the difference between my surviving as a writer, and my not surviving as a writer. On the other hand, it could be that the appointment would have destroyed me if I had received it. Stately elms sometimes have the same effect as poppies. Or is that sour grapes? [30]

Nowlan would soon answer the "sour grapes" question for himself. Two days later, mild despair replaced spleen. He wrote to Cogswell:

Thanks for the letter. I got the same kind of letter the same day from Desmond Pacey. I answered his. Why go through it all again.

In all my years of writing, the only tangible thing anyone has done for me simply because I am a writer was lend me $85. It was you who lent me the money, of course. At a time when I needed it desperately. I'll repay it eventually. But I will always be grateful to you for lending it.

Of course, many people have done things for me in my

life. But they did it because they felt decorum demanded it, or because they were personal friends. You know me only as a writer. Yet you lent me the money.

That, as I say, is the only time anyone ever did anything tangible for me, as a writer.

The rest, really, has been only a pile of horseshit — reviews in magazines that nobody reads and nice letters that cost only a five-cent stamp. All horseshit, I see that now, as I grow older.

You say you should have "some say in selecting the candidate" because there wouldn't have been any resident writer if your group hadn't gone for it. Of course, you had the right to select whoever you wanted. I didn't question that. Let's forget it. I have more important things to worry about.

And I was grateful for the $85.

Being told you're a good poet doesn't put any bread on the table.[31]

Nowlan was in a bind. The *Telegraph-Journal* was earning him a living while taking away his life. A promotion in 1964 to full-time provincial editor gave him the means to move the family into a larger, newer apartment on Mitchell Street, a better neighbourhood in the North End that was also about a twenty-minute walk from the office. He was promoted again a year later, to night news editor. But he dreamed of the freer life that the university could offer, while at the same time his working-class heart shrank from the incomprehensible mindset of the ivory tower.

The hard fact was that, though Nowlan had churned out six books between 1958 and 1963, he had little new work to offer readers, except for *The Glass Roses*, which had mostly been written in Hartland. Though he did keep publishing a steady stream of poems in magazines, his first two years in Saint John were too fragmented to allow him to embark on new projects. He also wanted to devote whatever free time he had to his family. In July of 1964, he packed Claudine and Johnnie into their 1959 Chev and drove to Windsor for a weekend vacation. It was Freeman's first acquaintance with his son's new family, and he remained on his best behaviour. As it turned out, Johnnie was quite taken with the old man. But the hurt remained between Nowlan and his father. "He talked with me like a peasant conversing with the son of a squire," he wrote Sylvia. "But I could see he despised me a little too. When we parted he almost wept and I almost wept."[32] But on the way out of town that night, he could not resist a harmless bit of fun. Under cover of darkness, he took Claudine and Johnnie inside the sawmill, then awakened the mechanical god by throwing the switches on all the lights and machinery. He laughed at their frightened reaction to the lights and the scream of the saw blades. "Don't worry," Nowlan said. "I'm an old mill hand from way back."

Back in Saint John, his frustration with his relentless schedule and dwindling opportunity to write started to affect his relationship with his friends. Ray Fraser was unlucky enough to find himself a target. By the fall of 1964 he had finished his degree and moved to nearby Belleisle, New Brunswick, to teach. The community was close enough to Saint John to afford him the opportunity to visit Nowlan on weekends, so the two of them could have a drink and a chat. But by that winter, as Nowlan was awaiting word on whether he would land the UNB writer-in-residence post, his friend was loafing around the apartment and grating on Nowlan's nerves. As Fraser tells it:

> Alden didn't want to *tell* me I was interfering with his schedule — he couldn't, for fear it would hurt my feelings. I might get mad at him, I mightn't like him. I can under-stand this sort of reasoning; in his place I'd probably have done exactly as he did.
>
> What he did was start an argument. I didn't see it coming, I just thought he was growing a bit disputatious and contrary the more we drank, as drinkers sometimes will. But it got worse. In no time he was disagreeing with everything I said. . . .
>
> "Are you questioning my sincerity? Mr. Fraser, where I come from that's as good as calling a man a liar."
>
> "You're telling me Hitler should have won the Nobel Peace Prize?"
>
> "What I'm telling you, sir, is that I resent your ques-tioning my sincerity. You come into my house and drink my wine and sit there smugly accusing me of . . ." And so on.[33]

The intellectual-baiting that had worked so well with his friend Wayne Tompkins out in a farmer's field in Hartland was now turned with effectiveness against Fraser. Nowlan's explanation to Cogswell underscores just how much his life had changed from what now seemed his carefree Hartland days:

> Raymond Fraser hates me. He has a good poem in the current *Delta* incidentally. And he wrote me a wonderful venomous letter, the gist of which was that I'm a fake. Which, of course, is true. The trouble was he wanted to stay here every weekend and consume limitless quantities of wine which I couldn't afford. He is a promising poet and short story writer and also a class A deadbeat.[34]

Relief would soon come for Nowlan in an unexpected form, a trial which would lead him to greater heights of writing and permanent escape from journalistic drudgery.

from **In the Operating Room**

The anesthetist is singing
"Michael, row the boat ashore,
Hallelujah!"
And I am astonished
that his arms
are so hairy —
thick, red, curly hair
like little coppery ferns
growing out of
his flesh
from wrist to shoulder. . . .
And soon
everything
is dark
and nothing
matters
and when I try
to reach up
and touch
the hair
which I think of
now as
little jets
of fire,
I discover
they've strapped
my arms
to the table.

The year 1966 marked Nowlan's fifteenth year as a published writer and journalist. By that time, he had written everything from book reviews to poems, from town council reports to short stories, from editorials to a novel to a magazine article about seed dryers. On January 25, his thirty-third birthday, he could look back on his life with some satisfaction. He now had a wife and an adopted son and was making a modest living as the night news editor of a major Canadian daily. It is true that he had had a few setbacks with publishers, granting agencies and the University of New Brunswick writer-in-residence program, but his poems and short stories had been published all over North America. He was becoming a writer of national prominence, and he could count among his friends other well-known writers and journalists, professors, politicians, and even a former premier of New Brunswick. His service to the *Telegraph-Journal* was taking a toll on his productivity as a writer, but in 1966 an unlikely saviour ended his career as a newspaperman and set him on the path to full-time writing.

It started as a small, asymmetrical lump that had appeared on his neck in the fall of 1965. He went to one physician to have it examined, only to be told that it was just an infected gland, nothing to worry about. By the end of 1965 he began to experience a persistent sore throat. His co-worker and friend John Mulcahey remembers that, around February of 1966, Nowlan started complaining about having trouble swallowing. At that time he was not given to talking much about physical ailments and continued to work through his discomfort. As he explained later, he felt he belonged "to a long tradition of people who only go to a doctor when they are carried there."[1]

But Claudine had other thoughts about this family tradition. She worried about the way the lump was visibly growing and urged her husband to get a second opinion. In March, 1966, Nowlan acceded to his wife's wishes and went to see another doctor. This one did not write the lump off right away as an infection. Instead, he performed a biopsy and sent the sample off to the lab for tests. A week later he called his patient in to his office to deliver some grave news. It was indeed a problem with a gland, the thyroid gland, which straddles the larynx — not an infection but a malignant tumour.

Nowlan's immediate reaction, as he recalled, was to burst out laughing at the ludicrousness of it all. Here he was feeling as healthy as he ever did while his physician told him he had a disease that would surely kill him in a matter of weeks. But the seriousness of his predicament quickly overtook his sense of irony. Cancer had claimed both of his grandmothers. He soon became convinced it would kill him, too, and he began to make arrangements for his funeral, to choose his pallbearers and to fret about how Claudine and Johnnie would fare without him.

There was no question that the situation was dire. As his doctor explained the course of treatment, Nowlan calculated his chances for survival and took strange comfort in the prognosis. As he figured them, the odds of surviving the operation were about the same as a Canadian soldier's odds of surviving the assault on Dieppe. Thinking of his young self waving to the pilots and soldiers back in Stanley, the metaphor ennobled the struggle in his mind, lending it heroic dimensions. He would need the comfort of such a fantasy. In reality the operation had as many hidden mines as a World War II battlefield. To remove the thyroid gland, the surgeon had to pick his way around a very sensitive area of the neck, avoiding nearby lymph nodes, nerves and, most serious of all, some blood vessels, including those that drain into the carotid artery and the jugular vein. The cure seemed almost as hazardous as the disease itself, even if the cancer had not already spread beyond the thyroid, a possibility which as yet remained unexplored.

Dazed, Nowlan went back to work, always nervous that the next ring of the telephone in the bustling newspaper office would be his summons to go to St. Joseph's Hospital. Adding to his worries about himself and his family was his guilt at having to break the news to his employers. Few journalists belonged to unions then, and emotionally Nowlan could not shake off the knowledge that had been instilled in him from birth: the boss, "the Big Man," would fire an employee if he so much as missed an afternoon tending to a hand that had been mutilated by a saw blade. Finger stumps could be hidden in a handkerchief, but Nowlan could not hide the ordeal he had to undergo. Ralph Costello, however, was no Dickensian industrialist; he guaranteed Nowlan his regular salary during his illness and recovery and his job when he was ready to return to work.

Nowlan did not have to wait long to find out if such a day would ever arrive. By the end of March, he was admitted to the hospital for the operation, scheduled for Monday, March 28. He could see now, clearer than he had in past months, the little ironies of life as they unfolded around him. He surrendered his clothes and donned the inadequate hospital gown with a sense of amusement. With a last squeeze of the hand, Claudine let the orderlies wheel her husband away on the gurney. The pre-operative tranquilizer began to take effect as

Nowlan watched the faces of the nurses and the ceiling lights as they sailed past. While his attendants waited for the elevator, he overheard a nurse speaking into a nearby pay phone. She was giving someone — presumably her husband — a shopping list. "And don't forget to pick up a can of Italian-style tomatoes," she stressed. Nowlan chuckled. He realized that the world could go on without him.

But, for the time being, the Earth would revolve with Nowlan still on it. He came out of the operation with his throat sorer than before. He needed a smoke and begged a nearby intern for a cigarette. The intern complied, lit it for him, and then gently extinguished it, for the patient had already passed out from his exertions. Upon regaining consciousness, he was hit with more bad news: the cancer was more extensive than doctors had hoped, and he might need more operations. Thyroid removal is normally accomplished in one operation, and Nowlan does not leave a precise record of what the succeeding operations were supposed to accomplish, but he went under the knife two more times during his stay at St. Joseph's. In a likely scenario, the surgeon, seeking to minimize the trauma to his patient, might have removed only one half of the thyroid during the first operation, taking samples from the other half and from the nearby lymph nodes to be sent to the lab in order to determine the extent of the cancer. A positive result on these tests would have meant operating again.

In the unreal world of the hospital, with its nurses, doctors, drugs, confinement and pain, time began to stretch out for the poet. He revisited worlds he had not seen for a long time, and saw everything with new eyes:

> All sorts of child-like myths helped sustain my egotism or stoicism, whichever it deserves to be called. I used to tell myself, as my grandmother told me when I was a small child, that I was the descendant of Irish soldiers and kings and that I owed it to them to die with dignity. I'd almost forgotten my grandmother's stories, incidentally, yet when I was sick they all came back, the story about the old Celtic cheiftan who was told that his son had been killed in battle and asked simply were all his wounds in the front? and dozens of others, and it seemed to me, then, as I lay there, that these stories weren't just parts of a romantic myth, but a great tradition that deserved to be upheld.[2]

If I could turn and meet myself

In the prime of his adulthood, at the peak of his strength, he had been made weak and helpless. But in this helpless state, with his defences lowered, he found a measure of love and caring that his struggles as a writer had made him forget, dim echoes of a childhood when pleasure and surrender were one and the same. The poem "Escape from Eden" echoes the bath scene that he had written earlier in *The Wanton Troopers*, when young Kevin, powerless, submits to the affections of his mother. In "Escape from Eden," the near-dead speaker is stripped naked by the nurses and bathed. As he recovers his strength (and thereby his adulthood), so do the nurses accord him less and less intimacy, first "cover[ing]/ my loins/ with a sheet," then "wash[ing] my back/ without removing/ my pajama jacket," and at last "knock[ing] loudly. . . before slowly opening/ the door/ of my room."

Another of his hospital poems, "Rivalry," has a similar theme; the nurse "who is neither young nor pretty/. . . massages my flesh as though coaxing a tired lover." But at the end, when everything is stripped away, the speaker finds the place where his heart resides. The nurse "smiles mysteriously across my naked body/ at my wife, who holds my hand in both of hers,/ her own smile becoming tighter and tighter." The crisis brought him and Claudine closer in ways that he did not expect, she assuming a prominence in his life that she did not have when he practically lived at the *Telegraph* office. He had been raised with the manly code that drew a line between family and work. Now the line was blurred. Emotionally, Claudine became the mother, the one person who would not abandon him. "Claudine is wonderful," he wrote to Fred Cogswell. "She is so innocent and, secretly, so strong. I could never have gone through all this without her. One of the discoveries I've made since I got sick is the humbling discovery that I need her more than she needs me."[3] Allowing himself to write more intimately about his life, Nowlan now started to use the word "we," himself and Claudine. Not just a word, "we" represented a whole new concept for him. But Johnnie was kept in the dark about his father's condition, his parents electing not to say the word "cancer" around him until Nowlan's prognosis was more certain.

Cogswell, who was teaching a night class at the nearby Saint John campus of the University of New Brunswick, visited St. Joseph's whenever he could drop by before or after class. Another English professor at UNBSJ, John Drew, asked Cogswell one evening what had become of the author of that chapbook he enjoyed so much, *The Rose and the Puritan*. He had picked up the book at UNB in 1958, but he left to spend time in the US, India and his native Britain. Now he had returned to New Brunswick, but Cogswell had bad news: the poet was in St. Joseph's Hospital clinging to life. Drew immediately made his visit and was confronted by a gigantic man practically immobilized by bandages, tubes, drugs and pain. "The doctors say if I live for the next twenty-four hours, there's a good chance I might last two weeks," Nowlan croaked amicably from the bed.

Suicide was in the poet's mind, though not despair; killing himself seemed the honourable, rational thing to do, rather than endure the humiliation of dying in a miasma of pain-killing drugs, writhing in his own filth. He imagined a more elegant way to die: if he could make it out of the hospital while still capable of walking he would go to the nearby community of Maces Bay — to him the most beautiful spot on Earth — and calmly walk into the surf. But he was nowhere close to walking. The second operation (probably the one in which the other half of the thyroid was removed) was successful, although his trial did not end when he regained consciousness. By doctor's orders, he was not allowed to ingest anything during the night following the operation. He remembers a terrible thirst and understood what Jesus meant when he said from the cross, simply, "I thirst." But there was no sickbed conversion for Nowlan. He stared at a crucifix on the wall and fruitlessly willed himself to believe in God, to no avail. He did, however, have a wonderful religious hallucinatory vision, one of many hallucinations he experienced under the influence of drugs. He seemed to float above his bed and out his eighth-floor window into the dark night. Then he drifted up to the top of the building, where he could reach out and touch the brightly lit cross.

He would need to draw courage from his faith, for the third and final operation would be the most serious of all, a more aggressive procedure to remove cancerous lymph nodes on the side of his neck. The surgeon would also remove a muscle in his neck as well as part of the jugular vein, rerouting the blood through other vessels while all the while minimizing nerve damage. Nowlan's strangled attempts to speak confirmed what doctors had feared: the laryngeal nerve leading to the voice box had been damaged by the thyroid removal. The mellifluous baritone that had nearly landed Nowlan a job as a radio announcer would sound rattling and raspy for the rest of his life.

The hospital environment was not, as Nowlan had hoped, a good one for catching up on reading. Claudine brought him Gibbon's *History of the Decline and Fall of the Roman Empire* and Frazer's *The*

Golden Bough from the library. But he could not read any farther than the beginning of *The Golden Bough*, the part about the priest-king who must be sacrificed to make way for a successor. In his situation, the story hit close to home. Much of the time he was too sedated by medication to concentrate on literary matters. "I watched *Bonanza* on television in the hospital once when I was high as a kite on various kinds of drugs," he wrote. "It was like watching a wild Jean Cocteau surrealistic kind of thing in which nothing that happened had any relation to what had happened before. It was as if someone had sliced up the videotape of a hundred or so western movies and then stuck the pieces together at random."[4]

The little absurdities the medical world imposed on the ill offered another surrealistic distraction, and he compensated for his helplessness by poking fun at the serious demeanor of the hospital establishment. Clothing especially was a source of amusement, since it was so like a uniform separating the doctors from the nurses, the sick from the well. When he submitted to X-ray tests to determine whether his cancer had spread to other parts of his body, he laughed out loud at the pomposity of a little sign by one peg of a clothing rack: "This space reserved for the doctor's topcoat." It seemed to him after a while that patients' garments were designed less for utility than to rob patients of their dignity and thereby make them easier to control.

Nowlan rebelled. He was particularly obsessed with the plastic identity bracelet that the nurses would check without fail before giving him medication, even though they knew his name. That seemed the ultimate expression of the bureaucratic mindset: to take away individual identities, codify them, and place them in a giant computer which spat out tags to attach to human beings, giving them new, sterile identities. He became mildly paranoid about dying and being buried with the tag still attached to him, so he cut it off one day and taped it to the head of his bed. "Hospitals are horrible bureaucracies," he wrote.

> I had an idea for a story along this line. Patient moving in a completely dehumanized hospital. A satire — with the hospital even more dehumanized than the real thing. Everybody in hospital talks in abbreviations, so I thought of entitling the story Term Canc Clinc for Terminal Cancer Clinic. And at the end of the story everybody, doctors, nurses, orderlies would be quite efficient, and utterly merciless. Not cruel, but merciless. They wouldn't even

know the patient existed — just be acquainted with his disease. The patient would be introduced to various doctors as Term Canc No. 5567 or some such.

Or maybe the plot could be that someone in perfect health wandered into the clinic by mistake and couldn't get out because of the bureaucracy etc. Say a telegraph boy takes the wrong door and suddenly a couple of nurses strip him naked and shoot a sedative into his arse and away he goes. Ends up two months later (during which he's been kept in isolation and kept from reaching a phone etc) in the morgue with a tag on his toe. Hell of an idea in this if I can get the energy, time and health to make anything of it.[5]

He would later write a poem called "Term Can Clinc"around this theme, one of many poems, stories and newspaper and magazine columns that described his experience or championed the idea of patients' rights.

Fear of deafness has stopped my ears.
Fear of blindness has sewn up my eyes.
Fear of nakedness has stripped me bare.
Fear of the desert has made me abjure drink.
Yet even now, bad joke for a black morning,
fear of silence has not stilled my tongue.
                    (from "Five Days in Hospital")

Nowlan still found himself alive after his third and final operation, and he looked as though he really had assaulted the beaches at Dieppe three times. But when the bandages that swathed his neck finally were unravelled, he wished that they could be put back on again. It was as if his old self had been killed and replaced by a new creature. The rerouting of the blood vessels caused his face to swell and gave him a permanently jowly appearance. As the scar tissue healed, it tightened to feel like a stiff leather collar. He started to wear an ascot and soon grew a reddish beard, sometimes explaining that it was uncomfortable to shave, at other times admitting that if he could no longer look pretty, then at least he could look picturesque.

Nowlan had sustained further nerve damage in the last operation and had to relearn how to lift his arms, requiring as much effort to lift a spoon to his mouth as he previously did to lift a heavy trunk, at least until his body became accustomed to the new muscular arrangement. He had a sort of sneer etched on his face until he learned how to use his facial muscles. Most debilitating of all was the loss of his thyroid gland, which controls the body's metabolism. Doctors experimented with various hormone replacement drugs, an experience that left the patient intermittently moody and shaky until a suitable one, Eltroxin, was found. Nowlan would have to take it for the rest of his life. Even so, his condition could cause mood swings and low energy levels that made extended activity, such as a book tour, difficult to undertake, along with leaving him prone to obesity. Another drug he became acquainted with was Librium, a central nervous system depressant used to help patients cope with the trauma of surgery. Librium is also used to help alcoholics wean themselves off the bottle.

Nowlan was admitted to the hospital at the end of March, when there was still snow on the ground. Now it was the beginning of May, the buds were on the trees, and flowers were bursting from the ground. He had been in St. Joseph's for nearly six weeks. One day, his doctor was checking the incision scars on Nowlan's neck when the poet croaked, "Doctor, when am I going to be able to leave this awful place?"

"When you are well, Alden."

"And when will that be?"

"Tell you what. The first day that you are able to walk down to the nursing station, sign yourself out, get on the elevator and walk across the lobby to a taxi, you can leave."

"It's a deal."

Putting his shirt on was the hardest part, but Nowlan was determined not to ask the nurses for help. He held on to the wall as he made his way to the nursing station, and again as he stumbled through the lobby to the taxi he had phoned for earlier. The cabbie had to help him with the door.

There was one more thing to do.

"I'm going to the Mitchell apartment building," Nowlan said. "But first I want you to take me to the Charlotte Street liquor store."

The cabbie rolled his eyes slightly: another refugee from the detox program.

When they arrived at the store, Nowlan found himself too weak to get out. Struggling not to slur his words, he made another request. "As you've noticed I'm in pretty shaky condition . . ."

A few minutes later the cab pulled up in back of the Mitchell Street apartments, and the poet counted out the fare from the liquor store change. The cabbie helped him get out of the car, Nowlan stumbled to his apartment door, holding the wall all the way, and let himself in to a room he had not seen in six weeks. He took a glass from the cupboard, slumped down at the kitchen table, poured himself a stiff shot from his pint of rum, bolted it, and immediately passed out.

Alden Nowlan was home at last.

Support from the literary community for the stricken author was not long in coming, and it arrived in a big way. Get-well cards poured in from most of the who's-who of Canadian literature. Jay MacPherson, whose Emblem Books had published *Wind in a Rocky Country*, sent him a book as a get-well gift. His friend Sandy Ives kept in close touch with him from the University of Maine at Orono, as did Elizabeth Brewster, a poet and contemporary of Fred Cogswell who had returned to her native Fredericton to work at the Legislative Library. She, too, had been included with Nowlan in Fiddlehead Press's anthology *Five New Brunswick Poets*. One of the writers who meant the most to him during that stressful time was the American novelist Henry Miller. Nowlan wrote him a fan letter and was surprised to receive a warm reply, along with an autographed photo and a small print of a watercolour the novelist had painted himself.

Nowlan wasted no time trying to revive his writing career during the free time before he would have to return to work at the *Telegraph-Journal*. A little note from May 12, 1966, no doubt written shortly after he regained consciousness at his kitchen table the morning after his return from the hospital, is a testament to how eager he was to write on a full-time basis. The note was for Pacey — written in Claudine's hand since Nowlan was still too shaky from his hormonal medication to use a pen — telling the professor that he just got out of hospital and would like his name to stand as a candidate for the 1966-1967 writer-in-residence. But Pacey, acting on Cogswell's advice, had already selected Dorothy Livesay as Norman Levine's successor. Cogswell had apparently told Pacey that Nowlan would be too sick to fulfill his duties. Nowlan was again frustrated in his attempt to be chosen for the University of New Brunswick post, and frustrated again with Cogswell, since, however sick he was, Nowlan faced returning to a job he found more stressful than writing. But this time his reply to Pacey held no rancour. "If you are in Saint John come see me. Like to see people now I'm in bad shape. When I was well I didn't give a damn. Selfish bastard aren't I? I guess the thing was I never needed anyone before. Or maybe wanting to have human contact is the symptom of the threatened self wanting to hold on to life consciousness etc etc."[6]

Ray Fraser started corresponding with Nowlan again just before the operations. He had taken the savings from his teaching job to Montreal, moved in with his girlfriend, Sharon Johnston, and started Poverty Press with LeRoy Johnson. On the side, he wrote for the tabloid *Midnight*, a job that dovetailed nicely with Fraser's sense of humour. His new literary magazine, *Intercourse*, debuted that year, and he sent Nowlan a copy of the inaugural issue. *Intercourse* mocked the more serious literary periodicals; that first issue featured poems by four Montreal hobos named Buck Layton, Art Purdy, Charlie Souster and Jack Nowlan. At that time, the real Nowlan was too preoccupied with his cancer operations to respond, but his June 23, 1966 letter to Fraser expressed his delight with the parody.

The two friends renewed their epistolary relationship, and Nowlan contributed some poems to Fraser's magazine, although it took him a year to offer an apology for their quarrel:

> I've always been sorry that things couldn't have worked out better the year you were in Belleisle — between us, I mean. . . . The ironic part of it is if you walked in tonight and we started drinking together we'd probably end up quarreling. And, generally speaking, we neither of us like poets very much. And so when we meet we keep searching in each other for symptoms of phoniness.[7]

Facing his own mortality, Nowlan tried to lower his defences with his friends and acquaintances. He re-established contact with his father, to whom he had not written in months. "Last night I was thinking how terrible it would be if I died. Then I thought how much worse it would have been if I had never been born," he wrote to Freeman. "Considering the start I had, these achievements seem almost miraculous. Almost every dream I ever had has come true. Not many people can say the same thing. So I don't complain about the bad luck."[8] Brewster continued to visit Saint John over the summer, and she brought a new friend along, Dorothy Livesay, the poet who had won the coveted UNB writer-in-residence post. Nowlan's letters to Brewster that summer show his continuing attempts to open up, as in this account of an excursion he and Claudine made:

I've tried to avoid thinking as much as possible — spend most of my time reading and watching television, although today we drove out into the country and sat on a hill overlooking the sea and listened to the birds and the wind in the grass and the foghorns, and I counted seventeen different shades of green. I don't think there's any colour as happy as green, especially green made from grass and leaves and sunlight. The colour of life. Eden. Someday, perhaps, I'll get this feeling in a poem.[9]

It was quite a change for the man who, a few weeks earlier, would work all night and then write all afternoon. And his new closeness to his wife is evident.

The prospect of death turned the vinegar of life into honey:

I am a product of a culture that fears any display of emotion, and attempts to repress any true communication. Perhaps the most beneficial effect of my discovery of the reality of death was its enabling me, for almost the first time, to express my honest feelings, outside of poetry. It's a painful process and probably never will be complete. But now I'm able, sometimes when I'm lucky, to tell certain people quite simply that I love them.[10]

On another trip with his family, this time to the seashore, he and Claudine watched while Johnnie sported in the ocean, "the waves like great dogs hurling themselves against him,/ beating their wet forepaws against his chest," as he writes in the poem "Down Shore." The speaker reflects on the joy of living life in the now, the eternity of a small moment trapped in time "falling around them like the shadow/ of a single cloud crossing the sun/. . . . *I, a man, have tamed even death.*" But, on his way home, he came across an injured seagull flapping helplessly on the sand. In the poem "On the Nature of Human Compassion," he reflects that his identification with the larger world might be mere egotism after all, "the conceit/ that all living things are Alden Nowlan in disguise."

While Nowlan recovered and found a new love of humanity, Fred Cogswell formulated his own plan for lending support to his friend. Although he scotched Nowlan's attempt to secure the writer-in-residence position, there was no doubt that Cogswell stood firmly in

Nowlan's corner. That June, working from behind the scenes, Cogswell engineered a $300 UNB library purchase of some of Nowlan's manuscripts. This as much as anything convinced Nowlan of the wisdom of Purdy's advice that he save all of his papers. Next on Cogswell's agenda was a strongly worded application to the Canada Council for a grant of $5,000, enough for Nowlan to get by for one year. Cogswell wrote to the Council about the tenacious hold his friend still had on life:

> My personal opinion is that Alden Nowlan is a poet of similar order to the American poet, Robert Frost, that he has already accomplished much more than Frost had done when he had reached a comparable age, and that his potential as a poet is by no means exhausted.
>
> He grudges any energy and time that must be spent at routine work and wishes to devote all his energy to fulfilling his creative impulses which have become more alive and sharp in the shadow of impending death.

He concluded, "If you feel that the Canada Council is not warranted in granting the Fellowship I ask, would you please suggest to me some other means of help for Alden Nowlan?"[11] He assembled a group of distinguished referees, including Pacey, Layton and Ives, to lend their support to the application, enjoining them to secrecy, lest the shock of being denied a grant damage Nowlan's shaky health.

His health was indeed shaky, but Nowlan had more spiritual strength than Cogswell gave him credit for. Tests that summer showed that there was still thyroid tissue in his body; it would have to be destroyed with radiation treatment. Again, he endured a terrible wait for a summons to the hospital. This time it would be the Saint John General Hospital, a looming fortress located not far from St. Joseph's. Finally, in early August, the word came that he would be admitted for one week. There he felt a renewal of the terror he had experienced during his operations, which for all he knew might have done no more than prolong his life by a few months. Remembering the power of clothing in the world of medicine, he donned his street clothes one night and went wandering alone through the dimly lit corridors of the General. No one bothered him; everyone assumed he was healthy. In the dark corners of his mind, he knew that assumption was far from true.

The radiation treatments over, his health improving by the day, he could put off the newspaper grind no longer. Starting in late August, he began working on the news desk for about twenty hours a week. But even this left him exhausted. He would typically go home after putting in a shift and then sleep for most of the following day, until a couple of hours before he had to get up for work.

Somehow, he found the strength to write again. It was now more important than ever to write and publish, for financial as well as literary reasons. That summer, working from an old book by Reverend Silas T. Rand loaned to him by Aida Flemming, Nowlan began writing short fictional adaptations of Rand's Micmac legends for publication in the *Atlantic Advocate*. He did a series of five such stories, which helped flex his fiction-writing muscles. And, for the first time in years, he assembled enough material for another poetry collection. He worked against time, aware that this collection could well be his last. By the end of August, the manuscript had been sent away. Its title, *Bread, Wine and Salt*, had been knocking around in his head for a few years, the bread and wine representing the sacramental food of life, the salt representing his satirical poems. The collection contained not just his newest writing but also a considerable number of poems that had been published years ago in little magazines. He did not hold back on his choice of publisher for his most ambitious collection, choosing Canada's largest literary publisher, McClelland and Stewart, even though they had rejected *The Wanton Troopers*.

The return to his newspaper and writing schedule drained what little energy Nowlan had. He needed a boost to validate his literary ambitions, and Al Purdy was just the sort of person to give it to him. The poet and his wife were travelling through the Maritimes in early September on the way back from Newfoundland, and he wanted to stop at Saint John to look around and to meet this Nowlan fellow he had been reading for so long. But their great, drunken meeting turned out to be a sober disappointment. When Purdy and his wife came to Nowlan's apartment that morning, they were greeted by a shy, tongue-tied bear of a man who could scarcely get past initial introductions. Claudine filled in the gaps in the awkward conversation, but not for long. The visitors quickly made their excuses and left, Purdy saying that he wanted to write a poem about the Loyalist Burial Ground in downtown Saint John. Purdy recalls:

He was a younger guy, twenty-six or twenty-seven I guess [actually thirty-three]; large, about my size but with an imposing presence I don't have. I kept feeling expectant of him, hoping for the marvels of intimate human converse; then I looked away, thinking I'd made him nervous. But if he wasn't, I was. It occurred to me: maybe he's conceived an instant dislike for this visitor from the wilds of hogtown Toronto (but I ain't from Toronto). I don't know, I don't know. Mere simplistic shyness? No, that couldn't be. Not this marvellous lyric poet I loved and was now beginning to hate for putting me through a tortuous boring endless era prior to human speech.[12]

Usually, Nowlan drowned his awkwardness around people whom he perceived to be literary types with a shot of gin or rum, which in fact he was planning to do that evening. He understood that Purdy would return after his shift at the paper ended, and he purchased a bottle of rum for the purpose. But Purdy was not aware of this plan, and he phoned Nowlan before pulling out of town the next morning to bid farewell. Nowlan could not take the call, however, having downed the rum by himself.

Some of Nowlan's publishing experiences that fall were sour. The August issue of a small literary magazine from Florida called *Human Voice Quarterly* made it to the review desk of the *Telegraph-Journal*. It was devoted entirely to Canadian poets Layton, Souster, Birney, Reaney, Avison, Purdy, McRobbie, Cohen, Dudek and Alden A. Nowlan. But Nowlan had sent no poems to *Human Voice Quarterly*. A bit of investigation revealed that the poems submitted by that issue's editor, R.H. Flood, were simply lifted from McClelland and Stewart's anthology *Poets of Mid-Century*. A typographical error in the title of one of his poems in the anthology was even reproduced in the magazine version. Nowlan's work had been pirated. He canvassed some of the other "contributors" to find out what they knew. Some had no idea their work had appeared in *Human Voice Quarterly*, not surprising considering the magazine's obscurity. Layton was mildly annoyed, but Earle Birney, who already knew, was furious. Nowlan, for his part, wrote a letter to the publisher, Vincent Smith, deploring the theft. "I wonder," he wrote of Flood, "if he bothered to retype the poems before sending them to you or simply scissored them out of the McClelland

and Stewart Ltd. book?"[13] A week later, on October 13, 1966, Smith sent back a grudging apology leavened with self-pity:

> Trying to promote poets appears to be a big mistake at this time even when the audience for poetry is microscopic. I guess it is simply that we suffer from delusions. Anyhow, you may rest assured that HVQ will never find itself in a position to earn your ire again if this may be of any consolation.[14]

"I wrote you to protest your infringement of copyright," Nowlan responded. "I also protest, most violently, the suggestion that you are doing me, or any other poet, a service by printing our poetry. I feel the poet does you a service, by allowing his work to appear in your magazine."[15]

But, in writing to Layton, Nowlan put the matter into perspective. "Getting upset over trifles such as this takes my mind off my real problems and makes me feel better." He was also writing to Layton to ask for support for an application to the Guggenheim foundation. The idea came from Ives, who had recently received his own Guggenheim grant. The deadline had just passed for 1966, but at Cogswell's urging Ives phoned the chairman anyway, mentioned his friend's dire circumstance, and secured Nowlan an extended deadline. So, much to his surprise, Nowlan received a call one day from Ives telling him to expect some forms in the mail. He took the project on with gusto. Whereas Cogswell's defence against failure had been secrecy, Nowlan affected jaunty dismissiveness. "I think of Guggenhiem as the name of a giant computer with the face of a robot," he wrote to Layton. "But I'm fully aware that I'd be far more apt to get some money if I could tell them I was a Ph.D. who had done post-graduate studies at Oxford and wanted a grant to finance a study of Anglo-Saxon punctuation as exemplified in the use of the semi-colon in *Piers Plowman*."[16]

But a letter to John Drew, who proof-read and copied Nowlan's application at the University of New Brunswick at Saint John, reveals the return of his deep-seated insecurity about his role as a writer, an insecurity that may account for his awkwardness with fellow writers such as Purdy. "Just under the surface there is a millhand in overalls with one strap missing and manure on his boots. And this millhand or farmboy looks out through my eyes at the educated world and wonders how he can keep them from finding him out."[17] There was another sort of blue-collar guilt at work in Nowlan's psyche. As he explained to

Drew, his Guggenheim application must be kept secret lest the people at the *Telegraph-Journal* find out what he was up to. Even though he was recovering from a potentially fatal illness, he still felt guilty that he was not working full-time to earn the money the paper was paying him. Though nothing in the *Telegraph* correspondence validates this attitude, it is clear that Nowlan still thought of himself as an "investment" that the Big Man was making in expectation of future profits.

At the end of October, as the Guggenheim application was working its way through the giant computer in New York, Nowlan received an unexpected letter:

> Perhaps you remember the time about six years ago when I dropped in at your newspaper office in Hartland, to talk with you for a few minutes. A few weeks later you wrote me a letter about some poems I'd sent you that was very encouraging and helpful.
>
> I'm still a great admirer of your poetry, and I notice that you haven't published in book form during the last four years or so. I was wondering whether you have a new manuscript, poetry or prose, ready for publication yet. If you do, we'd be very interested in having a look at it at Clarke, Irwin, where I'm an editor now. And if you don't have anything ready right at the moment, I'd be pleased if you'd keep Clarke, Irwin in mind for the future.[18]

Nowlan did remember Roy MacSkimming, the seventeen-year-old kid who had dropped into the *Observer* office one summer day in 1962 on a cross-country journey to meet some of Canada's writers. "He wrote this letter where he really unburdened himself in a way that I could understand, in a way that he probably figured would mean something to an adolescent," MacSkimming recalls. "It was a very moving thing to do. I was totally floored by it, because it was in contrast to the way he had been when we met. He'd been pretty shy.[19] Now it was MacSkimming's turn to surprise Nowlan. McClelland and Stewart had been silent about *Bread, Wine and Salt*, and Nowlan seems to have all but given up on them: "It's possible I'll have a book-length manuscript of poems available for submission in the next month or so. If so, I'll send it to Clarke, Irwin for consideration." Then he proposed a project he had long hoped would see the light of day: "Also, I have some stories for a book. Do you think there's any chance Clarke, Irwin would be at all interested in these?"[20] Ever the professional, he was eager to prove his versatility. Nowlan's guess that M&S would not accept the poetry book proved to be correct, and *Bread, Wine and Salt* was in Clarke, Irwin's hands by the end of that month.

And there were more surprises to come. Nowlan learned just before Christmas of Cogswell's secret plan to have him awarded a Canada Council Fellowship. Cogswell worried needlessly, it turned out, about how the shock of winning the award would affect his friend. "I guess I was the only person surprised," Nowlan told Fraser. "Because a day after I got the call [from the Canada Council] I started getting congratulatory messages from people in Montreal and Toronto."[21]

He had for years dreamed of being awarded that much money and being able to take Claudine and Johnnie to Europe, but he abandoned the idea once he realized that his health might not be up to the journey. The outcome of his Guggenheim application would make him dust off these plans. In March of 1967 Nowlan received word that he had again hit the jackpot: he had been awarded a Guggenheim Fellowship. He would have enough money to devote himself to writing full-time until the end of 1968. On March 31, 1967, a local radio station recognized the writer's achievement by declaring Nowlan the CFBC Citizen of the Day. The prize for the cancer survivor? A carton of Craven A cigarettes.

SEVEN

Playing the Jesus Game

Playing the Jesus game
I don't smile at strangers
because that might frighten them
into summoning the police.

Playing the Jesus game
I open the trapdoor in the top of my head
and let out the angel
that everyone believes
is an optical illusion.

I see an angel, they think
I must be going blind or crazy.

So my angel can touch them,
once, gently, with the flat of his sword.
He can play his guitar for them.

But if anyone asks me what I'm doing here
I'll tell them I'm waiting for a bus
because that is a lie that almost anyone would believe.

The time had come for Nowlan to break the news to the *Telegraph-Journal* that, because of his Canada Council and Guggenheim grants, he was flush with cash and would not be coming back to work until at least the end of 1968. In January, 1967, cap in hand, Nowlan thanked his employers for their generosity, outlined his improving health, and proposed a plan to keep one finger in journalism while using the other nine for his own writing. He offered his services for writing the occasional feature story in return for a minimal salary that would keep him on the Group Insurance and the Blue Cross health plan. As when they first heard of Nowlan's cancer, the managers of the paper were more than willing to accommodate the man they were starting to think of as "their Alden." Ralph Costello agreed to keep Nowlan on as a part-time employee who would come into the office for one night per week and contribute feature stories from time to time. Since November of 1966, he had been writing editorials, and he continued to do so up until the end of March, 1967 — his first quasi-volunteer venture.

Early in the new year, Greg Cook decided to get back in touch with his friend, with apologies for not returning Nowlan's phone calls and with big plans for the future:

> Your collection of stories. God help me, I hope you haven't retyped them unless you had a sure sale. I'm looking at a letter from you Aug 13/66. Most (all) of them were previously published. Frankly, I've bankrupted one of my two god damn companies — last month. I've given your originals to Ernest Buckler to write an introduction. Why? You'll kill me. Because if I fluke any more prize money in the next two months I'll put the collection out of that. I don't back down on promises, especially if they're personal commitments. Perhaps you won't let me then. Maybe I'll look the situation over and do it anyway and we can have a real brawl. It might help to promote the stories![1]

But Nowlan, with a new energy and drive to see his fiction in book form, had already started to retype the stories that were in Cook's possession. Though Cook was correct in saying that the stories had been previously published, Nowlan's journalistic professionalism would not allow him to submit a manuscript consisting of fiction clipped out of various magazines, complete with typographic mistakes. Retyping also allowed him to make minor alterations such as the character names in his story "The Foreigner." By now, he had no intention of allowing Cook to publish his fiction collection. In his February 14 reply, Nowlan absolves him of any responsibility for *The Glass Roses*: "You were under no obligation to publish my stories. In fact, I felt a little guilty about your undertaking the project because I knew, deep down, you couldn't afford it any more than I could." But he still could not resist nibbling at Cook's bait:

> One thing I would appreciate very much, and that's seeing Ernest Buckler's introduction. I've always admired him greatly and would very much like to see what he's written about the stories. If by some fluke one of the commercial companies accepts the book, do you think Buckler would let them use the introduction — or would you be agreeable to its being used, since it was you who persuaded him to write it? Incidentally, how much do you think it would cost to print an attractive edition of the stories?[2]

Nowlan's interest in Buckler's opinion was genuine, but, in addition, Buckler's support would be useful in persuading larger publishing houses to take a second look at *The Glass Roses*. On March 1 Nowlan finished retyping the stories and sent the new manuscript off to Ryerson, but without the Buckler introduction.

Meanwhile, Roy MacSkimming at Clarke, Irwin was just as eager as Cook to be the one to publish Nowlan's next book, but he faced his own challenges. The Toronto publishing firm was mostly engaged in publishing textbooks and the like for the lucrative educational market. The owner, Irene Clarke, kept up the firm's commitment to trade publishing, which had been a special interest of her late husband and partner, but the type of material the company published for that market held no interest for MacSkimming; he had to cut his editorial teeth on the memoirs of an eighteen-year-old equestrienne. The new editor-in-chief, however, was open to MacSkimming's proposal that Clarke, Irwin undertake to publish more poetry and fiction by the growing crop of Canadian writers.

This new editor-in-chief was Irene Clarke's son Bill, who had returned to his family's business after pursuing a PhD in astrophysics. Although Clarke had grown up with books, he was still new to managing a publishing firm with ninety-five employees. Clarke gave MacSkimming the go-ahead to solicit manuscripts from Canadian authors while he consulted with his mother about whether to take the firm in this new direction. By February 12, 1967, MacSkimming was becoming impatient and wrote to Nowlan to express his frustration with "the endless messing around over your ms."[3] This letter may have influenced Nowlan's decision two weeks later to send the manuscript of *The Glass Roses* to Ryerson instead of Clarke, Irwin. But the "messing around" with *Bread, Wine and Salt* took different forms. In the same letter, MacSkimming asked Nowlan for some new poems that had just been published in the *Canadian Forum* and the *Tamarack Review*, one of many such requests the young editor would make as he tinkered with the manuscript to make it as strong as possible.

The Clarkes' decision to publish the book came in early April, shortly after Nowlan learned of his success in winning the Guggenheim grant. MacSkimming intensified his efforts to solicit new poems and to jettison old ones; in all, only two-thirds of the poems submitted for *Bread, Wine and Salt* appear in the published version. Clarke, Irwin emphasized design almost as much as content. The hardcover edition was complemented by beautiful woodcut illustrations by Mary Cserepy that Nowlan described as "medieval." And it would have a larger print run and a wider distribution than any of his previous collections. "Who knows?" he speculated later that summer as he warmed to the attention Clarke, Irwin was giving to the project. "This book may mark a turning point for me, the way *A Red Carpet for the Sun* marked a turning point for Layton."[4]

Although Nowlan's first poetry collection in four years was progressing apace, his fiction met with less immediate encouragement. *The Glass Roses* came back from Ryerson with a rejection slip. In a May 4, 1967, letter to Ray Fraser, he mentioned sending the stories off to Clarke, Irwin. He would not let this manuscript die as he had *The Wanton Troopers*, even if he had to publish it himself, an option he was considering. "I've toyed with the idea of selling advance subscriptions, say, 100 at $5 a shot. Subscribers to get an autographed numbered copy or some such thing." In fact, later that summer he would follow through with this idea by writing the Villiers printing company for an estimate of how much such a book would cost. But he seems to have ruled out one option by then. He told Fraser, "Cook says he could still do it if he had $300. But I'm not sure I trust him. In fact, to be frank, I'm sure I don't."[5]

In the same letter to Fraser, Nowlan assessed the American poet Allen Ginsberg:

> I think Ginsberg is over-rated. As a poet, don't think he is any better than his father, Louis, who publishes in the *Fiddlehead*. Both are competent, minor, romantic poets. As the professors say . . .
>
> As I told [John] Drew, I may have panned Ginsberg's poetry simply out of spite and jealousy. I suppose I am jealous of him. After all, I'm a better poet than he is but I've never had my picture on the cover of *Esquire*. That's a stupid attitude, but I'm human enough to have it — even if only subconsciously. I mean I don't really *think* that I have such an attitude, but I *feel* that, deep in the recesses of my subconscious, I probably do think that way some- times.

Ginsberg was the very type of poet Nowlan and Fraser might have pictured when discussing literary "phonies." He was the beatnik of all beatniks, with his prayer beads, wild hair, unkempt beard and groovy devotion to Hinduism. Nowlan was reacting to Ginsberg's March 25, 1967, visit to Saint John, an event he covered in an article for the *Telegraph-Journal*.

Fred Hazel, not knowing Nowlan's views on "phonies," assumed that their resident poet would be just the person to write an article about Ginsberg's visit. Nowlan had reason to feel cocky as the day approached. Not only had he just heard about winning the Guggenheim, but he had also just finished a stint at the *Telegraph* working four nights a week to fill in for vacationing staff. From that moment on, according to his accommodation with the paper, he would work only one night a week. He was about to start having fun with journalism.

For John Drew, spiriting Ginsberg into the country was as much a challenge as organizing the reading. Two days before the reading, the UNBSJ vice-president G. Forbes Elliot received a phone tip from a friend in immigration saying that they intended to stop the controversial poet at the border and that Elliot should plan to cancel the reading. When Elliot conveyed the message to Drew, the professor decided instead to phone his member of Parliament, Gordon Fairweather. Fairweather in turn told Drew that he could arrange a telegram from the justice minister within the hour, but that Drew had to promise that Ginsberg would not corrupt any young people during his visit.

Ginsberg, as it turned out, was anything but a corrupting influence upon the youth of Saint John. He even bought a frumpy suit for the occasion in order to blend in with the citizens. When Nowlan met him in his room at the Admiral Beatty Hotel, he was reading from the Gideon Bible. "Ecclesiastes," Ginsberg explained. "One great, long, bitter poem."

Ginsberg, Nowlan, Drew and a visiting professor from India, Chanchi Mehta, toured the port city. Ginsberg mostly chatted with Mehta about Hinduism and made the most of what Saint John had to offer. "Ah, New Brunswick marijuana!" he exclaimed on tasting dulse in the City Market.

The poets walked through the old Loyalist Burial Ground. "Look, Allen," Nowlan pointed out, perhaps thinking of Purdy's visit. "Every poet who comes to Saint John writes a poem about the Loyalist Burial Ground. There have been thousands of them. You'll have to write one."

Ginsberg took a minute to ponder the darkened, moss-encrusted tablets. "Many drunks have slipped on this snow and bloodied their heads upon these stones." He paused. "Is that a haiku?"[6]

One of the places the group visited was the UNBSJ campus, in those days a large brick house at the end of Charlotte Street. In the library, Drew introduced Ginsberg and Nowlan to a young student who liked to write poetry, Louis Cormier. Cormier was impressed by Ginsberg but hardly remembers Nowlan from that afternoon. True to form, Nowlan said little in the company of strangers.

Of course, the church basement that had been rented for the reading was packed to the doors that evening. And, of course, Ginsberg corrupted the youth by launching into "Howl," which sent several of the less-corruptible towards the exits. Cormier squeezed into the back of the hall that night; he remembers seeing Nowlan sitting up front with Claudine.

Afterwards, walking home through a late-winter snowfall, Cormier saw a large car up ahead stuck hopelessly in a snowbank. The driver got out to inspect the situation. It was the quiet poet Cormier had been introduced to earlier that day, Alden Nowlan. Cormier offered his help and freed the stricken car, Nowlan in return offered the young man a ride back to his place to have a beer, and a friendship was born.

Cormier and Nowlan had more in common than they might have expected. Cormier, too, grew up in relative poverty and ignorance, but in the slums of Saint John; the Nowlans' basement apartment on

Mitchell Street was swanky by his standards. His father was also an alcoholic. But Cormier had fought his way through school, seeing education as his only ticket out. "Did you actually read all those books, or are they for decoration?" Cormier asked Nowlan, referring to the older man's stuffed bookcase. Nowlan let out a booming laugh and assured Cormier that he had indeed read them all. The booze flowed, and Nowlan opened up, talking about his bout with cancer and giving Cormier a couple of his poetry books. After Claudine had gone to bed, the two men cautiously approached the refrigerator, Nowlan motioning the young man to be quiet lest they wake her up. Conversation turned to literary and philosophical matters. At last, the sun rose, putting an end to their ruminations. Nowlan cooked breakfast for Cormier and sent him home, his young head spinning with new ideas and strange emotions.

John Drew loved the article that appeared in the paper the next day about the Ginsberg visit, although he had no illusions about his friend's prejudices about "phonies." "I was able to point out to Alden that one reason we had Allen was because Alden himself had repeatedly turned us down [for readings]," the professor recalls. "Perhaps Allen's visit and the awards and the stream of his own poetry publications did have the effect of causing Alden to 'come out' a bit more."[7] This was probably the first time Nowlan had seen a showman of Ginsberg's calibre in action. Despite the positive impression the American made on his Saint John audience, Nowlan wrote a satirical short story called "The Innermost One" for the new fiction collection. In it, an American writer named Martin Rosenberg seeks wisdom in the temples of India, only to be frustrated by the lama's very earthly interest in Western pop culture.

With one book of poetry on the way and a book of fiction under consideration, with the cancer banished to a dark corner and a wad of grant money sitting in his bank account, Nowlan revived his desire to travel in Europe. He now had the leisure to do so, and, although he fretted about periodic medical tests, he no longer feared being stuck in a hospital in a lonely corner of France or Spain. But France and Spain, he now felt, were too ambitious; just looking at the pamphlets for coach tours — the Nowlans' preferred method of travel — made him and Claudine dizzy. So they abandoned the European coach tour idea in favour of a less ambitious plan: he, Claudine and Johnnie would spend three weeks knocking about England and Ireland, and he would go in search of his roots, both genetic and literary.

The Nowlans arrived in London on July 25, and the family took in most of the principal tourist sites of London, including St. Paul's Cathedral and Westminster Abbey. Nowlan had an eye not just for the historical significance of these churches, but also for the human element to be found nearby. It was not the Chair of State in Westminster Abbey that sparked his interest as much as the graffiti that had been carved into its wooden frame over the centuries. Not the tombs of kings and lords but rather the casts made of their faces at death. The German and American tourists smoking casually in the pews drew the poet's attention as much as the great paintings and statues.

Upon seeing Buckingham Palace, with its prim toy-soldier guards and its ornate trimmings, Nowlan reflected on the monarchists he knew back home, such as his former landlady, Mrs. Shaw, and how little they meant to the people who lived at this grand address. In the park surrounding the palace there were, as in parks everywhere, great flocks of pigeons. One dropped a foul present on Johnnie's head. "You should be honoured, Johnnie," Nowlan deadpanned. "That's royal pigeon shit." At the Tower of London, Johnnie met with another minor mishap. On the way to see the Crown Jewels, he complained of feeling sick. The family had to stand in the queue of tourists for over an hour before descending the long staircase to the jewel vault. When they finally reached the darkened corridor where the jewels were kept, Claudine turned from the vast golden display to see two guards trying to revive her fainting son.

After that, the family decided to maintain a more leisurely pace. For Nowlan, London offered more than historical sites. In Soho, Hyde Park and Piccadilly Circus, the real attraction for him was the bizarre collection of people and the little everyday dramas. A Dickensian crone at Hyde Park handing out taffy to the London bobbies, stuffing it into their pockets when they would not take it from her. The same crone singing a ribald refrain to a street corner evangelist. And, of course, the hippies who congregated in Soho, some wearing little more than army blankets, tiny dresses and strings of beads. One character in a kilt, a rain cape and a stovepipe hat blew soap bubbles at passersby. For Nowlan, London was a feast for the senses.

Of course, England was a literary Mecca, and Nowlan wanted to make his pilgrimage. But, unlike most, he bypassed the shrines of

Stratford and the Lake District and instead made his way to Eastwood, Nottinghamshire, the birthplace of one of his heroes, D.H. Lawrence. Eastwood was not a tourist industry attraction, and that was all the better for the poet from Canada. "Sigh-ite see-ahs, sigh-ite see-ahs!" the local children shouted after the trio as they roamed the streets. "There's no sigh-ites to see he-ah!" The children did not realize that a man who had visited this village so often in his imagination saw a treasure of sights. Within moments of Nowlan's arrival, a man pulled up in a car and asked for directions to Ripley. Nowlan responded without a hitch, "Go straight ahead, turn right at the Sun Inn, follow the Nottingham Road to Langley Mill Lane, and keep bearing right." "If I'd stopped to think about it," he later wrote in an essay, "I'd have said: 'Sorry, I'm a stranger here myself.'"[8]

He was indeed a stranger in this rural village so unlike the ones he had known. Women peeked out through their curtains at the family roaming the lanes. Nowlan found several houses from Lawrence's world still standing, including the one where Lawrence grew up. After several hours, he had to admit that he found Eastwood, which Lawrence had described as ugly, in fact rather pretty. Eastwood was a coal-mining town made up almost entirely of uniform company cottages, but each one could boast a little garden of its own, and the surrounding countryside was beautiful and green. The man from Desolation Creek had seen worse. "But of course he'd never/ seen Springhill or Sudbury" he writes of Lawrence in the poem "The Pilgrim's Tale."

By that time, the Nowlans had been in England for two weeks. For the final week of their trip, they visited Ireland, the land of Nowlan's ancestors. This was a pilgrimage of a different sort.

> Ireland is another world. It really is. I think we may go back there someday to live for a while. And it *is* greener than North America. A dream-like, misty golden-green. Gypsies with piebald ponies and wagons; sheep wandering back and forth across the roads; the smell of peat drying; great treeless mountains with the clouds resting on the peaks as though they were tired; ruined round towers, Celtic crosses, little fairy tale farms — you keep expecting Jack of Beanstalk fame to walk out of one of the farm-houses and meet Cinderella coming out of another. A very beautiful and mysterious country.[9]

And a conservative one. Young girls here would not think of wearing what their hippie counterparts wore in Soho, or even of wearing slacks or shorts. Skirts of modest length were still the order of the day, even for working girls who rode their bicycles to and from their jobs. Men wore jackets and ties for every occasion, although these would be finer or shabbier depending on whether they were farming, collecting garbage or working in an office.

Nowlan was on the whole more accepting of Irish quirks than he was of English ones. A small-town boy at heart, he preferred the marginal and traditional culture to one that was, to him, more central and sophisticated. He expressed this preference in the familiar Maritime way: "I'd say that about 90 per cent of the Dubliners are friendly and about 90 per cent of the Londoners are bastards," he estimated to fellow Maritimer Ray Fraser. But even among the friendly Dubliners he encountered the same type of duplicity that he often noted in small towns such as Hartland. "It is very funny," he continued. "The Irish kept mistaking us for Americans and as soon as they found out we weren't, they started telling us what arrogant boors the Yanks are."[10]

Later in the month of August, after the family's return from their adventure in the British Isles, they were visited in Saint John by Greg Cook, who was driving back to Nova Scotia from Expo 67 in Montreal with his wife, Miriam, their three children, and a teacher friend, Anne Greer. Cook had another literary project in mind. He had decided to return to Acadia University to study for his master's degree and was trying to persuade Greer to do the same thing. Acadia's one-year MA program allowed students to write a thesis on a living Canadian writer. Cook would write his thesis about Ernest Buckler. "And I have just the writer for you," he said to Greer on the way to New Brunswick, handing her a copy of the *Amethyst* issue containing his interview with Nowlan. She read it in the car, and the poetry spoke to her of her own background in rural Nova Scotia. When they arrived in Saint John, she and Nowlan hit it off right away, but she did not then broach the topic of a thesis. Instead, she waited until she gained admission to Acadia; then she approached him by letter that fall. Nowlan was bemused by the request, as Greer recalls "He said he would allow me to write a thesis on him as long as I promised to use the word 'adumbrate.' He thought it was a great joke that academia should be taking an interest in him, and yet he was touched. . . It made him realize that people were taking him seriously."[11] At her desk, she searched the dictionary to find out what "adumbrate" meant: to indicate faintly, to outline, to fore-shadow, or to obscure.

Bread, Wine and Salt came out in the fall of 1967 to favourable reviews and brisk sales. Nowlan's confidence in its eventual success was not unfounded. In a *Tamarack Review* article, Purdy praised the book as Nowlan's best to date and banished the regional bugbear for Nowlan by noting, "Regional subjects still make up the bulk of Nowlan's poem material, but there are enough pieces dealing with childhood, Ottawa, his own illness, etc., to destroy any pat generalization of him as a strictly regional poet."[12] "Because of its style and its compelling medley of certain personal, social, and historical themes, [the collection] is distinctively North American," Robert Cockburn echoes in *The Fiddlehead*, adding, "he must now be numbered among our very best poets: read this book, and you will see him shouldering half-poets and lesser men aside as he moves up to the front rank."[13] The five hospital poems at the end of the collection, plus the poem "I, Icarus" at the front of the book are often singled out for special praise.

Readers in New Brunswick had a difficult time finding the collection on bookstore shelves, although this was as much the result of poor book distribution in the province as it was an indication of *Bread, Wine and Salt*'s popularity. What few book retailers there were in New Brunswick could not obtain enough copies to keep up with the demand. To make matters worse, one major retailer in Saint John, the Manchester, Robertson and Allison department store, pulled *Bread, Wine and Salt* from their shelves after some patrons returned the book, complaining about the language in some of the poems. Nowlan blamed the "genteel old maids" of Saint John who could not stomach "poetry, real poetry, and have had the shit knocked out of them."[14]

At Clarke, Irwin, MacSkimming was having similar problems per-suading the Clarkes not to censor Nowlan's short stories. MacSkimming remembers, "What really bothered me was that, if they objected to an image or a passage on the grounds of taste — on grounds of gentility or morality — that was enough for them to reject the story. So they weren't necessarily rejecting it on grounds of quality, they were rejecting it because it had something in it that they found offensive."[15] MacSkimming also took an active editorial hand in culling the best Nowlan stories, both old and new, for the collection; in the end, only eight of the original fifteen stories in *The Glass Roses* survived. Nowlan finally received the

Buckler introduction from Cook in November and sent it on to Clarke, Irwin, but by that time the Clarkes had decided to publish it complete with its crude imagery, choosing its title from one of the other stories in the collection, *Miracle at Indian River*. It had taken over five years, but the public would at last be able to read a collection of Nowlan's fiction.

Anne Greer, meanwhile, had started an intimate correspondence with her subject as part of her thesis research. Freed of his earthly obligations by the generosity of the Canada Council and the Guggenheim Foundation, and on a peaceful plateau after his battle with cancer and his struggle to publish his last two books, Nowlan began anew to contemplate his place in the Canadian literary scene, something he had not had the chance to do since his Hartland days. "You know, I think most literary criticism is based on the fallacy that the writer writes his life as well as his books," he muses to Cook. "Once you've eliminated this fallacy you'd knocked the props out from under 90 per cent of all the literary criticism that's ever been written, and destroyed most of accepted history."[16]

And yet Nowlan could not forbear giving Greer only his version of the events of his life, sending her among other things the unpublished manuscript for *The Wanton Troopers*, which had been gathering dust in a drawer since he moved to Saint John. "My Boswell," he sometimes called her. With Greer, Nowlan articulated his stance on regionalism more effectively than he could as a tongue-tied young poet reading for the first time in Toronto:

> While my background is different from the North American norm it is closer to the *world* norm than that of any other North American writer. I am one of the new [few?] North American writers who really knows anything about the world outside the affluent society. In many ways I have more in common with a peasant in Vietnam or a militiaman in Cuba than I have with John Updike, for instance. And I'm dead certain I can understand Mao Tze-tung better than Salinger ever could. So which of us is the provincial?[17]

Nowlan was not just clarifying facts for Greer, he was also drafting his definition of himself. He hints to Greer that he does not always tell the factual truth, but rather a mythic truth. Greer, for her part, sensed this need in her subject: "I think he knew that this was important. I think he knew that this was his opportunity to have things recorded."[18]

With his friend Fraser, however, he was much less self-conscious in his ruminations. In October, 1967, Nowlan went to Montreal to read at Sir George Williams University. While there, he looked up Tyndale Martin, a Zen Buddhist poet, because of the strength of a batch of poems the guru had sent him, and Martin escorted Nowlan, Claudine and Johnnie through Expo 67. Fraser did not attend the reading; he had seen Nowlan in September before leaving Canada on his own European adventure in Scotland and Ireland. Irving Layton was there, and he entertained Nowlan later that evening and the next morning at his home. Nowlan's unguarded letters to Fraser reveal a different evolution of his persona than is seen in his more considered approach with Greer.

His account to Fraser of the reading at Sir George Williams shows that, though still deferential to the elder members of the Canadian literary scene (with the significant exception of Dorothy Livesay, for whom he was developing a dislike), his unsatisfying encounters with his peers during the early 1960s was leading him to adopt a less-than-collegial attitude towards them. Margaret Atwood shared the stage with him that night at Sir George Williams. Nowlan told Fraser, "Margaret Atwood read, and everyone was very soulful, and it got on my nerves so that I read mostly my satirical poems and when everybody started laughing and relaxing, the ham in me came out and I gave them more and more."[19] After reporting his meeting with Layton, he continued, "Marijuana makes me feel the way I felt when I started drinking, when I was a teenager. I haven't had enough of it to know if that's a permanent thing, or if the feeling would change, as the feeling that comes with alcohol has changed."[20] That this remark immediately follows his news about Layton suggests that Layton might have introduced him to marijuana, or that he wanted Fraser to believe this. In any case, such gossip was characteristic of the relationship he and Fraser enjoyed, to which Greer was not a party.

Greer arrived in Saint John just before New Year's to collect what biographical information she could for her thesis on Nowlan's life and art. Claudine gave her Johnnie's room, he being away for his usual holiday trip to see his grandfather in Hartland. They sat up late into the night as Nowlan played with his beloved cat, Hodge, and spun his tale. "We were drunk," she remembers. "Drunk with words." And, like someone who is now sober, Greer today is aware of the problematic "openness" of their collaboration. "He told me about what I've come to think of as the myth, his own myth of his birth and mother. . . . That's what interests me about him. His life is such a fine example of an archetypal life. And he knew that already, to the point that he was creating something of a myth about his own beginning."[21] Nowlan had found a sympathetic and credulous member of what he saw as the academic world, someone who would tell his story in an academic paper and would tell it the way he wanted it told. For he was again gearing himself up to confront academia.

Nowlan had been invited to take part in a writers' conference at the University of New Brunswick in February, 1968, which would feature himself, John Newlove, George Bowering and an American poet, John Gill. The event was organized by a new UNB faculty member, Kent Thompson, who was himself an American expatriate and short fiction writer. That year, Thompson and Dorothy Livesay started a writers' group that met on Tuesday nights in a tiny old building that used to serve as the university's ice house; it came to be called the Ice House Gang. Some of the Ice House Gang were also faculty members, including Bob Gibbs and another expatriate American poet, Bill Bauer. Nowlan knew what this conference could mean to him. Dorothy Livesay was in her second year as UNB writer-in-residence, and it was certain that the university would want a new face, since the Canada Council had funded only her first year. The UNB academic and literary community would be there in full force. Before Nowlan loomed the prospect of returning to full-time newspaper work when his grant money ran out at the end of 1968. It was time to sing for his supper.

To do so, he would have to come out of his shell both as a reader and as a mingler. In effect, he would have to become as "clubbable" as when he was secretary of the first Potato Festival committee in Hartland. Luckily, he had learned much since his awkward reading at the Contact poetry series in Toronto. He had seen how Ginsberg and Layton could win over an audience not only through their skill with the written word, but also by adopting an appealing public persona. But what kind of persona would he choose to project? Not boastfully virile like Layton or esoteric and hip like Ginsberg, but something in keeping with his bear-like appearance and anti-academic sensibility. A clue was provided by

Ray Fraser, who had returned from his British adventures in November, 1967. In late January, 1968, Fraser gave his own reading at Sir George Williams and brought the house down with his antics, which included reading while smoking a cigar and pulling from a bottle of wine, playing the guitar, and running out into the hallway to invite passersby join the audience. All of this played in Nowlan's mind as he prepared for the February conference.

Meeting John Newlove no doubt demonstrated to Nowlan that a poet's persona need not be appealing to be effective. Newlove had just published an acclaimed collection of his own, *Black Night Window*, and his persona seemed to match the dark title. Nowlan told Greer, "There was Newlove, looking like St. Dismas, the Good Thief who was crucified beside Christ."[22]

Four of them, Nowlan, Newlove and two UNB professors, John Zanes and Barrie Davies, went down to the River Room in the Lord Beaverbrook Hotel, where they imbibed a few beers and some abuse from Newlove. "You're a bunch of phony bastards and your conference is a bunch of horseshit," he told the professors. "The only reason I'm here is because I wanted to meet Nowlan and I need the $100 fee."

But when Nowlan tried to say how much he liked Newlove's poetry, the other shot back, "Oh, well, why don't the two of us get married?"

"Look, Newlove," John Zanes broke in, "You're a very sweet, gentle guy trying to convince us you're a son of a bitch, but you might as well lay off because we're not buying it."

Newlove smiled sweetly back at them.

Nowlan felt he understood Newlove in a way the others didn't. "Actually I know he's a son of a bitch," he would later write to Cook. "I'm fond of him because I'm the same sort of son of a bitch, except that with me the fevers are sporadic and with him they seem to be chronic."[23] Nowlan admitted to being moved at the reading by Newlove's poetry." But when another writer's persona rubbed Nowlan the wrong way, he immediately branded him or her a "phony." He told Greer:

> Leonard Cohen says what the new generation needs is not
> artificial adolescents but tribal elders. I like that. The idea
> of being a tribal elder rather appeals to me. Although I
> suppose that's basically another kind of phoniness. It is
> very pathetic to me, though, people like poor old Dorothy
> Livesay struggling so hard to be under 35 — under 25, for

that matter. At Fredericton she unbent her poor creaky old bones and sat on the floor at my feet and I wanted to tell her: Look, if you need an image you should try for the Earth Mother not the Teeny-Bopper.[24]

Compared to their male colleagues, female writers and intellectuals such as Livesay and Atwood were in greater danger of making Nowlan's "phony" list, although a few, such as the more retiring Elizabeth Brewster, met with his approval.

The conference not only exposed Nowlan in person to the UNB faculty, it also accommodated him to the idea of leading a public life. But where with Greer he could almost allow himself to be honest about his past — or at least bring the nature of his personal mythos into question — in Fredericton he found Newlove's abrasive and defensive posture more appealing. In counterpoint to his intimate and confessional writing, he could not resist playing up to an audience. He wrote to Fraser, "From the little public speaking I've done I can see how it intoxicates people like Diefenbaker or, in his different way, Dylan Thomas. It's a little like bullfighting, I guess, and the audience is the bull, at least the audience has a collective personality of its own that you can feel and respond to."[25] Gradually, his own public image began to gel. Further on in the same letter, Nowlan mentions his growing girth. True to the doctor's warnings, he had grown fatter because of his missing thyroid. His drinking and lack of exercise did not help, either. Nowlan knew he stood outside fashions and trends, in terms of temperament, intellect and appearance. But he also revelled in his role as an outsider in literary circles; *Bread, Wine and Salt* proved he could, in essence, beat "them" at their own game. His recent adoption of Greer as his Boswell reminded him of Samuel Johnson, another portly and unfashionable — but brilliant and multi-talented — literary figure. And he had already named his cat Hodge in honour of Johnson's cat. Nowlan decided to cultivate this Johnsonian image.

Unfortunately, Nowlan lacked what Johnson possessed in abundance: verbal wit. One month after the conference, at the end of March, he appeared on stage again, this time at a literary event at Acadia University. Some of the same people were there, including Newlove and Livesay, who was trying to impress a professor who was considering whether to write an academic article about her, "playing up to him as blatantly as an old doll on the make." The professor waited until Livesay wafted away, then quizzed Nowlan on how much of a literary reputation she enjoyed. Nowlan realized that the professor was fishing to find out whether his reputation could be helped by a Livesay article. "People like that make me crawl into my shell like a snail. . . . And I'm never able to demolish such people: I just freeze into a lump, damn it."[26] Frustrated by his tongue-tied, un-Johnsonian performance in "sophisticated" situations, he took refuge in backwoods rowdiness, which he demonstrated at another party at Acadia that weekend. He reported to Ray Fraser:

> I met John Newlove there again and the first night he and
> I consumed all of our host's spirits before the others arrived,
> he drank the scotch and I drank the rum, so everybody else
> drank beer and thought dark thoughts about us. Newlove
> insults everybody, turns on television soccer games in the
> middle of conversations, finally threw a cigarette package
> and struck a very dignified old English lady-professor in
> the side of the head and got ordered out. Almost everybody
> but me dislikes him. I like his poems too except they're as
> nihilistic as hell. My wife hates him.[27]

Fraser could not have known that the host, Greg Cook, had already ejected Newlove for his misdeeds before the Nowlans arrived that night; Nowlan did not let that detail stand in the way of a good story.

The pains he took to accommodate himself to academic and literary life were not in vain: the University of New Brunswick was considering him as the writer-in-residence for the 1968-1969 year. As with the Guggenheim application, he superstitiously avoided talking about the possible appointment in any but the most disparaging terms. "I'm scared of the whole academic, establishment thing. So much of it is moist horseshit," he told Roy MacSkimming.[28] At the same time, he prepared himself to be mentor to young student poets, a role he gravitated towards naturally. Already he had a protégé in Louis Cormier, who had become a regular visitor at the Nowlan home. John Drew and, especially, John Grube had been Cormier's previous mentors, but they had left UNBSJ in the spring of 1967, Drew for Ryerson and Grube for the University of Windsor. Nowlan saw it as his mission to ensure that Cormier would adopt the right attitude, which included reversing the "phony" academic attitude towards literature. "A tough-minded little Acadian with a lot of good sense," he told Fraser.

The trouble is that a couple of very good English teachers who used to be at UNBSJ "discovered" Louis and told him he was good so often that he has become very self-indulgent and is on the point of thinking himself as a poet — you know what I mean, if he's not careful he'll go around posing as a poet and writing worse and worse poems. That hasn't happened yet but it could easily happen to him. One of the dangers of isolation in a two-year college where there are no older and better student-poets and where the professors are either indifferent or afraid of being critical for fear of destroying a budding talent.[29]

Part of Nowlan's "cure" was to expose Cormier to the right kinds of influences, including Fraser and his magazine, *Intercourse*, which by then had become the *Mad* magazine of literary periodicals. Cormier and Fraser started to exchange letters regularly, and Cormier became, in Drew's absence, the Saint John distributor for Fraser's Poverty Press.

Another part of Nowlan's cure for phoniness was to be brutally frank about what he saw as the pitfalls of Cormier's poetry. Cormier's best friend and fellow writer, Eddie Clinton, also received this treatment when the two gave their poems to Nowlan to read. If anything, Clinton got worse treatment because of Nowlan's disregard for him. "Criticism is good, but not for Ed," Cormier told Fraser. "He asked for it but it really hurt him. He cried for a while, but I don't think they were childish tears."[30] On the contrary, Clinton's letter to Fraser a week before shows he was made of sterner stuff:

> He cut me from anus to the top of the head. Made such comments as ". . . largely very commonplace thoughts and very perfunctory emotions expressed in very banal terms," "old stale porridge," "old dead fish" etc. I'm somewhat annoyed but what he said was the truth and I hate the truth, specially when it's about me. But I'm taking his advice. LOOK AROUND. SIMPLIFY. and so on.[31]

Although Nowlan did not have Johnson's conversational wit, he was discovering a weapon that could be every bit as devastating: the power to pinpoint a person's emotional weakness and skewer it.

But he could also be an indulgent master. Picking through Nowlan's bookcase one evening, Cormier decided to test Nowlan's insistence that he had, in fact, read every book in it. He selected one and asked Nowlan if he could borrow it. Nowlan let the young man take it home, and on Cormier's return the young man quizzed him about it and discovered that Nowlan did indeed know the contents in detail. It was a book on Zen Buddhism.

As Nowlan honed his mentoring skills that spring and awaited word on whether he would be accepted at UNB, another honour unexpectedly fell into his lap. At the end of April, he received a mysterious summons from the Governor General for him and his family to attend a ceremony at Rideau Hall in May. Although clothed in secrecy, there was no question what the invitation was for. As John Drew waggishly put it:

Queen's Messenger: There's a Governor General's for you.
Nowlan: Lord Jesus to Kingdom Come.
Queen's Messenger: You'll go to Ottawa for it?
Nowlan: I'll go anywhere for rum.[32]

There would be no rum for this occasion. He was on his best behaviour to receive his country's highest literary award for *Bread, Wine and Salt*. He also met his publisher, Bill Clarke, for the first time. When Clarke arrived at the Château Laurier, Nowlan phoned his room so that they could meet in the lobby and go to Rideau Hall together. "How will I know what you look like?" Clarke asked. "I'm the one who looks like a bear," Nowlan replied.

There was no award for fiction that year, although there were two awards for poetry, Nowlan sharing the honour with Eli Mandel and his collection *An Idiot Joy*. At the ceremony, the recipients were called up, one by one, to hear their citations and to receive a discreet envelope containing a $2,500 cheque. At the reception in the garden afterwards, Nowlan walked about with his brand-new leather-bound copy of *Bread, Wine and Salt*, perhaps thinking of the irony that cancer might have been the catalyst that made this day possible. By now, he exhibited few physical signs of his brush with death. In the photograph accompanying an article in *Time* magazine about the ceremony, he is walking beside Mandel, bearded, a huge man in a dark suit, towering over the other poet. More honours awaited him on his return: a letter in June from Desmond Pacey invited him at last to be the University of New Brunswick's writer-in-residence.

Alden Nowlan and Eli Mandel, Rideau Hall, May, 1968.

If I could turn and meet myself

The Bhikku

I ask for nothing,
*   he tells me, except*
*   to be freed from*

all desire.
*   No wonder*
*   his voice shakes:*

even Lucifer's
*   desire was less*
*   insatiable than that.*

That summer, as the Nowlan family made preparations to leave Saint John, they received bad but not unexpected news from Hartland. In the early part of July, Claude Orser, Claudine's father, died. Johnnie, in Hartland as a normal part of his summer vacation, had spent a lot of time with his grandfather in the hospital. The Orser clan rallied around, and Nowlan once again stole a glimpse into the inner workings of his wife's close-knit family that was such a contrast to his own.

Nowlan had not visited Hartland for several years. The cancer operations had made driving uncomfortable, and his neck and shoulders would ache for days after a long drive. But he knew that he could not back out of such a sacred family duty as the funeral of the father-in-law for whom he had such a high regard. But he shied away from the close touch of familiarity he felt in Hartland. His beard, considered too hippie in Carleton County, was an object of mild disapproval from some family members. Nowlan was forced to explain it as an unfortunate side effect of his facial swelling, which made shaving painful. But what struck him most was the insular and unchanging nature of village relations, how his friends chided him about still driving his 1959 Chev and commented on his appointment to UNB only by saying, "Well, I guess you'll be a little closer to Hartland next month, eh?"

Nowlan found the loss of his small-town trappings surprising. On his return home with Claudine, he almost hit a pair of moose on the dark road, a cow and her calf. Perhaps thinking of his poem "The Bull Moose," written at a time of frustration with his writing career and with the small New Brunswick town that had saved but stifled him, he wrote a gentler poem about the encounter, and this time the moose lives:

> *and the instant*
> *he's safely over, she runs and he*
> *runs behind her,*
> *and I drive on,*
> *happy about it all,*
> *bursting to tell someone about the great sight I've seen,*
> *yet not sure why it should seem so important.*

Despite Nowlan's recent success, he did not sever his connection with the *Telegraph-Journal*. He still needed the security of a permanent job, a legacy of his impoverished childhood. The idea of living purely off his writing, without the safety net of a grant or a writer-in-residency, secretly terrified him, so he arranged with Ralph Costello to provide a column for the Saturday edition of the paper for twenty dollars per week and continued inclusion in the company health plan. "It might be fun to do a little satirical piece based on the Toronto complaints about Maritime migrants," Nowlan suggested to Costello. "Perhaps the satire would consist of pretending that the Maritimes has its own problems with Upper Canadian immigrants."[1] As he initially envisioned it, the column would cover Fredericton stories in the same vein as his article on Ginsberg's visit to Saint John. These would be supplemented by humour or opinion pieces that could be written in advance for weeks when he was too busy or for times when the news was slow.

There was his working-class soul to appease, too. Nowlan loved writing poetry, but knew that he could reach more readers through journalism than he could through verse. He liked to think of himself as a salt-of-the-earth craftsman, and in his mind good, solid non-fiction prose was somehow a more honest craft. Also, journalism, not poetry, made him a household name, and Nowlan knew this despite the awards and recognition for literary achievement that had come his way over the past three years.

Nowlan approached his move to the University of New Brunswick with caution, inspecting even his new accommodations with economy in mind. The university provided him with a little house on the edge of campus behind the bookstore that had been rented to short-term professors. At 676 Windsor Street, it was designed along the same lines as the houses built for veterans after the Second World War, with four rooms downstairs and two bedrooms upstairs. Nowlan especially liked the little patch of trees in the back yard that separated the house from the campus; sitting in the back yard on a quiet night, he could almost imagine he was in the country. But financially he found cause for complaint. The writer-in-residence received $5,500 from the Canada Council for a year; that was fair enough. UNB added $1,500 to the pot, but then charged $120 per month in rent, unheated. Nowlan toyed with the idea of finding a place at the Wilmot Apartments, which were of the same design as the Mitchell Street apartments. He could have paid less in rent, but then UNB would have taken away its stipend for accommodation. Besides, Johnnie, who was always stuck with the smallest quarters, looked forward to having his own more spacious room. Nowlan took the UNB house and never regretted his decision. Thinking of his recent trip to England — or perhaps of his grandmother Nora — he dubbed it "Windsor Castle," and it shortly became a well-known address among writers both young and old in Fredericton. Becoming "the world's oldest unofficial undergraduate"[2] did not cure his shyness, but it enabled him to become highly sociable nevertheless.

The city that greeted the Nowlans was certainly conducive to literary life. The Loyalists who settled the capital of the new province in 1785 brought with them a love of the humanities and fine arts, and one of their number, Jonathan Odell, was already a recognized poet. In 1824, Julia Beckwith Hart published *St. Ursula's Convent*, the first novel written by a native-born Canadian. From the early 1880s until the 1930s, Fredericton natives Charles G.D. Roberts and his cousin, Bliss Carman, were the most celebrated poets in Canada.

Roberts was well aware of the effect his childhood in Fredericton had on his and Carman's poetry:

The Fredericton of those days was a good place for a poet to be. The lovely little city of the Loyalists, bosomed in her elms and half encircled by the sweep of her majestic river, was stirring with a strange aesthetic ferment. With not more than six thousand inhabitants, she was not only the capital, with Government House, the House of Assembly, the Law Courts, and all they stood for, but also she was the cathedral city, as well as the educational centre of the province. . . . This sudden outflowering of the poetic impulse which, for perhaps a score of years, made the name of Fredericton conspicuous in the world of letters, is a thing which some critics have been puzzled to account for.[3]

In front of the library on the UNB campus is a monument that reads:

POET'S CORNER
Bliss Carman
1861-1929
Sir Charles Roberts
1860-1943
Francis Joseph Sherman
1871-1926

*Born in or near Fredericton, these three poets
were educated in this University and are
buried in the cemetery of Forest Hill. Their
gifts of verse enriched Canadian literature
and gained for their common birthplace the
designation "The Poet's Corner of Canada."*

Fredericton was wrestling with change at the time of the Nowlans' arrival. Politically, New Brunswick had just undergone its own modest version of the Quiet Revolution under Premier Louis Robichaud, whose Equal Opportunity reforms gave the provincial government the authority to collect and distribute municipal tax monies on behalf of local governments. In practice, this meant siphoning off excess funds from richer (and usually English) communities in the south and disbursing them to poorer (and usually French) communities in the north. Discontented English-speakers described Equal Opportunity as "robbing Peter to pay Pierre," although the reforms went a long way towards redressing the economic inequalities that had been a given of provincial life for everyone.

The university campus was not immune to the revolutions rocking the world in 1968, in Prague, Paris and Chicago. Closer to home, Pierre Trudeau was elected Prime Minister, and the *Front de Libération de Quebéc* was planting bombs in Quebec mailboxes. At Sir George Williams University in Montreal, students staged a protest in which the university's new computer was thrown out of a window.

The University of New Brunswick's major student protest hit the campus as soon as classes started in September of 1968, just a couple of weeks after Nowlan's arrival. It, too, had an anti-technological theme. A junior physics professor named Norman Strax thought UNB's new policy of issuing student identity cards was oppressive and Orwellian. Many students agreed. Among the uses of the new cards was to control borrowing library books. So Strax organized a protest in which students went into the library, grabbed an armload of books, and tried to check them out without an ID card. When they were refused, they left the books on the counter and walked out. The library was soon paralyzed, as were the administrative offices, which Strax and his protesters occupied. The university crushed the revolt quickly, and Strax was fired. Nowlan's bemused reaction to the affair made it clear that the new writer-in-residence would be no campus radical: he wrote a satiric short story about university activists entitled "The Year of the Revolution." He did not approve of "movements," even if the cause was something he otherwise supported.

The parade of young students who aspired to be writers soon made Nowlan abandon his original intention of keeping office hours; in any case, he preferred to meet students at his home. Nor was he interested in teaching any creative writing classes. Playing the tribal elder role to the hilt, his approach was student centred, though different in style from that of his predecessor Dorothy Livesay. Going to classes and hanging around the office or the faculty lounge was too professor-like and, for him, a waste of time.

Windsor Castle's informality seemed to be more convenient for the students anyway, especially for the type Nowlan attracted: mostly males with an appetite for grog. Louis Cormier was one of these. He

Leo Ferrari, Al Pittman, Ray Fraser, Alden Nowlan, Eddie Clinton, and (front) Louis Cormier, 1968. SHARON FRASER

and Eddie Clinton had spent the summer in Saint John impersonating nineteenth-century soldiers at Martello Tower. Now Clinton remained in Saint John while Cormier took up residence in Harrison House at UNB to complete the last two years of his degree. One of the most promising student poets had arrived in Fredericton a year before Nowlan. Alphonse Pittman, a St. Thomas University student from Newfoundland, was already a friend of Ray Fraser's and a regular *Intercourse* contributor. STU had by then moved from Chatham to the UNB campus, so poetic mentors such as Fred Cogswell were more accessible for St. Thomas students than they would have been in Fraser's day. Cogswell, in fact, liked Pittman's poetry so much that he published the student's first collection, *The Elusive Resurrection*, as a Fiddlehead Poetry Book.

Pittman was eager for his new friend Nowlan to meet his favourite professor at STU: Leo Ferrari, an internationally respected Augustinian scholar who taught philosophy. Nowlan's acquaintances would not have expected the poet to become fast friends with a philosopher, but then Ferrari did not fit the academic stereotype. Nowlan described their first meeting at a party in a student's apartment: "The first time that I saw Leo Ferrari he was pounding his head against a stack of bricks. So violently that I winced. Not only his throat and lungs but his entire body was laughing."[4] In fact, their first meeting was probably more sedate; Ferrari told Fraser, "It's great to have Al [Pittman] back again, and just what the place needs. He and Alden Nowlan gave a poetry recital last night here at STU and there was about a hundred people present, more or less at the drop of a hat, so to speak."[5] Ferrari remembers going out for a quiet beer on that first night, but Nowlan's version of their meeting may have occurred early in their friendship, since it is in keeping with Ferrari's bacchanalian character. The philosopher was as good at making homebrew as he was at consuming it, and he gladly taught Claudine the craft.

Other academic friends, though less flamboyant, were good company. Bob Cockburn and John Zanes were both young professors and poets. Zanes wrote a doctoral thesis at UNB in which he compared the "Fiddlehead group" of poets to other famous literary circles including the Bloomsbury and Algonquin Round Table groups. Cockburn, like Zanes, Kent Thompson and Bill and Nancy Bauer, was an American who had fallen in love with the Maritimes as soon as he arrived. His poetry in particular dwelt on the traditional features of Maritime life, such as the lore of the lumbermen.

Donald Cameron was another imported Maritimer, in his case from British Columbia. He was also a writer-professor, but his interests were less poetic and more political. When he arrived at UNB in the fall of 1968, he was working on a book-length series of interviews with Canadian writers, and Nowlan was uppermost on his interview list. Cameron and another new acquaintance, the painter Tom Forrestall, were somewhat atypical Nowlan friends, not blue-collar types or people who enjoyed revelry, but more cerebral and reserved; even so, they could be intellectual in a non-academic way, and Cameron would leave the ivory tower a few years later to write full-time as Silver Donald Cameron. Nowlan liked to chide Cameron for his left-leaning political views. "I, a High Tory, send to you, my dear Presbyterian friend, my warmest and most affectionate regards," he wrote, concluding, "I love you despite the fact that you are a Calvinist and probably a Whig. No, that's not true about your being a Whig . . . in your heart of hearts you are also a Tory."[6] Nowlan also had a high regard for Cameron's skill at journalism. In 1969, Cameron began editing a left-wing, pro-Maritime magazine called *Mysterious East* that lasted until 1972.

Considering all the friends Nowlan made among the UNB and St. Thomas faculty, his phobia of "sophisticates" seems to have been on the wane or at least highly selective. His tenure at UNB opened his world to people he might not otherwise have allowed himself to meet, and the sentiment was returned. Writing to Elizabeth Brewster on October 25, after Nowlan's well-received first reading as UNB writer-in-residence, Bob Gibbs had nothing but praise:

> Alden is so completely honest and unpretentious that some are taken in by his manner and get an impression of his work that doesn't do him justice. He has been coming on Tuesday nights [to the Ice House meetings] — saying little — but everything he does say is so perceptive & helpful that we're glad to have him.

Gibbs then goes on to express the level of moral support the UNB faculty would muster on his behalf, even against the literati.

> Did you read that piece of trash in *The [Canadian] Forum* concerning Alden's short stories (really questioning his audacity for reviewing Hood's (bad) novel). I was incensed & woke up at five o'clock & composed a letter which turned out to be worse than the article — so I didn't send it. Apparently Alden himself, in some heat, replied, as well as Kent & Fred — so perhaps the fellow has already got more attention than he deserves. The implication of his review is that nobody could expect a Maritimer to see how infinitely superior a writer like Hugh Hood must be — by virtue of living in civilized Canada — to anything we could produce. It's the quintessential condescension of the Upper Canadian toward all of us down here — that really hurts.[7]

The review of *Miracle at Indian River* was the focus of a regular feature in the *Canadian Forum* called "Piquefort's Column" that discussed literary matters. "Piquefort" devoted the September 1968 column to giving Nowlan the worst critical thrashing of his career.

The story behind the review actually goes back to the March issue of the magazine, when Nowlan reviewed, not Hugh Hood, but Dave Godfrey's short story collection *Death Goes Better with Coca-Cola*. "I don't think [Godfrey's] all that good, myself, but I don't feel strongly enough about it to argue with [the critics]," Nowlan had written. "The only major weakness I find in his stories is that all the characters sound alike . . . and there are many almost embarrassingly bad similes and metaphors."[8] He did not know that Godfrey was actually "Piquefort." Nowlan wrote of Hood's novel *The Camera Always Lies* in the May issue: "Personally, I think that Mr. Hood would have written a much more entertaining book if he had followed the suggestion of James (*From Here to Eternity*) Jones, forgotten the 'delicate niceties' and just 'sort of bullassed right through.'"[9]

Godfrey entitled his September "Piquefort's Column" "Bullassin' Lord Brunswick-o":

> Now what I admire, really admire, about your own stories, Ald, is that they're timeless. They have that real genuine simplicity of the timeless. I can go out and look at the world up here in Ste. Crape and it's just like your stories. Or I can open up my collection of the *Saturday Evening Post* almost anywhere and test your stories against theirs and find the same wide vision of the world. It's reassuring, Ald, reassuring. I won't wax the sentiment, but let me say that I'm going to head down for Toronto town sometime this year and have a little chat with Robby Weaver and Mrs. Clarke and maybe we'll get the GG's mother on the telephone and I'll just make sure they see all that timeless, Alden Nowlan, wide-angle vision of yours, as I do, and then see if we can't just arrange another prize or two for you. I can sure think of one or two you deserve.[10]

Godfrey's smear enraged more people than just Nowlan, who was given space to reply in the January issue: "The only unusual thing about this latest bit of anonymous crank mail is that it was not written in ballpoint on ruled paper but printed in a respectable 'independent journal of opinion and the arts.'"[11] The review went beyond misunderstanding his writing as merely regional, it attacked an achievement he had taken five years and much trial and error to accomplish: to earn respect as a fiction writer. To attack in support of Hugh Hood was, for Nowlan, the poison on the dagger, since he admired Hood, who had once gotten in touch with Nowlan because of the young man's fiction writing. The Godfrey review taught Nowlan a bitter lesson about how far one was allowed to go in the literary world.

Nevertheless, Nowlan's first fiction collection was praised in most circles. Donald Cameron took the "choleric little Piquefort" to task with a well-reasoned defence in *The Dalhousie Review*:

In the best of Nowlan's stories, the impact grows out of the objectivity with which people and events are presented, and the selectivity of details by which they are evoked. Nowlan isolates a sequence of events and recreates them without distractions, as though he were framing a little panel of life. Each small stroke adds to the completeness and relevance of the picture, so that one has at last the effect of events speaking for themselves. This is not to say that his fiction is not fiction: but the solidity and authenticity of these stories are as persuasive as the authority of fact.[12]

Nowlan, writing to Ray Fraser about the title story, claimed that he based it on a true incident and mused about his abilities as a fiction writer. "I've often thought that I don't have much imagination. Truly. It's almost impossible for me to write a story that isn't true."[13] A month later he recanted somewhat: "Maybe I'm kidding myself a little when I say that I can't write fiction and that all my stories are true. It would be truer to say that everything I write has to be *sparked* by something true. Truth, I'm beginning to think, is pretty relative and subjective anyway."[14]

For Nowlan, the consolation for being a public figure was the positive influence he could exert on student poets. Cormier blossomed under his tutelage. That year, Cormier's third in university, he won UNB's Bliss Carman Prize for student poetry and had his first collection, *The Silent Cowboys of the East*, published by Fraser's Poverty Press. But the dedication in the book, to his girlfriend Debbie and to John Grube, must have pushed Nowlan's nose a little out of joint, since he had come to identify Cormier as a younger version of himself. From the University of Windsor, Grube was providing the young poet with advice about *Silent Cowboys*, and Nowlan did not approve. "Only thing I'm a bit afraid of," he said, "is that John Grube will choose all the wrong poems and maybe even edit some of them, and by 'edit' I mean partly rewrite. I don't trust his taste."[15]

In February, 1969, Nowlan had taken his protégé for his first public poetry reading in front of an audience of about eight hundred Fredericton High School students. Al Pittman was also on the program. Together, they made a disreputable trio for some of the FHS teachers, who saw their beards and long hair as evidence that they were nothing but a group of hippies. One teacher was overheard to say that someone should give them a good scrubbing. While their reading was by no means foul-mouthed, they felt no need to hold back, either. Nowlan finished his performance by bringing a record player on-stage and treating the students to what he felt was one of the best popular poets in the world: Bob Dylan, singing "Lay, Lady, Lay." He found out later, to his satisfaction, that one of the teachers had walked out during the reading. He reported to Fraser: "Louis was the star of the show and enjoyed himself immensely. A real performer there."[16]

Nowlan also attracted out-of-town guests. The poet Patrick Lane always made it a point to stop in and see the Nowlans whenever he was in town. John Gill, who read with him, Bowering and Newlove at UNB, came to visit him in the summer of 1969. Gill ran Crossing Press, a small publishing house, from his home in upstate New York. Crossing Press actively promoted Canadian literature, having published, among others, Patrick Lane, and now Gill wanted to bring out a selected edition of Nowlan's previously published poems for the American market, to be called *Playing the Jesus Game*. The collection's introduction would be an essay about Nowlan's poetry by American poet Robert Bly that also appeared in the *Tamarack Review*. Taking his cue from D.H. Lawrence's image of the umbrella of reality in "Chaos in Poetry," Bly praised Nowlan as one of "the umbrella rippers": "I think his work is the work of a brave man."[17] Gill published *Playing the Jesus Game* in 1970, and it sold well in the US and in New Brunswick, although one of the clerks at the UNB Bookstore, a religious lady, chided Nowlan for its blasphemous title.

Shortly after Gill's visit, Sylvia decided to drive up to New Brunswick from Connecticut and visit her cousin after not having seen him for over ten years. Through their extensive correspondence, Nowlan was already apprised of the changes in her life. She had become a teacher and an artist's model before scandalizing her foster parents by marrying an artist for whom she had been modelling. The source of the scandal was that her husband, Jim Pride, was black. However, Jim had no problem being accepted into the Nowlan family. It was Sylvia and Alden who were initially tongue-tied, and Claudine helped to fill in the silences during the awkward meeting. The cousins gradually warmed up that evening, especially Alden, who discovered that Jim shared his fondness for drink.

Claudine made an unsettling discovery that night. Not able to stifle her curiosity about her husband's vague and unpleasant stories of his life in Stanley, Claudine took Sylvia aside to ask her about Grace, whom Nowlan had always insisted was dead. Sylvia, who had maintained some contact with Grace through the years, confirmed Claudine's suspicions that Grace was in fact still alive. Sensing the pain that would have led her husband to create such a tale, and appreciating how one person can be dead to another in all but actual fact, Claudine helped her husband maintain his version of the truth about Grace, and nothing more was said about the matter.

Sylvia understood. Jim shared some of the delusions that Nowlan so often suffered, born out of the pain of the past and sometimes whetted by drinking. Late that night, after both couples had retired, Jim awoke with an overwhelming sense of paranoia. He woke up Sylvia and insisted that there was something wrong and that they had to go back to Connecticut immediately. Carefully, without waking their hosts, they slipped into their car and started the long drive home. Far from being shocked and hurt by the mysterious scene that greeted his eyes the next morning, Nowlan was sympathetic to the man he now considered his brother.

The social life among the congenial spirits of Fredericton gave Nowlan a second (or, in a sense, a first) adolescence, a mixture of the bizarre, the romantic, the intellectual and the inebriated. A party he threw in March, 1969, for Cormier's twenty-first birthday is typical of the parties for which he would become famous. Greg Cook and his wife, Miriam stayed over for the weekend. Al and Marilee Pittman were also honoured guests, and Marilee brought her father along from St. Stephen, who sang Irish folk songs to entertain the crowd. Bernell MacDonald, another young UNB poet in the Nowlan circle, was a sensitive young man who loved nature and entertained fantastical visions that rivalled Nowlan's own. On this night, after bottles of sherry and blueberry wine and some of Leo Ferrari's homebrew, MacDonald would not walk home for fear that a werewolf was lying in wait for him. Cook, as an ex-clergyman, joined the fun by trying to exorcise it for him. A good time was had by all.

Among some of the UNB faculty, however, the writer-in-residence still had the scent of death about him. When Pacey wrote the Canada Council in January, 1969, to request a renewal of the $5,500 writer-in-residence grant, it was almost as if he were writing about an old man, not the social animal Nowlan had become:

> I believe that a recommendation to renew Mr. Nowlan's
> grant should be based primarily upon his quality as a
> writer rather than on the contribution he has made or is

likely to make to the university. . . . He is a shy man, and feels ill at ease in any formal academic context. He has, of course, undergone major operations, and his health is still, I gather, delicate and uncertain. I think the Council should ask itself whether it is prepared to support Mr. Nowlan because of the contribution he is likely to make to Canadian literature rather than because of the contribution he is likely to make to the University of New Brunswick. I personally believe that he is very worthy of support, for his writing seems to be unique in quality and context.[18]

The sympathy that had helped secure the Canada Council and Guggenheim grants now worked against Nowlan. In frustration, he wrote to Elizabeth Brewster:

I don't know how much good, if any, I've done here. But I know I've met at least six kids who love me and whom I love, and there are damned few professors who can say the same. In fact there are at least two kids who have dropped out of university altogether except that they show up on weekends to see me.

I don't say that to boast but in rebuttal to suggestions that Desmond, for instance, used to make that "Alden Nowlan is too shy to communicate with the kids." Well, shy old Alden sometimes has as many as three students sleeping on the floor of his house in sleeping bags, all of whom call me "Al," and him, when they mention him at all, "Old Pacey."[19]

Nowlan's paradoxical position as both Johnsonian tribal elder and the world's oldest undergraduate could be a delicate balancing act.

While Nowlan loved the leisure his position at UNB gave him, he hated the insecurity that accompanied it. He began to get frustrated with Pacey and what he saw as the unbearable delays in finding out whether UNB would have him for the following year. He made up his mind: he would not go back to full-time journalism if he could help it. While waiting for the Canada Council's approval of UNB's application, Nowlan sought an alternate escape route. An art critic friend from his Saint John years, Barry Lord, was teaching at the new Conestoga College in Kitchener, Ontario. Lord wrote Nowlan early in 1969 to say

He is Entertained by the Chairman of the Department

It's not the same here, the chairman
of the department cautions me.
We're close enough to drive
to Toronto and back
in an evening. Did you know
that in Toronto you can have
the Sunday edition of
the New York Times delivered
to your door the day it comes out?
Life here moves at a faster tempo
than where you are, Down East.
One must adjust to the rhythm
of a different century, one
might almost say.
But you understand that,
I'm sure. Have you been following
this thing in Ethiopia?
A sad business.
I was there
three years ago,
one of a delegation.
We had tea with the Crown Prince,
as he then was.
                      A charming fellow
although, obviously, not
the man his father was.
Are you often in Boston?
You'd have no trouble, then,
learning to live with us
in Kitchener.

that the college was looking for a writer-in-residence for its 1969-1970 academic year and asking whether he would be interested in coming up for a poetry reading and a look around the campus.

Conestoga was also new in its academic approach, perhaps a little too new for Nowlan's tastes. The English department, for instance, was called the Department of Communications Design. "Barry Lord is obviously out to save my soul in the same way those old missionaries tried to save the souls of the Polynesians," he told Fraser. "Well, in almost the same way. The missionaries wanted to put Mother Hubbards on the Polynesians, and Barry wants to give me the veneer of Upper Canadian culture."[20] Nowlan, again feeling he was being forced to play a "Mug's Game," was not at his best for the meeting with the department and left pessimistic about his chances of securing a position there.

The modernity of the college worked against him in other ways. The wings of the college building converged on a common area, where Lord had arranged for Nowlan's reading to take place. The area also served as the student lounge, the cafeteria, and the main artery for student traffic between classes. Nowlan, with the aid of a microphone, competed with commuters and students playing bridge. But those students who came, especially those from Lord's creative writing class, demonstrated enormous sensitivity to the beleaguered poet. One composed a poem about the reading then and there, decrying the distractions from the passersby, and presented it to Nowlan upon the conclusion of the reading. A beautiful young woman gave him a package of flower seeds. "I thought about giving you a flower, but they die, so I thought I would give you seeds instead," she explained.

After his mixed success in Kitchener, Nowlan spent a night in Toronto before returning to New Brunswick. He had many people to visit, including his publisher, but he felt compelled to phone Raymond Souster, the poet who had been such an influence on him when he was a struggling young writer in Hartland. Nowlan wanted to come over and visit. Souster agreed enthusiastically, but his guest arrived later than expected. Nowlan had to fortify himself before meeting one of his literary heroes. Souster finally heard a heavy thump at his door. Opening it, he was simultaneously enveloped by a cloud of gin fumes and the great arms of Nowlan. "God . . . god," the bear kept repeating as a tribute to the older man. Souster was moved by Nowlan's effusive greeting and the courage it took for him to say, "Raymond, I love you." The two sat down, Souster made some coffee, and they had one of

Alden Nowlan reading from *The Mysterious Naked Man.* IRWIN PUBLISHING INC.

If I could turn and meet myself

those great literary and philosophical discussions. Then Nowlan excused himself, went to the bathroom, and threw up.

Shortly after returning to Fredericton, to his mild surprise, he was told that the Canada Council would renew his grant for the 1969-1970 year, and that UNB would contribute the $1,500 that covered the rental of the house. The Lord of Windsor Castle would reign for another year at least.

His adventures during his first year as writer-in-residence would inspire reams of poetry, but for the time being Nowlan still mined the mother lode of his Saint John and Hartland years. In 1969, Clarke, Irwin brought out another collection, *The Mysterious Naked Man*. The title poem, though based on a news report he heard one night in the *Telegraph* office, reflects the dual identity his fame had made him adopt: reporter by day, literary superstar by night. In the poem, the police and the entire neighbourhood hunt for the mysterious naked man:

> *And the mysterious naked man*
> *is kneeling behind a garbage can or lying on his belly*
> *in somebody's garden*
> *or maybe even hiding in the branches of a tree,*
> *where the wind from the harbour*
> *whips at his naked body,*
> *and by now he's probably done*
> *whatever it was he wanted to do*
> *and wishes he could go to sleep*
> *or die*
> *or take to the air like Superman.*

In November of 1969, after *The Mysterious Naked Man* was published, the Nowlans went to Toronto for a reading, and Irene Clarke, whom Nowlan called "the grand dame sans merci,"[21] invited her award-winning author and his wife to have dinner at the Clarke home. It was the first time they had ever eaten in a household that employed a maid. "I don't think I am at all reactionary," Mrs. Clarke explained to her guests. "For instance, I never thought we should have held on to India."

Nowlan nearly gagged, but not with laughter. He thought the drinks the Clarkes were serving were real drinks, since they were in fancy bottles. One contained ginger ale — that was certain — but the other?

"Would you like some more grape juice with your ginger ale, Mr. Nowlan?" Bill Clarke's wife, Marie, asked.

"Yes, certainly I would." It really was grape juice, of course. No one had told him the Clarkes were teetotal.

Despite her patrician demeanour, Irene Clarke and Nowlan actually developed a strong affection for each other. "She is very much the Toronto Loyalist-Anglican matriarch," he said, "but sort of appealing, really — so out and out, so sure of her convictions and indifferent to ideological fads."[22]

On November 25, Claudine started a job working at the university daycare centre, which was across the street from Windsor Castle. From the time they lived in Saint John, she had taken part-time work to supplement the family's income. There, she had worked as a clerk at Simpsons-Sears. Now, their financial position was healthy, but a cloud of insecurity hung over Nowlan's position at UNB. Through some unforeseen miracle, the Canada Council agreed to renew Nowlan's tenure for the 1970-1971 year, although this would certainly be the last time. In the spring of 1969, he finally broke down and bought a newer car, a 1965 Pontiac. Or rather he waited in the lot while Al Pittman haggled with the owner over the price. As a reward for Pittman's bargaining savvy, Nowlan and Claudine offered him and Marilee a ride to Saint John to attend the New Brunswick Progressive Conservative leadership convention, which was held in June. The car broke down on the way there, making them late for a planned meeting with Nowlan's old friends at the *Telegraph-Journal*.

Richard Hatfield had come a long way since winning his first seat in 1961. In November of 1966 he ran for the leadership of the provincial Tories, but lost to Charlie Van Horne, a maverick businessman from northern New Brunswick. Nowlan hated Van Horne, whom he called "the Kingfish." He wrote to Hatfield after the defeat:

> This man is completely unprincipled, completely vile. It may be presumptuous on my part, but I think I'm in a better position in some ways than you to judge the full implications, the full danger of his vileness. I grew up among the redneck crackers, the poor white trash, that will be his most fervent supporters. Almost all my relatives in Nova Scotia, all my close relatives, are people of that

same social, cultural, economic class — the rural proletariat that the Kingfish woos. Perhaps that's why I hate the man so much — because he preys on such people.[23]

Hatfield's fortunes would not flag for long. After a stinging defeat by the Grits in 1967, Van Horne, who lost even his own seat, resigned and moved to the United States. Hatfield was victorious at the June, 1969, convention, and in October, 1970, he defeated Louis Robichaud and became premier. "He's a fine fellow," Nowlan wrote of his friend. "One of the most intelligent people I've ever met, candid and humorous. But I'm not very enthusiastic about the Tory crowd, too many of the same old faces, each with a cigar planted in the centre of it. If Dick weren't a personal friend I'd vote for Robichaud."[24]

Nowlan's friendship with Hatfield gave him connections. He was often invited up to Hatfield's room at the Lord Beaverbrook Hotel to have a drink with such political notables as the Lieutenant Governor, or with Robichaud on the occasion of his retirement. Hatfield also became a regular guest at any of the parties at 676 Windsor. These connections yielded practical benefits. Starting with Hatfield's 1970 campaign, Nowlan added another profitable number to his literary repertoire: he became an occasional speech writer.

In the fall of 1970, Nowlan began to feel desperate about his position at UNB. By this time, Elizabeth Brewster had moved to Edmonton, where she was a librarian and part-time English instructor at the University of Alberta. The English department there was considering starting its own writer-in-residence program. To Nowlan, this represented a lifeline to future security. He asked Brewster to float his name to Rudy Wiebe, the department head, as a possible contender. "I don't know what I'll do when my year here expires," he confided to her. "Claudine is working and I make a little, pitifully little, I'm afraid."[25] In addition to his weekly column in the *Telegraph-Journal*, he started another regular gig with the monthly *Atlantic Advocate*, for which he wrote a longer column for $75 per month. He welcomed the extra income, but it could not replace the writer-in-residence position. Still, he was reluctant to travel all the way to the University of Alberta to read, perhaps thinking of his less-than-stellar performance at Conestoga College the previous year. Besides, Wiebe would be at UNB from November 2 until

November 6 for another writers' conference organized by Kent Thompson. One of the authors who would read at that conference was John Metcalf, an editor and writer of fiction, highly respected in his field and, as it was whispered in some circles, Nowlan's heir apparent at UNB.

As the November conference approached, Nowlan struggled with the loss of two of his friends. Al Pittman moved to Fogo Island, Newfoundland, to teach. Louis Cormier took a much different path. After graduating from UNB in the spring of 1970, he cast about before deciding to head to Ottawa with the idea of finding a job as a translator and continuing his writing. On his way there he stopped in Montreal to see a few people and to take in the scene. But the usual people were not to be found. Ray and Sharon Fraser were then in Spain for a couple of months — in fact, the previous issue of *Intercourse* had been edited by Cormier, with the assistance of Bernie MacDonald, and assembled on Nowlan's kitchen table. And the scene in Montreal had changed radically. There was nothing to keep Cormier from going astray:

> i never wrote any sooner because i haven't exactly been myself in the last few days. or perhaps it would be most accurate to say that i've been certain parts of myself magnified while others have been suffering from under-exposure, which sounds kind of abstract, but maybe you get the gist of it . . . . ya never know what i'll do next.[26]

Cormier's next letter solved that mystery. He had looked up Tyndale Martin, the Buddhist poet Nowlan knew, and started studying Zen philosophy.

Hiding his alarm at losing his protégé to yet another teacher, Nowlan tried to distract Cormier by bringing up a harebrained project the two had discussed while putting *Intercourse* together, the possibility of starting up a Canadian nationalist society. Nowlan discovered that July 1 is the feast day of St. Simeon the Mad, who would go about naked and steal from the shops to give to the poor. Pamphleteering on behalf of St. Simeon was just the sort of tomfoolery to keep the two amused while waiting for Fraser to put out the next *Intercourse*. Nowlan tried to keep his advice light when discussing Tyndale Martin: "Generally I'm suspicious of people who profess to be Zen Buddhists, but I feel a great affection for him; I think he's a good fellow, and I like his poems very much."[27] There was more than religious choice at stake. Martin operated the Great Heart Zen centre in Montreal, where acolytes went to meditate, pray, do chores, forget about the outside world and typically donate to the collective most or all of their earnings from whatever jobs they held. Cormier had just landed a part-time job as a proof-reader for the *Financial Times*. His next letter indicates how badly Nowlan lost this battle. "It was ironic that you should begin your letter talking about Tyndale Martin and Zen Buddhism," it begins. "Because, of all things, i've decided to stay at his Zen centre for a month to practise zazen and see what it's all about."[28]

Nowlan knew for certain that no more poetry, real poetry, would come from his young friend. No Society of St. Simeon the Mad, either, although Nowlan gamely tried to keep the idea alive as an indirect way of coaxing Cormier away from a commitment that Nowlan thought he would regret. "Despite what I said in my last letter I think it's quite possible to be sincere even if one goes to the extreme of adopting the robe and scalp lock the way the Krishna Consciousness people do,"[29] he told Cormier, trying to put the best face on the matter.

Nowlan worried about Cormier, not just because he had been seduced by Zen, but also because of the explosive political situation erupting in Montreal that month. FLQ terrorists had kidnapped the British trade minister, James Cross, two blocks from the Zen centre, and the nation just watched as Prime Minister Trudeau declared martial law and shut down Canada's largest city. Ray and Sharon Fraser, back from Spain, planned to duck the crisis and come to the writers' conference to regale Nowlan with stories about Ibiza. Closer to home, Leo Ferrari had taken refuge at Windsor Castle for a couple of weeks after leaving his wife, Kathleen. But Greg Cook, who was also supposed to stay there during the writers' conference at UNB, had to cancel at the last minute due to appendicitis. "I think such conferences are mostly bullshit, frankly," Nowlan had grumbled to Cormier. "The real writers write. The phoney writers confer. But maybe I'll meet some interesting people — and probably insult them."[30]

It was November 6, Friday, the final night of the conference and, as usual, Windsor Castle was hosting the best party. Real writers and phony writers mingled while Nowlan sat in his special armchair in the den holding forth on whatever topic struck his fancy. "Holding forth" was Nowlan's version of conversation; his discourse could become like a pronouncement of the Truth, especially when he was in his cups. This tendency had increased since he had become writer-in-residence. The younger people knew that one did not talk or voice opinions in such a conversation, much less challenge him about the mythos of his life.

One sprawled at the elder's feet and listened. To do otherwise invited a glare from The Nowlan. Frequent visitors knew this; infrequent visitors learned the hard way.

Kent Thompson was not a frequent visitor to the Nowlan household. The man he brought that night, John Metcalf, was a first-time visitor. He had made a good impression among the UNB faculty, so good that it was generally understood that he might soon become a familiar face. Nowlan was holding forth in the den about a topic central to his mythos: the poverty of his youth. He catalogued his various deprivations like a mantra. "We had no indoor plumbing, no running water. I didn't even learn how to use a telephone until I had moved away at the age of nineteen . . ."

"Yes, I know how that is," Kent Thompson said from the corner where he had been listening. "I, too, had a pretty impoverished childhood."

The guests could not listen to Thompson; they were too focused on Nowlan, who fixed the professor in his stare while Thompson spoke. People started looking away. There was a void of silence before Nowlan responded.

"Oh, yes, Kent," he said, his voice steady. "I know that you know just what it was like. Take your family for instance. They were so poor they could only afford to trade the car in every second year . . ."

"Oh, come off it, Alden," Thompson protested.

But Nowlan was relentless. "You were so poor that you could only afford a party line for your telephone, so poor that you sometimes had only beans and bacon to go with your potatoes . . ." And on and on, every word twisting the knife deeper.

Thompson had not had an easy week, either, what with the stress of organizing the conference. He put down his glass in disgust and walked towards the door. "That's right, Kent," Nowlan persisted. "Go back to where you are wanted, because it's not here."

Metcalf had had enough, too. "Alden, you've obviously had way too much to drink, and have no right to subject Kent or anyone else to your blatherings."

But Thompson had already grabbed his coat, nearly in tears, muttering on his way out, "I know one thing: I'm sick and tired of taking all this shit." Metcalf followed. Sharon Fraser got up in the silence and watched their backs receding into the night. She turned, wandered back into the room and leaned against one of the bookcases, making the mistake of meeting Nowlan's eye.

"And you," he said to Fraser's wife, extending his accusing finger. "You," he repeated. "You standing there with your hand on your hip. You with all your pretensions and affectations. You come here and eat my food, drink my wine, sleep in my house. Who invited you here? What makes you think you are welcome in this house?"

Then Claudine intervened. After a quiet conference, she persuaded her husband that the party was over and that it was time he got some sleep.[31]

The next day Nowlan remembered enough about the night before to know that he owed Thompson a huge apology. There were a few people brave enough to remind him. "You were wrong and I'd be a shit to myself and to Kent if I didn't say so," Metcalf wrote on Monday, after cooling down. "Which, being said, I hope we can proceed as before and that you'll reply to this. You must know that I admire your work this side idolatry."[32] Nowlan had written Thompson a very contrite apology the same day, but he could not forbear reminding Thompson that he was an outsider among real Maritimers such as himself:

> When you told us you were tired of being shat upon and that we could go fuck ourselves — well, probably, under the circumstances you should have done that an hour earlier. Then probably we'd have all laughed and started singing folksongs or wrist wrestling or some such equally drunken but more companionable thing. Maybe I haven't expressed that well.[33]

Thompson accepted the apology with good grace. But a year later Nowlan was still trying to explain the situation to Metcalf:

> Kent Thompson hasn't darkened the door of my abode since that other night, although I actually grovelled for his forgiveness and for a while rather bombarded him with invitations to dinner, parties etc. Nor did he invite me to the gathering at his place following the reading, although I wore his old school scarf to it as a subtle mark of my continued regard for him. (He gave me a Swansea College scarf in happier days, as they used to say in Victorian novels.) God bless the poor bugger, it doesn't seem he is a very good forgetter.[34]

Then later still, in a less-repentant vein:

> There's no feud. Incidentally I wrote the poem, "He Attempts to Dignify a Quarrel with His Guests," as a result of the original incident — and a piddling incident it was; where I come from men have been known to break one another's noses and afterwards walk away arm-in-arm. But that's enough on't, as Sam Johnson might have said.[35]

In his attempts to make up, Nowlan continued to imply that he could not accept Thompson as a real Maritime writer — or even an honorary one — as he had other imported writers such as Bob Cockburn, Bill Bauer or Donald Cameron. The communal activity of drinking might have had something to do with Nowlan keeping the professor at the margins of his circle; Thompson seldom drank. In the faculty lounge of the UNB English department hangs a painting by Bruno Bobak called *Kent's Punch*. Thompson is the middle figure in the painting, serving some concoction to the circle of writers and professors gathered around him: UNB English professor Allan Donaldson, Desmond Pacey, Robert Gibbs, Bill Bauer, Fred Cogswell and Alden Nowlan. Whatever Nowlan may have thought about who truly belonged within the circle of Maritime literature, Thompson did not share his views, nor did he ever return to Windsor Castle.

That tumultuous November was not over. On the Tuesday evening after the conference, Ray and Sharon Fraser, back in Nowlan's good graces, were sitting with him and Ferrari, getting ready for a night of thinking and drinking. The events of the previous week, with all the academics and *artistes*, were no doubt not far from their minds. Ferrari mulled over his marital problems, Sharon listening sympathetically. But Nowlan and Fraser were discussing philosophical questions of faith and science, and how people have allowed themselves to be deluded by both. The lost wisdom of the old had been replaced by the cold science of the new. As the night wore on, they became more excited about these ideas. What was needed was a new way of looking at the world, a way that validated knowledge that ordinary people could see for themselves.

"Leo," Nowlan shouted out from his corner of the room. "Is the Earth flat?"

Kent's Punch, by Bruno Bobak. Clockwise from lower left: Allan Donaldson, Robert Gibbs, Alden Nowlan, Kent Thompson, Desmond Pacey, Bill Bauer and Fred Cogswell. BRUNO BOBAK

Without missing a beat, Ferrari replied. "Of course the Earth is flat. Everyone knows that."

The philosopher's maxim had a nice ring to it. The idea caught fire. Fraser suggested that what was needed was an organization to support their views. Nowlan, whose Society of St. Simeon the Mad Cormier had recently abandoned, pricked up his ears. The mind that had managed a country and western band and had taken minutes for the Hartland Fish and Game Association went into high gear. Why not a society, with membership cards and dues and the like? They could even host their own conferences and produce their own academic papers, all the while tweaking the nose of established wisdom whenever doing so could produce the most laughs. The sun rose the next morning to find itself no longer the centre of the solar system and the Earth no longer a spinning blob of dust on the periphery of a cloud of stars. The stars themselves were on the periphery. The Flat Earth Society was born.

The FES was the refuge Nowlan needed. It had all the mysterious and esoteric lore of the Freemasons, except that it was not a respectable diversion for used car salesmen and store clerks; it was, if anything, unrespectable. And it offered all the fellowship of the Knights of Pythias, "fellow" being the operative word for this mostly male fraternity. Ferrari was perfect for the presidency, with his knowledge of ancient and medieval thought, his formidable debating skills, his wild appearance and his doctorate. Nowlan was to be the Symposiarch and Ray Fraser the Chairman. Sharon Fraser, the only woman present at the founding, was chosen as Executive VP, and, after some canvassing among Ontario writers, the Toronto poet Gwendolyn MacEwen agreed to serve as vice-president, making the FES a national organization.

Ferrari and Nowlan quickly drew up a document describing the aims of the society:

> 1) To restore man's confidence in the validity of his own perceptions. For more than fifteen hundred years man has been blinded by metaphysics and coerced into denying the evidence of his senses. The Flat Earth Society stands for a renewed faith in the veracity of sense experience.
> 2) To combat the fallacious deification of the sphere which, ever since Galileo dramatized the heresies of Copernicus, has thwarted Western thought.
> 3) To spearhead man's escape from his metaphysical and geometrical prison by asserting unequivocally that all science, like all philosophy and all religion, is essentially sacramental and, therefore, all reality, as man verbalizes it, is ultimately metaphorical.[36]

Of course, the FES had a frivolous side. The following spring, Ferrari travelled to the 1971 Learned Societies conference, which was held that year at Memorial University in Newfoundland. His poster and pamphlet display yielded some sixty enquiries, a few signed "Flatly yours" or "Up with flatness." The media caught wind of this, and Ferrari was briefly a local celebrity. He rounded off his trip by a visiting Al Pittman on Fogo Island. They agreed that a flat Earth must have an edge or, in FES parlance, an Abysmal Chasm. So, fortified by quantities of screech to steel their nerve, Pittman and the president ventured out to visit the edge of the Earth, which happened to be not far from the Pittman house. Secured by a rope tied to Pittman, Ferrari plucked a large boulder from the Abysmal Chasm and brought it home as a souvenir of his exploits.

The flat Earthers then had to decide what to do about the Absymal Chasm: put a fence around it? How could they deal with an invasion by the Chasm-dwellers? Such preoccupations belied the society's motto: "We're on the level."

Two weeks after the FES was founded, Brewster wrote from the University of Alberta with some bad news. The talk going around the department was that Nowlan might not be chosen as a writer-in-residence after all. They had the impression he was not interested, since he did not come out to give a reading. Besides, Cogswell had confided to Wiebe that Nowlan's health might not be up to moving to the other end of the country. "Ah, Fred, Fred," Nowlan wrote to Brewster. "I love him, but sometimes I wish he didn't quite talk so much."[37] But harming his friend's career was the last thing on Cogswell's mind. On the contrary, he was at that moment working, again in secret, on Nowlan's behalf, and the plan would not work if he took a job in Alberta. The new premier, Richard Hatfield, was approached by UNB with a plan: that the province recognize the cultural treasure it had in Nowlan by taking over the Canada Council's portion of the funding that kept Nowlan as writer-in-residence. In return, the province would have, in effect, its own poet laureate who could take on certain small writing projects for the province. Hatfield agreed. Nowlan would stay at UNB for one more year.

Meanwhile, amid the swirl of activity, Johnnie had become a young man. Though he and Nowlan had developed a close and loving bond, Johnnie did not feel the need to follow in his father's literary footsteps, and Nowlan felt no desire to push him. Where he cajoled and pushed young student writers to follow his example, he allowed Johnnie to develop as he would, all the while offering loving support. But this support had its limits.

Johnnie, even by teenage standards, was innocent and easily swayed by his peers' reasoning. One day when Nowlan and Claudine were in Sackville for a poetry reading, Johnnie was approached by one of his friends at Fredericton High School. They told Johnnie that they had met a guy their age who said he was an American draft dodger. Since Johnnie's father was a poet, he must be against the war in Vietnam and willing to harbour a draft dodger, right? Johnnie supposed Nowlan would. So Johnnie and this stranger boarded the bus to go home, the young man all the while regaling Johnnie with stories of how he flew a helicopter in Vietnam, which actually made him a deserter. But the bus was stopped by the authorities, who ushered the mysterious fellow off. Johnnie's parents found out when he phoned them long-distance to ask, "Dad, is there any penalty for harbouring an American draft dodger?" Nowlan later summed up Johnnie's adventure:

> What's amusing to me is that Johnnie couldn't be less interested in politics, he's just a very hospitable kid and, besides, he likes to talk with exciting people, he'd have brought George Lincoln Rockwell or Stokely Carmichael home, or for that matter Jesus Christ or Adolph Hitler, and I'd probably have welcomed any of the foregoing, had I been there — but I could imagine explaining that to a judge.[38]

As it turned out, the kid was not a draft dodger after all but an imposter from Ontario.

Nowlan, once a shy and outcast teen, mildly envied his son. "He looks as though he'd stepped from a photograph in a history of the American west," Nowlan told Sylvia. "Not like a fictional gunfighter, but like a real one, with one of those narrow-brimmed trilby hats with the crown poked out so it looks like a bowler on the back of his head, bare-chested with a long vest made from a piece of cotton with a leopard skin pattern, a sort of Mexican moustache and Wyatt Earp sideburns." He added, "He'll never be a poet with words but I think it's possible he may be a poet of actions. In some ways he is much more mature than most of the university students whom I know and in some ways he is such a little boy. He'd like to go off to Ireland and fight for the IRA."[39]

In one way, however, their lives followed parallel paths. Johnnie had never found school very interesting and longed for a life of adventure. In March of 1971, just months away from his high school graduation, he dropped out of school. Nowlan had always given Johnnie as free a hand as a parent could, and he could not bring himself to force him back into an institution he had rejected. But, on the other hand, when boys dropped out of school in Stanley, they worked in the mill. Would his son travel down the same road Freeman took?

Hoping that Johnnie would pass through this phase and return to complete his education, Nowlan asked Hatfield about possible job opportunities for a young man in his position. Hatfield suggested a summer job program where students cut trees and tended the grounds at Canadian Forces Base Gagetown in nearby Oromocto. But the experience only reinforced Johnnie's desire to see the country and gave him the financial means to do so. That September, after working briefly as a farm labourer in Hartland, he hitchhiked to Montreal on his way to Vancouver. He stayed in the big city for a week or so, long enough to give his parents one last chance to see him off. The Nowlans spent a weekend together at the Laurentian Hotel, where they treated Johnnie to a big steak dinner and then parted, leaving him standing alone on a Montreal street. A week later, Nowlan confessed his worries to Anne Greer:

> Part of me wishes he'd stayed in school. In fact part of me would have been proud to have him become the kind of *successful man* that another, deeper part of me despises. I've always been afraid he'd slip back into the kind of life from which I escaped. I suppose that's partly selfish of me. But I'm happy that now there seems to be no chance of it happening. Whatever else he may become I can't see him ever sinking back into the ancestral pattern — married at nineteen, five kids by the time he's twenty-five, a $50 a week job in a feed mill and a double case of beer on Saturday night. . . .
>
> Being a parent is like being an artist in that everybody who tries it fails — but, shit, there are degrees of failure and we shouldn't flagellate ourselves for not being gods.
>
> At least that's what I tell myself.[40]

His fears were somewhat allayed by a phone call he received just before writing the letter — Johnnie, phoning from Montreal to let his parents know that, because he found hitchhiking too cold for that time of year, he would take the train to Vancouver instead. It seemed the kid would be all right after all.

In the summer of that year, 1971, the last issue of *Intercourse* was published. Fraser had long since turned the magazine over to Louis Cormier, who ran it from Tyndale Martin's Zen centre in Montreal. But Cormier had not put out a new issue in months. On March 4, 1971, around the time Johnnie dropped out of school, Nowlan wrote Cormier a desperate plea to renounce Zen:

> If it is important for you to stay at the Zen Centre then by all means stay. To me it seems sort of silly. But that's to *me*.

I am not *you*. No, I guess it doesn't seem so silly as it seems a *waste*. But I'm not going to argue the point with you. I love you. Do what thou will is the whole of the law, said Mr. Rabelais.

But don't be *preachy*. Because that's not you. Let the rest of us poor bastards go to hell in our several ways. . . .

It doesn't disappoint me that you've gone in for this Anglicized, faddish, psychedelic, Rollin' Stones, Beatles kind of orientalism — what saddens me is that you *needed*, obviously, to do this. *I thought you were stronger.*

But if you need it, more power to you. And God bless you.

Ah, Louis, Louis, Louis. You speak of the "pain" and the "torture" of school when what you mean is the "frustration" and the "annoyance."

Pain is what makes you scream.

And then lose consciousness.

Pain is when you drown in your own vomit.

Pain is when you pray to a god in whom you don't believe that you'll die.

That is pain, Louis. God spare you from it.

But before he put the letter into the envelope, he read it over again and thought better of it. Purged of his frustrations over this wayward son, he put a fresh piece of paper into the typewriter and copied a poem called "Twenty-Three" that he had written for himself when he was twenty-three years old, which was also Louis's age. Then, after some discussion of John Grube, he said:

I think you should be more careful about the manner in which you apply the words "pain" and "torture." School may very well be frustrating and annoying and depressing. But pain is another matter altogether. Pain makes you scream and, sometimes, it makes you beg for death. It's a word to be used with great care.

Mindful of emotion unexpressed, he closed with "MUCH LOVE."[41]

Cormier visited Fredericton in June; however, Nowlan did not gain much by trying to speak with him face to face, although Cormier was staying at Windsor Castle. First there was the hair. Lama Louis had cut his flowing locks and was now virtually bald, a fact Cormier bragged about in his phone conversations with friends. When Nowlan or Claudine prepared dinner and then went in search of their guest he would as often as not have vanished to some other part of Fredericton. "I don't know whether to cry for him or kick his arse, frankly," Nowlan groused to Fraser. "When he left I told him that I'd pray that he'd be restored to Our Holy Mother the Church and led to enter a Trappist monastery. He's in such a fog that he appears stupid, which he isn't, or didn't used to be."[42]

When the last issue of *Intercourse* — dedicated to, among others, the Zen Centre and "all who care about becoming deeply honest people" — finally came out late that summer, it had changed as much as Cormier himself had. It was no longer the magazine that featured Layton, Souster and Nowlan, along with a new crop of up-and-coming poets, a bit of satire and the odd crude cartoon of Miss *Intercourse*. Instead, it featured a tedious three-page editorial by Cormier praising Martin's own Buddhist poetry magazine, *Sunyata*, and explaining his devotion to Zen. Fraser evidently thought little of his magazine's new direction. Years later, poets attempting to submit to the defunct periodical received replies from Fraser that would say something like this:

> Sad to say *Intercourse* is kaput — at least as far as I can divine. I left it in the hands of a young gentleman who subsequently turned into a Buddhist monk — a lama no less — and whatever else Buddhist monks might be good at, they are not suited for running a magazine called *Intercourse*. Or called anything, perhaps.[43]

Nowlan's response to Cormier's perfidy was less good-natured. In the winter of 1974, Cormier and three people from the Zen centre visited Fredericton for a couple of months in an attempt to establish a Great Heart franchise east of Montreal. By that time, Martin's followers had adopted not only the familiar shaven head but also long robes. One cold day, while walking about campus, Cormier decided to visit Nowlan with two of his Buddhist friends in tow. He rang the bell while his friends hung back. A hulking shape soon appeared at the door; it was his old mentor, Nowlan.

"Hello, Louis," the poet greeted him. "Well, look at you. Why don't you step in?"

"Can my friends come in, too?"

For the first time, Nowlan noticed the saffron-robed young men standing in the yard. His demeanour changed like a cloud passing over the sun. He could not meet Cormier's eyes.

"No," he mumbled and shut the door in the young man's face. It was the last time Cormier saw Alden Nowlan.

In the Night

Best to put off
going back to sleep
until the dark stops
asking questions
— so thinks the man
who has been awakened
by the sound of his own voice
calling out to his wife
who lies within reach
of him:
                    Stephanie, Stephanie
—which is not hers
but his sister's name.

As if he did not have enough on his plate in early November, 1970, what with his feuds with academics and other writers, his fretting about the lost University of Alberta position and the founding of the Flat Earth Society, Nowlan received the first of a series of intrusive communications from the people of his Nova Scotia past. His career had taken to the air, as in his poem "I, Icarus," but he started to find himself dragged down by an accumulation of ghosts. The communication was the first of a half-dozen letters sent to him between 1970 and 1972 by his Aunt Hazel, the woman who had the hydrocephalic son — Nowlan's cousin Robert — when Nowlan was just a boy. Now, her charring days behind her, Hazel lived in the house of one of her former employers, supported by the community of Windsor. Her letters are barely legible pleas for money from her now-famous nephew, whom she believed to be a "smart and wealthy man." Nowlan communicated regularly with Freeman, who sometimes acted as a conduit for news of Harriet and other relatives. Nowlan would not respond to Hazel's letters, much less send her any money, explaining to Freeman, "I would send her five dollars. But I'm afraid that would be just the beginning. I'm scared she'd pester the life out of me."[1]

Freeman was not all that well himself. In January of 1969 Russell Palmer had decided to sell the mill where Freeman had worked for most of his life. The sale of the dying enterprise would certainly mean its closure as well. Throughout the winter of 1968-69 Nowlan had been trying to secure an old-age pension for his aging father, which involved locating parish records that would give some proof of Freeman's birth date, of which Freeman himself was unsure, having no birth certificate. Nowlan at last found the date, November 2, 1904, which meant Freeman would be able to draw a small pension starting in November of 1969, his sixty-fifth birthday. But news of the mill's closure caused Nowlan to worry about how his father would make it through the summer. Once again, a job on a road crew saved the day; Freeman found work assisting highway surveyors for a better wage than he had been earning at Palmer's mill. In the spring of 1971, after his retirement, Freeman traded houses with his neighbour, Grant McCullough. Nowlan, in a literal as well as a spiritual sense, would not be able to go home again.

The mental and spiritual effects of Nowlan's battle with cancer lingered long after the physical threat had passed. His dread of hospitals, awakened long ago when he was an inmate at the Nova Scotia Hospital, had solidified. He believed that the cancer was by no means defeated but still lurked in his system like a monstrous white crab, ready to bite him again when his guard was down. He wrote John Grube in June of 1971 (the five-year anniversary of his successful surgery, the point at which a cancer survivor's odds of dying old are the same as anyone else's) that he still felt he was being "stalked by an assassin: the disease that will almost certainly kill me in a horrible manner or, eventually, confront me with the necessity of killing myself."[2] This letter, written in a moment of anger and despair, was not mailed. A minor ailment could send him into agonies of worry. When he noticed a hearing loss in his right ear due to infection, he confided to Greg Cook, "Naturally

I'm afraid it's a symptom of my old antagonist, getting the knife in again. . . . I'm afraid of doctors now. . . . If they tell me it *is* what I'm afraid it might be, then, I'll have been deprived of hope. That's a situation I dread facing."[3]

To be sure, the poet still suffered some side effects from his cancer battle — his hoarse voice, his swollen face and his thyroid problems — plus the added burden of his unhealthy habits: excessive smoking and drinking and a combination of eating and lack of exercise that increased his weight and diminished his strength. He was prone to infections, especially ear infections; he often woke up in the middle of the night struggling for breath and would easily tire on long trips. These ailments, while real enough, could at times be turned to his advantage, allowing him an easy escape from uncomfortable or inconvenient situations, or providing a handy tool to elicit sympathy. "I remember one night we were talking about death, and he said he had only six months left," Bernie MacDonald recalls. "I went over to see Louis [Cormier], bawling my eyes out. . . . I'm sure Al was milking it for what it was worth."[4]

Greg Cook found himself on the losing end of Nowlan's new propensity to make excuses. Acadia University had decided that the 1971-1972 academic year would be the last one for Cook as a full-time faculty member unless he agreed to go back to school and get his PhD. Instead, he decided to fight the matter through his union and was granted a formal hearing with the university. He asked Nowlan to appear at the hearing to speak on his behalf, but instead he received a letter of support from the poet to be presented in his stead, along with this explanation:

> Since my sickness — and what a bore it gets to be, always having to adapt myself to that — it's hard for me to cope with any strain, physical, mental or emotional. If I went down to Acadia the chances are strong that I'd get drunk and then wouldn't be able to appear at all or would insist on appearing and, quite possibly, making an ass of myself. If I didn't get drunk I'd likely be so damned tongue-tied they'd think I was an idiot.[5]

While he was probably justified in seeing such a journey as not worth the financial and physical toll it would take, his lack of confidence in the impact his visit might have had suggests that more than health concerns kept him from such battles.

Nowlan's professed aversion to physicians was about as genuine as his professed aversion to academics. For a man so leery of hospitals, Nowlan cultivated a number of close friendships with physicians, possibly because the friendships were mostly conducted on his terms; if death were to come, then it could take him with a drink in one hand and a cigarette in the other. One of these doctors was Ian Cameron, a keen amateur bagpiper with an interest in poetry. "I want you to play checkers with me when I'm dying," Nowlan once told him. Only Leo Ferrari, who swam regularly in the UNB pool, made sporadic attempts to persuade his friend to reform his unhealthy habits.

Cameron was more interested in Nowlan the poet than Nowlan the patient, as was Dr. Nicholas Catanoy, a Romanian radiologist with a vocation for writing. After working in Romania, the Soviet Union, China and North Korea, Catanoy immigrated to Canada in 1962 and lived in Montreal, where he met writers such as Irving Layton and Louis Dudek and immersed himself in Canadian literature. When he came to Fredericton in 1968, he met Fred Cogswell and the new writer-in-residence, Alden Nowlan, who gave him a book by William Carlos Williams inscribed, "For the Romanian Doctor Zhivago with esteem." Throughout the early to mid-1970s, after Catanoy's return to Europe, Nowlan helped the doctor edit *Modern Romanian Poetry* (1977), an anthology of one hundred poems. Catanoy translated the poems literally into English, and then, with Nowlan's help, he contacted twenty-two of Canada's finest poets to work the literal translations into beautiful and evocative English poetry. By the time the doctor left for France in the fall of 1971, the project was well under way.

Nowlan's only contact with a number of significant Canadian writers, including Dennis Lee, Tom Marshall and Ron Everson, was through Catanoy's project. Now secure at the University of New Brunswick, he was more preoccupied with shoring up his position in Fredericton than seeking new challenges in the wider world. In May of 1971, the university awarded him an honorary degree, which he accepted proudly, and, in contradiction to his anti-academic sensibility, he would often call himself "Dr. Nowlan," no doubt conscious of the potential to subvert "university types" and certainly bearing the image of his idol Dr. Samuel Johnson in mind.

Heeding his maxim "real writers write, phony writers confer," he used his pen to do what his person could not and developed his national presence through his writing — not through literary criticism or essays in avant-garde publications, but instead through his old standby, journalism. Having established a regular sideline as a local newspaper and magazine columnist, he started to write for national magazines. He was initially asked by *Maclean's* editor Peter C. Newman late in 1970 to write an article as part of a series in which well-known Canadians discuss their conception of Canada. Nowlan, whose sense of national identity was inextricably linked to his region and his past, devoted the first part of the article to describing Stanley:

> If a nation is a communion between the dead, the living and the unborn, then I was aware even as a child that I belonged to a nation. I don't recall that anybody I knew as a child ever gave that nation a name. Certainly nobody ever talked about "my country" or "Canada" except the teacher in the one-room school, and she didn't count. The inhabitants of my native village seldom if ever discussed abstractions; I doubt if many of them were capable of abstract thought.[6]

Even before the article appeared in the June 1971 issue, Newman had Nowlan working on another one about the newly elected premier of New Brunswick. This proved to be a more difficult task, Newman being one of the most exacting editors Nowlan had ever worked for. The Hatfield article was sent back for revision three times before *Maclean's* would print it. Ever the professional craftsman, Nowlan was intrigued by the challenge of mastering a new way of writing and adapted easily to the glossy magazine's combination of superficiality and depth. *Maclean's* paid him $300 for the article about Canada and $600 for the Hatfield article. Two 1972 articles, one about country music star Stompin' Tom Connors and the other about a travelling evangelist named Floyd Cruse, earned him $800 apiece. Even better, *Maclean's* paid when an article was accepted, not when it was finally published.

The June 1971 issue of *Maclean's* had barely appeared in the nation's mailboxes when his article saying that the opinions of the local schoolteacher did not count in Stanley received its first response. It was from Hilda Palmer, his former schoolteacher. Before tearing the letter open, he thought it was going to contain congratulations. "It turned

Richard Hatfield, Stompin' Tom Connors and Alden Nowlan. PATRICIA A. BROWN

out to be a semi-official communiqué from the villagers telling me I was a son of a bitch for writing the kind of thing I do," he told Ray Fraser.

> I gather that she — as a former school marm — had been assigned to write it. Funniest part of it was from reading between the lines I could see they also think I'm making enormous amounts of money. They virtually demanded a donation [to the Stanley community centre] to soothe their wounds inflicted by my prose. Blackmail. I finally decided to ignore it, after toying with possible replies, one of which I liked was: "Dear Madam: Because of Dr. Nowlan's absence in Japan his private secretary is directed to thank you for your letter and good wishes. Signed: Lieut. Col. Julian Tempest-Stewart, Private Secretary."[7]

He scrawled his only response for posterity at the top of Palmer's letter, a note to any scholars who might later be interested in his papers: "Not answered. This silly bitch was my Grade V teacher. — AAN."[8]

Nowlan's name was mud in Stanley. First Hazel began hounding him, then Hilda Palmer attacked him. At last his long-lost sister, Harriet, tried to resume contact. Nowlan's papers contain only one letter from her, written in August of 1971. Harriet — now living in Calgary and married to a man named Richard Ottie — broke years of silence by telling her brother, "I won't make any excuses for my life and I found out it's not very good to feel sorry for one's self because no one feels sorry for me. I only wish that you would write me and let me know [how] you are."[9] This, like the letter from Hilda Palmer, went unanswered. There is little doubt that Harriet's attempts to re-establish contact with her brother were sporadic, but Harriet claims that she tried unsuccessfully to talk to her brother on the phone, and that she sent other letters, some containing photos of her children and herself. Why did Nowlan — who included in his collected papers even those items that cast him in an unfavourable light — not also include these? If, on the other hand, he intended to expunge all traces of Harriet from the record, then why did he allow this one letter to survive?

His complaint to Freeman about another aunt — this time Roxie — provides a clue. Just as Hilda Palmer had been offended enough by his description of Stanley in *Maclean's* to write in protest, so too was Roxie "disgusted with me for fattening my purse/ by selling lies about my relatives,/ not excepting my poor old grandmother who took me in/ when I was eight years old and homeless." Her angry letter to her nephew in January, 1972 — what would prove to be their final communication — was prompted by his short story "There Was an Old Woman from Wexford," which had won the University of Western Ontario President's Medal for best short story published in 1970. The story was a sensitive portrait of a boy lying awake listening to his grandmother sing old songs and tell stories on the last night of her life. "I didn't answer any of Hazel's letters and I don't intend to answer any of Roxie's either," Nowlan writes to Freeman, and then adds: "In fact Claudine talks of simply mailing them back to her, without showing them to me — because they *do* depress me, at least for a little while."[10]

The possibility that Claudine may have intercepted some of her husband's mail, either without his knowledge or with his tacit consent, adds a new dimension their relationship as it is suggested in his poems and described by various visitors to Windsor Castle. For Claudine was not just Nowlan's helpmate but his keeper as well, steering him towards bed when he became obnoxious at his parties and preventing his drinking from getting out of hand when she accompanied him outside the home. But some of the young women in Nowlan's circle sensed something else from Claudine when they stayed up with the poet talking long into the night. "I was a young, single, academic woman, and I came into their home," says Anne Greer. "I felt that she was not academic; she was simpler, in a way . . . I never felt comfortable with her."[11] The danger was not so much potential physical intimacy as the emotional intimacy he shared with young women such as Greer and Sharon Fraser; in his conversations with Anne Greer, for instance, he exposed his contradictions and the truths about his origins to a greater degree than he ever did with his readers, with Claudine, and even with himself. It was Nowlan's young, pretty cousin Sylvia, and not Nowlan, who informed Claudine that Grace was still alive.

Since her visit over Christmas in 1967, Greer had abandoned her thesis, moved to Ontario, had a daughter, and become a teacher at Seneca College, all the time keeping up an intimate correspondence with her mentor. In the summer of 1971 she re-started her thesis and submitted it to her supervisor at Acadia, who rejected it because it was too disorganized. She adopted an unorthodox way of bringing herself around to her subject again. In the spring of 1972, she and Jim, her fiancé, organized a special investigative class at Seneca on Atlantic Canada. Students would live and learn on a bus trip through the Maritimes, meeting interesting people and seeing the sights along the way. As the one in charge of the cultural portion of the tour, Greer put Nowlan on the top of her list. So, to the poet's delight, a bus pulled up in front of his house one afternoon, and twenty-five college students tumbled out. Claudine made Irish stew for the party as they sat around Nowlan's chair and listened to him talk about and read his poetry, but Greer also remembers Claudine's concern that the excitement might tax Nowlan's energy. Looking back, Greer struggles to account for her sense of unease:

> I found Claudine a puzzle. I think one of the reasons why I found it difficult to continue to have a friendship with Nowlan after I did my thesis was partly because of Claudine. I felt that Claudine was very important to Nowlan. She always looked after him. And I felt that my agenda was so opposite to that. . . . Around this biography [her thesis] there was this intimacy, and I think I felt that Claudine felt that I was intruding.[12]

She had the inspiration she needed to complete the thesis in 1973, but her relationship with her subject did not last much beyond its acceptance.

As always, Nowlan's antics with his male friends still held centre stage; his fantasy world provided a retreat from the troubling questions he found himself confronting in the company of sympathetic young women. There was little danger of confronting these questions in the Flat Earth Society, a fraternity that kept Sharon Fraser and Gwendolyn MacEwen's involvement marginal and Nowlan, Fraser and Ferrari at the centre. As Symposiarch, the poet spared no pains to promote his hobby. Through correspondence, he and Fraser discussed the day-to-day business of running the club. Brochures had to be printed, dues had to be collected and membership had to increase. Naturally, the top priority for Nowlan and Ferrari was producing a publication, and they soon wrote a brochure and published the first issue of the society's official organ, entitled, appropriately, the *Official Organ*. The private joke soon became public. Ferrari was a natural performer, all wild hair and an ability to get under the skin of serious scientists who attempted to refute the FES position. The CBC-TV program *Take 30* featured Ferrari in April, 1972, and he was a guest on *Front Page Challenge* in January, 1973. When Nowlan wrote an article about Ferrari for the December 14, 1974, *Weekend* magazine, he could not resist exploiting the FES angle at the expense of the professor's internationally respected accomplishments in Augustinian philosophy. The cover featured a photo of Ferrari jumping on a globe with the banner "Would You Buy a Used Globe from This Man?"

Meanwhile, the group had invented another club that was as much fun as the FES, if not more fun, since it was truly private. It revolved around another student poet who came under Nowlan's tutelage, Jim Stewart, who spent his first evening at Windsor Castle mute and unable to overcome his shyness. Casting about for a way to bring the young man out of his shell, Nowlan subjected him to one of his own enthusiasms, records of Scottish and Irish folk music played at maximum volume on his record player. It turned out that Stewart already loved the music and was, furthermore, very knowledgeable about his own Scottish heritage. "My family is distantly related to the Earl of Fife," he boasted.

As Stewart started coming around more and more in the spring of 1970, Nowlan's imagination set to work. The boy who had once created the houses of imaginary royal families, and who had memorized the genealogy of the Hapsburgs from *Appleton's Encyclopedia*, was now a man with formidable esoteric knowledge of royal lineage. He played a recording of Scottish folk song with the refrain, "Rise and follow Charlie" — Charles Stuart, "Bonnie Prince Charlie," the Young Pretender who was defeated at Culloden in 1746. "Stewart" was just a variant spelling of "Stuart," after all, and with the death of Charles Stuart's line, did not the crown revert to the Earl of Fife? And if one did not accept the legitimacy of the Hanoverian line as the rightful rulers of Britain (as many did not, or at least did not two hundred and fifty years previously), then that meant that Jim . . .

"God Save Your Majesty!" Nowlan greeted Stewart on his next visit. The Jacobite cause was resurrected in the little house called Windsor Castle.

People in the Nowlan circle slowly started to amass titles as more people were inducted into the peerage. The titular head of the Stewart Monarchy in Exile, of course, was Stewart himself, or James IV, King of England, Scotland, Ireland and France, as he came to be known. Nowlan liked to emphasize his own heritage sometimes by calling Stewart "High King of All the Celts." Nowlan was the Duke of Wexford and Prince of Fortara. Ferrari's background in religious philosophy earned him the title Archbishop of Canterbury, and he vowed that, once the monarchy was restored, he would assume the government's monopoly on the sale of alcohol and remove all taxes on booze.

Another friend, artist Tom Forrestall, whom Nowlan once lauded as "the last mystical ploughboy in Amerikay," became Baron Middleton (after his hometown in Nova Scotia) and Painter-in-Ordinary. So too was Nowlan's physician friend Dr. Ian Cameron knighted. At one of the Windsor Castle parties, Cameron was walking down the short hallway between the kitchen and the living room, and Nowlan and Stewart were walking the other way, discussing weighty matters of the royal court. When they met, Nowlan commanded Cameron to kneel. "Arise, Earl of Woodbine," Stewart intoned, invoking the name of Cameron's street. "To what do I owe this honour?" Cameron asked, but the duo had already reached the kitchen, talking about the possible royal significance of dulse. Unlike the FES, this was an all-boys club, although a woman might be referred to by her husband's or boyfriend's title if she had a male partner in the club. Sharon Fraser, for instance, was sometimes known as the Duchess of Northumberland. The Duke of Dungarvon was one of the quieter peers, in keeping with his reserved style. He was otherwise known as David Adams Richards.

Richards, another Miramichi lad, enrolled at St. Thomas University in 1969. Unlike Cormier or Stewart, he was fairly independent of Nowlan's influence, finding advice and guidance from a variety of sources including Fred Cogswell, the Ice House group, and his own voracious reading. His poetry and fiction quickly made him a star among student writers, and he did not start frequenting the Nowlan house until his second year at STU. The Ice House group, spearheaded by Nancy Bauer, had by then formed its own small press, New Brunswick Chapbooks. Richards's poetry collection *Small Heroics* was published in 1972, one of the first books in the series. But Richards was not satisfied with his poetic development and decided to devote himself entirely to writing fiction. In 1973, he also began to devote himself to marriage and his new wife, Peggy. His experiences with growing up in the Miramichi and marriage were the creative engines driving his powerful debut novel, *The Coming of Winter* (1974). Nowlan found he could offer Richards little in the way of literary support, since the younger man was intent on working in a medium and with a voice outside Nowlan's expertise. "I'm a sprinter, not a long-distance runner," Nowlan would often tell people as a way of accounting for his own method of writing fiction, page after painful page. But he did offer garrulous companionship that Richards loved. "Ah, David, David, you write like an angel . . ." Nowlan sometimes interjected into his discourse with the young writer. Richards was too shy to mention that he understood the reference to Johnson, which concludes, "but you talk like poor Poll."

In a way, Richards and Stewart replaced the young friends Nowlan had lost due to graduation or religious devotion. Another new student writer was Brian Bartlett, a UNB student and literary wunderkind who had started showing up to Ice House meetings while still in high school. As Fred Cogswell observed, Nowlan's influence on these young men was not always beneficial:

> Of the promising young writers — Al Pittman, Terry Crawford, Bernell MacDonald, Louis Cormier, Eddie Clinton, James Stewart — who frequented Nowlan's house, none has fulfilled, in my own opinion, his poetic promise, and I think that in this Nowlan was inadvertently at fault. Having discovered Nowlan's superficial voice without his depth, they never tried — nor did he suggest that they try — to explore further possibilities of development.[13]

In fact, the young men did not go to Nowlan in search of editorial suggestions but to enjoy the respect Nowlan accorded them as fellow writers, respect they could not find among older writers and academics.

The few who can recall taking their unpublished writing to him say that they did not keep up the practice beyond their first meeting with Nowlan, who probably wanted to avoid a repeat of his experiences with Louis Cormier and Eddie Clinton. At 676 Windsor Street they had a second set of parents: the father who would talk or argue long into the night and play loud music, and the mother who would not let them go out into the night without treating them to supper or to sandwiches.

Perhaps the most significant of the friendships Nowlan made in Fredericton was with a man from outside the academic and literary community. Alden Nowlan was not the only new artist to come to Fredericton in 1968; that year also marked the beginning of what became a cultural mainstay of the province, Theatre New Brunswick, Canada's only professional touring theatre company. TNB performed shows in all corners of the province, but its home base was (and remains) the Playhouse in downtown Fredericton. The Playhouse was one of many public buildings donated by Lord Beaverbrook, a former Fleet Street newspaper tycoon, Churchill's minister of aircraft production, and New Brunswick's most famous son. The Playhouse was built in the mid-1960s on the site of the Governor's House, a former coffee house and hotel that once served as the New Brunswick legislature. But the Playhouse lacked one important feature, a fly gallery where large scenic backdrops, curtains and props can be stored until lowered to the stage with a system of ropes and pulleys. It was omitted at the whim of Lady Beaverbrook, who thought that the large, box-like structure sitting on top of the new theatre would destroy its elegant look.

When Theatre New Brunswick opened its doors at the Playhouse in January, 1969, the new artistic director insisted that Lady Beaverbrook's decision about the fly gallery be overturned. Walter Learning possessed a gift for persuasion and invited controversy. The young and energetic Newfoundlander was determined to make theatre popular in New Brunswick, something that people would talk about, even argue about. After making his dream of a professional touring company a financial and artistic success, Learning convinced the Playhouse board to invest $1 million in renovations, of which the fly gallery was the centrepiece. The renovations were undertaken in 1971-1972 and inaugurated with the opening of TNB's fourth season. The large box that Lady Beaverbrook felt would look incongruous was built on top of the theatre, painted white, and accented by oblique multicoloured stripes in a design by artist Tom Forrestall entitled *Surprise Package*. Local legend has it that *Surprise Package* was painted on the fly gallery because soldiers from CFB Gagetown who occasionally spent the night at the Lord Beaverbrook Hotel across the street had discovered that the plain white box made a perfect projection screen for pornographic movies.

Nowlan first saw Learning on stage at the Playhouse as part of a dance program. During the pauses when dancers were changing into new costumes, various performers from around the city read their favourite poems. Learning chose to read "Britain Street," and after the performance he received a note from Nowlan congratulating him on a fine interpretation. Their first face-to-face meeting occurred in 1970, when Leo Ferrari and his wife, Kathleen, invited Nowlan and Claudine for dinner at Walter and Lea Learning's home. Learning and Ferrari already knew each other and had a lot in common. Learning had done his undergraduate and master's degrees in philosophy at the University of New Brunswick before starting a doctorate in Australia. Ferrari, an Australian, had studied theology before coming to Canada to earn a doctorate in philosophy.

Learning had been eager to meet Nowlan in the flesh. The dinner party proceeded pleasantly until after dessert, when hosts and guests moved to the living room. Learning and Nowlan discovered a shared love of country music, and as they spun albums and chatted about their favourites, they fell into an argument about a Kitty Wells song. Learning said that one of her songs was called "It Wasn't God Who Made Honky-Tonk Angels." Nowlan maintained that the real title was "It Wasn't God That Made Honky-Tonk Angels" and accused Learning of phony genteelism. It was one of those Nowlan arguments over nothing in which the participants were supposed to change sides halfway through, just as he and Buss Oliver had done at the *Observer* many years before. With Claudine's prompting, he made his exit with the Ferraris. "Well, that's probably the last time I'll ever be invited there," he remarked to the professor.

But Learning was made of more jovial stuff than the academics Nowlan was accustomed to insulting, and each man was delighted to have found in the other someone equally disputatious. With his impresario's eye, Learning saw a way in which their "animosity" could be used to create drama almost as good as the performances on the TNB stage. As the renovations were under way in February of 1972, a reporter asked Learning why TNB had never staged a Canadian play and if it would do so in its next season. He replied off-handedly that he had not read any good Canadian plays; at any rate, ninety per cent of the new drama written every year was garbage, and it was difficult to cull the ten per cent that was any good. "Learning Says '90 Per Cent of Canadian Plays Are Garbage,'" the February 21, 1972, *Daily Gleaner* announced; the press ran with the story, and it went national. This was not the type of controversy the director had in mind, especially when Nowlan chided him in his next *Telegraph* column: "It isn't as if Theatre New Brunswick produced only American and English masterpieces. Many of the plays performed here have been sheer froth and bubble, no different from the ordinary television fare except that the actors appeared 'live and in person' instead of on a screen in the living room."[14]

The gauntlet was thrown down. Learning found opportunities to harass his friend in other ways: when Nowlan showed up late to a performance of *Dracula*, dressed in a top hat and long black cape, Learning very publicly ejected him from the theatre. More unflattering references to his nemesis, Walter Learning, followed in other *Telegraph-Journal* columns penned by Nowlan. It was all in good fun — and good publicity — but not everyone shared in the joke. One prominent elderly lady offered the director the free services of her lawyer in case he wanted to sue Nowlan for his slander; the offer was never accepted.

With Learning, Nowlan had become the centre of New Brunswick's cultural community. In the summer of 1972 a crew from the CBC-TV program *Telescope* came to film a documentary about the poet, and made him do such things as waiting an hour for a heron to take flight while he repeated the line, "I write poems as a child might talk to an imaginary playmate." The experience caused him to reflect on the process of creativity and the artist's sometimes limited power over his subject. "[I] understand their trickery is no different/ from mine," he writes of the film crew in his poem "On Being the Subject of a Documentary." "It is only in films/ that the animated tube complains/ aloud at the manner/ in which the user squeezes it."

The deal between the University of New Brunswick and the provincial government that allowed Nowlan to remain writer-in-residence during the 1971-1972 year did not make onerous demands on New Brunswick's "poet laureate." No longer was there any question about keeping Nowlan at UNB, but now that he was installed there — permanently, as far as anyone could tell — what was to be done with him? In the spring of 1972 he had completed a guidebook to the New Brunswick legislature. "Not art, I assure you. Hack work, thrown my way by our beneficent provincial government," he wrote to Sylvia. "But if you ever want to know anything about the NB Legislative Assembly Building, just ask."[15]

John Metcalf was invited to be UNB's writer-in-residence (or rather, co-writer-in-residence with Nowlan) for the 1972-1973 academic year. The English department came up with a strategy to maintain the connection with Nowlan by making him a Canadian Studies consultant, a semi-academic position in which he would consult with graduate students and adjudicate theses; in this way, he would earn his provincial government stipend. Nowlan approved.

The government had other ideas for the use of its money. Hearing that the Roosevelt Campobello International Park Commission wanted someone to write a history of Campobello Island, Hatfield suggested that Nowlan undertake the task. Campobello sits off the extreme southwest coast of New Brunswick. Although it is connected to the rest of Canada by a seasonal ferry, it is accessible in winter only by causeway from Lubec, Maine. The commission invited Nowlan and Claudine to be their guests on the island for a week in early September, 1972, so they could explain what they wanted in this book. The Nowlans did not know that being "guests" meant having the use of a luxurious twelve-bedroom cottage next to the famous Roosevelt cottage, where FDR and his family spent many carefree summers. The amenities included the services of a maid, a cook, a gardener, and a security man who opened the gate for the Nowlans' old Pontiac while tourists gawked and snapped photos of what they thought was a celebrity couple. It took Nowlan a couple of days to summon up the courage to fix himself a drink from the well-stocked bar. "Gawd," he wrote when he returned on September 6. "How that glittering taketh me."[16] Even so, he would have liked the UNB job instead of doing "a piece of straight journalistic hack work that I'd prefer not to have to do."[17] But the Canada Horizons grant that the commission had applied for on Nowlan's behalf succeeded and the UNB scheme did not, and so he was saddled with a long-term, sustained prose project that he was secretly afraid to tackle.

For at least two years, he had been trying to knit together another novel, with limited success. He wrote disconnected chapters which he published separately as short stories. The prize-winning "There Was an Old Woman from Wexford" was one of these, and in 1972 the story "Life and Times" also won the President's Medal. Despite the accolades his short fiction received, Nowlan picked away unenthusiastically at a larger fiction that would unite them in a single work.

> I'd like to have a book-length manuscript ready by the fall [of 1970], but I don't know, I'm all thumbs when it comes to doing fiction. Besides the stories are set in the Nova Scotia village of my childhood and youth, and that's growing dimmer. I've got other obsessions now, which I work out in poems. It's almost as though my childhood had begun to bore me. Maybe that means I'm at last approaching maturity! But I still feel I have to get the book out of the way. It's something I have to do. But it's mostly drudgery, except for bits and pieces where I'm writing well.[18]

The drudgery continued through the autumn of 1972. He was busier than ever as he worked simultaneously on two frustrating projects: the Campobello history and a novel that seemed to have no focus. He could not find time for his favourite occupation, poetry, nor for the congenial company of friends he had come to depend on. He told Stewart, "It feels — as it has before on similar occasions — as if I were never going to write another poem."[19]

The King had gone to Britain that fall for a year — not to reclaim his throne but to work and to see a bit of Europe. In fact, Johnnie (by now "John" to everyone but his parents), the Frasers and Dave Richards had all migrated to various parts of Europe. After coming home from Vancouver for the Christmas of 1971, John went to work in the woods near Moncton during the winter of 1972. As during the previous winter, he saved his money for a personal odyssey, this time to Europe. In August, 1972, he flew to France, toured the continent and returned home for New Year's. Ray Fraser received a Canada Council grant in the spring of 1972 to complete his first short story collection, *Black Horse Tavern* (1973). He and Sharon moved to Chatham for the summer and lived on a small fishing boat that he bought for $650. Perhaps thinking of his forthcoming trip to Europe, he named the boat *Spanish Jack*. Ray and Sharon left for Spain in January, 1973; Dave and Peggy Richards joined them there until the Frasers returned in the spring.

Left with little to distract him from the arduous task of finishing two book-length prose works, and with family discord playing in the background, Nowlan worked away at the manuscript of his novel, *Life and Times*, putting aside the Campobello project for the time being. The

Jim Stewart and Claudine Nowlan aboard Ray and Sharon Fraser's boat, *Spanish Jack.* <small>SHARON FRASER</small>

conditions in which he wrote this novel were very different from the ones in which he wrote the *The Wanton Troopers*. In 1961 he was a promising but still largely unknown writer with a burning need to recreate the story of his youth, a story which still lay in his desk drawer, read by only a few people. More than ten years later, he was a writer of national importance, struggling to maintain a Johnsonian persona in a provincial university town while confronted by the ghosts of his past, which had become reanimated to haunt him again. Nowlan had always written unselfconsciously about himself and the life he knew around him. Now he cast about for some way of accounting for his fictional and poetic worlds, the public persona, and the private life on which all of these were based.

Although Nowlan referred to the book as a novel, it turned out to be a series of short fiction pieces that he linked thematically with one or two pages of a frame story in which the narrator, a journalist named Kevin O'Brien, reminisces about various events from his youth during his first trip home in many years. The disjointed form of the novel reflects the almost schizophrenic way the author was by that time forced to make sense of his identity:

[Kevin] has tried over the years to find the meaning of various incidents in his life and to give form to them. The briefcase that he carries with him on this trip contains a number of manuscripts in which he has attempted to explore and explain his past. But though the plot may be fixed the pattern is constantly changing. The childhood Kevin remembers at twenty-five is different from the childhood he remembered at twenty. The childhood that he will remember should he happen to be alive twenty years from now will be something else again. Already he has watched his youth undergo its first transformation. Certain persons and places have grown in importance, while others have dissolved into insignificance and are almost forgotten. The protagonist changes too. The teenaged Kevin O'Brien that the twenty-five-year-old Kevin O'Brien remembers was piteously young for his years, whereas that person considered himself to be unusually mature; there were even times when he thought of himself as an old man. The matter is complicated further by the fact that none of these former selves will die until the final Kevin O'Brien is dead. (pp. 23-24)

This is what Nowlan wanted his audience to believe about the author, too, as the subtitle of the novel, *A Fictional Memoir*, strongly suggests. The novel's title, *Various Persons Named Kevin O'Brien*, reinforces the possibility that a writer, be it Kevin O'Brien or Alden Nowlan, may change his past and present at will.

Years after Nowlan's death, academic examinations of Nowlan's writing have focused as much on *Various Persons Named Kevin O'Brien* as they have on Nowlan's poetry, a credit to the man who always downplayed the success of his own fiction. In particular, the different narrative voices of the various Kevin O'Briens competing against one another have provoked scholarly criticism. Paul Milton sees Nowlan's novel in light of the literary theories of Mikhail Bakhtin, who promoted the idea that all novels are populated by different narrative voices, various persons who compete with each other in an effort to tell the reader the same story. In Milton's opinion, Nowlan purposely constructed his novel in this way to represent the voices of various critics who had commented on his poetry and short fiction. He thinks that, because the

The Encounter, The Recognition

There's a path through the woods, or a corridor
in an empty building. I enter it
at both ends and walk slowly toward myself.
I am wholly drunk.
                    I am wholly sober.
We meet midway
                    and recognize one another.
"Hello, Alden," I say.

That's how my best poems are created.

name of the man that Kevin punches out in the final chapter of *Various Persons Named Kevin O'Brien*, Bob D'Entremount, recalls the setting of Ernest Buckler's novel *The Mountain and the Valley*, Entremount, Nowlan symbolically wishes to overcome Buckler himself. Milton evidently did not realize that Nowlan's only overall plan for the novel was to stitch together his group of short stories in a convincing way.[20]

In her 1987 study of Maritime literature, Janice Kulyk Keefer accorded high praise to Nowlan's work, *Various Persons Named Kevin O'Brien* in particular. While acknowledging that "it is certain that no case can be made for the 'superiority' of a text like *Various Persons Named Kevin O'Brien* over Buckler's acknowledged masterpiece," she nonetheless singled out Nowlan's use of language as more successful at conveying the harsh realities of his fictional world than Buckler was in describing his:

> In *Kevin O'Brien* Nowlan uses language to create an anatomy of poverty, making us see and know "his" people, and as importantly, interrogating his own relation to literacy, that power which has both rescued and alienated him from "his own." This "fictional memoir" is the story of a returned prodigy, not prodigal; it is a self-conscious narrative in a much different sense than is *The Mountain and the Valley*. Buckler's narrative consciousness is supersaturated with the sense of his role as priest of the Annapolis Valley imagination, its aesthetic smithy. Nowlan's O'Brien, on the other hand, is obsessed both with his own sense of dislocation . . . and with the problematic nature of truth wherever memory and human relations are involved. He is out to present Lockhartville as he finds it and not, like Buckler, to "make the light shine kindly" on its people.[21]

The mask Nowlan (as opposed to Kevin) would now assume was his seemingly total honesty, the thesis that he, too, could be several different people at once. His first poetry collection of the 1970s, *Between Tears and Laughter*, strikes a more conversational tone than his previous collections; the poetic structure is looser, mimicking the rhythms of human speech almost as if the poet was "holding forth" to the reader while sitting in his comfortable chair. "In a very definitive sense Nowlan *is* his poems, the majority of which seem to be ostensibly casual transcriptions of his experiences," Sam Solecki said in a review of the collection for *Queen's Quarterly*.[22] But is the poetic "I" or Kevin O'Brien separable from Alden Nowlan the man? No contract exists between a writer and his audience stipulating that the author write only the factual truth. Nowlan nonetheless felt more and more compelled to insist that what he was writing *was* the truth, that "Nowlan has seen and heard and touched and smelt and tasted everything he ever wrote about." In an interview conducted shortly after he finished *Various Persons Named Kevin O'Brien*, Nowlan said:

> It's embarrassing that you should bring up this point about the truth because there was a period at which I was actually handicapped because I had such a commitment to truth. When I was writing a short story or a poem, no matter how incongruous or how absurd some development was, if it actually happened I'd be committed to put down the thing. I felt it was sort of a betrayal or sin to tamper with reality in any way. I finally discovered that sometimes in art you can tell the truth best by lying. But it was a very difficult discovery for me to make.[23]

The fact that he cared at all whether a reader accepted the literal truth of his fiction is indicative of the extent to which Nowlan believed that writers ought to tell the truth — or at least a near approximation of it — in their writing. Despite his claim to feel more at ease with the slippery nature of his own version of the truth, he was still uncomfortable with those who impinged upon his self-created mythos.

By the beginning of 1973, Nowlan had signed a contract with Clarke, Irwin for his first published novel. Now he had other contractual obligations to honour, neither of which he relished. One was to his publisher, who had arranged a national reading tour in 1972 to promote *Between Tears and Laughter*. Nowlan had cancelled half an hour before his plane took off from Fredericton; he again gave poor health as his excuse. Now, in March of 1973, he decided that he would be able to tour western Canada for the League of Canadian Poets, as long as Claudine accompanied him. Elizabeth Brewster would also tour with him to promote her latest Clarke, Irwin poetry collection, *Sunrise*

North. For Nowlan the tour was perhaps the lesser of two evils. Work on *Various Persons Named Kevin O'Brien* allowed him to duck working on the Campobello book, but by 1973 there was no place left to hide. He tried to write about the Owen clan and the Roosevelts, two families whose stories dominate the history of the island. Mostly, in those early months, he worked from a manuscript by a Mrs. Gallagher, a local lady who had compiled but not published a Campobello history; the commission had bought the rights to the manuscript. But the material did not excite him; his important work was as a creative writer, not as a historian-for-hire. The continuing need for distraction might have been one of the factors that persuaded him to undertake the long and ambitious western Canadian reading tour.

"Welcome to the Gateway to the Golden West," the cowboy greeted him, Claudine and Elizabeth Brewster at the Regina airport on March 17, 1973. By that point, they did not feel in a mood to be welcomed. In the past five days Nowlan and Brewster had read at colleges and universities in Winnipeg, Brandon, Saskatoon and Red Deer, and at two in Vancouver. They had waited in Vancouver International Airport for two and a half hours for the fog to lift, Brewster and Nowlan trying unsuccessfully to pass the time writing. Nowlan, squeezed into a little plastic chair, switched to doodling. Now, in Regina, they were lost in a swirl of costumed people who looked as though they were having a Wild West Mardi Gras: Mexican banditos, cowboys, sheriffs, outlaws and saloon girls. Some of these people embraced Nowlan's party or handed them buttons and pamphlets. A band played in the background. It turned out that they were in the middle of arriving conventioneers.

They had come to expect this type of foul-up. Touring and The Nowlan did not get along; typically, he read in only one or two centres over a period not exceeding a couple of days. Claudine acted as his assistant on this tour, carrying books along with her to sell after the readings, making sure he did not tire himself out, and, just as important, preventing him from drinking too much. Stuck in the melee at the Regina airport, they searched for the man from the University of Saskatchewan who was supposed to meet them, Professor Lloyd Person; they had no idea what he looked like. It was Saturday — St. Patrick's Day as far as Nowlan was concerned — and so the university was closed. Directory assistance was of little help; there was no listing for Person. So they waited. Then they took a taxi to the hotel.

Their reading, scheduled for Sunday evening, did not come off at all, since they had still not made contact with the professor. Brewster, who by then taught at the University of Saskatchewan in Saskatoon, left on Monday morning. Before catching his flight to Toronto, Nowlan made one last try; he called the university switchboard.

"Oh, yes," Person said from his office. "We read some of your poems — yours and Miss Brewster's — to the audience, but then it seemed you wouldn't come, so we cancelled."

The mess was not Person's fault, either. This was Nowlan's first tour under the auspices of the League of Canadian Poets, and it seemed to be their first tour, too. Person had indeed gone out to the airport on Saturday, but the League did not tell him which plane they would be on, where it was coming from, or where the poets were staying in Regina. The poets' list of contacts did not include home phone numbers or campus maps. Worse, upon making up his list of expenses for the league, he discovered that the $25 he was allotted per day was supposed to cover his hotel accommodations as well as his meals. But the league had often booked him into hotels that cost more than his entire daily allowance. With Claudine along at his expense, he found that the $125 he was paid for each reading barely put him ahead at the end of the day.

Even his publisher was after him. A March 19 reading at York University in Toronto was his last stop on his way home. Phoning ahead from Winnipeg, he was chided by Clarke, Irwin's promotion manager, Mary Lawson, for a publicity photograph he had sent to promote *Various Persons Named Kevin O'Brien*.

"You ass," she said. "That picture makes you look like a bloody bank manager." The picture showed him neatly coiffed and wearing a shirt and tie. "Don't you have a turtleneck sweater?"

"No, turtlenecks emphasize my paunch," he said.

"All right, I'll buy you a bloody turtleneck."

When he and Claudine landed in Toronto, Lawson met them and drove them to George Richards Big and Tall Shop, where Nowlan, helpless, modelled sweaters and a couple of shirts that Claudine wanted him to try. Lawson negotiated with the clerk for the sweater, Claudine for the shirts, and the poet amused himself by pretending he was mute. Later, he posed in the St. Lawrence Market for the photographer, dressed in his turtleneck and trying to look writerly.

Upon his return from the exhausting tour, Nowlan lay in bed for over a week with a viral infection. It was not just excuse-making when he wrote from his sickbed to the Campobello Commission to say that he would not be able to meet their original June 1, 1973, deadline for the book. David Walker, the chairman of the Campobello history book committee, gladly extended the deadline to August. By June 30 Nowlan was back on the island for a week to take another crack at the research. He and Claudine shared the twelve-bedroom cottage with his "research assistant," Dave Richards, and his wife, Peggy, back from their trip to Spain. This sojourn was not the luxury vacation of the previous Campobello trip. The history of Campobello had not held Nowlan's interest up to that point because it lacked a human element. What had happened at Campobello in the past was a matter of record, but what was happening now? He and Richards combed the island, interviewing people, visiting graveyards and taking in the atmosphere. Nowlan's strength as a non-fiction writer was the human angle, giving his subject a face and a heart. He finally began to warm to his subject, and, back in Fredericton, he again asked Walker for an extended deadline. His request was again cheerfully granted. The first draft of the Campobello book was submitted to the committee on November 6.

There were other obstacles to surmount, such as finding a publisher. The commission intended to publish the book themselves, but they lacked experience. Nowlan suggested his own publishers, who could offer a wider distribution network than the gift shop at the Roosevelt Cottage. He trusted Clarke, Irwin and Louise Dennys, the editor who had worked with him on *Various Persons Named Kevin O'Brien*. But he did not trust the judgement of some of the other committee members, who had their own well-intentioned but narrower agendas that did not necessarily embrace the demands of the trade book market. Bill Clarke wanted to secure the rights to the book and to ensure a royalty for Nowlan, even though it was a commissioned work. That spring, he flew down to Fredericton, and he and Nowlan hitched a ride to Campobello with the lieutenant-governor of New Brunswick, Hédard Robichaud, who would negotiate on the province's behalf. The party travelled in style in the lieutenant-governor's limousine, but the posh surroundings this time grated on Nowlan's proletarian sensibility.

Robichaud talked about the trials of being the Queen's representative in New Brunswick. "It's not all that easy, you know," he said from the back seat of the limousine, where he was sitting with Nowlan. "You are always in the public eye, you have to live far from your hometown at the official residence, and then there's all the pomp and circumstance."

"Isn't one of your functions to be the commander-in-chief of the New Brunswick militia?" Clarke asked from the front seat. By this time they had crossed the American border on the way to the causeway at Lubec.

"Yes, it is. Why?"

"I'm just wondering what the Americans might think about the commander-in-chief of a foreign militia cruising through their country with the Union Jack flying on his limo."

"By God, you're right. I hadn't thought of that."

So Robichaud had his driver pull over and take the little flags off the front of the car while Nowlan watched, speechless.

David Walker awaited the party at the FDR cottage, where the contract was to be discussed. There were drinks and a table set up downstairs, and the staff had prepared some rooms on the upper storey where the men would stay. The men took a few minutes to put their things away and freshen up. But Nowlan took a little longer than a few minutes to come down and join the others. Suddenly they heard the crash of Nowlan stumbling down the stairs. Somehow he had managed to get himself completely drunk. "Assholes, assholes," he muttered as he stormed past Walker and Robichaud, who were terrified at the transformation.

It was close to dinnertime, so the men sat down, Clarke next to Nowlan's empty place. Dinner had just been served when Nowlan floundered back in, plunked himself down beside Clarke and devoured an entire fish. Clarke could not allow his friend to sign any contract in his state, so he suggested a stroll after dinner. Nowlan vented his frustrations about all rich phonies, then suddenly embraced Clarke and said, "The aristocrats and the peasants must rise together." Then they went back in and negotiated the contract. The next morning, when he was supposed to sign it, Nowlan arose bright and early and went down to have breakfast. He was chatting and laughing with the kitchen staff as Walker and Robichaud stumbled down into the dining room, looking as if they had slept poorly. Nowlan was equally friendly with the chauffeur on the way back to Fredericton. The limousine was one passenger lighter, the lieutenant-governor having elected to find another way home.[24]

Nowlan delivered the final manuscript of *Campobello: The Outer Island* to Clarke, Irwin on May 13, 1974. Nowlan's relief at having completed this most difficult project was palpable. He summed up his feelings to Louise Dennys: "With this book, I feel that I am about to be discharged from a minimum security prison where while paying my debt to society I used toothpicks, rubber bands and paper clips to build a rather impressive model boat."[25]

That day was actually more like the end of his parole than his release from prison. He had been working on another major project since the previous fall, after he submitted the first draft of the Campobello history. Walter Learning had taken up his friend's challenge about producing a Canadian play and had thrown it back at him: if Nowlan thought the plays at Theatre New Brunswick were so frothy, then why did he not write one himself? The two of them had begun to consider writing and producing their own play at TNB. The success of *Dracula* had excited Nowlan, whose young mind had been nurtured on horror dramas heard over the battery-powered radio at his house in Stanley. They settled on an adaptation of Mary Shelley's *Frankenstein*, a classic novel that they felt had been corrupted by Hollywood's influence, Boris Karloff staggering about the screen in grotesque makeup with a bolt through his neck. The two men wanted to do the story justice, including reversing the popular impression that "Frankenstein" is the name of the Creature, rather than of the Baron. Nowlan engaged Learning as a collaborator, someone who could help him convert his ideas into dramatic form. "I think of Walter as the deformed Igor and myself as the Baron,"[26] he told his son, John. But as the writing continued, he saw himself more and more as the Creature, gigantic but emotionally helpless, rejected by those around him.

Family events in the autumn of 1973 forced Nowlan to revisit the feelings of rejection he had endured as a child. One shock came in a letter from Freeman. A fire had burnt him out of his new house. He was unhurt but had lost most of what little he owned, so the people of Stanley had brought in an old cabin from the woods and set it up on his land. Another shock was a surprise visit from Aunt Ervette and Uncle Albert.

There was to be a party at Windsor Castle that night, September 22, to celebrate "the 228th Anniversary of the sacred, glorious and immortal victory of the forces of His Royal Highness the Prince Charles Edward over the hirelings and dupes of the usurping Elector of Hanover at the Battle of Prestonpans."[27] He reported to Sylvia:

[I] started to drink at two o'clock that afternoon after I got a telephone call informing me that your and my Aunt Ervette and Uncle Albert were in town and were coming to see me! As soon as I put down the telephone I poured myself a triple Beefeater. I hadn't seen Ervette in, oh, maybe fifteen years and hadn't seen Albert since I was ten. The thought of seeing them again after so many years terrified me. That is no exaggeration. While waiting for them to arrive I had another triple Beefeater and when I looked out the window and saw that their group was large enough to fill two cars I dashed to the kitchen and downed a third triple Beefeater while Claudine answered the door. There was Ervette. There was Albert. There was Albert's wife, Doll. There was Albert's wife Doll's sister. There were Albert's two sons. There was Ervette's daughter, Dora, and Ervette's daughter Dora's husband and two children . . . And there was poor old Alden confronted by a sea of ghosts. Not that it would have been unpleasant, if it hadn't been for the ghosts — Ervette did most of the talking and her daughter seems very warm and nice and quite sensitive and intelligent. Poor old Albert seemed to be almost stone deaf. "It's a Reese ailment," Ervette said. "All the Reeses go deaf." One thing that struck me as both incredible and poignant was the information that this was Albert's first time outside Nova Scotia.[28]

Nowlan, too worn out from the afternoon to preside over his Prestonpans party, retired well before midnight and allowed the revels to continue without him.

As autumn fell into winter, Learning and Nowlan cooked up a play designed to move and frighten the audience. Nowlan trusted his friend's judgement completely. A partnership developed: Nowlan became the man who wrote (and often acted out) the dialogue; Learning knew how to edit the ideas, turn them into a workable script, put the script into production and sell the play to other theatres. Typically Nowlan would write an act, and his collaborator would take it home to read it and make notes. The two men would then get together for an evening or an afternoon and smoke packs of cigarettes while hashing out what had been written. Learning initially did most of the talking, his partner often interjecting a grunt of understanding. But after a while Nowlan warmed up to the material and expanded on his own thoughts about the play. By the spring of 1974, it looked as though they had a hit on their hands, TNB's first world premiere.

Nowlan was just as excited over the production of *Frankenstein* as he was over creating it. He sat in on rehearsals whenever he could. The actor who was to play the Creature, David Brown, impressed him immensely, and they became friends. The poet was touched at how the actor could embody emotions he had had to live with his entire life. "You must have suffered terribly at some point in your life to be able to project such anguished loneliness,"[29] he later wrote to Brown. Director Timothy Bond sometimes suggested line changes during rehearsals, which Nowlan would draft on the spot. On one of his wanders through the bowels of the Playhouse he happened upon a young man building a fence. He looked up from his work.

"You Nowlan?" he asked.

"Yes, I am."

"A human brain in a bell jar is no problem and a trick staircase is a cinch," he said solemnly. "But an exploding light bulb — man!" This was the properties man.

In Nowlan and Learning's hands, the Creature lost the monster connotations inflicted by Hollywood. Nowlan started to invest a lot of himself in the Creature's personality. He would write later to a friend:

> I don't think you ever saw the stage version of *Frankenstein* that I did in collaboration with Walter Learning. I did most of the actual writing (apart from what we stole from Mary Shelley). I mention this because I used to tell people who asked if *Various Persons Named Kevin O'Brien* was auto-biographical that, no, I had done my autobiographical writing in the stage version of *Frankenstein*.
>
> They'd always laugh. But the real joke was that I was telling the truth. I could readily identify with The Creature (I never think of him as a Monster and he isn't a Monster in the play, not really) who was absolutely and hopelessly alone. The Creature was me when I was 16.[30]

This identification became almost obsessive, especially as the opening date drew nearer. On July 12, 1974, Ferrari told Fraser:

Of course Alden has so identified with the Creature that Claudine is getting increasingly apprehensive about being alone with him. He goes round the house dragging his foot behind him and saying, "You called, Master?" Claudine says that he even wakes up in the middle of the night saying it. All the world's become his stage. He refuses to draw his living room curtains and acts out the parts of the play for the benefit of the people in the apartment across the street.[31]

Acting the part of the Creature did not fade with time. Years later, a friend might get a phone call late at night, or any victim in any setting (it once happened to a taxi driver) might suddenly feel meaty fingers around his or her neck and hear Nowlan's strangled whisper as he uttered the Creature's line, "It will all be over quickly. There will be almost no pain." Some people thought he was going insane, just as his Stanley neighbours had when they heard him crying out to God from his darkened house in the middle of the night. In drama, he found another way besides writing to externalize his inner fantasy world. But the date of Ferrari's letter suggests that other events might have been driving Nowlan towards at least a temporary madness.

Though Ferrari could not have known it, just as he was writing his letter Nowlan was trying to deal with some momentous news. On July 11 Freeman had passed away, quickly and quietly, in his cabin. "The poor old man's death was no tragedy, it was his life that was unutterably sad," he eulogized to John, then in Vancouver. "He lived seventy years, worked like a slave and left nothing but an empty pocketbook and the deed to a quarter acre of land." But Nowlan never delivered a eulogy in person. "Your beautiful and precious mother was a tower of strength for me," the letter to John continued.[32] What he did not say was that she was also his stand-in. He wanted things done right, but he would not go to the funeral himself. He phoned his friend Ian Cameron, who was vacationing that weekend in Nova Scotia, and asked him to go and play the bagpipes at Freeman's graveside. Claudine carried his instructions to the mortician: there would be no suit and tie for his father. Freeman met his Maker wearing what he wore every day, his work clothes.

On top of the last-minute pressures of dealing with his father's death, Sylvia and Jim paid another visit to see her honorary brother and to take in opening night of *Frankenstein*. They arrived just before

My Father's Body Was Found by Children

My father's body was
found by children.
Boys from the neighbourhood
who thought he was asleep
in his chair until
they came back the next day
and saw he hadn't moved.
Children often visited him,
I'm told. He'd wrestle
with them if he was drunk,
converse with them soberly
at other times. His shack
was the sort of dwelling
a twelve-year-old would
build for himself,
in his last years he lived
the way a small boy would
if allowed to live alone.
Huck Finn at seventy.

To think he might have been
a child all his life
if less had been asked
of him and more had been given.
To think I'm afraid
of him, even now,
half-expecting to look out
some night and see him
standing there:
I fear that most.

Nowlan received news of his father's death. Though Claudine flew to Halifax alone, she and Sylvia had made arrangements for Nowlan to follow if he had a last-minute change of heart. But he did not. Instead, he slept furtively in two or three-hour bouts. Sylvia and Jim went out for Chinese food — one of Nowlan's favourite treats — and persuaded him to eat. No doubt some of the words of his play haunted him, especially the scene in which the rejected Creature confronts a Frankenstein who thought his creation was dead.

> CREATURE (*Moves a step towards VICTOR*): You cast me forth, a poor helpless miserable creature tormented by hunger, thirst and cold.
> VICTOR: I could not bear the burden of what I had created.
> CREATURE: And what of my burden? I could distinguish no sensation but pain. I lived in a pig-sty and ate the slops which are their food. For a time I could not speak but only babble like a beast.
> VICTOR: I didn't wish it so. (*Woefully*) I wanted to create something beautiful. . . .
> CREATURE (*Losing control*): Accursed creator! Why did you form a monster so hideous that even you turned from me in disgust? God in pity made man in His own image. But my form is a filthy imitation of yours, made more horrible by its very resemblance. (p. 43)

Nowlan was a nervous wreck on the day before the play's opening. The open dress rehearsal, known as "buck night," gave people a chance to see the play for a reduced price before it officially opened the next night. "You'd better go home and come back tomorrow night," Tim Bond advised Nowlan when he arrived Tuesday night, July 16, for the dress rehearsal. "This one's going to be hell."

Nowlan peeked in at the audience. Among the crowd of college students was a rowdy group of elementary and junior high school kids who were shooting spitballs and paper planes, a far cry from the audience they had envisioned. It was definitely a tough crowd, but he had to stay to see if his Creature could win them over.

And win them over he did. The properties man had made the play a dazzling event, with the brain in a bell jar, the trick staircase, the exploding light bulb and many other magical moments besides. But it was the authenticity of the story that won their hearts. The kids tittered only during the love scenes, and they gave the performance a standing ovation at the end. *Frankenstein* was indeed a hit.

Despite the success of the preview, Nowlan dithered around the house the next day, catching up with Sylvia and Jim and trying to forget about how Fredericton's adult audience would react to the Creature. Sylvia remembers his dread. "He couldn't stop time, but he wanted to pass over the opening and let time continue. He wrote the play from the heart. Alden was like the Creature in so many ways; the play was personal to him."[33] He balked at getting dressed up for the occasion, but Claudine, back from Freeman's funeral, had Sylvia and Jim persuade him to don a jacket and tie. He compromised with a turtleneck and a pair of dress pants.

Once seated in the balcony, he started to relax. He gripped Sylvia's hand with his left hand and Claudine's with his right. In the audience were many who had known the author from various times in his life. Claudine's brother John and his wife came down from Hartland, and Fred Hazel and his family came up from Saint John. Virtually everyone in the theatre had read his poetry, but his soul was about to be more exposed than it had ever been. After the curtain rose, Nowlan began to do a curious thing, a habit that would continue whenever he sat in an audience watching one of his plays. He began a sort of mumbling chorus commenting on the audience's reaction to the play, which was as enthusiastic as it had been the night before. If they applauded at a point where he felt applause was inappropriate, the people nearby could hear him murmuring his disapproval. They might also hear him comment on the way a character spoke a line, and he was especially vocal in moments of silence when he felt the audience should have laughed at one of his jokes.

None of this deterred the audience from a four-minute standing ovation at the end of the play, and the cry of "Author!" At first he remained seated and acknowledged the applause of the people below him, but Lea Learning at last led him to the stage, where he embraced Walter Learning, David Brown, and the actor who portrayed Viktor Frankenstein, Peter Jobin. As the curtain went down, a champagne-laden table came up through the stage trap door, and the party began. Fred Hazel was one of the many who came back to the green room after the play. Claudine was walking around with a single rose in her hand and a look of bliss on her face. Hazel's two daughters had Nowlan sign their programs, and for weeks afterwards they re-enacted *Frankenstein* scenarios in Hazel's garage. The poet circulated with a glass of champagne in one hand and a glass of gin in the other, introducing people he knew to the Creature and then, later, introducing David Brown (out of makeup) to the very same people, an indication of how deeply he entertained the fantasy of the Creature's literal existence.

The success of the play, his reunion with Sylvia and the death of his father made for a bittersweet week. Still, he felt bathed in a glow of love that he had seldom before experienced. He would later write to Sylvia:

> It was so bloody wonderful to have you and Jim here. After all those hundreds of letters and dozens of telephone calls it would have been too bad if we'd been disillusioned with each other when at last we met face to face. . . . Now you are truly my sister, having seen me drunkenly incoherent and in mindless rages — and yet continuing to love me. The frosting on the cake being that we all love each other, you, Jim, Claudine and I. I couldn't tell you how touched I was that he wanted me to sign the book: "To my brother."[34]

But, at the same time as Nowlan accepted Sylvia as his adoptive sister, he shut the door at last on his biological one. The evening of the day Sylvia and Jim left for home, Nowlan answered a phone call.

"Alden, this is your sister, Harriet. Why in God's name haven't you told me that our dad just died?"

A chill ran through his veins at hearing Harriet's voice again after so long. "Well," he began. "For one thing, I haven't heard from you in twenty years, so how could I tell you anything? I don't even know where you live anymore, or even what your married name is . . ."

"I wrote you two years ago telling you that, but you didn't answer. Is it too much for you to write back to your own family?"

He responded by hanging up.

At three o'clock in the morning, the phone rang. This time, Claudine answered it. It was Harriet again. "I want to talk to that son of a bitch of a brother of mine."

After a few minutes of trying to be polite but getting angrier at long-lost family members intruding on her husband's life, Claudine finally snapped, "Listen, you, don't give me any of that welfare whine. I've heard about you, my girl. You didn't give a damn for your poor old father when he was alive. Why the hell would you want to look at him when he's dead? If it's the estate you're concerned about, he owned a $500 shack. You're welcome to it. Now get the hell out of our lives." This time Harriet hung up.

Again the phone rang and Claudine answered.

"This is Richard Ernest Ottie," the voice began. Harriet's husband. "You've insulted my wife."

"I don't give a goddamn if you're Franklin Delano Roosevelt. Nobody could insult your wife." And she hung up.

Claudine returned to bed. "Sometimes it's best not to be too subtle," she told her husband.[35]

After the excitement of July, there was time in August for a bit of repose. The King, Jim Stewart, had chosen his Queen, Jane, and was to be wed in Rothesay, New Brunswick, a suburb of Saint John. And he would have none other than his faithful Prince of Fortara and Duke of Wexford as his best man. Nowlan was delighted, having served as best man to another former University of New Brunswick student and friend, Lindsay Buck, two years earlier.

Appropriately for a Celtic king, the entire wedding party dressed in tartan, and the bride was piped into the church to the tune of "Mairi's Wedding." The kilts for Nowlan and Stewart had to be ordered from Halifax and did not arrive until two and a half hours before the ceremony. The delay added another level of stress for the groom, who was planning on going regimental (that is, without underpants) instead of wearing his usual boxer shorts. Nowlan stayed away from the drink, did not lose the ring, and gave a wonderful speech at the reception. From his vantage point, the continuity of the monarchy and the good times and fellowship that went with it were assured. He was with his real family, the "Royal Family," and his imaginary kingdom was made flesh.

TEN

The Night of the Party

Never have I seen women
wiser or more beautiful.

Never have I known men
so witty, so sensitive.

Here in my living room
are the twenty most remarkable
persons in all the world.

And me, the one fool,
who must dance
although too heavy
on his feet, sing
although his vocal cords
are out of tune.

But that is the price
I pay for such
companionship.

My friends,
I do not get drunk for myself,
I get drunk for you.

Amid the drama of 1974, with the death of Freeman and the resounding success of his and Learning's play *Frankenstein*, Nowlan sounded a much quieter note with the release in the fall of his eighth collection of new poetry, *I'm a Stranger Here Myself*, and praise for the book was modest.

John Robert Colombo in the *Tamarack Review* is genuine in his admiration when he writes about *I'm a Stranger Here Myself*, "Whether the Nowlan-self is flitting mischievously through time and space, philosophizing, moralizing or storytelling, it does so in a convincing though deceptively simple manner, sprinkling the recorded thoughts with grains of irony and laughter."[1] His comments are restrained compared with the buzz about Nowlan's poetry in the 1960s, when his contemporaries, though overly engaged with the question of regionalism, nonetheless predicted greatness rather than "philosophizing, moralizing or storytelling." In the *Canadian Forum*, Scott Lauder tries unsuccessfully to support his opening statement, "Alden Nowlan is the sort of talent who gives poetry a good name." At last he stumbles into the realization that the reader's trust sometimes "is abused elsewhere [in the book] by the infrequent intrusion of cloyingly precious children"; he concludes, "Certain poems in this collection might seem too slight and flimsy to warrant inclusion. . . . To be prepared to accept and embrace such trivia is small compensation for the decency and legitimacy of feeling Nowlan consistently offers us."[2]

A growing cadre of writers was not satisfied with the new direction Nowlan's poetry was taking. John Metcalf, who shared the 1972-1973 writer-in-residence position with Nowlan at UNB, was one of these:

> I've always admired [Nowlan's] early poetry, the poems in *The Rose and the Puritan, Under the Ice, Wind in a Rocky Country*, but with his *Bread, Wine and Salt* — which won the Governor General's Award — an aspect of his temperament which I consider detrimental to his poetry began to receive intensified expression. Some of the poetry became far too prosy and he gave in to the desire to be warm, wise, and "philosophical" — cracker-barrel philosophy. At the end of that road lies *Reader's Digest*.
>
> The arguments that Alden and I had on sentimentality were ferocious.[3]

Nowlan was creating his own poetic evolution. Most obviously he no longer relied on the metre and rhyme that made poems such as "God

Sour the Milk of the Knacking Wench" amusing and memorable. The shorter and looser line structure had mixed results, in some cases weakening his poetry by making it prosaic, in other instances strengthening and personalizing his authorial voice. In a 1975 interview with Metcalf, Nowlan explained his changing approach to line divisions as "attempts to find a typographical substitute for the purely visual and oral things that play such an important part in conversation — facial expressions, gestures of the hands, intonations of the voice."[4]

Michael Brian Oliver's 1978 study of Nowlan's poetry, *Poet's Progress*, stands alone in its attempt to chart the evolution in Nowlan's intimately conversational voice during his later period. "Nowlan has become, in fact, a domestic poet in the best sense of the term," Oliver writes of his poetry of the early 1970s. "His poems invite people into his home to share with him moments of insight, poignancy, despair, and laughter."[5] Critics who once faulted the poet for his preoccupation with regional subject matter now did not know how to take Nowlan's new preoccupation with that most universal of subjects, the struggle of everyman to make sense of life's little ironies. But Nowlan had by this point entirely stopped writing for critics, which is by far a more significant development than a mere change in subject matter. His first two collections of the 1970s show that he had made an important choice, as he explained to Metcalf: "*If* there comes a time when truck drivers read poetry, mine will be the poetry they'll read."[6]

The pile of fan letters from "ordinary readers" during this period attests to the success of this approach, and the most radical aspect of Nowlan's poetic sensibility is that he did in fact measure literary success by popularity. In an age of television, he could tear his readers away from their TVs long enough to read and think for a moment, a feat most of his contemporaries could not duplicate. His "art" may have suffered as a result, his poetry may at times have become prosaic and sentimental, but he made a conscious, clear-headed decision, unlike his indecision about Truth in his prose. Unnecessary as it may have been, he willingly sacrificed praise from the ivory tower so that people who would not normally read poetry would read his.

A weakness in this new approach dismayed academics and fellow writers alike: the signs of old-fashioned laziness. Some poems in *I'm a Stranger Here Myself*, such as "Four O'Clock in the Morning" and "The Chianti Drinker's Poem," seem to be thin efforts stretched over two pages of type. When read against his newspaper and magazine columns from the same period, some poems, such as "We Were Younger Then," contain almost verbatim passages from *Telegraph-Journal* or *Atlantic Advocate* columns.[7] Ever the professional scribbler, Nowlan would claim to friends that he had no qualms about recycling material for fun and profit, a troubling hint that his continued devotion to mass-audience journalism tempted him to make literary compromises.

Frankenstein paid off in several ways. Not only had it given Nowlan the thrill of learning to write in a new genre, but it also became a steady source of income as the play was produced by other theatres, including the Centaur Theatre in Montreal, Theatre London in London, Ontario, and the Vancouver Playhouse. Theatre New Brunswick remounted the production in the 1974-1975 season and toured it around the Maritimes and Newfoundland. When Clarke, Irwin published a book-length version of the play with an abridgement of Mary Shelley's novel in 1976, some critics preferred aspects of the Nowlan/Learning version over Shelley's.[8] Shortly after the play finished its first run at Theatre New Brunswick, Nowlan bought a brand new Plymouth Valiant and christened it "The Bride of Frankenstein," an indication of where he had found the means to get it. Claudine went on her own spree, buying a cupboard, a dining room table and six chairs. "Now we have a table that is worth more than our car,"[9] he told John.

His triumph with the play made Nowlan eager to take on new projects in previously untouched disciplines. *Shaped By This Land* (1974) was the catalogue of artist Tom Forrestall's nationally toured exhibition. Nowlan helped Forrestall find a publisher, Irving-owned Brunswick Press, through Ralph Costello. Costello suggested that the book might be strengthened if Forrestall's haunting images of Maritime scenes were accompanied by Nowlan's poems. Nowlan and Forrestall agreed to include a few older poems to evoke the stark scenes of rural life that inspired Forrestall. The result was a handsome coffee-table book.

Eager to capitalize on his dramatic success, Nowlan accepted an offer from CBC-TV to tackle a television script with Eric Nesterenko, a former NHL hockey player who was producing a film for CBC-TV. Tentatively called *The Last Game of the Finals*, the story is Nesterenko's semi-autobiographical tale of an ex-pro hockey player who tries to adjust to retirement while keeping one foot in the hockey world. Nowlan worked on it sporadically throughout 1975 but, as with *Campobello: The Outer Island*, he had a hard time writing on commission using someone else's ideas, and the script did not make it beyond the first draft. Even this netted him an extra $2400, $1200 on signing the contract and $1200 for completing that first draft. The pleasure of creation was an essential

Nicholas Catanoy with Tom Forrestall and Claudine and Alden Nowlan.

ingredient in Nowlan's writing process. He had trouble producing longer works on demand, as Robert Weaver discovered during the 1970s when he prodded Nowlan to write long, narrative poems for voices for CBC Radio. Nowlan eventually completed one of these, his long poem *Gardens of the Wind* (1982), but another Weaver enthusiasm, a narrative poem about the Irish Famine, failed to spark Nowlan's creative energies. "I suppose I was working against his instincts, but with the best of intentions," Weaver explains. "He didn't really like the idea of writing long poems, and yet he was prepared to do it as a kind of assignment."[10]

After the heady summer of 1974, Nowlan faced a lonely winter. As in 1970 and 1972, his circle of friends disintegrated as they left Fredericton to pursue their own dreams. Leo Ferrari took a sabbatical to study in Montreal during the 1974-1975 academic year, and the only comrade who dropped in from time to time was Walter Learning. "I feel a bit like the Last Survivor,"[11] he lamented. It was a familiar refrain. John was again out in Vancouver, working as a merchant sailor. He wrote home on June 4, 1974, to tell his parents that he and another fellow were picketing his ship over unpaid back wages. They chose an opportune time, since the ship was in dry dock and the union workers would not cross even their small picket line. "It was really enjoyable to screw the company & the captain," John wrote. "He had a bad habit of referring to the below decks people as niggers or peasants. Therefore it was nice to show him what peasants could accomplish."[12] In the summer of 1974, Ray and Sharon Fraser bought a house on the Miramichi near the village of Black River Bridge, where Fraser worked on his first novel, *The Struggle Outside* (1975). Jim Stewart was living in Black's Harbour, not far from Saint John, working at the *Telegraph-Journal*. But this academic year Nowlan did not find a new group of young friends. "The students have changed, I think," he said. "Even the writing wallahs are very neat and very sane, the kind who plan to take graduate courses in Creative Writing."[13]

One of the old group of student poets, Louis Cormier, left Tyndale Martin's Zen centre in January of 1975, or rather escaped from it, taking along his new girlfriend, Kristine, who was pregnant with their daughter, Miriam. Cormier hid out in Ottawa for the next few months, for some reason in fear of his life. But Martin was no hitman, and in 1976 Cormier re-established contact with Ray Fraser. Writing to his old mentor Nowlan, however, was a more challenging prospect. "I don't feel good about contacting him again," he told Fraser. "I think he's a really sweet guy, but he's also fast on the draw when it comes to putting someone down, so I'm not sure I would want to have that kind of communication with him."[14] But Fraser was encouraging. "I think if you wrote Alden in the way you wrote me you'd find him very receptive. I'm sure he'd very much love to hear from you."[15] Fraser knew the truth of this advice, since he had told Nowlan of Cormier's escape.

Nowlan's assessment of the new crop of literary students at the University of New Brunswick might have had something to do with his own aging sensibility and his renewed feelings of loneliness. On January 25, 1975, he turned forty-two. He had fulfilled his dream of becoming a nationally respected literary figure, and yet the changes in his Fredericton lifestyle made him feel abandoned. People around him were less understanding of his eccentricities and moods than they once were. Even Leo Ferrari became annoyed with him from time to time. Ferrari's new wife, Lorna Drew, did not get along with the poet, and this would sometimes cause friction between the two men; back in

January of 1974, Ferrari had been irritated enough about a slight that he had written to Fraser, "Yes, my patience has worn thin with Alden. He has been insulting at home, but to indulge in the same in public is crossing the Rubicon in my book."[16]

Nowlan's young friend Brian Bartlett, who left Fredericton in the fall of 1975 for Montreal, coined a term for being subjected to a Nowlan attack. He called it "getting the treatment." Another part of "the treatment" was to endure Nowlan's repeated and abject attempts to apologize afterwards. Bartlett once became so frustrated at trying to shake off an exaggerated act of contrition that he snapped, "Alden, you apologize once more and I'll throw something! Really, I find your continual apologizing more embarrassing than the initial incident."[17] Learning stood alone among the poet's intimates, noting the early warning signs of another "treatment" approaching and leaving his friend's company before the storm broke. Being Nowlan's friend demanded a large emotional investment that some were unwilling to make. UNB professor Barry Cameron, an occasional guest at Nowlan's parties, was one of these, recalling, "It wasn't possible to be just a casual friend of Alden's because he was someone who had an ability to emotionally devour people who got too close."[18]

In July, 1975, the close relationship between Nowlan and Sylvia soured, costing him the last friendly link with his Nova Scotia roots. The flashpoint was Jim, who at the insistence of his doctor had been trying for a couple of years to quit drinking. By 1975, he seemed to have the problem licked. Now, from his sober standpoint, his "brother's" emotional attachment to Sylvia presented itself as a nuisance. One night in July, Nowlan attended a summer festival of readings hosted by the University of Prince Edward Island. He was holding forth at a party hosted by PEI's premier artistic couple, Hilda Woolnought and Réshard Gool. Gool, a South African writer with a multiracial heritage, was arguing about race with Nowlan, whom he accused of being a racist. Nowlan insisted that he was not.

"You say you are not," said Gool. "But I am sure that if push came to shove and, let us say, your sister married a black man, you would disown her."

Nowlan had his trump card. "Aha! As a matter of fact, my sister did that very thing, and I still love her and her husband. And just to prove it, I'll phone her up right now."

Had Sylvia been at home that night, things might not have gone awry. But she was away at a conference, and even at the best of times

Jim did not take well to Nowlan's late-night phone calls, since he had trouble getting back to sleep. Nowlan pressed on, telling Jim that he had a black man there and asking him to confirm that he was also black and that he was married to Sylvia. Jim and Gool actually did chat amicably for a few minutes, but Jim refused to talk to Nowlan again. When Nowlan phoned back a few minutes later, Jim accused him of being a racist and hung up. Sober, Nowlan realized his mistake; he drafted the same letter of apology, over and over again in slightly different ways before he found the words that satisfied him, each version an attempt to achieve a reconciliation with Sylvia and Jim. Despite this outward appeal for forgiveness, however, he kept up his habit of phoning Sylvia at odd hours. Jim finally insisted that Sylvia break off contact altogether. Sylvia's problem with her cousin exacerbated the struggles in their own marriage, and she and Jim separated a few months later. When they reunited in 1976, Sylvia knew she would have to make a choice between the two men. She chose Jim, and her correspondence with her cousin ended.

Nowlan, however, had his own theory to explain how he lost the cousin whose friendship he had treasured since his lonely days in Hartland. "Jim Pride seems to have turned into a bit of an arsehole since he gave up the booze," he remarked to John. "Now he's searching for his black identity, cutting off all his ties with the white oppressor, and all that crap."[19] He told Fraser:

> Jim (husband of my cousin-sister Sylvia) Pride gave up the poison bowl a few months ago. (Diabetes and cirrhosis — the doctor said, it's teetotalism or death.) He'd been more or less sozzled ever since I'd known him — ten years — and probably long before that. Now he's become passionately black-conscious and tells Sylvia he doesn't want to have anything to do with her honkey relatives. He works most of the time and when he's not working he's campaigning for the Black Federation of Blackness or some such damn thing. I suppose sooner or later he'll ditch his honkey wife unless he goes back to the jar, in which case he'll climb the golden stairs. As a drunk he was a sweet guy, as a reformed drunk he's a grade "a" arsehole, black variety.[20]

There was more at play than Jim's abandonment of the bottle. Nowlan, stung at losing his sister and confidante, needed to find another culprit to account for Jim's actions; he blamed ideology. Whether or not Jim was as committed to black causes as Nowlan imagined him to be, Nowlan's Tory nature seized the explanation that Jim's devotion to a political crusade made Jim (and thereby Sylvia) abandon him just as surely as Louis Cormier abandoned him for a religious one.

His account of Jim's apostasy to Ray Fraser was meant to be instructive, for his trusted friend was facing the very same wagon ride to sober oblivion. In January, 1976, Fraser visited his old stomping grounds in Montreal for a week and was drunk for virtually the entire time. Life in Black River Bridge had not been healthy for Fraser:

> I'd been going months for a stretch getting up at five or six in the morning — rarely later — vomiting, pouring a shot of rum, then having several beers, then another rum, and so on; and in the afternoon flaking out for an hour or two, then resuming my activity, and by nine in the evening I had about as much energy as a limp rag.[21]

When he returned home from Montreal, he was having auditory hallucinations. He answered the voices by cleaning out his liquor cabinet, pouring the contents down the sink, and writing his friends to let them know that they could not show up at his door with an armload of booze.

But alarms bells rang in Nowlan's head. In the same letter containing his account of Jim, he offered Fraser some advice:

> Now that you've forsaken our brother Al Cohol — if you have forsaken him and are still swigging cranberry juice and bog water when you receive this — don't turn into a Prick as many ex-lush-heads do. Hell hath few furies equal to some of the reformed drunks I've known. I've often thought that I might become a complete arsehole if I turned teetotal; of course I've been a son of a bitch many times when I'm drunk, but that's not the same thing. If I turned teetotal I might become one of those awful pinhead intellecktuals. On the other hand, I may be telling myself that I have to get drunk because it's for my own good, which doesn't sound too convincing when it's put like that.[22]

In Nowlan's mind, the danger that inevitably followed forsaking the brotherhood of the bottle was betraying one's true self by adopting a Cause — and thereby becoming "an arsehole." Fraser's response indicates that the subject of teetotallers had come up before and had been an object of fun. He assured Nowlan that he had nothing to fear from him: "I haven't even got my prohibition speeches written yet, nor has my agent yet finalized arrangements for the lecture tour. Your ordinary reformed alco would have had these matters attended to long ago."[23]

Even Nowlan had made desultory attempts to lay off the sauce, but not specifically for health reasons. "I've been doing pretty damn good with Colonel Booze," he had written Fraser a year earlier. "Thanks in part, I think, to massive doses of niacinamide and dolomite, which are supposed to be good for hangovers and also for staying sober. I decided something had to be done after waking up one morning and realizing that I'd been drunk for eight days."[24] By February 6, 1976, it was clear that this cure had not been effective:

> I find I can drink in moderation, or in something close to moderation (three double gins before supper and maybe a beer later in the evening) so long as *nothing* happens. I mean if I work all day and then Claudine comes home and we eat and watch television or read — if nothing more than that happens — I can go all week on a forty ouncer of Beefeater. But as soon as *anything* happens I start tossing them back and if anything *disturbing* happens, whether pleasant or unpleasant, I may toss them back until I'm pixilated. Not always, but damn near always.
>
> The trouble is you can't say to anyone, "No, thanks, I'd better not do that because I don't want to get on the booze." Can't even say it to myself, except on rare occasions. "Sorry, Maud, I can't be a pallbearer at my old friend Ed's funeral because if I do I'm sure to get drunk as four barrels of shit" (one of my poor old father's similes) "not at the funeral but after I get home." How could anyone say that?
>
> Another problem for me is that I'm physically capable of consuming enormous amounts of booze. Those people who can get plastered on a glass of sherry don't do much harm to their bodies — I can down a forty-ouncer before I pass out. I used to be able to do that, drink a few cups of coffee the next morning, take a cold shower and a

couple of aspirins and go whistling on my way. Now I spend the next day in bed — crawling downstairs occasionally to guzzle a beer.[25]

It is hard to say whether he is complaining about his alcohol addiction or boasting about his drinking prowess. Perhaps Nowlan was unsure himself, in some crevice of his mind equating drinking with masculinity. It was just this kind of paradox, in fact, that he tried to come to grips with during the mid-1970s. While rejecting other people's ideologies, he consciously tried to develop his own, rooted in his earlier preoccupations with his rural and working-class heritage and influenced by his later contacts with the academic and literary world. After trying for years to distance himself from his Stanley roots, he now came full circle and embraced them — or rather he redefined for himself what it means to be a Maritimer. After years of trying to prove that he was not a regional poet, he began writing poetry celebrating his vision of the Maritime way of life. After a lifetime of condemning Freeman's alcoholism, he had to face his own.

Having fought against the "regionalist" label during the 1960s, the Nowlan of *I'm a Stranger Here Myself* has taken himself far away from writing about his rural roots. "Kevin O'Brien" had at last been left behind. At this point in his life when he was least tempted to sentimentalize and romanticize his past, he began to take a fresh look at where he had come from, a process largely unmarked by his former bitterness. Freeman's death worked a strange effect: now that the father was dead and buried, the son could at last admit how much he resembled his father.

During 1975 and 1976, Nowlan spent more time travelling around Atlantic Canada than he ever had before. *Legion* magazine contracted him to write three articles about the Legion, one for each of the three Maritime provinces. He visited Prince Edward Island in the spring of 1975, wrote the New Brunswick article over the winter, and visited Nova Scotia the following spring. Although his focus was the activities of veterans in the Maritimes, his poetry of that period describes the things he saw along the way. For the first time since he lived in Hartland, he would again lend his poetic voice to the working-class people of the Maritimes, describing their beliefs and inner strength.

As his young friends drifted away and his parties became tamer and less frequent, Nowlan tried to find in Maritime culture what he lacked in his personal life. Windsor Castle was losing its former status as crossroads of the world, and so he was determined to recreate that atmosphere wherever he went. During his February, 1976, reading tour of Atlantic Canada, he renewed his acquaintance with old friends, and was especially glad to see Al Pittman, who was now teaching at Wilfred Grenfell College in Corner Brook, Newfoundland. He sat in the Pittmans' parlour after a feed of Marilee Pittman's fish and brewis, getting hammered on gin while chatting with Sister Wilhelmina, a friend of the Pittmans' who was drinking Irish whiskey. In the local hotel he found himself charmed by the maid's accent, so like those he had heard in Ireland, where everyone invoked God in their conversation: "God love you, me old dear, you're not in the way at all." But such parochial details and folkloric colour had no place in that part of his literature that had a Maritime setting; instead, Nowlan imbued his region with an almost transcendental quality. The sacraments of alcohol, laughter, food and conversation celebrated at Windsor Castle were now, as he saw it, the very essence of Maritime culture, a culture residing, not in the artists or poets, but in ordinary people.

Nowlan always saw traditional music as the hallmark of the Maritimes, music ranging from Celtic to country, bluegrass and folk, and including even old woodsmen's ballads like the version of "Howard Carey" that Freeman liked to sing. "Ryan's Fancy are going to be at the Playhouse Friday," he told John. "I hope to get a chance to meet Denis Ryan as an old drinking buddy of Captain Pittman."[26] Ryan's Fancy was a Newfoundland-based Celtic music trio whose members — Denis Ryan, Dermot O'Reilly and Fergus O'Byrne — had all emigrated from Ireland. They became good friends of Nowlan as well as one of his touchstones in expressing his love of the Maritime region:

> Maps don't always tell the whole truth. There's a sense in which the Atlantic Provinces aren't where the atlas would have you believe they are. Culturally speaking, they're a group of islands in the North Atlantic, about halfway between the Gaspé Peninsula and the west coast of Ireland. "These are our people," Denis says. "I couldn't live anywhere else in North America." He hopes that the upcoming television series "will help give the people of this part of Canada a greater sense of self-respect, a sense that they have a distinctive culture that's worth preserving.

The Red Wool Shirt

I was hanging out my wash,
says the woman in North Sydney.
It was a rope line I was using
and they were wooden pins,
the real old-fashioned kind
that didn't have a spring . . .

Then I looked up and saw
Charlie Sullivan coming
towards me.
He'd always had a funny walk.
It was as if he was walking
sideways.
       That walk of his
always made me smile except
for some reason
I didn't smile
that day.
       He had on a hat
with salmon flies
that he'd tied himself
in the brim.

Poor old Charlie.

It's bad, Mary, he said.

I finished
hanging up the red wool
shirt
       and then I said,
Charlie, it's not
both of them, and he said,
Mary, I'm afraid it is.

And that was that.

This may be a depressed area, economically, but I can't think of any place on earth where the people love life more than they do here."[27]

Nowlan went to see the band again in March, 1976, and in May he drove to St. Stephen, New Brunswick, and spent three days there interviewing and partying with the band as they made a television music special. In a brief, typewritten log he kept for that year, Nowlan noted an entire week devoted to writing about them. "Worked on Ryan's Fancy article — June 30, July 1, 2, 3, 5, 9, 10, 11," he notes, then later: "August 21, 22 — Revising Ryan's Fancy piece, also Aug. 24." The care and attention he gave to the profile of his new friends — two weeks out of a busy year — underscores the article's title: "A Hard Day's Night with Ryan's Fancy."

At the same time that Nowlan was exploring the Atlantic region, he showed signs of disenchantment with the Fredericton scene. In *Canadian Literature's* 1976 issue on Maritime literature, he says in his essay "Something to Write About" that his culture is not something that can be easily defined by immersing oneself in books, but that one must immerse oneself in Maritime life:

> There is no Maritime school, no Fredericton school and no Fiddlehead school [of writing]. . . . The best thing about living and writing in the Maritimes, as far as I'm concerned, is that there's no place on the continent where so broad a range of social and human relationships is so readily accessible. When I meet writers in Montreal, Toronto and Vancouver, writers I admire, I'm continually reminded of the narrowness of their experience. Most of them have lived all their lives in one sub-caste of the bourgeoisie. . . . I have friends who can't read or write, friends who can read and write in six languages, friends who are fishermen, farmers, bikers, waiters, professional soldiers, semi-professional thieves, cabinet ministers, priests, nurses, actors, painters, whores, musicians, friends who are doctors, lawyers and Indian chiefs, friends ranging in age from seven to eighty-seven. Living in the Maritimes, one not only meets and gets to know other people who live here; one meets and gets to know an astonishing percentage of the people who visit here.[28]

But once again, many of Nowlan's closest friends started to move on to other things. David Adams Richards's success with *The Coming of Winter* was followed in 1976 by the publication of *Blood Ties* by Oberon Press. The wild and wicked launch party in September was just like old times — almost. "An event likely to take its place in the history of Canadian Literature as the equivalent of the famous drunken first meeting between Charles Lamb and John Keats in the history of English literature," he reported to Ray Fraser, who was not present. He almost taunted his friend for his sobriety and for missing out on the fun. But the party exposed the fault lines in Fredericton's happy literary circle. The house of Ice House Gang stalwarts Bill and Nancy Bauer provided the launch's setting. According to Nowlan, Richards, the star of the evening, showed up that night very drunk and proceeded to accost various women. Richards, for his part, denies that he accosted anybody. Still, no one denies that the event quickly got out of hand. John, home from Vancouver on a visit, tried with little success to abscond with the money Michael Macklem, the publisher, had collected from the evening's sale of books. The highlight of the evening occurred when Jim Stewart held a copy of *Blood Ties* aloft and announced, "Ladies and gentlemen, your attention please. This is a book-warming and therefore I intend to burn one of these stupid books. You published this crap, Mr. Macklem, but you didn't want to publish one of mine." Then he lit it on fire and flung it out into the yard; someone retrieved it and urinated on it on the bathroom floor. "To be honest, it wasn't that much fun to attend," Nowlan at last admitted. "Most of the fun comes from talking about it. A lot of things in life are like that."[29]

The Flat Earth Society and the Stewart Monarchy were also starting to pall. In January, 1976, the private joke of the Jacobite peerage went public when Fraser's article about Jim Stewart appeared in *Weekend* magazine. The article was written with the blessing and participation of the Royal Court, who thought that the publicity would be just as beneficial for the younger writers as the Flat Earth Society had been for Ferrari and Nowlan. The gang played their roles to the hilt, with Stewart brandishing a sword and wearing a crown and kilt for the front cover photograph. The photo accompanying the article was a rogue's gallery of Maritime Jacobites. Nowlan had dug out his highland dress for the photo. Ferrari opted for religious robes and a mitre fashioned by Tom Forrestall. Fraser posed in a simpler captain's hat and navy jacket in keeping with his title, "First Lord of the Admiralty." The men stand on a rocky coastline, looking suitably grim and regal. Of course, Fraser's

"A New James III," published in *Weekend*, January 17, 1976. Raymond Fraser, James Stewart, Dr. Alden Nowlan and Dr. Leo Ferrari. NATIONAL ARCHIVES OF CANADA

article was completely tongue-in-cheek, but, like the Flat Earth Society pamphlets, it made a compelling argument for the veracity of their claims.

The article, unfortunately, led to the dissolution of the very thing it was trying to promote. The trouble with making a private joke public, as they discovered, was that it exposed the group to any outsiders who wanted to get involved. Nowlan's conscience bothered him about the letters he received from people who took the article seriously. A couple of these were truly pathetic. One, a waitress from Vancouver, wanted to enlist the help of "Dr." Nowlan, the great genealogist, to help track down her lost father, offering to pay him from her meagre wages for his services. Another letter came from an Archbishop Thomas J. Fehérváry of Montreal. He belonged to a sect of the Catholic Church that did not accept papal infallibility and celebrated the mass in Latin. The Archbishop saw the King as a ray of hope for a Hungarian nation oppressed by Communism, and he encouraged him to press a claim for the throne of Hungary as well, since there was also a tenuous Stewart link to it. Nowlan, embarrassed, sent each a brief, impersonal letter thanking them for their support.

Even CBC personality Peter Gzowski wanted a piece of the action. The same month in which Fraser's article came out, Stewart received a phone call from Anne Crichton-Harris, one of the producers of Gzowski's television show, *90 Minutes Live*. She asked him and Nowlan to come to the Halifax taping of the show, dressed in their highland regalia. After a brief interview, a bathtub would be brought out, Gzowski would sit in it, and Stewart would confer the Order of the Bath on him. The idea was a little too campy, even for the Windsor court, and besides, the producers would pay them only seventy-five dollars each to travel to Halifax for the taping. As the producer persisted, the court resisted. Nowlan stopped answering the phone and Ferrari unhooked his altogether.

By March, 1976, the CBC lost interest. Leo Ferrari and Lorna Drew, his wife, were at the Nowlan house having a few drinks when the call came from *90 Minutes Live*, cutting them from the show but offering the men fifty-dollars for their pains. Off the hook, Nowlan still found cause to be incensed, cursing the CBC and cursing Fraser for inventing the whole Stewart Monarchy charade. Lorna made the mistake of reminding Nowlan that his facts were wrong; he thought up the Stewart Monarchy, not Fraser. This earned her a dose of "the treatment" from the poet; she would not tolerate it and left with her husband. By mutual agreement, that ended the Monarchy. For Nowlan, the club had served its purpose as a stress-release valve during the early 1970s. Now it waned in importance, just as the Masons and the Knights of Pythias had done a decade earlier when he tired of Hartland.

The venerable Flat Earth Society had also become too successful. When the Learned Societies conference came to UNB in the summer of 1977, Ferrari was anxious to repeat his success at the St. John's Learneds. He and Nowlan devised an associate membership for those willing to part with their three-dollar dues right away, and later the executive would decide whether the individual would be accepted as a full member, a strategy to keep cranks from infiltrating the club. Ferrari arranged to give a series of lectures and had a thousand associate membership cards and certificates and two thousand pamphlets printed. But the lectures did not generate the enthusiasm — or the money — that the society had hoped for. Some professors were even hostile to the FES. One went so far as to tear down posters advertising Ferrari's lectures. But it was the little things that made the FES fizzle out. "While everyone wanted to share in the fun, nobody wanted to share in the work or help with the finances," Nowlan later wrote. "My wife and I simply got tired of doing all the clerical work (and paying the printing bills)."[30]

Besides, Nowlan had enough contact with the Hanoverian monarchy to distract him from his loyalty to the Stewart pretender. Far from being overwhelmed by the glitter, Nowlan took his contacts with the real Royal Family as further proof that the Maritimes offered the chance to meet people from all walks of life. His first contact with royalty occurred, of all places, at a Johnny Cash and June Carter concert in May, 1975. The two musicians had performed in Fredericton on their way to Toronto, and Nowlan, a country music fan with connections at the Playhouse, managed to smuggle himself and Claudine backstage to meet Cash in his dressing room. He was not the only one interested in meeting Cash that night. Prince Charles, who had just completed a three-week tour of the Canadian Arctic, had also taken in the concert. To Nowlan, the nicest thing about the meeting was its informal nature. Mostly, he and Prince Charles talked about beards, since Nowlan already had one and His Royal Highness was trying to grow one. "My mother doesn't like it," the Prince confided. "For the rest of my life, I will hold in reserve the ultimate piece of name-dropping," Nowlan wrote to his publisher, Bill Clarke. "'That reminds me of the time when I was talking to Johnny Cash and the Prince of Wales happened to walk into the room and he said . . .'"[31]

But he reached the zenith of his lifelong fascination with royalty during the following summer of 1976 on the occasion of Queen Elizabeth II's visit to New Brunswick. Nowlan, who still wrote out the occasional speech for Richard Hatfield, received the plum assignment of writing the speeches for Her Majesty's New Brunswick tour. He also met the Queen and, with Claudine, attended a gala dinner. He later admitted that his greatest satisfaction came from the fact that the Queen had never once spoken the much-parodied phrase, "my husband and I"; his greatest frustration was with a royal aide who, fearful of Her

Majesty unintentionally offending Americans, excised passages praising the Loyalists from one of Nowlan's speeches.

Nowlan and Learning, meanwhile, brimmed with ideas for a new drama project to follow up on *Frankenstein*'s success; this time the play would be set in Canada and have Canadian characters. They batted around a plan for a play about Sir John A. Macdonald, but instead a nearly forgotten piece of New Brunswick history captured their imaginations: the manner in which poor people were looked after by the county. In the days before province-wide welfare, the local overseer of the poor held an annual auction of paupers in which the household that bid the least — that is, would charge the county the least for the pauper's upkeep — won guardianship. This practice, according to critics, was akin to slavery, and perhaps in some respects it was worse, since the bidder had no real investment in his charge. Young paupers tended to "sell" for the lowest price, snatched up by farmers looking for cheap labour, and these guardians would sometimes try to skim some of the county's money by spending as little as possible to feed and accommodate their paupers. An old pauper might fetch a higher or lower bid depending on the likelihood of his or her death within the year. If the pauper died, the bidder could keep the full year's payment, and sometimes unscrupulous householders went so far as to subtly encourage their charge's demise. The play that Nowlan and Learning wrote during the summer and fall of 1976, *The Dollar Woman*, adds an even less savoury element to the mix: a lecherous man who bids the absurdly low price of one dollar for the upkeep of a beautiful young intellectually handicapped woman.

"Citizen" George Train, an American liberal reformer, toured the province in 1898 speaking out against the pauper auctions. In the play, Nowlan used Train to illustrate his own convictions about the danger of ideology, especially an ideology imposed on Maritimers by people from away. He paints Train as a character who is morally smug and possessed of a missionary fervour to convert unbelievers. *The Dollar Woman* centres around a visit by Train to a fictional small town in King's County that is about to have its annual pauper auction. Pitted against Train is the protagonist of the play, Lewis White, the county's overseer of the poor. White is a salt-of-the-earth Maritimer trying to make the best of a bad situation, balancing human dignity with the responsibility of caring for the county's poor.

Alden Nowlan and Walter Learning on the set of *The Dollar Woman.* THEATRE
NEW BRUNSWICK

In *The Dollar Woman*, Nowlan and Learning turned their twentieth-century middle-class audience against themselves. White has the moral sympathy of an audience who sees that he is only trying to do the right thing; Train sways the intellect with his appeal for social justice. But Train is also a shyster and a showman who stoops to low tactics to prove his point. At the climactic scene of the play, as the lecherous Tom Roach bids for what amounts to a helpless, live-in concubine, Train rips off the front of her dress before the crowd, exposing both the young woman and the injustice of the provincial poor laws.

This scene ignited a terrific controversy. *The Dollar Woman* opened in January, 1977, to appreciative — or, at least, mostly appreciative —

audiences. A few people objected to the salty language in the play and especially to the exposed breasts of the young woman playing the title character. Foremost among these was an Anglican priest in Sussex, New Brunswick, the supposed setting of the play. The priest, Reverend F. Harold Hazen, denounced *The Dollar Woman* from his pulpit as pornographic. Actually, the degree of the actress's exposure varied widely from one performance to another according to the firmness of the stitching in the costume. But the controversy did not mar the play's success. For his part, Nowlan agreed with Hazen's comment that Lewis White would never have used rough language in front of his wife and child; in the published version of the play, he brought White's language more into line with what he felt was appropriate for a nineteenth-century gentleman.

Nowlan's 1977 poetry collection, *Smoked Glass*, was the product of all the changes he had undergone since the debut of his first play and the death of his father. These poems are tighter, both thematically and poetically, than those in any collection since *Bread, Wine and Salt*. The book reflects a mature, fresh new vision of himself and his own cultural context. Nowlan had won some approval in the early 1970s as a "universal" poet, but *Smoked Glass* turned out to be his most self-consciously "regional" poetry book to date. It is not regional in a merely colourful, charming or folkloric way, however; here is no lighthouse-and-seagull version of Maritime culture.

Reviewers for the most part seemed oblivious that Nowlan's poetry was undergoing any evolution at all. John Drew's observation in the *Canadian Forum* that the book "does not make any great departures from the sort of poetry found in his earlier collections" is typical, although he allows that "there is perhaps in this collection more of a sense of the mythical Nowlan the goat-bearded figure who takes cover behind the facade of a Nova Scotian peasant."[32] Only Michael Brian Oliver in *Poet's Progress* recognized the departure Nowlan makes in *Smoked Glass*, hailing it as "his best book to date":

> Here is Nowlan's old theme, escape from the village, and he seems to be on the verge of pointing out how far he has travelled from home — mentally, emotionally, and spiritually — how independent he is as a man from the

crippling restrictions of Puritanism, poverty and ignorance. Instead, and this is truly wonderfully strange, he suddenly turns and identifies with the people from his past.[33]

Of particular note is the poem "On the Barrens," which was based on the stories Freeman used to tell of farmers letting their cattle roam wild in a desolate area close to the sea. The poem is almost a reversal in point of view from "The Bull Moose." Now it is the farmers, the "sinewy men in rubber boots and tweed caps/ with their dogs beside them" who are the heroes and their wild cattle the natural aberration to be destroyed: "all the stories/ agreed/ in this: now there was nothing to do/ but kill them." The storytellers are responsible for the change in the speaker's point of view. The speaker of the poem privileges the viewpoint of the men gathered around the fire telling about hunting cattle on the barrens; they are transmitters of culture, just as Freeman was, and just as his son is. Nowlan's attitude has come full circle.

The poem "Full Circle" is, in fact, the anchor of the collection and in many ways the touchstone for Nowlan's later life. Here his speaker articulates the poetic and personal process Nowlan had been undergoing since his father's death. "In my youth," he begins, "no one spoke of love/ where I lived, except I spoke of it,/ and then only in the dark." The line takes him back to the harsh world of Kevin O'Brien, to the boy on the darkened stair, enraptured with the wonder of being himself but shut off and alone in his knowledge, harbouring the desire for escape: "It was not enough for me." But for the first time Nowlan contrasts this state with the new world that has accepted him:

Now, like everyone else, I send
postcards to acquaintances, With Love —
Love meaning, I suppose, that I remember the recipients
kindly and wish them well. But I say it
less often and will not be surprised
at myself if the time comes when I do not say it,
when I do not touch, except desperately, when I ask
nothing more of others, but greet them with a wink,
as my grandfather might have done, looking up
for an instant from his carpenter's bench.

With Freeman's death, Nowlan could at last let himself see the more meaningful aspects of his father's existence. In the poem "A Certain

Kind of Holy Man," the winos outside the store — whom Nowlan once equated with Freeman — are "oblates": "They have looked into the eyes of God,/ unprotected by smoked glass."

Despite the confidence he shows in re-mythologizing his people, comfort about his past still eluded him. If anything, his defensiveness about himself grew as his drinking increased. To his arsenal of insults and put-downs he added a new twist: despair at what he saw as "abandonment" by his friends. Not only had the FES and the Stewart Monarchy all but dissolved, but the drinking culture that sustained it had waned. As Fraser later explained, "When you're an alkie you don't want to see another [alcoholic] stop [drinking]. That's abandonment and you feel you're going down the drain anyway; you know that inside. Misery loves company. You don't want to be alone if someone else escapes."[34]

Misery did have company one September afternoon in 1977, as *Smoked Glass* was going to press. The day was a special one. That very night Nowlan would see the well-known Irish band, the Chieftains, in concert at the Playhouse, and, judging by his past luck, he would probably be allowed backstage to meet them in person. And he would be accompanied by Stewart, Richards and Fraser, who was drinking again. His three young friends had come down from Black River Bridge, Stewart having just moved there to join the other two. The only fly in the ointment was the strike that had shut down New Brunswick's liquor stores. Fraser had picked an inopportune time to fall off the wagon. Nevertheless, the group managed to procure some booze and made very merry in Nowlan's living room. The poet held forth again about the things in his past for which he could never forgive himself. Fraser made the mistake of jumping in, telling him that if one wrote honestly enough about those things, they could be dispelled. The two men started to quarrel, Nowlan interpreting Fraser's remark to mean that he, Nowlan, was writing insincerely.

The two were fuming — and also tipsy — when they went to see the show. When it was over, the group headed backstage for some conversation and Irish hospitality, neither of which was to be had. Fraser drew the ire of the band for helping himself to some of their Guinness, and he proceeded to quarrel with one of the band's members about a folksinger Fraser knew from his trip to Dublin. This caused all four writers to be ejected from backstage, which started them on a pub crawl of various watering holes in the city. But Nowlan was a sitter, not a crawler, and protested having to keep up with the younger men.

As the evening wore on, Nowlan began to fall behind, and the younger men pressed on and at last ignored their older companion. In a pique, he left, climbed into his car, and went for a ride out on the highway. Never a good driver at the best of times, his weaving attracted the attention of a police car. He was stopped, deemed impaired and taken to the police station to be charged. Returning to Windsor Castle to sleep off their revels, the trio found that Nowlan was not there. Later, Claudine received the phone call to come down (by taxi, since she did not drive) and pick her husband up. As a result of his folly, Nowlan was fined and lost his licence for six months. His three young friends could not help but feel somehow responsible. Upon his return, Nowlan focused his wrath on Fraser for abandoning him, and they resumed their earlier fight more loudly. The next morning, before Nowlan had arisen, Fraser left the house.

Claudine made sure that she accompanied her husband on his next League of Canadian Poets tour in the spring of 1978. He still did not like touring. His letters to reading organizers in the mid-1970s started asking for better reading conditions; these show not so much his growing fussiness as how sloppy universities and libraries had become at organizing literary events. As a minimum, he asked that the reading be held in a smaller room with many people rather than a larger room with few people. There must be a lectern and some sort of sound system, since he could not always project very well. And there must be a pitcher of water and a glass. Hosts typically neglected even these basic details and sometimes did not even meet him at or drive him to the airport.

He had not forgotten the snafus of the previous league tour in 1973. The twenty-five-dollar per diem that had irked him in 1973 had not kept pace with inflation, and he tried to negotiate a higher rate. When this effort failed, he attempted with better success to set a reading fee higher than the customary $125. His March, 1978, tour of western Canada paid him $200 per reading, and for the Great Canadian Poetry Weekend in Collingwood, Ontario, that same year he was paid $300.

The league and the hosting institutions had learned little since 1973. Nowlan's March 8 reading at the University of Calgary was postponed because of a locked room and then marred by a squawking sound system. The refreshments that were supposed to follow the reading did not arrive because the waitress took the time off without telling anyone. The reading on March 9 at the University of Saskatchewan at Saskatoon was an even worse debacle: the few handmade posters advertising the event had spelled his name "Aldan Knowland," the room booked for the reading was simultaneously booked for a math class, and the professor organizing the event was late. When she met the poetry crowd waiting outside in the hallway, she promptly initiated an argument with the math professor and stalked off. Luckily, someone found a room, but the professor had not yet returned to introduce the poet. Nowlan introduced himself and tried to ignore the crew that tried frantically to set up the sound system and then to videotape the event with glaring lights and a lapel microphone stuck to his jacket. The next day, before the Lethbridge Public Library reading, Nowlan phoned the librarian from the airport. It seemed the librarian had forgotten all about the event, including advertising for it. Nowlan read for an audience comprised of the librarian, his family, and two of his friends.

The stress of the tour sent Nowlan into the hospital upon his return to Fredericton with his old enemy, a viral infection. From his customary post-tour sickbed he urged the league to consider making some changes. "Let me repeat that I think *you* are doing a damn fine job," he wrote on April 8. "The fault lies with the local sponsoring people — who should be pasting up posters and arranging to unlock doors and worrying about parking space etc etc." His suggestions included a nominal admission charge and gimmicks like door prizes (evidently the hustling part of his personality that had propelled the Hartland KPs and the Flat Earth Society was still in fine form). "By damn, I'm glad I made the trip!"[35] he added, and indeed he would continue to do readings with the league, despite the occasional fiasco.

While Nowlan lingered in the hospital, Louis Cormier continued to struggle with whether he should get back in touch with his friend. Ray Fraser's response shows the extent to which the sympathy of Nowlan's friends had eroded:

> I just heard that Alden is in hospital after a reading tour out west. It doesn't surprise me, boozing the way he does. What does surprise me is that he hasn't collapsed from the drink long before this, as I myself have done on several occasions. I'm not drinking now, not since early Dec. (except for a few weeks in Spain). At least I assume it's the drink that explains his hospitalization . . . I'm not bothered in any way, it's just the reverse: I can't be bothered. He's fine when sober but he goes completely out of his mind

after a certain stage of drunkenness. If he comes out of his illness and straightens up it will be much better for himself and everyone else. Leo doesn't see him much anymore for the same reason, which shows you how bad Al can get: it would seem almost impossible to be insulting to such a lovely man as Leo, but Alden's done it, and once too often.[36]

Fraser's choler, still keenly felt eight months after their quarrel on the afternoon and evening of the Chieftains concert, was enough to convince Cormier to put off contacting Nowlan until another day, a day that would never arrive.

Far from being oblivious, Nowlan was all too aware of the problems his alcoholism was causing him. In the October 29, 1977, entry of the diary he kept sporadically, he had pondered his erratic behaviour:

In the past fifteen days I've fallen asleep dead-drunk eleven times. By dead-drunk, I mean almost completely detached from reality, absolutely indifferent to the effects of one's behaviour. Twice I've gone to bed slightly drunk and twice sober. Physically, this doesn't seem to affect me greatly but this is an illusion stemming from the fact that I exert myself so seldom. Most days my chief exercise is walking downstairs for breakfast, upstairs to work, downstairs for dinner and upstairs to bed. I was sweating with exhaustion when I walked to the campus post office and back the other day.

Why do I get drunk? Because in drunkenness there comes such blissful and yet knowing indifference. Drunk, I'm still alone but I'm no longer lonely. Then there's the delightful process of getting drunk, especially the phase in which one derives so much pleasure from other people's company, including the company of people who would otherwise bore one to desperation. Generally speaking, other people bore me when I'm sober and I bore other people when I'm drunk.

The worst part of getting dead-drunk is the way I feel afterwards — not the dehydration and all that but the shame at having made a fool of myself, as I did when I got picked up for impaired driving last month and, again, when I stripped naked while spending the night with Greg and Miriam Cook a week or two ago in a hotel room in Halifax.

It's not guilt that I feel at such times, but shame. I regret what I did only because it lowered me in the estimation of others. But, perhaps, it's not that easy to distinguish between shame and guilt.[37]

As he now realized, his continued happiness and perhaps even his life was at stake. Having beat the tremendous odds against him from birth — his poverty, his emotional and physical abandonment by his parents, his aborted education, his battle with cancer — he at last faced defeat at his own hands.

ELEVEN

1977-1983

from **He Enters His 50th Year**

I feel myself dissolving like a snowman,
coming to pieces like an old book.
But I'm not complaining.
It's not as bad as it sounds.
There are compensations.

For one thing, I've accumulated such a company
of past selves, enough of them to fill the stage
in a sizeable theatre, that it is easier to believe
the person I am is only one among many, to look at him
in almost the same way I would look at anyone else.

As a public figure, Nowlan had attracted fan mail since the late 1960s, and the pile grew throughout the 1970s as his public exposure increased. He treated this correspondence initially with the care and respect of any writer still unused to the glare of the spotlight. And for good reason; most of the letters were laudatory and were written by other young writers trying to make contact with a peer or a mentor. He understood, having gone through the same epistolary process with his own mentors, Cogswell, Souster and Layton. Often, his correspondence led to meetings and friendships (as was the case with Ray Fraser), and occasionally to animosities (as with Tyndale Martin). But the quality and tone of his fan letters changed over the years, in most cases for the worse.

Letters usually fell into two categories: would-be writers seeking easy advice and praise, and cranks looking for a sounding board or punching bag. Or, alternately, into the nice and not-so-nice. He writes to one woman from the "nice" group: "It is a funny thing but when I receive really touching letters from people who have read things that I've written, they almost always apologize and say that I'll probably think they're silly. On the other hand, people never apologize when they write nasty letters."[1] There was another way to divide the lot: letters to Nowlan the poet/fiction writer and letters to Nowlan the journalist. Many correspondents writing to the one seemed to be unaware that the other existed. Even the old newspaperman was surprised at how few people read his poetry — or any poetry — but how many read newspapers and magazines. His *Telegraph* and *Advocate* columns made him public property, like any train station or pay phone whose use and condition depends entirely on the whims and good nature of the general user. And, like old newspapers, his work took on a disposable quality in the eyes of some of his correspondents.

Letters from would-be writers are generally polite and deferential, but in their way they could also be the most annoying. The writers' biggest sin was presumption. Most assumed that it was part of Nowlan's job to read their (sometimes voluminous) submissions carefully, comment on them and praise them in detail, even if the authors were not University of New Brunswick students. Nowlan usually gave in, motivated by the guilty feeling that UNB was paying him with public funds and, therefore, he had to be available to the public. Being available meant pawing through sheaves of bad poems and stories. Return postage was rarely included.

As he became more popular, he learned to be more selective in his kindness towards strangers. Requests came from students asking for help with assignments. One grade twelve student from Yarmouth, Nova Scotia, posed a list of nine theoretical and technical questions about humour and wit that is exhausting to read, let alone answer. This student at least enclosed a self-addressed stamped envelope. At the top in Nowlan's hand is the note "NO ANSWER," but it is crossed out, indicating that he may have relented and written some reply. Often, students wanted explanations or interpretations of a poem or story. Not surprisingly, his two most anthologized poems, "The Bull Moose" and "The Execution," figure prominently in this group of letters. The writers sometimes reveal interesting possibilities that he had not considered. Some, for example, asked if the bull moose died at the hands of the rangers or if he just collapsed at the same time as the rangers raised their rifles. A couple of students in British Columbia wanted to know if the speaker in "The Execution" really was a member of the press, or if the police and the hangman were just humouring a delusional convict.

But most of the literary correspondence was accompanied by the letter-writers' poetry, fiction and sometimes unhappy and complicated life stories. Nowlan often wrote "NO ANSWER" at the top of such letters.

By no means were all queries ignored; he continued to give personal attention to those few correspondents who seemed sincere in their love of poetry. These were not necessarily the best poets, as can be guessed from his frank but kind comments. "You use far, far too many adjectives," reads the opening sentence of one letter to a poet. "I'd suggest that you rewrite these two verses, using adjectives as sparingly as a cook uses cayenne pepper or Tabasco sauce."[2] In another he is blunt in telling a young poet that his poetry is not very good, but adds that at his stage of development talent is unimportant compared to the desire to work and to derive some enjoyment from writing. "One doesn't waste one's time in making love even if one isn't as good at the mechanics of it as Casanova. One does it because one has to do it."[3] Most of his replies boil down to the same few nuggets of advice assembled in different ways to suit the situation. Always conscious of making poetry more accessible and enjoyable, he stressed that the satisfaction of writing verse should supersede any questions about whether their poems were any good or not; he also advised them that their poetry and prose should be grounded in their own reality and feelings rather than decorated with literary artifice; and he encouraged aspiring writers to read as much good literature as they could. Eventually he prepared a form letter, which he used many times. His efforts did not please everybody, as this diary entry shows:

> Telephone Call, July 7, 1972 at about 7 o'clock in the evening.
> Nowlan: "Hello."
> The Caller: "Is this the great poet on Mount Olympus?"
> Nowlan: "I'm afraid I don't get the point of your question."
> The Caller: "I mean is this the man that says other people's poetry is shit?"
> Nowlan: "Could you come to the point, please?"
> The Caller: "You insulted me a year ago and you don't even remember me!"

Nowlan: "The trouble is I insult so many people during the course of a year . . . Sometimes I don't even catch their names."

The Caller: "Go ahead, hang up on me."

Nowlan: "Don't tell me that you called me just so I could hang up on you. What are you, some kind of masochist?"

The Caller: "Go ahead, hang up on me."

Nowlan: "Try to pull yourself together, man."

The Caller: "Now you're getting uptight! You're getting uptight now! Now you're going to hang up on me."

Nowlan: "You seem to be the one that's upset. I feel quite calm."

The Caller: "Don't try to play it cool with me. Hang up on me."

Nowlan: "Look, I suggest that you discuss your problem with your priest."

At which point Nowlan does hang up.[4]

The correspondence from readers of newspaper and magazine columns was either very supportive or very insulting. In rare letters, the writer politely disagrees with one of Nowlan's essays. These were a treat, for Nowlan enjoyed dissension and debate. Readers almost universally acclaimed his lament in the *Telegraph* for the disbanding of the Black Watch regiment in 1970. In the mid-1970s his cat Hodge started to "share" the occasional column with his master, whom the cat referred to as "The Lump." Hodge attracted his own small epistolary fan club among New Brunswick cats. Nowlan's September 1979 *Telegraph* column on Hodge's death elicited a dozen sympathetic responses from humans and cats alike. However, his *Telegraph* and *Advocate* columns championing the anti-abortion cause attracted the most response, positive and negative.

Readers who did not share Nowlan's opinions were often irrational. A Hartland couple mildly suggested that he shave his beard because only gay men wore beards, while outraged zealots consigned his soul to hellfire for a less-than-pious article about religious matters. One lady responded to a *Telegraph* column in which he compared rude Fredericton theatre goers to bizarre species of birds. A handful of letters reacted negatively to his essays about growing up poor. Rather than sympathize, these readers seem almost to scorn Nowlan because his deprivation could not match theirs, putting Nowlan on the receiving end of a "treatment" similar to that which he had meted out so many times to any who dared talk about poverty in his presence.

The worst of all of his mail was cryptic and even threatening.

Dear Sir,

How did you find me out? I can guess. Spys. Except your spys are pretty stupid to think I believe in witches. There is no such things. Your writing is mostly junk and lies. And I never wrote to the pope or the queen either.

Obvious you are as you put it a communist rat and I don't understand why Mr. Irving don't fire you. Obvious he believes in freedom of the press. But communists have no right to use our press for their godless uses. You gave yourself away good saying you wanted to sell filthy books to children. There is no use praying for your soul, you have gone too far. And don't talk about anonymous letters either. Do you think we are stupid enough to believe your real name is alden nowlan.

It is pretty bad when a man can't write a letter without communist spys all over the place. I don't think you are really from this province. You are probably from Toronto or Russia. Why don't you go back. You are no fucking good anyhow. To use your own words you are probably a catholic frog communist. And your turn is coming too.

A enemy[5]

Although this letter has no date, the content suggests that "A enemy" wrote in response to a newspaper or magazine column. In the December 22, 1973, *Telegraph-Journal*, Nowlan did write a column denouncing anti-French bigotry in New Brunswick. At that time anglophones in New Brunswick feared losing jobs to bilingual workers, and Nowlan's pro-French stance drew some controversy. His January 19, 1974, column discusses crank letters he receives from irate readers, and he invents a parody of such a letter, complete with poor spelling, block capital letters to emphasize key words, and the epithet "catholic frog communist." The content of "A enemy"'s letter suggests that he or she wrote in response to this column, not vice-versa, and infers that he or she may have written an earlier letter in similar language that provoked Nowlan's January 19 column. Nowlan did not save this earlier letter, if indeed it existed.

Hate letters, at least from strangers, did not seem to bother Nowlan very much, and some even amused him. Complimentary letters, especially the rare ones that did not ask him for anything, could more than compensate for a crank's spleen. "I usually read the mail as I'm having breakfast — which is how I read your letter," he replied to one woman. "It made me feel good all the rest of the day. It's nice to be reassured that there's somebody out there listening."[6] One correspondent responded to a 1976 column in which Nowlan confessed an addiction to licorice by sending him a box of 120 black licorice cigars. Another woman wrote that she, her husband and their eighteen-year-old son had sat around the table one night reading parts of *Miracle at Indian River* aloud to each other. That this legacy of a family breakup could bring a family together must have made his heart glad.

As the 1970s faded into a new decade, Nowlan grew more confident about his position as a writer. He had a scare at the start of the 1977-78 academic year, when the University of New Brunswick considered cutting back on the writer-in-residence post as part of an austerity program. Desmond Pacey, who died in 1975, was no longer there to guarantee Nowlan's continued employment with the university, but the rest of the English department rallied around their poet laureate, and, with the support of the Vice-President of the University of New Brunswick at Saint John, Tom Condon, Nowlan kept his job. Although at the department's request he began to submit yearly reports of his activities, Nowlan became much more relaxed and confident about keeping the roof of 676 Windsor Street over his head. Nor did he feel that he had to prove himself to critics and other writers, having achieved success in nearly every genre on a wide variety of subjects and in a variety of styles. His theatrical successes with Walter Learning and his lucrative freelancing efforts seemed to convince him that there would be bacon and flour in the pantry for some time to come.

Nowlan could now afford the luxury of laughing at himself more than usual, and the Great Canadian Poetry Weekend in Collingwood, Ontario, gave him an opportunity to do so in the summer of 1978. He re-established friendly contact with other icons of the Canadian literary scene, including the two poets to whom he was most often compared, Al Purdy and Milton Acorn. Comparisons between the men, however, were sometimes more comical than literary. At a buffet lunch, he and

Alden and Claudine Nowlan. FREDERICTON DAILY GLEANER

Claudine were standing behind two women who watched in amazement as Acorn reached into the potato salad bowl, scooped out a dollop and began eating it out of his hand.

"Who is that man?" one whispered, so as not to offend a Distinguished (if eccentric) Canadian Writer.

"That's Alden Nowlan," the other whispered back.

Nowlan and Learning did not waste any time planning their next play. They had batted around various historical subjects, including a one-woman show about Queen Victoria and a play about Churchill, Beaverbrook and Somerset Maugham as old men vacationing in the south of France, a project tentatively entitled *Winnie, Willie and Max*. As *The Dollar Woman* finished its run at Theatre New Brunswick in February, 1977, they had made up their minds and were excitedly plotting a drama based on Sir Arthur Conan Doyle's immortal Sherlock Holmes. The great detective was another of Nowlan's enthusiasms, a legacy of the days when he sat glued to the radio, enhanced by his adult taste for Victoriana. He also shared Doyle's love of the supernatural. It was a perfect fit.

The play that emerged, *The Incredible Murder of Cardinal Tosca*, continued a pattern set by *Frankenstein*; it was also an adaptation of existing literary material, specifically, nineteenth-century literature with a modern spiritual cast, and, like *Frankenstein*, it was enormous fun. While the first play relied on special effects and the melodramatic tragedy of the Creature for its effect, *Tosca*'s delight lay in its verbal play, colourful characters and bizarre plot twists. Plays about Frankenstein and Sherlock Holmes gave Nowlan a chance to let his hair down and fill his wallet up.

TNB planned a more ambitious touring schedule for this play than it did for its other productions; the company would take *Tosca* to Nova Scotia, Newfoundland, Prince Edward Island and Ontario after its New Brunswick premiere. The good wishes from Holmesian societies around the world — some with strange names like The Afghani Perceivers and Dr. Watson's Neglected Patients — reflected the popularity of the Holmes cult, although a note from Moriarty scolded the authors for perpetrating such lies: "As though the world has not already been glutted by the excess of pulp regaling the 'adventures' of my sometimes rival, Sherlock Holmes. I should have hoped that you would know better."[7]

The Incredible Murder of Cardinal Tosca opened to packed audiences in Fredericton on January 14, 1978, the night of the worst blizzard to hit the city that winter. The show, which had been sold out for days, nevertheless went on, and people lined up in the lobby to snatch up the few tickets that were cancelled. Greg and Miriam Cook did not let the weather stop them from attending the opening, and they brought along Cook's brother Harry Thurston and his wife, Cathy. The production starred Jack Medley as Holmes, Dan MacDonald as Watson and Vernon Chapman as the sinister Moriarty. Also in the cast was a young actress named Wenna Shaw, who happened to be the girlfriend of one John A. Nowlan. *The Incredible Murder of Cardinal Tosca* was as big a hit as *Frankenstein*.

It was a night of good clean fun, although Nowlan again chorused his remarks during the play whenever the audience did not react to it as he wished. At one point, Holmes recounts to Watson some of his cases, including the recovery of a packet of compromising letters written by Oscar Wilde. Holmes says, "In one of them he describes a very plain cockney stable boy as being 'like a hyacinth, all white and gold.'"

"Abominable!" Watson replies. "The fellow ought to be in prison."

"Don't you think that a severe, harsh punishment for a bad simile?" Holmes asks dryly. On opening night there was no laugh for this remark.

"Jesus Christ," Nowlan muttered to Learning as they stood at the back of the theatre. "Either these idiots don't know who Oscar Wilde was or they don't know what a goddamn simile is."

A melodramatic speech by Holmes about the glory of Victoria's empire caps the play. This elicited plenty of laughs, but Nowlan wrote to his friend David Brown, the Creature in *Frankenstein* and Colonel Dashwood in another theatre's production of *Tosca*:

> I'll tell you a secret. I wish we could have done a serious Holmes. I wish that present-day audiences would stand for it. But of course they wouldn't. I'll tell you an even more shameful secret — one that I haven't told anyone else — I don't really feel that Holmes' speech at the end of *Tosca* is funny. No, I don't. I'm such a bloody old Anglophile Victorian that I truly do believe that the glory of England will remain forever bright — like the glory of Greece, that nobody laughs at — and I'd almost bet that if *Tosca* were to be staged a century from now, nobody would [laugh] at that speech — by then the Victorians will have been put into a truer perspective.[9]

The play was later produced in Toronto at the St. Lawrence Centre for the Arts Centre. Nowlan and Learning at last showed themselves off as the Victorians they were — they arrived for the opening with Ontario's lieutenant-governor, pulled in a horse-drawn carriage and dressed in top hats, tails and long, flowing capes.

For Learning and Nowlan, *Tosca* would be a last hurrah. In May of

1978, Learning joined what seemed to Nowlan an exodus when he accepted a position in Ottawa with the Canada Council. Ray Fraser had stopped writing and visiting entirely since the night of the Chieftains concert, but in 1978, after he completed his critically acclaimed novel *The Bannonbridge Musicians* (1978), Fraser once again dropped by to see his old friend, and once again they made up. But their friendship was not the same. Fraser's battles with the bottle remained a source of annoyance. In 1980, when Fraser phoned to tell Nowlan that he would be moving to Fredericton because Sharon had a job with the CBC, Nowlan became irked at how much Fraser talked about his new devotion to teetotalism. He had joined Alcoholics Anonymous, and he brought pamphlets around to the poet's house, urging him to join, too. Fraser recalls how Nowlan took pains to keep the pamphlets out of Claudine's sight; Nowlan quipped to friends that Fraser compulsively edited the poor writing on the pamphlets with a ballpoint pen. Things were worse during periods when Fraser went back to drinking. "He never visits us unless he is dead drunk or in the throes of a terminal hangover and in search of spirituous solace,"[9] Nowlan groused to Al Pittman. Sometimes Nowlan would phone Fraser to say that he was out of cigarettes or gin and ask Fraser to bring some over. Fraser says, "I'd look out in the kitchen and he'd have all kinds of gin there. He just wanted company."[10]

Nowlan drank as much as he ever did at the Windsor Castle parties. More often than not, the poet became drowsy sometime around midnight, then let the party continue while he retired to bed. His deceased feline companion, Hodge, was quickly replaced with young, rambunctious cats, Flashman and T'other. In 1978, John moved "a little closer to Hartland" when he left Vancouver to study social work at Ryerson Polytechnical Institute, Toronto. Nowlan's secret wish that his son would one day return to school had been granted. "I've been meaning for a long time to write you a letter telling you how proud I am of you," he said in May, 1979.

> There was a brief period, a few years ago, when I was disappointed in you; but that wasn't your fault, it was mine. I had pictured you getting all the degrees that I'd never had a chance to get. So it was disappointing when you dropped out of high school. But I long ago came to realize that if you had taken all those courses and received all those degrees then you might become the sort of person that I can't stand. . . .

What makes me proud of you is your appetite for life, your sensitivity and your capacity for love. You would have been a beautiful human being even if you and I had never met. But I like to think that I did you more good than harm.[11]

The move made it easier for John to see them, and for them to visit him on their frequent trips to Toronto.

Nowlan's role as New Brunswick's "poet laureate" was changing, and he himself was only too glad to adapt if it would give him some new literary ventures to explore. Fredericton was starting to become a little stale, as Hartland had earlier. The writer-in-residence did not have the cachet for UNB students that he once did, either. In his yearly report for 1979-1980, written for UNB English department chairman Robert Cockburn, Nowlan described the changing character of the post. "It's very different from the way it used to be, when we had students like Louis Cormier and Bernie MacDonald and Eddie Clinton practically living with us. Now I see more people from the community than from the university."[12] Instead of encouraging student poets, he found himself more and more giving advice to soldiers writing regimental histories, old people writing memoirs and teenagers with science fiction manuscripts tucked under their arms. The kind of counsel he offered was of a different nature, too, not grand philosophical discussions about art but instead advice about vanity publishers, song publishing and copyright. "I have also been approached by a surprising number of social workers who have asked me to read manuscripts from their 'clients,' who were in gaol or on welfare," he wrote in his 1980-1981 report. "I have tried to be helpful, although I must confess that I'm dubious about the value of writing as social therapy."[13] But one MA student in UNB's Creative Writing program bucked this trend. Yvonne Trainer had come all the way from her native Alberta to meet her favourite poet and, accompanied by Bob Gibbs, helped restore some of Windsor Castle's former glory as a congenial place for writers to chat, laugh and eat trays of Claudine's sandwiches. He also struck up a friendship with Lesley Choyce, a young poet who had moved from the United States to the Eastern Shore of Nova Scotia, where he surfed and founded a new literary journal, *Pottersfield Portfolio*, to which Nowlan contributed.

Not only did Nowlan spend less of his time talking about literature, he spent less of it creating literature, while his old standby, journalism, played a steady and even growing role in his writing life. The income from it increased proportionally; in 1979 his fee for a *Telegraph-Journal* column rose to fifty dollars from the thirty dollars he was paid in 1974; in 1980 this would grow to sixty dollars, then in 1981 to eighty dollars. He and Ralph Costello talked for years of Brunswick Press publishing a collection of Nowlan's best *Telegraph* columns. The success of *Campobello* proved that he could write appealing non-fiction, and Brunswick Press's *Shaped By This Land*, essentially a coffee-table book, had sold over seventeen hundred copies by 1979. As the idea took shape, the idea of collecting newspaper columns waned in favour of publishing a collection of his more substantial magazine pieces, mostly from the *Advocate*. Nowlan was not as involved with this project as he had been with others; he helped to choose which columns went into the book, he proof-read and he dickered over a title. He originally suggested *Stompin' Tom Connors Meets the Flat Earth Society*, after two of the book's more colourful articles. The editor rejected this in favour of *Two-Way Mirror*. A mock-up of the cover included this title and a montage of linked illustrations facing their doubles in mirror image. But the title had already been used for another recent book, so they retained the cover design and changed the title to *Double Exposure*.

The book of magazine articles earned Nowlan the Writers' Federation of Nova Scotia's Evelyn Richardson Award for non-fiction. His trip to Halifax in the spring of 1979 to attend the awards ceremony provided a good occasion for the kind of drunken blast with friends that had lately been too infrequent. The award itself was a $500 cheque and a large iron trophy in the shape of a lighthouse. Journalist Harry Bruce, the previous year's winner, had the job of making the speech and presenting the award to Nowlan. When the winner's name was called out, there was silence in the audience. Bruce, who was mildly inebriated, spoke into the microphone again, "Alden, Alden, are you there?" This provoked titters from the restive audience. At last, amid a small commotion, a large man squeezed into the aisle and lumbered up to the stage. Nowlan, feeling no pain, stumbled as he approached Bruce and fell into him, throwing the two men into an awkward embrace. After the ceremony, he and another honouree, Farley Mowat, drunkenly sang Mowat's old regimental song as they went out to see Denis Ryan, Dermot O'Reilly and Al Pittman, who were playing in town that weekend. The next day the boys left Nowlan — still clutching his large iron trophy — in the care of Eastern Provincial Airways staff, who poured the distinguished author onto a plane back to Fredericton.

Nowlan's association with Harry Bruce was more professional than their encounter at the WFNS ceremony suggests. Bruce's new magazine, *Atlantic Insight*, made its appearance that year on newsstands across the region. *Insight* was a punchy, modern-looking glossy devoted to investigating and promoting Atlantic Canadian news and issues, considerably more lively than its frumpy cousin the *Atlantic Advocate*, for which Nowlan continued to provide his regular column. Nowlan wrote his *Telegraph* and *Advocate* columns in much the same spirit as he wrote his poems, not a labour, but a labour of love. Though some of his essays, especially in the *Telegraph*, are disposable, he evidently wrote most of them with a great deal of care; in his desultory attempts at diary writing he often notes which columns he produced on which days. Even so, the spirit of Bruce's new magazine rekindled Nowlan's love of journalism. For his part, Bruce was overjoyed to find such a solid writer for his team, and Nowlan acted for a time as his unofficial New Brunswick correspondent. The editor remembers Nowlan as a meticulous and professional writer, submitting flawlessly spelled and punctuated manuscripts, for Bruce a mark of true professionalism. *Atlantic Insight* allowed Nowlan to stretch his journalistic writing in previously untried ways. One of his first articles was an entertaining piece for the food section of the magazine, Claudine's recipes for Blueberry Cobbler and Blueberry Bangbelly, two rival desserts that had caused some "confrontation" ("feud is too strong a word") among different branches of her family.[14]

Atlantic Insight published Nowlan's most outstanding magazine feature, a travel piece about Cuba. Throughout the 1970s, his travelling had been mostly business-related. He had crossed Canada a few times on reading tours, experiencing the country from a succession of hotel rooms, but, all told, book touring was a poor substitute for a vacation. After the headaches of the 1978 reading circuit, he was long overdue for a break, and he chose an uncharacteristically adventurous visit to Cuba in March of 1979. No doubt the low price tag was part of the appeal, along with the Caribbean antidote to winter, and the adventure was mitigated by the rest of the Canadian tour group. Touring Cuba with a group of Canadians presented less risk than striking out alone to some villa in Spain, where the Frasers and Richardses once soaked up the sun, but at least Cubans did speak Spanish, of which Nowlan had a rudimentary knowledge.

Bruce gladly offered Nowlan $600 for an article about his trip. As Nowlan and Claudine discovered, $600 could take a couple a long way in Cuba. Few attractions there encouraged impulsive overspending, and what consumer goods they found were very cheap. "A city of two million — and not a single store!" was Claudine's comment after wandering around Havana. At Ernest Hemingway's old house, she reached into a window and scored a souvenir, a cutting from a plant that she rooted in a pot back home. Nowlan found the locals as friendly towards strangers as Newfoundlanders and the Irish, although there were isolated incidents of rudeness towards the "gringos." "No gringo," he tried to explain in Spanish when, say, a bartender refused service. "Oiga! Soy de el Canada!" The gambit usually did not help, although in one restaurant the waiter, when he discovered his patrons were not American, rebuked the rudeness of the nearby Cuban diners towards their comrades from Quebec. Tourists from *la belle province* did, in fact, comprise a sizable part of the Canadian tour group, which created little dramas that must have amused their Cuban hosts. The Québécois refused to join their fellow travellers from the rest of Canada in a pick-up baseball game against their Cuban hosts. One night in a bar, the Nowlans and the other Canadians were plunged into darkness because of a power outage, an all-too-common occurrence. In the gloom some Québécois began to sing "Gens du Pays," only to be drowned out by a group of Albertans singing "This Land Is Your Land."

As a journalist, Nowlan could not ignore the political overtones of his situation: a well-fed writer from a capitalist country visiting the Western Hemisphere's premier Communist nation. Everywhere he went he was conscious of the revolution, especially at the Bay of Pigs museum, where locals balefully eyed the Canadians. To his regret, he ended up missing a speech by Fidel Castro by only minutes, although he did not miss the crush of humanity streaming into Cienfuegos, mostly on foot, to hear their commander-in-chief. He saw the other side of Cuban society, too, through a Cuban writer called "Daniel." They met secretly, Nowlan dodging in and out of hallways, waiting for signals from apartment windows, and meeting his contact "accidentally" in nearby parks. But his only fear was of getting stuck lying on the beaches beside the overfed Russians. "Cuba Is a Great Place to Visit," he called his *Atlantic Insight* article, but, he said, "Freedom is a luxury I'd find painful to live without. . . . Thinking of those Cuban writers I come close to tears. Not from sadness. Call it gratitude."[15]

Despite the departure of his collaborator, Walter Learning, Nowlan continued to develop his scriptwriting skills. Starting in the summer of 1978, he began working on a film script for a CBC-TV variety special called *All On a Summer's Day*, a loosely connected series of vignettes, songs and poems filmed at the nearby King's Landing Historical Settlement. The idea was to depict a typical day in the lives of nineteenth-century rural Canadians through the eyes of a young boy, played by Warwick Learning, Walter's son. Several of Nowlan's poems would be narrated by an older actor representing the young boy as an old man, and Nowlan also wrote some of the script that linked the poems to songs performed by Ryan's Fancy. Film provided an exciting new world for Nowlan, and he hung around the set as much as he once haunted the backstage area of the Playhouse.

But nothing could replace the creative association he enjoyed with Learning. Malcolm Black, Theatre New Brunswick's new artistic director, had approached the poet for a new play, but Nowlan found he could not put his heart into it. He told David Brown, "I've got several good ideas. But going ahead without my trusty confidant and colleague, Dr. Learning, would be a bit like a divorcée who is about to start dating again after a 10 or 15-year interval."[16] He and Learning began a long-distance working relationship along the same lines as the one they enjoyed together in Fredericton. After working out a general idea, Nowlan sent his friend chunks of script and Learning phoned or wrote back his comments. The director's frequent trips to Fredericton usually allowed for an afternoon to sort out particularly difficult revisions face to face.

In their first long-distance collaboration, they acted as consultants for a new CBC-TV dramatic series set in a Newfoundland boarding house. Learning and Nowlan collaborated on the pilot of the show, called *Up At Ours*, and also wrote a couple of later episodes. They advised the producers about other scripts, which were mostly written by fledgling Newfoundland scriptwriters. Nowlan knew the quality of the show — even of his own scripts — was uneven. "Right now, I would say that it is better than *Flappers* but no better than *King of Kensington*," he wrote to John in 1980. "Sometimes better and, alas, sometimes worse."[17] But he maintained his enthusiasm for the work he and Learning were doing. In 1981, he sent his friend a draft of a new radio play, called *La Svengali*, and this message:

> I hope that I didn't unintentionally give you some sort of
> false impression while blathering away drunkenly on the

telephone about how happy I've been about our collaboration.

Ever since I teamed up with you, there have been those who, sometimes in public like Dennis Duffey in *The Canadian Forum* after *Frankenstein*, but more often in private conversation, have said that I was making a bad mistake — and behaving in a manner unworthy of my talents — in collaborating with Walter Learning on gothic horror stories and the like.

That is absolute bullshit, as far as I'm concerned. But it occurred to me that with so many people seemingly eager to turn me against you, there must surely be some who are eager to turn you against me. I simply wanted you to know for certain and in advance that, as far as I'm concerned, my decision to go into partnership with Walter Learning was one of the better decisions I've made during my life.[18]

Nowlan and Learning collaborated for the last time in late 1982, when Nowlan travelled to Vancouver to work on a stage adaptation of Gordon Pinsent's pilot for the television series *A Gift to Last*; the play had its premiere in Vancouver at Christmas, 1982. Even when Nowlan was not working in partnership with Learning, he enjoyed the accolades of the film and television community. In 1981 he was nominated for an ACTRA award for Best Writer of a Television Variety Show, and in 1982 he was nominated for the follow-up to *All On a Summer's Day*, the film *Christmas at King's Landing*.

The early 1980s was a period for exploring exciting new writing frontiers, but it was also a period of mending fences, or at least trying to do so. Nowlan had more or less come to terms with the region and the culture that produced him, but in doing so he had alienated some of the friends who had sustained him during his hardest times. Reconciliation with his actual family and his personal roots in Nova Scotia remained more elusive still.

Beginning in the spring of 1980, he mended the rift that had grown between him and his cousin Sylvia. In the five years since Nowlan's disastrous phone call to Jim, Sylvia and Jim had managed a marital reconciliation. While Jim was emerging from his fight with alcoholism, he began to look around and ask Sylvia, among other things, what became of her cousin Alden. It was he who urged her to get in touch with Nowlan again, which she did in April, 1980. But by then she had adopted a new identity, Rachel Paulson Pride. During the years repairing her marriage with Jim, she had sought spiritual comfort in a religious organization called Inner Light Consciousness and had been ordained as a minister. The group held that choosing one's own name helped a person choose his or her own path in life, so Sylvia chose Rachel (after a baby of hers that was stillborn) and Paulson (after Paul, her spiritual adviser). Nowlan's fears that he would lose another beloved friend to a religious movement were allayed when she sent him a book of dirty limericks for his forty-ninth birthday, though he persisted in calling her Sylvia or, as he sometimes preferred, Sylvie.

Making peace with Hants County and his family presented a greater challenge, but not everyone back home was sharpening their pencils to take a stab at their native son. Nowlan's success had not escaped the notice of those who supported the awkward young man back when he still carried the stigma of being "retarded." He had always disliked reading in Nova Scotia, particularly at Acadia University, not because he did not like the people or the institution, but because it was so close to Stanley. In February, 1979, for example, he had refused an invitation by Greg Cook, then working with the Writers' Federation of Nova Scotia, to attend a literary event called "Nova Scotia Homecoming," saying, "To be perfectly frank, dearest Greg, I'd rather be in Hell with my back broke, as they say in Carleton County, rather than read verses upon my native heath. A kind of madness comes over me as soon as I cross the Nova Scotia border and worsens as I approach the place where I was born."[19] But in the fall of that year, he received an invitation he could not refuse.

It came from Ken Miller, the writer from the *Windsor Tribune* who had started him in journalism thirty years ago. A committee in Windsor had proposed to erect a plaque in his honour at the Windsor Library, where he had spent so many hours as a teenager. Eleanor Geary, the librarian, was one of the people spearheading this initiative. Miller wanted to know if the library's most famous alumnus would attend and read at the event. In March, 1980, Nowlan and Claudine boarded a plane to Halifax, where Miller picked them up in his car. The room that served as the library was actually too small for the crowd that had gathered for the reading, so Nowlan read in a room across the hall. The poet was taken aback by the turnout: a full house of ghosts from his past, along with other local people dressed up for the occasion. Eleanor Geary attended, of course, and even his old teachers Hilda Palmer and

Marty Walker made an appearance. Midway through his reading, he looked up to see a stooped figure coming through the door, accompanied by his Aunt Ervette. It was Uncle Sylvester. "As you must have noticed, I had a very hard time to keep from bursting into tears during the testimonial," Nowlan wrote to Miller.

> Everybody was so nice to me and, what is even more touching, so proud of me and, what is most touching of all, some of those people who were so good to me when I was a kid — you and Eleanor Geary and, although I didn't get to know them well back then, Don Wetmore and the Loomers. And then there was Marty Walker who, as I now realize, taught me not in Grade I but in the grade that comes *before* Grade I in Nova Scotia, and my poor old aunt, who is stone-deaf, and my poor old uncle, who got out of his sickbed and what will probably be his deathbed (he has cancer of the bowel) to drive into Windsor. And, later, on the way home, I learned that my wife, Claudine, had taken the carnation that she'd been given to the cemetery where my poor old father lies and laid it on his grave. So much love.[20]

The most touching part of all was holding Sylvester. "That day I hugged my poor old uncle for the first time in my life — we weren't a demonstrative family — and to my amazement, he hugged me back. I would have thought that he'd pull away in embarrassment, if I had thought about it at all, but I didn't think about it, I simply hugged him."[21] Sylvia, too, planned a reconciliation with her father, whom she had not seen since leaving Nova Scotia at the age of fourteen. But Sylvester was every bit as ill as Nowlan said, and he succumbed to cancer in February of 1981, before Sylvia could visit.

Back at home, Nowlan tried to work through the flood of contradictory emotions aroused by the visit. He fictionalized the experience through the eye of a more detached and cynical Kevin O'Brien in his short story "About Memorials," in which Ken Miller appears as "Max Worthington," a stuffy and self-important big fish in a small pond who brings the poet back to "Balmoral" for the literary dedication. The speaker reflects on the irony of his situation, surrounded, as he sees it, by people who once disliked him:

Would Max and Mrs. Forrester and Mrs. Rhodenizer have even remembered me if I hadn't achieved what they imagined to be Success? I asked myself. It was a rhetorical question. I knew they'd have forgotten me years ago. And, as Aunt Agnes said, Uncle David hadn't got off his deathbed to see me again, he had got off his deathbed so he could talk with a member of the Legislature and other elders of the tribe of *The Big Man*, as an equal, in his own eyes at least.

Only Aunt Agnes was there simply because I was family. No, on second thought, she was there because Uncle David could not have come without her.

I almost wept.

Life had given these people so little that it was important to them to believe they were each of them a part — not of me, but of a person to whom a plaque could be erected. Because I had made this possible, they loved me. (p. 165)

It would be tempting to conclude that Nowlan was expressing his own feelings about the dedication ceremony directly through the persona of Kevin O'Brien, but, given the complexity of his feelings about the event and about Stanley, such a conclusion would be simplistic. More significant than the bitterness he allows his fictional persona to express is the real Nowlan's continuing inability to let go of his past. He did not attempt to follow up on his embrace with Sylvester by visiting him in the eighteen months between the dedication and the old man's death. Nor did he ever see Ervette again, or any of the other people from Hants County who turned out in such force to see him. Decades after his struggle to leave Stanley, Nowlan still could not overcome the habit of biting the hand that fed him. "About Memorials" was published in the Autumn, 1983, *Fiddlehead*, but by then there was no point in the better families of Hants County writing angry letters of protest.

In his last poetry collection, *I Might Not Tell Everybody This*, published in 1981, the poet reveals fears of his impending death. The evocative title emphasizes the intimate and even confessional quality of many of the poems. But, unlike his previous "conversational" poetry in *Between Tears and Laughter* and *I'm a Stranger Here Myself*, these poems hearken back to an earlier phase when he expressed the dread of the random violence that affects us all. He envisions a world where children "were clawing at one another, screaming," where vampires walk amongst us ("There is blood on his lips./ You fought back./ It is you they blame"), where "there is a horrible wing to the hotel" in which a relationship that might begin well "ends badly, with the Pimpernel/ beaten bloody, the Red Shadow turned into/ a monstrous parody of a baby-fat two-year-old,/ blubbering, and naked except for an undershirt." Many deal in some way with looking back, be it to the ancestral past in "Bobby Sands," the horrific past of Nazi Germany in "The Perfectibility of Man," or a wide-sweeping look at how history itself can be changed in "Word From the Losers." "We don't linger long in the present," he writes in "His Day in Court." "It can be rough there." Things fall apart, not only in society, but in the poet himself, haunted by "Cousin Wilfrid's DT Blues," hearing imaginary voices that, "God help me, I think I'd have to answer," and resisting the decay of a mortal body that can no longer support him.

Critical opinion of Nowlan, once divided over the question of regionalism, now entrenched itself around Nowlan's philosophical musings on the universal joys and pains of life. "Opening Nowlan's *I Might Not Tell Everybody This* is like meeting an old friend, wiser and more expansive for the intervening years," Ann Munton wrote in the *Fiddlehead*, finding "no hint of sentimentality in this latest volume."[22] In another camp, Anne Morton , writing in *Quarry*, stopped just short of equating the poem "Subway Psalm" with "ads for long-distance telephone calls." But she admitted, "He employs a persona so thoroughly ordinary, yet so warm-hearted, so just plain nice, that you find yourself wanting to like his poetry possibly more than it deserves."[23] In the *Canadian Forum*, Patrick O'Flaherty also singled out the Nowlan persona for comment, noting that "this horny-handed parading of what he honestly thought and felt in certain situations is part of Nowlan's candour, part of his game." He concluded, "Nowlan is a poet who takes risks. 'This is what I am, like it or lump it.' And in some of his rarer moments . . . he delivers the goods as only a true poet can."[24]

In January of 1982, Nowlan had another health scare, the most serious one since his cancer diagnosis. His blood sugar tested dangerously high, and he risked developing diabetes. Nowlan reported to his physician friend Nicholas Catanoy that the threat "didn't scare me until I read a couple of books on the disease and found that it could result in blindness and amputations and all sorts of horrible things."[25] The doctor ordered him to cut back severely on fat, sugar and alcohol until more tests could be done in a month's time. He told John:

The surprising thing about it [giving up alcohol] was that it hasn't bothered me all that much so far. There is a craving, mind you, but it isn't very different from the cravings that I occasionally have for root beer, say, or some favourite dish such as corned beef and cabbage. Nothing anything like as bad as the craving I've felt for a drink when I've simply told myself to stop drinking for a while. I guess that's because my taking a drink at this point would be like raising with nothing in the hole against an open pair. When you're beaten on the board it's time to fold, and wait for the next deal.

Mindful of his admonitions to Fraser, he adds, "I'm determined not to become a Reformed Lush. They're such a pain in the arse. I've always said that."[26]

Nowlan did reform, however, even after his second test results showed improvement. In fact, he forsook alcohol completely that spring, followed his diet and lost forty pounds. Yvonne Trainer remembers how Nowlan, denied his usual pleasure of sour cream, made a great show of cutting up his lemon and squeezing the juice onto his potatoes. He liked to show off his wristwatch to friends, not because it was fancy, but because the watch band now slid easily up and down his forearm. There were other beneficial side effects. His teeth, which he had complained were loose, were now firmly set in his jaw, and he could walk four times as far without tiring. Not that he made a point of walking any distance; he was still as resistant to exercise as he was before the diabetes scare.

His recovery prompted him to take another vacation to Ireland while his health was still good. This time he would see the island in detail over two weeks, including the torn city of Belfast and the village in County Wexford from which his ancestors had come. Of course, he arranged to write articles on his travels for both the *Telegraph-Journal* and *Atlantic Insight*. In fact, it was his article on Cuba that indirectly gave him the means to make the journey: it had won the National Magazines Award gold medal for best travel article of 1980. The award was sponsored by Air Canada, and Nowlan was successful in persuading the airline to give its "award-winning author" two return tickets to Ireland.

The timing of the trip made friends think he was mad. He elected to be in Belfast for the July 12 holiday, the commemoration of the Protestant William of Orange's victory over the Catholic James II at the

Treasures on Earth

Put on pajamas, go outdoors
and join the joggers. Do not eat
butter or eggs. Beware of drink.
Avoid excesses of cold or heat.
Abjure tobacco. Watch for lumps.
Get enough rest. Control your fears.
And, barring accidents, you ought
to live for years and years and years.

That is what the doctors told her.
The lady did as she was told.
In return for her exertions,
she knows the joys of being old.
Installed in Sunset Manor House,
she now partakes of such delights
as crosswords, paint-by-number kits
and semi-monthly Bingo nights.

Battle of the Boyne. It was the height of the season when Orange lodges undertake to march through Catholic neighbourhoods and the Catholics try to resist, sometimes with bricks and placards, at other times with guns and bombs. But Nowlan's sense of romanticism would not allow him to miss witnessing the drama of his heritage played out on a real-life stage. The hotel where he and Claudine stayed, the Belfast Europa, had been bombed thirty-eight times in the past ten years, and it was armoured with a seven-foot barbed wire fence and a heavy gate against a repeat performance. Everywhere they went their persons and belongings were searched. Yet in one *Telegraph* article Nowlan makes the same point about Belfast as he made in his article about Cuba: that people can still be friendly and human in the face of adversity. He noted of the July 12 parade: "The mood of both the marchers and onlookers was one of boisterous camaraderie. . . . It would have been bloody stupid to shout, 'Up the IRA!' And the 50,000 marchers did include a good many rather grim old men with bowler hats and furled umbrellas. But the dominant mood was good-humoured. Like a carnival."[27]

In contrast to his feeling after his 1968 trip to England and Ireland, he now thought that Dublin was the villain, with its fast-food franchises, modern buildings, modern dress, supermarkets and other conveniences unsightly to tourists from abroad. Worse, Dubliners were evidently not as "good-humoured" as their northern cousins. "Shop assistants, waitresses and chambermaids no longer address customers as 'luv' and say things like, 'thanks be to God, it's a fine large morning.'" The title of this *Telegraph* article laments, "Oh, How Dublin Has Changed!"[28]

Nowlan explores his other reason for going to Ireland — the search for his roots — in the *Insight* article: "We grow more interested in the past as we get older and draw closer to the time when we'll become part of the past ourselves."[29] His search for the past took him to the village of Bunclody in County Wexford, the ancestral home of the Nowlans. It turned out to be a sleepy agricultural village with twelve public houses, not very different from other such villages in Ireland. Nowlan went to one of these pubs, Conolly's, and chatted with Michael Kavanagh, the barman and, fortuitously, an amateur genealogist. Kavanagh looked up Nowlan's family records at the parish office, and Nowlan sent him a copy of *I Might Not Tell Everybody This* in return. The photograph accompanying the *Insight* article shows a very different-looking poet, tall, slim, and not bear-like at all. But upon his return from Ireland, he again fell off the wagon and gained back most of the weight he had lost.

Nowlan's March, 1983, League of Canadian Poets tour of western

Alden Nowlan in Ireland. CLAUDINE NOWLAN

Canada was just as hectic as previous tours, though he suffered no catastrophes save those he created himself. At Kwantlen College in Surrey, British Columbia, he gave the taxi driver wrong directions to an old part of the campus, not recognizing his error until he clambered up on some boxes and peered through a window to spy empty classrooms. The fact that he could clamber at all testifies to the robustness lingering from the previous summer, as does his account of winning a draft beer-drinking contest in Victoria while unaware (he claimed) that such a contest was under way. Claudine did not accompany him on this tour to set limits.

On January 25, 1983, Nowlan had celebrated his fiftieth birthday. Despite his preoccupation with mortality in his later poems, such as "He Enters His 50th Year," there is no indication that Nowlan harboured a subconscious intention to die, as some people do after retirement, the death of a loved one or some other milestone (statistically speaking, people are most likely to die after Christmas, New Year's or birthdays). But Nowlan had too many projects to pursue. On January 1, 1983, CBC, BBC and National Public Radio in the US made their first simultaneous program broadcast: *La Svengali*, a radio play written by Learning and Nowlan in the early 1980s. That spring, he gave a reading with Yvonne Trainer, the two of them sitting on high stools trading poems written in their own unique, yet similar, voices. Observers say it was perhaps the best of Nowlan's readings. A little book, *Nine Micmac Legends*, a collection of the Micmac legend adaptations he wrote while recovering from cancer, would be issued in the fall. The previous October, he had done a series of interviews with filmmaker Jon Pederson, who was planning on making a documentary about him. His May 5, 1983, letter to Sylvia sums up the contentment he felt with the opportunities his life had given him:

> I think the finest single moment in my life was sitting in the balcony at the theatre on opening night [of *Frankenstein*] and thinking to myself — very childishly, I know — how when I was a kid and used to go to Windsor on Saturday nights, the older boys (who thought of me literally as a retardate) would sit in the balcony with their girls, and I'd envy them — and now here I was, sitting in the balcony with two wonderful ladies, you and Claudine, with an arm around each of them, and a theatre crammed with people was applauding my play.
>
> Put like that, it probably sounds like a very egocentric experience — but it wasn't. Not really. It was more like experiencing an ecstasy purely on the strength of knowing that I was a member of the human race after all. Because when I was a kid I never really and truly felt that I was a member of the human race. Do you see what I mean?
>
> One problem I have as a result of becoming a member

of the human race so late in life — you're supposed to smile at this point, my love — is that I like being part of all sorts of different branches of the human race, which means that I feel a little out of place almost everywhere. . . .

And Claudine would be happier, I know, if I were something more straightforward and working class — a truck driver, for instance. One who went to the pub on Saturday nights with the other truck drivers while she and the other truck drivers' wives went off to play Bingo. . . . I sound as if I were complaining. I'm not; at least I don't think I am. It is something I've adapted to.

Actually, I'm in quite a cheerful mood. The tulips are out and we have one daffodil and one crocus. No sign of the others we planted. But one daffodil and one crocus may be aesthetically superior, anyhow.

Your loving brother,
Al[30]

A few days after Nowlan wrote to Sylvia, he and Claudine brought a gallon of fiddleheads to Trainer's going-away party, Nowlan sporting an eye patch because of broken blood vessels in his eye. Trainer recalls that the poet had difficulty breathing.

Later that same month Nowlan received an unexpected setback. Clarke, Irwin, his publisher and mainstay for the past sixteen years, went into receivership with a $1.6 million debt. Its assets had been frozen by the Ontario government until some manner of compensating creditors (including authors) could be arranged. As Nowlan explained to Cockburn in his 1982-1983 report, "I hadn't realized that receivership — unlike outright bankruptcy — is a kind of catalepsy. It's like being stung by one of those spiders that stings its prey and thereby puts it into a state of paralysis until it comes its time to be eaten."[31] Nowlan had one of his own treasured flies caught in that web: his next full-length book of fiction, a story collection called *Will Ye Let the Mummers In?* He wrote about the shock in his June 4, 1983, *Telegraph* column, "Requiem For a Book Publisher": "This is getting to sound more and more like an obituary, and I don't want it to be. . . It's just that I've been dealing with this all week, to the exclusion of practically everything else, and it would have been difficult and insincere of me to choose a different subject for a column."[32] But it was the way in which he was dealing with the crisis that was worrisome. Rumours swirled that Nowlan had been drinking steadily since news of the receivership reached him.

On the night of June 10 Nowlan was drinking with John, who had taken time off from his job with the Metro Toronto welfare department to visit his parents. Nowlan's latest bender, coupled with his usual nagging infections and his breathing problems, had taken their toll on his health. Even in better times, he snored and often woke up in the night fighting for breath, a consequence of his weight and his drinking. When he woke up on the morning of Saturday, June 11, he went to the bathroom to run a hot shower, the steam being his only relief from his breathing problems. After a few minutes, Claudine heard her husband calling out for her. He had collapsed in the shower. An ambulance was quickly summoned.

Nowlan insisted on dressing and walking out to the ambulance, although he needed assistance. But after reaching the hospital he went into full cardiac and respiratory arrest. Resuscitation was difficult owing to the rerouting of the blood vessels more than seventeen years ago. The medical staff could not maintain the blood flow to his brain, and he lapsed into a coma. They restarted his heart, put him on a respirator and finally diagnosed the cause of his breathing problem: pneumonia. Nowlan may have been walking around with it for weeks before his collapse, and a number of factors could have caused it. His friend Dr. Ian Cameron speculates that he might have had that most lethal kind of pneumonia, inflammation of the lungs due to aspirated vomit; this would be consistent with the excessive drinking of the previous few weeks. Bob Gibbs wrote later in a poem, "Dear Yvonne": "His doctor called it pickwickian syndrome after/ Dickens' fat boy his lungs flooding with CO2/ unbreathed trapped in fluid." Another contributing factor might have been the drug he sometimes used to combat his drinking and calm his nerves, Librium, which, as one of its more unusual side effects, may cause respiratory problems. Whatever the cause, pneumonia was the result, and the rerouted blood vessels, part of a procedure that once saved his life, now threatened it.

Nowlan's *Telegraph* column that morning was about that day's national Progressive Conservative leadership convention. It begins: "Like many of you, I'll be seated in front of the telly today, taking in the mixed boredom and excitement characteristic of political leadership conventions."[33] He predicted that Brian Mulroney would win. That afternoon, on the shore of Nova Scotia, poet Lesley Choyce encountered a mysterious bird, a cattle egret seldom seen in those parts, which followed Choyce for an hour as he worked in his garden. For some reason that he cannot explain, Choyce says the bird made him think of Nowlan. That night, in Halifax, just after Ryan's Fancy finished their farewell gig before breaking up the band, Al Pittman took the call from his wife, Marilee, announcing the news of Nowlan's collapse.

Dave Richards was often at Claudine's side as the week wore on and his friend languished in a coma. Richards's mother was a patient in the same Fredericton hospital. Sharon Fraser also visited and offered support in other ways, such as picking up Al Pittman from the airport and keeping Ray Fraser, who was in France, abreast of the latest developments. Sylvia and Jim even made the trip up from Connecticut, determined not to let another family member slip away without a final word of goodbye. A pile of homemade get-well cards arrived from a local elementary school. Not all visitors were welcome; Harriet phoned from Vancouver, but Claudine would not speak to her.

Nowlan was in no condition for speech either, unconscious and breathing with the help of a machine. Claudine and John watched, waited and wondered what to do. Searching for some evidence that his cardiac arrest did not irreversibly damage his brain, doctors sent Nowlan to the Saint John Regional Hospital for a CAT scan. But Al Pittman knew his friend's fate before he returned home to Newfoundland. Ducking the rule observed by most of Nowlan's circle to remain outside his room with Claudine, Pittman could not forbear asking a nurse to allow him access to his friend. Seeing the immobile mass in the bed, Pittman could tell it was over. "All that was missing was the coffin," he says.[34] Claudine thought of an old poem, "Aunt Jane," which Nowlan had written about his dying grandmother.

> *Aunt Jane, of whom I dreamed the nights it thundered,*
> *was dead at ninety, buried at a hundred.*
> *We kept her corpse a decade, hid upstairs,*
> *where it ate porridge, slept and said its prayers.*
>
> *And every night before I went to bed*
> *they took me in to worship with the dead.*
> *Christ Lord, if I should die before I wake,*
> *I pray thee Lord my body take.*

Claudine had her husband's instructions. She requested that the respirator be disconnected. But he continued breathing, and Sylvia finally decided to depart for home. Nowlan expired a couple of days afterwards, on June 27, 1983.

From that point, John assumed the responsibility for seeing that his father's remains were buried in the proper way. He took this responsibility seriously, although, in the opinion of some, his behaviour was somewhat dictatorial. The invitation list — who would come to the funeral and who would not — was a bone of contention. Ray Fraser was too far away to attend and Sharon, who had kept vigil at Claudine's side, was not among those invited. Hurt and angry, she attributed the slight to John's (and, by extension, his father's) belief that the women in his circle were mere adjuncts of their husbands. As when the Flat Earth Society was founded, Sharon was left out. But the limited size of the church chosen for the funeral service, the Edmund Jacob Chapel of the Old Arts Building at the University of New Brunswick, probably cramped the guest list as much as any preferences the family might have had.

Whatever the case, the high emotions in the family made rational decisions difficult. John's feelings no doubt account in large part for the fierce energy with which he handled the funeral arrangements. Ian Cameron and a bagpiper from CFB Gagetown were engaged to stand outside the Old Arts Building and play the pipes while mourners filed in. When the hour for the ceremony arrived, one important person was missing: Richard Hatfield, who was not only a guest but also the first speaker. The mourners sweltered in the crowded and stuffy chapel. John could wait no longer. "Where's that arsehole Richard Hatfield?" he asked Cameron as he stormed out of the building. He went back inside and arranged for Learning, the other speaker, to go first instead. When the ceremony was almost over, a black limousine at last turned from Dineen Drive towards the building, pulled up, and discharged Hatfield. The pressures of the past week made John snap. As Hatfield hustled in, Cameron could hear John berating him for his tardiness. "You arsehole! You were supposed to be here thirty minutes ago!" A seasoned veteran of public disapproval, Hatfield ignored him and went in to deliver his address.

Later that afternoon, after the ceremonial interment at Forest Hills Cemetery, the mourners assembled at Windsor Castle for one last Nowlan party, sharing drinks and fond memories, many laughs and some tears as well. Jim Stewart, driving home after the funeral, noticed only then that his whistle had cut him when he broke it over his knee. Claudine sat in the front room, acknowledging the condolences of the guests, and, after the stress she had been through, looking forward to the time when it would be over. She mulled over the events of that morning, before the funeral, when she had been alone and thinking about her husband clinging to life in the hospital in 1966, writing his poem "Morning of the Third Operation":

what if
I die
and go home
and Claudine
is crying:
will she know
what it means
even if I
have the strength
to knock
a pencil
off the table.
Listen, Claudine,
look at me!
I'm alive!
Don't be
so damned
stupid, woman.
I'm here
beside you.
But she keeps on
crying
and then
a friend comes
and takes her away
because it isn't good
for her
to be alone.

That morning, before the funeral, she had been sitting alone in her quiet house when for no apparent reason a pencil flew off a nearby table and landed at her feet.

Soon a new writer-in-residence, David Adams Richards, assumed the position at the University of New Brunswick that had been held by the man he loved and admired. But 676 Windsor Street reverted to its former function as spare office and accommodation space for the university. Richards chose to live on St. John Street, near Queen Square Park and close to the base of the UNB campus. Claudine moved to a larger house on McKeen Street on the city's north side. Most of the Nowlans' friends, with the exception of Bob Gibbs, say they have had little contact with Claudine since the poet's death.

Before he died, Nowlan had chosen Bob Gibbs as the executor, not of his will, but rather of his literary estate: published and unpublished stories, books, articles, plays and thousands of poems, as well as letters, diaries, and other writings. Gibbs kept Nowlan's memory alive with the publication in 1985 of *An Exchange of Gifts*, which remains the most ambitious collection of Nowlan's poems, new and selected. His introductions to this book and to the 1992 catalogue of Nowlan's papers at the University of Calgary Archives are perhaps the most sensitive and perceptive critical essays about Nowlan's life and work. Nowlan's stature as a poet of national prominence seems to have shrunk since 1983, but this shrinkage is more noticeable among the academics and literati who try to mould public taste than among the public who actually read the many books and magazines that have featured and discussed his work since his death.

Outside the ivory tower, Nowlan's writing enjoys a popularity expressed in continuing sales of his work. Creative writers have taken up the Nowlan banner, as can be seen by the collections published during the 1990s and edited by writers, most notably Thomas R. Smith's 1993 collection for the American market, *What Happened When He Went to the Store for Bread* (containing a new introduction by Robert Bly), and Governor General's Award winners Patrick Lane and Lorna Crozier's 1997 collection *Alden Nowlan: Selected Poems*. In New Brunswick, the former poet laureate's light has not dimmed. In 1988 *The Wanton Troopers*, the novel that Nowlan had kept in a drawer since his Hartland days, was at last published by Goose Lane Editions, and it has sold steadily, particularly as a textbook for senior high school and junior university students. Gibbs continues to manage the Nowlan literary estate, editing most recently a two-volume collection of Nowlan's newspaper columns: *White Madness* and *The Road Dancers*.

The poet still draws controversy, too. Paul Hanna's 1987 drama *Lockhartville*, a semi-biographical play about Nowlan based on his poetry and the novel *Various Persons Named Kevin O'Brien*, was produced jointly by TNB's Contact Theatre and St. Thomas University. Some people who knew Nowlan were offended at the play's suggestion that an incestuous relationship between Freeman and Harriet formed part of Nowlan's emotional baggage. Richards, in his last year as UNB writer-in-residence, wrote, "In [*Lockhartville*], art has become social work. Nothing more than holding forth on a morally superior lifestyle. Much of it contrary to [*Various Persons Named Kevin O'Brien*'s] genius. A genius few of the players were compassionate enough to understand."[35]

This is another aspect of the legacy Nowlan left to those who knew him and those who have known him only through his writing. With the love of his work comes a duty to defend him, to explain him against those who might understand him too quickly and make unconsidered judgements about his work. There is justice in Michael Brian Oliver's claim that "Alden Nowlan may well be the most misunderstood poet in Canadian literature."[36] Part of the paradox comes from trying to disentangle the threads of what made him a poet from those that made him a man. In his writing, he was committed to honesty, to seeing things as they are; in his life, he could not bear the truth about himself. He became an adept escape artist, avoiding situations that troubled him or, when cornered, learning how to turn the tables and fight his way out, often not realizing when fighting was unnecessary. Throughout his life he created a multitude of selves to increase the richness of his experience, but he ended up cheating himself by trying to believe that the lie was true. What made his writing a triumph made aspects of his personal life tragic. Above all a survivor, he was willing to cut away those painful parts of himself that would destroy him, yet he continually examined those castaway fragments, reassembling them in a way that might explain their origins and enable him to discover why they hurt him so much. At every milestone of his life, with every accomplishment, before he could meet the eye of anyone else, he could not help but turn and meet the eye of himself as he once was.

ACKNOWLEDGEMENTS

"A Mug's Game," "Morning of the Third Operation," "Britain Street, Saint John, New Brunswick," "In the Operating Room," "My Father's Body Was Found by Children," "What Happened When He Went to the Store for Bread," "The Mysterious Naked Man," "The Red Wool Shirt": Copyright © Irwin Publishing Inc., 1967, 1969, 1977, 1982. First published by Clarke, Irwin & Co. Ltd. Reprinted by permission of House of Anansi Press Ltd. "The Encounter, The Recognition": Copyright © 1967 Clarke, Irwin & Co. Ltd. Reprinted by permission of Irwin Publishing Inc. "In the Night" and "The Night of the Party": Copyright © 1974 Clarke, Irwin & Co. Ltd. Reprinted by permission of Irwin Publishing Inc. "Treasures on Earth" and "He Enters His 50th Year": Copyright © 1982 Clarke, Irwin & Co. Ltd. Reprinted by permission of Irwin Publishing Inc. "On the Stairs" and "The Bhikku": Copyright © 1969 Clarke, Irwin & Co. Ltd. Reprinted by permission of Irwin Publishing Inc. "He Is Entertained by the Chairman of the Department," "The Kookaburra's Song," and "Living in a Mad House": Copyright © 1977 Clarke, Irwin & Co. Ltd. Reprinted by permission of Irwin Publishing Inc.

"My Sister's Boyfriends," "A Letter to Tomorrow," "The Mists," "The Mind is Turkestan and Proud," "The Final Prophet," "The Expatriate," "Johnny Five," "A Poem to My Mother," "After the First Frost," "Disguise," "Saturday Night," "The Bull Moose," "Aunt Jane," "I Knew the Seasons Ere I Knew the Hours," and "Playing the Jesus Game" are published by permission of Claudine Nowlan. Extracts from manuscript materials and letters by Alden Nowlan are published by permission of Claudine Nowlan.

Letters to Alden Nowlan are published by permission of the writers. A few writers could not be found; the publisher and the author would be grateful for information that would enable us to contact them.

Photo sources and copyright holders are as follows: Cover photo and frontispiece: Copyright © Kent Nason, 1982-83, reproduced by permission. Pages 34 and 298, material relating to Alden Nowlan collected by Rachel Paulson Pride, Special Collections, University of Calgary Library, reproduced by permission of Claudine Nowlan. Page 186 and page 299, reproduced by permission of Sharon Fraser. Page 180, Duncan Cameron/National Archives of Canada/Accession 1970-015, and page 262, Frank Prazak/National Archives of Canada/Accession 1988-041, both reproduced by permission of the National Archives of Canada. Page 196, courtesy of *New Brunswick Telegraph-Journal*, reproduced by permission of Irwin Publishing Inc. Page 205, courtesy of the Department of English, University of New Brunswick, reproduced by permission of Bruno Bobak. Page 218, by Ian Brown, courtesy of Alden Nowlan fonds, Special Collections, University of Calgary Library, reproduced by permission of Patricia A. Brown. Page 251, reproduced by permission of Nicholas Catanoy. Page 266, by Ian Brown, courtesy of Walter Learning, reproduced by permission of Theatre New Brunswick. Page 281, reproduced by permission of *The Fredericton Daily Gleaner*.

NOTES

Chapter One: 1933-1940

1. Alden Nowlan, Letter to Louis Cormier. 6 May 1969. Alden Nowlan Papers #40.9.17.19. University of Calgary Library, Calgary.

2. Walter Learning, "Learning on Nowlan: Final Tribute to a Giant," *UNB Perspectives* (September 1983), p. 5.

3. Material on funeral taken from interviews with Claudine Nowlan and Robert Gibbs (24 February 1993), Ian Cameron (9 July 1998) and Bill and Nancy Bauer (22 December 1992); from Janice Tyrwhitt, "The Man From Desolation Creek," *Reader's Digest* 124 (March 1984), pp. 67-71; and from Ralph Costello, "Alden Nowlan's Love-in — They Called It a Funeral," *Telegraph-Journal* (2 July 1983), p. 8.

4. Clifton Whiten, Editorial, *Poetry Canada Review* 5 (Fall 1983), p. 3.

5. Fraser Sutherland, "Nowlan Meant Integrity to a Generation of Writers," *Globe and Mail* (28 June 1983), p. 19.

6. Milton Acorn, "Sealed with a Kiss and a Tear," *Cross-Canada Writers' Quarterly* 7.2 (1985), p. 17.

7. Irving Layton, "In Memoriam: Alden Nowlan — 1933-1983, *Poetry Canada Review* 5 (Fall 1983), p. 3.

8. Ken Adachi, "Poet's Work Aimed at Ordinary People," *Toronto Star* (28 June 1983), p. C1.

9. Eli Mandel, "In Memoriam: Alden Nowlan — 1933-1983," *Poetry Canada Review* 5 (Fall 1983), p. 3.

10. Douglas Fetherling, "A Work in Progress: Remembering Alden Nowlan," *New Brunswick Reader* (17 February 1996), p. 22.

11. David Adams Richards, "Nowlan," *New Brunswick Reader* (27 June 1998), p. 14.

12. Alden Nowlan, Letter to Anne Greer. 13 November 1967. Alden Nowlan Papers #40.13.52.8. University of Calgary Library, Calgary.

13. Alden Nowlan, "Alden Nowlan: Autobiographical Sketch," *Yes* 16 (October 1967), p. 19.

14. Ervette (Reese) Hamilton, Letter to author. n.d.

15. Rachel (Sylvia Reese) Pride, Telephone interview. 17 December 1995.

16. Ervette (Reese) Hamilton, Interview. 1 September 1996.

17. Alden Nowlan, Letter to Roy MacSkimming. 15 July 1967. Alden Nowlan Papers #40.6.37.35. University of Calgary Library, Calgary.

18. Alden Nowlan, Letter to Anne Greer. 14 January 1968. Alden Nowlan Papers #40.13.52.18. University of Calgary Library, Calgary.

19. Alden Nowlan, Letter to Anne Greer. 13 November 1967. Alden Nowlan Papers #40.13.52.8. University of Calgary Library, Calgary.

20. Alden Nowlan, Speech to the International Reading Association. 11 October 1980. Alden Nowlan Papers #40.75.9.2. University of Calgary Library, Calgary.

21. Albert Reese, Interview.

22. David Donnell, Interview with Alden Nowlan, *Books in Canada* 11.6 (June/July 1982), pp. 26-28.

23. Albert Reese, Interview.

24. Ervette (Reese) Hamilton, Interview.

25. Alden Nowlan, Letter to Rachel (Sylvia Reese) Pride, 10 November 1969. Alden Nowlan Papers #40.26.4.5. University of Calgary Library, Calgary.

26. Nora Reese, Letter to Edgar Hamilton. 26 May 1939. Author's collection.

27. Alden Nowlan, "Growing Up in Katpesa Creek," *Double Exposure* (Fredericton: Brunswick Press, 1978), p. 20.

28. Rachel (Sylvia Reese) Pride, Telephone interview.

Chapter Two: 1940-1952

1. Carol Church, Interview. 22 September 1996.

2. Alden Durling, Interview. 23 September 1996.

3. Alden Nowlan, Letter to Greg Cook. 29 June 1968. Alden Nowlan Papers #40.9.10.47. University of Calgary Library, Calgary.

4. Alden Nowlan, "Growing Up in Katpesa Creek," *Double Exposure* (Fredericton: Brunswick Press, 1978), p. 23.

5. Ethyl Ogilvie, Interview. 20 September 1996.

6. Alden Nowlan, "Something to Write About," *Canadian Literature* 68-69 (1976), p. 8.

7. Harriet (Nowlan) Ottie, Interview. 18 August 1995.

8. Alden Nowlan, Letter to Rachel (Sylvia Reese) Pride. 24 May 1963. Rachel Paulson Pride Papers #61.1.1.7. University of Calgary Library, Calgary.

9. Alden Nowlan, Letter to Rachel (Sylvia Reese) Pride. 29 November 1974. Alden Nowlan Papers #40.26.5.43. University of Calgary Library, Calgary.

10. Albert Reese, Interview. 22 September 1996.

11. Marty Walker, Interview. 23 September 1996.

12. Alden Nowlan, Introduction, *Gardens of the Wind*, by Alden Nowlan (Saskatoon: Thistledown Press, 1982).

13. Greg Cook, Interview with Alden Nowlan, *Amethyst* (1963), p. 17.

14. "Growing Up in Katpesa Creek," p. 21.

15. "Growing Up in Katpesa Creek," p. 20.

16. "Growing Up in Katpesa Creek," p. 15.

17. "Growing Up in Katpesa Creek," p. 19.

18. Gail (Sanford) Manning, Telephone interview. 26 June 1998.

19. A.H. MacDonald, *Mount Hope Then and Now* (Halifax: Nova Scotia Hospital, 1996), p. 102.

20. *Mount Hope Then and Now*, p. 101.

21. Alden Nowlan, Letter to Raymond Fraser. 28 June 1963. Raymond Fraser Papers. Harriet Irving Library, University of New Brunswick, Fredericton.

22. Ervette (Reese) Hamilton, Interview. 23 December 1992.

23. Renald Shoofler, Letter to the editor, the *Canadian Forum* 44 (December 1964), p. 204.

24. Alden Nowlan, Letter to the editor, the *Canadian Forum* 45 (January 1965), pp. 227-228.

25. Alden Nowlan, Letter to Freeman Nowlan. 8 November 1966. Alden Nowlan Papers #40.24.1.7. University of Calgary Library, Calgary.

26. Lawrence Anthony and Owen Lowe, Interview. 21 September 1996.

27. Rachel (Sylvia Reese) Pride, Telephone interview. 1 August 1999.

28. Alden Nowlan, Letter to Raymond Fraser. 26 January 1963. Raymond Fraser Papers. Harriet Irving Library, University of New Brunswick, Fredericton.

29. Alden Nowlan, Speech to the International Reading Association. 11 October 1980. Alden Nowlan Papers #40.75.9.2. University of Calgary Library, Calgary.

30. Alden Nowlan, Letter to Freeman Nowlan. 14 April 1973. Alden Nowlan Papers #40.24.1.169. University of Calgary Library, Calgary.

31. "Something to Write About," p. 8.

32. "Something to Write About," p. 9.

33. Harriet (Nowlan) Ottie, Interview.

Chapter Three: 1952-1956

1. Alden Nowlan, Letter to Laura Clark. 14 August 1971. Alden Nowlan Papers #40.6.33.1. University of Calgary Library, Calgary.

2. Alden Nowlan, "Growing Up in Katpesa Creek," *Double Exposure* (Fredericton: Brunswick Press, 1978), p. 24.

3. Alden Nowlan, "She Was Beautiful," *Atlantic Advocate* (August 1974), p. 53.

4. Harold Plummer, Interview. 8 April 1996.

5. Alden Nowlan, Document #40.112.8f25. Alden Nowlan Papers. University of Calgary Library, Calgary.

6. Alden Nowlan, "John Diefenbaker: Larger Than Life," *Atlantic Advocate* (October 1979), p. 11.

7. Hartland *Observer* (29 May 1952), p. 1.

8. Letter to Laura Clark.

9. Hugh Clark, Interview. 20 March 1996.

10. Alden Nowlan, "The Lodges: Down but Not Out, and Far from Forgotten," *Atlantic Insight* (November 1980), pp. 55-56.

11. Harold Plummer, Interview.

12. "The Lodges: Down but Not Out, and Far from Forgotten," p. 57.

13. Hugh Clark, Interview.

14. Harold Plummer, Interview.

15. Alden Nowlan, Letter to John Metcalf. 2 February 1974. Alden Nowlan Papers #40.18.50.47. University of Calgary Library, Calgary.

16. Alden Nowlan, "My Career in Baseball." Manuscript of CBC Radio broadcast. Alden Nowlan Papers #40.76.20f7-9. University of Calgary Library, Calgary.

17. Alden Nowlan, "John Diefenbaker: Larger Than Life."

18. Alden Nowlan, "Something to Write About," *Canadian Literature* 68-69 (1976), p. 9.

19. Glen Coffield, Letter to Alden Nowlan. 18 September 1951. Alden Nowlan Papers #40.3.24. University of Calgary Library, Calgary.

20. Rachel (Sylvia Reese) Pride, Telephone interview. 17 December 1995.

21. Alden Nowlan, Letter to Catherine Wilbraham. 20 July 1972. Alden Nowlan Papers #40.18.5.12. University of Calgary Library, Calgary.

22. Alden Nowlan, "Fred Clarke Remembered," *Atlantic Advocate* (December 1974), p. 63.

23. Alden Nowlan, "I Discovered a Mountain," *Family Herald and Weekly Star* (28 July 1955), pp. 24-25.

24. Jim Murray, Interview. 9 February 1996.

25. Harold Plummer, Interview.

26. Fred Hatfield and Kay Hatfield, Interview. 9 February 1996.

Chapter Four: 1956-1960

1. Alden Nowlan, "Something to Write About," *Canadian Literature* 68-69 (1976), pp. 9-10.

2. Fred Cogswell, "Alden Nowlan as Regional Atavist," *Studies in Canadian Literature* 11 (1986), p. 208.

3. Alden Nowlan, Letter to Fred Cogswell. 22 February 1955. *Fiddlehead* Papers, File: n.d., 1955-1960 #12. Harriet Irving Library, University of New Brunswick, Fredericton.

4. Fred Cogswell, Letter to Alden Nowlan. 3 April 1955. *Fiddlehead* Papers, File: n.d., 1955-1960 #13. Harriet Irving Library, University of New Brunswick, Fredericton.

5. Alden Nowlan, Letter to Fred Cogswell. 18 February 1958. *Fiddlehead* Papers, File: n.d., 1955-1960 #30. Harriet Irving Library, University of New Brunswick, Fredericton.

6. "Something to Write About," p. 10.

7. Alden Nowlan, Letter to Fred Cogswell. 31 December 1960. *Fiddlehead* Papers, File: n.d., 1955-1960 #97. Harriet Irving Library, University of New Brunswick, Fredericton.

8. Alden Nowlan, Letter to Fred Cogswell. 10 January 1958. *Fiddlehead* Papers, File: n.d., 1955-1960 #28. Harriet Irving Library, University of New Brunswick, Fredericton.

9. Fred Cogswell, Letter to Alden Nowlan. 8 January 1958. *Fiddlehead* Papers, File: n.d., 1955-1960 #28. Harriet Irving Library, University of New Brunswick, Fredericton.

10. Alden Nowlan, Letter to Fred Cogswell. 17 January 1958. *Fiddlehead* Papers, File: n.d., 1955-1960 #29. Harriet Irving Library, University of New Brunswick, Fredericton.

11. Alden Nowlan, Letter to Canada Council. Desmond Pacey Papers. National Archives of Canada, Ottawa.

12. Alden Nowlan, Letter to Fred Cogswell. 9 November 1960. *Fiddlehead* Papers, File: n.d., 1955-1960 #90. Harriet Irving Library, University of New Brunswick, Fredericton.

13. Harold Plummer, Interview. 8 April 1996.

14. Alden Nowlan, Letter to Fred Cogswell. 27 April 1957. *Fiddlehead* Papers, File: n.d., 1955-1960 #24. Harriet Irving Library, University of New Brunswick, Fredericton.

15. Alden Nowlan, Letter to Fred Cogswell. 19 September 1960. *Fiddlehead* Papers, File: n.d., 1955-1960 #86. Harriet Irving Library, University of New Brunswick, Fredericton.

16. Alden Nowlan, Letter to Fred Cogswell. 10 January 1962. *Fiddlehead* Papers, File: n.d., 1961-1972 #2. Harriet Irving Library, University of New Brunswick, Fredericton.

17. Alden Nowlan, Letter to Fred Cogswell. 27 May 1962. *Fiddlehead* Papers, File: n.d., 1961-1972 #34. Harriet Irving Library, University of New Brunswick, Fredericton.

18. Desmond Pacey, Letter to Al Purdy. 21 January 1975. Desmond Pacey Papers. National Archives of Canada, Ottawa.

19. Milton Wilson, "Letters in Canada: 1961: Poetry," *University of Toronto Quarterly* 31.4 (1962), pp. 432-454.

20. Michael Hornyansky, Review of *The Rose and the Puritan*, by Alden Nowlan, *Fiddlehead* 39 (Winter 1959), p. 44.

21. Alec Lucas, Review of *Under the Ice*, by Alden Nowlan, *Fiddlehead* 51 (Winter 1962), p. 62.

22. Miriam Waddington, "Japanese Flowers, Autumn Vistas," *Canadian Literature* 9 (Summer 1961), pp. 71-72.

23. John Robert Colombo, "Wit, Wisdom and Two Chapbooks," *Waterloo Review* 2 (Winter 1960), p. 79.

24. Eli Mandel, "Turning New Leaves," *Canadian Forum* (July 1961), p. 91.

25. Douglas Lochhead, Review of *Under the Ice*, by Alden Nowlan, *Dalhousie Review* 41 (Autumn 1961), p. 431.

26. Alden Nowlan Papers #40.113.1f118 verso. University of Calgary Library, Calgary.

27. Robert Weaver, Letter to Fred Cogswell. 9 September 1958. Robert Weaver Papers. National Archives of Canada, Ottawa.

28. Fred Cogswell, Letter to Louis Dudek. 2 January 1957. Louis Dudek Papers. National Library of Canada, Ottawa.

29. Alden Nowlan, "A Defense of Obscenity," *Delta* 3.1 (1959), p. 27-28.

30. Alden Nowlan, Letter to Louis Dudek. 16 February 1962. Louis Dudek Papers. National Library of Canada, Ottawa.

31. Alden Nowlan, Letter to Fred Cogswell. 21 March 1961. *Fiddlehead* Papers, File: n.d., 1961-1972 #10. Harriet Irving Library, University of New Brunswick, Fredericton.

32. Alden Nowlan, Letter to John Drew. 18 October 1966. Alden Nowlan Papers #40.10.49.34. University of Calgary Library, Calgary.

33. "Alden Nowlan as Regional Atavist," p. 208.

34. Edward D. Ives, "Alden Nowlan's Poetry: A Personal Chronicle," *Fiddlehead* 81 (1969), p. 62.

35. Alden Nowlan, Letter to Edward Ives. 4 February 1983. Alden Nowlan Papers #40.3.29.1. University of Calgary Library, Calgary.

Chapter Five: 1960-1966

1. Fred Cogswell, "Alden Nowlan as Regional Atavist," *Studies in Canadian Literature* 11.2 (1986), p. 208.

2. Harold Plummer, Interview. 8 April 1996.

3. Alden Nowlan, Letter to John Drew. 18 October 1966. Alden Nowlan Papers #40.10.49.34. University of Calgary Library, Calgary.

4. Ralph Costello, Letter to Alden Nowlan. 18 March 1960. Alden Nowlan Papers #40.29.23.7. University of Calgary Library, Calgary.

5. Alden Nowlan, Letter to Ray Fraser. 10 June 1967. Alden Nowlan Papers #40.12.23.29. University of Calgary Library, Calgary.

6. Alden Nowlan, Letter to Tom Miles. 15 April 1967. Alden Nowlan Papers #40.19.4.2. University of Calgary Library, Calgary.

7. Alden Nowlan, "Hatfield Country," *Maclean's* (November 1971), pp. 78-79.

8. Alden Nowlan, Letter to Carolyn Atkinson, Office of the Premier of New Brunswick. Alden Nowlan Papers #40.20.7.40. University of Calgary Library, Calgary.

9. Alden Nowlan, Letter to Fred Cogswell. 27 May 1962. *Fiddlehead* Papers, File 1961-1972 #34. Harriet Irving Library, University of New Brunswick, Fredericton.

10. Fred Cogswell, Letter to Louis Dudek. 11 June 1962. Louis Dudek Papers. National Library of Canada, Ottawa.

11. Milton Wilson, "Letters in Canada: 1962: Poetry," *University of Toronto Quarterly* 32 (July 1963), p. 377.

12. Eli Mandel, "Turning New Leaves," *Canadian Forum* (March 1963), p. 280.

13. Eli Mandel, "Turning New Leaves," p. 278.

14. Alden Nowlan, Letter to Fred Cogswell. 25 March 1963. *Fiddlehead* Papers, File 1961-1972 #49. Harriet Irving Library, University of New Brunswick, Fredericton.

15. Alden Nowlan, Letter to Fred Cogswell. 21 May 1963. *Fiddlehead* Papers, File 1961-1972 #53. Harriet Irving Library, University of New Brunswick, Fredericton.

16. Alden Nowlan, Letter to Tom Miles.

17. Alden Nowlan, "The New Brunswick Papers: What About the Irvings?" *Canadian Newspapers: The Inside Story*. Ed. Walter Stewart. (Edmonton: Hurtig Publishers, 1980), p. 66.

18. Alden Nowlan, Letter to Fred Cogswell. 22 October 1963. *Fiddlehead* Papers, File 1961-1972 #64. Harriet Irving Library, University of New Brunswick, Fredericton.

19. Alden Nowlan, Letter to Fred Cogswell. 1 October 1963. *Fiddlehead* Papers, File 1961-1972 #63. Harriet Irving Library, University of New Brunswick, Fredericton.

20. Alden Nowlan, "Of Course Oswald Did It," *Telegraph-Journal* (6 December 1975), p. 5.

21. Alden Nowlan, Letter to Fred Cogswell. 1 December 1963. *Fiddlehead* Papers, File 1961-1972 #65. Harriet Irving Library, University of New Brunswick, Fredericton.

22. Alden Nowlan, Letter to Fred Cogswell. 18 December 1965. *Fiddlehead* Papers, File 1961-1972 #74. Harriet Irving Library, University of New Brunswick, Fredericton.

23. Ray Fraser, Interview. 19 September, 1999.

24. Alden Nowlan, Letter to Fred Cogswell. 1 October 1963.

25. Brian Bartlett, Diary entry. 31 December 1982.

26. Alden Nowlan. Letter to Fred Cogswell. 22 October 1963. *Fiddlehead* Papers, File 1961-1972 #64. Harriet Irving Library, University of New Brunswick, Fredericton.

27. Robert Gibbs, Letter to Desmond Pacey. 6 October 1964. Desmond Pacey Papers. Harriet Irving Library, University of New Brunswick, Fredericton.

28. John Grube. Letter to Desmond Pacey. 22 September 1964. Desmond Pacey Papers. Harriet Irving Library, University of New Brunswick, Fredericton.

29. Alden Nowlan, Letter to Fred Cogswell. 26 April 1965. *Fiddlehead* Papers, File 1961-1972 #71. Harriet Irving Library, University of New Brunswick, Fredericton.

30. Alden Nowlan, Letter to Desmond Pacey. 4 May 1965. Desmond Pacey Papers. National Archives, Ottawa.

31. Alden Nowlan, Letter to Fred Cogswell. 4 May 1965. *Fiddlehead* Papers, File 1961-1972 #73. Harriet Irving Library, University of New Brunswick, Fredericton.

32. Alden Nowlan, Letter to Rachel (Sylvia Reese) Pride. 3 February 1965. Alden Nowlan Papers #61.1.1.13. University of Calgary Library, Calgary.

33. Ray Fraser, "Words," *Pottersfield Portfolio* 18 (Fall 1997), p. 33.

34. Alden Nowlan, Letter to Fred Cogswell. 6 February 1965. *Fiddlehead* Papers, File 1961-1972 #70. Harriet Irving Library, University of New Brunswick, Fredericton.

Chapter 6: 1966-1967

1. Alden Nowlan, Transcription of audiotaped interview with Jon Pedersen. Harriet Irving Library, University of New Brunswick, Fredericton. p. 18.

2. Alden Nowlan, Letter to Tyndale Martin. 25 August 1967. Alden Nowlan papers #40.18.22.10. University of Calgary Library, Calgary.

3. Alden Nowlan, Letter to Fred Cogswell. 20 April 1967. *Fiddlehead* Papers, File 1961-1972 #79. Harriet Irving Library, University of New Brunswick, Fredericton.

4. Alden Nowlan, Letter to Ray Fraser. 12 January 1968. Ray Fraser Papers #51. Harriet Irving Library, University of New Brunswick, Fredericton.

5. Alden Nowlan, Letter to Ray Fraser. 3 July 1966. Alden Nowlan Papers #40.12.23.4. University of Calgary Library, Calgary.

6. Alden Nowlan, Letter to Desmond Pacey. 16 June 1966. Desmond Pacey Papers. National Archives of Canada, Ottawa.

7. Alden Nowlan, Letter to Ray Fraser. 4 May 1967. Alden Nowlan Papers #40.12.23.25. University of Calgary Library, Calgary.

8. Alden Nowlan, Letter to Freeman Nowlan. 1 October 1966. Alden Nowlan Papers #40.24.1.6. University of Calgary Library, Calgary.

9. Alden Nowlan, Letter to Elizabeth Brewster. 29 June 1966. Alden Nowlan Papers #40.3.23.5. University of Calgary Library, Calgary.

10. Alden Nowlan, "In the Face of Death," *Atlantic Advocate* (May 1970), p. 69.

11. Fred Cogswell, Letter to Canada Council. n.d. Desmond Pacey Papers. National Archives of Canada, Ottawa.

12. Al Purdy, *Reaching for the Beaufort Sea: An Autobiography* (Madiera Park, BC: Harbour Publishing, 1993), p. 240.

13. Alden Nowlan, Letter to *Human Voice Quarterly*. 4 October 1966. Alden Nowlan Papers #40.15.15.1. University of Calgary Library, Calgary.

14. D. Vincent Smith, Letter to Alden Nowlan. 13 October 1966. Alden Nowlan Papers #40.15.15.2. University of Calgary Library, Calgary.

15. Alden Nowlan, Letter to *Human Voice Quarterly*. 22 October 1966. Alden Nowlan Papers #40.15.15.3. University of Calgary Library, Calgary.

16. Alden Nowlan, Letter to Irving Layton. 22 October 1966. Alden Nowlan Papers #40.16.24.5. University of Calgary Library, Calgary.

17. Alden Nowlan, Letter to John Drew. 18 October 1966. Alden Nowlan Papers #40.10.49.34. University of Calgary Library, Calgary.

18. Roy MacSkimming, Letter to Alden Nowlan. 27 October 1966. Alden Nowlan Papers #40.6.37.1. University of Calgary Library, Calgary.

19. Roy MacSkimming, Interview. 17 December 1997.

20. Alden Nowlan, Letter to Clarke, Irwin. 4 November 1966. Alden Nowlan Papers #40.6.37.2. University of Calgary Library, Calgary.

21. Alden Nowlan, Letter to Ray Fraser. 25 January 1967. Alden Nowlan Papers #40.12.23.19. University of Calgary Library, Calgary.

Chapter Seven: 1967-1968

1. Greg Cook, Letter to Alden Nowlan. 7 January 1967. Alden Nowlan Papers #40.9.10.4. University of Calgary Library, Calgary.

2. Alden Nowlan, Letter to Greg Cook. 14 February 1967. Alden Nowlan Papers #40.9.10.5. University of Calgary Library, Calgary.

3. Roy MacSkimming, Letter to Alden Nowlan. 12 February, 1967. Alden Nowlan Papers #40.6.37.10. University of Calgary Library, Calgary.

4. Alden Nowlan, Letter to Roy MacSkimming. 15 July 1967. Alden Nowlan Papers #40.6.37.35. University of Calgary Library, Calgary.

5. Alden Nowlan, Letter to Ray Fraser. 4 May 1967. Alden Nowlan Papers #40.12.23.25. University of Calgary Library, Calgary.

6. This account of Ginsberg's visit is based on Alden Nowlan, "Ginsberg: Truth is a Five-Letter Word," *Telegraph-Journal* (27 March 1967), p. 5; Letter to Ray Fraser, 4 May 1967; Louis Cormier, "Unstuck," *Pottersfield Portfolio* 18 (Fall 1997), pp. 36-39; and Louis Cormier, Interview, 14 December 1997.

7. John Drew, Letter to author. n.d. Author's collection.

8. The account of the trip to England and Ireland is based primarily upon Alden Nowlan, "On a Literary Pilgrimage," *Atlantic Advocate* (July 1970), pp. 74-75; Letter to Ray Fraser, 25 August 1967, Ray Fraser Papers #51, Harriet Irving Library, University of New Brunswick, Fredericton; Letter to Rachel (Sylvia Reese) Pride, 1 September 1967, Alden Nowlan Papers #40.26.4.15, University of Calgary Library, Calgary; Letter to Bertha Shaw, 5 September 1967, Alden Nowlan Papers #40.27.51.10, University of Calgary Library, Calgary; Letter to John Drew, 2 September 1967, Alden Nowlan Papers #40.10.49.48, University of Calgary Library, Calgary.

9. Alden Nowlan, Letter to Rachel (Sylvia Reese) Pride. 1 September 1967.

10. Alden Nowlan, Letter to Ray Fraser. 25 August 1967. Ray Fraser Papers #51.

11. Anne Greer, Interview. 21 December 1997.

12. Al Purdy, "Aiming Low," *Tamarack Review* 47 (Spring 1968), p. 93.

13. Robert Cockburn, Review of *Bread, Wine and Salt*, by Alden Nowlan, *Fiddlehead* 76 (Spring 1968), pp. 73-74.

14. Alden Nowlan, Letter to Roy MacSkimming. 19 December 1967. Alden Nowlan Papers #40.6.37.68. University of Calgary Library, Calgary.

15. Roy MacSkimming, Interview. 17 December 1997.

16. Alden Nowlan, Letter to Greg Cook. n.d. Alden Nowlan Papers #40.9.10.9 University of Calgary Library, Calgary.

17. Alden Nowlan, Letter to Anne Greer. 18 November 1967. Alden Nowlan Papers #40.13.52.11. University of Calgary Library, Calgary.

18. Anne Greer, Interview.

19. Alden Nowlan. Letter to Ray Fraser. 31 October 1967. Ray Fraser Papers #53. Harriet Irving Library, University of New Brunswick.

20. Alden Nowlan, Letter to Ray Fraser. 12 January 1968. Ray Fraser Papers #54. Harriet Irving Library, University of New Brunswick.

21. Anne Greer, Interview.

22. Alden Nowlan, Letter to Anne Greer. 27 February 1968. Alden Nowlan Papers #40.13.52.25. University of Calgary Library, Calgary.

23. Alden Nowlan, Letter to Greg Cook. 16 June 1969. Alden Nowlan Papers #40.9.11.5. University of Calgary Library, Calgary.

24. Alden Nowlan, Letter to Anne Greer. 27 February 1968.

25. Alden Nowlan, Letter to Ray Fraser. 6 February 1968. Alden Nowlan Papers #40.12.23.49. University of Calgary Library, Calgary.

26. Alden Nowlan, Letter to Anne Greer. 3 April 1968. Alden Nowlan Papers #40.13.52.29. University of Calgary Library, Calgary.

27. Alden Nowlan, Letter to Ray Fraser. 3 April 1968. Alden Nowlan Papers #40.12.23.60. University of Calgary Library, Calgary.

28. Alden Nowlan, Letter to Roy MacSkimming. 3 April 1968. Alden Nowlan Papers #40.6.38.10. University of Calgary Library, Calgary.

29. Alden Nowlan, Letter to Ray Fraser. 3 April 1968.

30. Louis Cormier, Letter to Ray Fraser. 14 April 1968. Ray Fraser Papers. Harriet Irving Library, University of New Brunswick, Fredericton.

31. Eddie Clinton, Letter to Ray Fraser. 5 April 1968. Ray Fraser Papers. Harriet Irving Library, University of New Brunswick, Fredericton.

32. John Drew, Letter to Alden Nowlan. n.d [fall 1970]. Alden Nowlan Papers #40.10.49.92. University of Calgary Library, Calgary.

Chapter Eight: 1968-1971

1. Alden Nowlan, Letter to Ralph Costello. 26 August 1968. Alden Nowlan Papers #40.29.23.16. University of Calgary Library, Calgary.

2. Alden Nowlan, Letter to Rachel (Sylvia Reese) Pride. 26 August 1970. Alden Nowlan Papers #40.26.4.45. University of Calgary Library, Calgary.

3. Sir Charles G.D. Roberts, "Bliss Carman," *Dalhousie Review* 9 (1930), p. 417.

4. Alden Nowlan, "Dr. Ferrari and the Flat Earth Society," *Double Exposure* (Fredericton: Brunswick Press, 1978), p. 132.

5. Leo Ferrari, Letter to Ray Fraser. 23 September 1968. Ray Fraser Papers. Harriet Irving Library, University of New Brunswick, Fredericton.

6. Alden Nowlan, Letter to Donald Cameron. 9 April 1973. Alden Nowlan Papers #40.1.2.3. University of Calgary Library, Calgary.

7. Robert Gibbs, Letter to Elizabeth Brewster. 25 October 1968. Elizabeth Brewster Papers. National Archives of Canada, Ottawa.

8. Alden Nowlan, Review of *Death Goes Better with Coca-Cola*, by Dave Godfrey, *Canadian Forum* 47 (March 1968), p. 282.

9. Alden Nowlan, Review of *The Camera Always Lies*, by Hugh Hood, *Canadian Forum* 48 (May 1968), pp. 46-47.

10. Piquefort [Dave Godfrey], "Bullassin' Lord Brunswick-o," *Canadian Forum* 48 (September 1968), p. 143.

11. Alden Nowlan, Letter to the Editor, *Canadian Forum* (January 1969), p. 230.

12. Donald Cameron, Review of *Miracle at Indian River*, by Alden Nowlan, *Dalhousie Review* 48 (Winter 1968-69), pp. 591, 593.

13. Alden Nowlan, Letter to Ray Fraser. 25 February 1968. Ray Fraser Papers #57, Harriet Irving Library, University of New Brunswick, Fredericton.

14. Alden Nowlan, Letter to Ray Fraser. 17 March 1968. Ray Fraser Papers #58, Harriet Irving Library, University of New Brunswick, Fredericton.

15. Alden Nowlan, Letter to Ray Fraser. 11 February 1969. Alden Nowlan Papers #40.12.23.100. University of Calgary Library, Calgary.

16. Alden Nowlan, Letter to Ray Fraser. 11 February 1969.

17. Robert Bly, "For Alden Nowlan, with Admiration." Introduction to Alden Nowlan, *Playing the Jesus Game* (Trumansburg NY: Crossing Press, 1970), pp. 5-6.

18. Desmond Pacey, Letter to Canada Council. 17 January 1969. Desmond Pacey Papers. National Archives of Canada, Ottawa.

19. Alden Nowlan, Letter to Elizabeth Brewster. 27 November 1970. Alden Nowlan Papers #40.3.23.42. University of Calgary Library, Calgary.

20. Alden Nowlan, Letter to Ray Fraser. 18 March 1969. Alden Nowlan Papers #40.12.23.106. University of Calgary Library, Calgary.

21. Alden Nowlan, Letter to John Drew. 24 November 1969. Alden Nowlan Papers #40.10.49.83. University of Calgary Library, Calgary.

22. Alden Nowlan, Letter to Ray Fraser. 26 November 1969. Alden Nowlan Papers #40.12.23.132. University of Calgary Library, Calgary.

23. Alden Nowlan, Letter to Richard Hatfield. 28 November 1966. Alden Nowlan Papers #40.14.47.4. University of Calgary Library, Calgary.

24. Alden Nowlan, Letter to Elizabeth Brewster. 10 September 1970. Alden Nowlan Papers #40.3.23.37. University of Calgary Library, Calgary.

25. Alden Nowlan, Letter to Elizabeth Brewster. 20 November 1970. Alden Nowlan Papers #40.3.23.40. University of Calgary Library, Calgary.

26. Louis Cormier, Letter to Alden Nowlan. 1 September 1970. Alden Nowlan Papers #40.9.17.37. University of Calgary Library, Calgary.

27. Alden Nowlan, Letter to Louis Cormier. 22 September 1970. Alden Nowlan Papers #40.9.17.40. University of Calgary Library, Calgary.

28. Louis Cormier, Letter to Alden Nowlan. 25 September 1970. Alden Nowlan Papers #40.9.17.41. University of Calgary Library, Calgary.

29. Alden Nowlan, Letter to Louis Cormier. 29 September 1970. Alden Nowlan Papers #40.9.17.42. University of Calgary Library, Calgary.

30. Alden Nowlan, Letter to Louis Cormier. 30 October 1970. Alden Nowlan Papers #40.9.17.46. University of Calgary Library, Calgary.

31. Material for this section from Sharon Fraser, Interview, 17 December 1997; Sharon Fraser, "Remembering Alden," *Pottersfield Portfolio* 18 (Fall 1997), pp. 40-43; Alden Nowlan, Letter to Kent Thompson, 9 November 1970, Alden Nowlan Papers #40.30.7.1; and John Metcalf. Letter to Author. 30 March 1998.

32. John Metcalf, Letter to Alden Nowlan. n.d. "Monday." Alden Nowlan Papers #40.18.50.26. University of Calgary Library, Calgary.

33. Alden Nowlan, Letter to Kent Thompson. 9 November 1970.

34. Alden Nowlan, Letter to John Metcalf. 22 November 1971. Alden Nowlan Papers #40.18.50.37. University of Calgary Library, Calgary.

35. Alden Nowlan, Letter to John Metcalf. 17 December 1971. Alden Nowlan Papers #40.18.50.39. University of Calgary Library, Calgary.

36. Alden Nowlan, "The Flat Earth Society of Canada," *Atlantic Advocate* (March 1972), p. 67.

37. Alden Nowlan, Letter to Elizabeth Brewster. 27 November 1970.

38. Alden Nowlan, Letter to John Gill. 10 November 1969. Alden Nowlan Papers #40.10.2.35. University of Calgary Library, Calgary.

39. Alden Nowlan, Letter to Rachel (Sylvia Reese) Pride. 3 September 1969. Alden Nowlan Papers #40.26.4.42. University of Calgary Library, Calgary.

40. Alden Nowlan, Letter to Anne Greer. 12 October 1971. Alden Nowlan Papers #40.13.52.57. University of Calgary Library, Calgary.

41. Alden Nowlan, Draft and letter to Louis Cormier. 4 March 1971. Alden Nowlan Papers # 40.9.17.57 and #40.9.17.58. University of Calgary Library, Calgary.

42. Alden Nowlan, Letter to Ray Fraser. 14 June 1971. Alden Nowlan Papers #40.12.24.13. University of Calgary Library, Calgary.

43. Ray Fraser, Letter to Elizabeth Lill. 21 March 1974. Ray Fraser Papers. Harriet Irving Library, University of New Brunswick, Fredericton.

Chapter Nine: 1971-1974

1. Alden Nowlan, Letter to Freeman Nowlan. 9 November 1970. Alden Nowlan Papers #40.24.1.118. University of Calgary Library, Calgary.

2. Alden Nowlan, Letter to John Grube. 22 June 1971. Alden Nowlan Papers #40.14.8.19. University of Calgary Library, Calgary.

3. Alden Nowlan, Letter to Greg Cook. 16 June 1969. Alden Nowlan Papers #40.9.11.5. University of Calgary Library, Calgary.

4. Bernell MacDonald, Interview. 21 December, 1997.

5. Alden Nowlan, Letter to Greg Cook. 14 February 1972. Alden Nowlan Papers #40.9.11.45. University of Calgary Library, Calgary.

6. Alden Nowlan, "Alden Nowlan's Canada," *Maclean's* (June 1971), p. 17.

7. Alden Nowlan, Letter to Ray Fraser. 14 June 1971. Alden Nowlan Papers #40.12.24.13. University of Calgary Library, Calgary.

8. Hilda Palmer, Letter to Alden Nowlan. 31 May 1971. Alden Nowlan Papers #40.25.21.1. University of Calgary Library, Calgary.

9. Harriet (Nowlan) Ottie, Letter to Alden Nowlan. 15 August 1971. Alden Nowlan Papers #40.25.8.1. University of Calgary Library, Calgary.

10. Alden Nowlan, Letter to Freeman Nowlan. 26 January 1972. Alden Nowlan Papers #40.24.1.146. University of Calgary Library, Calgary.

11. Anne Greer, Interview. 21 December 1997.

12. Anne Greer, Interview.

13. Fred Cogswell, "Alden Nowlan as Regional Atavist," *Studies in Canadian Literature* 11.2 (1986), p. 210.

14. Alden Nowlan, "He Doesn't Agree with Walter," *Telegraph-Journal* (26 February 1972), p. 5.

15. Alden Nowlan, Letter to Rachel (Sylvia Reese) Pride. 23 March 1972. Alden Nowlan Papers #40.26.5.6. University of Calgary Library, Calgary.

16. Alden Nowlan, Letter to Greg Cook. 6 September 1972. Alden Nowlan Papers #40.9.11.49. University of Calgary Library, Calgary.

17. Alden Nowlan, Letter to Bob Gibbs. 19 September 1972. Alden Nowlan Papers #40.13.32.19. University of Calgary Library, Calgary.

18. Alden Nowlan, Letter to Ray Fraser. 10 March 1970. Alden Nowlan Papers #40.12.23.14. University of Calgary Library, Calgary. ·

19. Alden Nowlan, Letter to Jim Stewart. 16 January 1973. Alden Nowlan Papers #40.28.45.48. University of Calgary Library, Calgary.

20. Paul Milton, "*Various Persons Named Kevin O'Brien:* Nowlan's Novel Response to the Critics." *Studies in Canadian Literature* 23 (1998), pp. 36-48.

21. Janice Kulyk Keefer, *Under Eastern Eyes* (Toronto: University of Toronto Press, 1987), pp. 166-167.

22. Sam Solecki, Review of *Between Tears and Laughter*, by Alden Nowlan, *Queen's Quarterly* 80 (Summer 1973) p. 312.

23. Robert Sorfleet, Interview with Alden Nowlan, *Manna* 4 (1973), p. 42.

24. William Clarke, Interview. 19 December 1997.

25. Alden Nowlan, Letter to Louise Dennys. 13 May 1974. Alden Nowlan Papers #40.7.1.79. University of Calgary Library, Calgary.

26. Alden Nowlan, Letter to John Nowlan. 12 March 1974. Alden Nowlan Papers #40.24.3.31. University of Calgary Library, Calgary.

27. Alden Nowlan, Invitation to Rachel (Sylvia Reese) Pride. n.d. Alden Nowlan Papers #61.1.2.12. University of Calgary Library, Calgary.

28. Alden Nowlan, Letter to Rachel (Sylvia Reese) Pride. 19 October 1973. Alden Nowlan Papers #40.26.5.23. University of Calgary Library, Calgary.

29. Alden Nowlan, Letter to David Brown. 3 October 1974. Alden Nowlan Papers #40.3.31.2. University of Calgary Library, Calgary.

30. Alden Nowlan, Letter to Lynne Clare Miller. 24 October 1980. Alden Nowlan Papers #40.19.7.2. University of Calgary Library, Calgary.

31. Leo Ferrari, Letter to Ray Fraser. 12 July 1974. Ray Fraser Papers. Harriet Irving Library, University of New Brunswick, Fredericton.

32. Alden Nowlan, Letter to John Nowlan. 20 July 1974. Alden Nowlan Papers #40.24.3.46. University of Calgary Library, Calgary.

33. Rachel (Sylvia Reese) Pride, Interview. 17 December 1995.

34. Alden Nowlan, Letter to Rachel (Sylvia Reese) Pride. 21 July 1974. Alden Nowlan Papers #40.26.5.37. University of Calgary Library, Calgary.

35. Based on Alden Nowlan, Letter to Rachel (Sylvia Reese) Pride. 21 July 1974.

Chapter Ten: 1974-1977

1. John Robert Colombo, Review of *I'm a Stranger Here Myself*, by Alden Nowlan, *Tamarack Review* 66 (June 1975), p. 106.

2. Scott Lauder, "Decency of Feeling." Review of *I'm a Stranger Here Myself*, by Alden Nowlan, *Canadian Forum* 55 (April-May 1975), pp. 61-62.

3. John Metcalf, *Kicking Against the Pricks* (Downsview ON: ECW Press, 1982), p. 122.

4. John Metcalf, Interview with Alden Nowlan, *Canadian Literature* 63 (Winter 1975), p. 11.

5. Michael Brian Oliver. *Poet's Progress: The Development of Alden Nowlan's Poetry* (Fredericton: Fiddlehead Poetry Books, 1978), p. 33.

6. John Metcalf. Interview with Alden Nowlan, p. 16. Metcalf's italics.

7. See Alden Nowlan, "John Diefenbaker: Larger than Life," *Atlantic Advocate* (October 1979), p. 11.

8. See reviews of *Frankenstein* by Al Kowalen, *Performing Arts Magazine* 13 (Winter 1976), p. 52 and Edward Mullaly, *Fiddlehead* 113 (Spring 1977), pp. 150-51.

9. Alden Nowlan, Letter to John Nowlan. 15 March 1976. Alden Nowlan Papers #40.24.3.62. University of Calgary Library, Calgary.

10. Robert Weaver, Interview. 20 December 1997.

11. Alden Nowlan, Letter to Greg Cook. 9 March 1975. Alden Nowlan Papers #40.9.12.8. University of Calgary Library, Calgary.

12. John Nowlan, Letter to Alden Nowlan. 4 June 1974. Alden Nowlan Papers #40.24.3.40. University of Calgary Library, Calgary.

13. Alden Nowlan, Letter to Greg Cook. 9 March 1975. Alden Nowlan Papers #40.9.12.8. University of Calgary Library, Calgary.

14. Louis Cormier, Letter to Ray Fraser. 22 August 1977. Ray Fraser Papers. Harriet Irving Library, University of New Brunswick, Fredericton.

15. Ray Fraser, Letter to Louis Cormier. 25 August 1977. Ray Fraser Papers. Harriet Irving Library, University of New Brunswick, Fredericton.

16. Leo Ferrari, Letter to Ray Fraser. 22 January 1974. Ray Fraser Papers. Harriet Irving Library, University of New Brunswick, Fredericton.

17. Brian Bartlett, Diary notes. Author's collection.

18. Barry Cameron, Interview. July 18, 1998.

19. Alden Nowlan, Letter to John Nowlan. 11 January 1976. Alden Nowlan Papers #40.24.3.63. University of Calgary Library, Calgary.

20. Alden Nowlan, Letter to Ray Fraser. 6 February 1976. Alden Nowlan Papers #40.12.24.95. University of Calgary Library, Calgary.

21. Ray Fraser, Letter to Alden Nowlan. 19 February 1976. Alden Nowlan Papers #40.12.24.96. University of Calgary Library, Calgary.

22. Alden Nowlan, Letter to Ray Fraser. 6 February 1976.

23. Ray Fraser, Letter to Alden Nowlan. 19 February 1976. Alden Nowlan Papers #40.12.24.96. University of Calgary Library, Calgary.

24. Alden Nowlan, Letter to Ray Fraser. 25 June 1975. Alden Nowlan Papers #40.12.24.82. University of Calgary Archives, Calgary.

25. Alden Nowlan, Letter to Ray Fraser. 6 February 1976.

26. Alden Nowlan, Letter to John Nowlan. 15 March 1975. Alden Nowlan Papers #40.24.3.62. University of Calgary Library, Calgary.

27. Alden Nowlan, "A Hard Day's Night with Ryan's Fancy," *Double Exposure* (Fredericton: Brunswick Press, 1978), p. 146.

28. Alden Nowlan, "Something to Write About," *Canadian Literature* 68-69 (1976), pp. 10-11.

29. Alden Nowlan, Letter to Ray Fraser. 30 September 1976. Alden Nowlan Papers #40.12.24.108. University of Calgary Library, Calgary.

30. Alden Nowlan, Letter to Tom Dolan. 24 February 1981. Alden Nowlan Papers #40.12.6.138. University of Calgary Library, Calgary.

31. Alden Nowlan, Letter to Bill Clarke. 6 June 1975. Alden Nowlan Papers #40.7.2.13. University of Calgary Library, Calgary.

32. John Drew, "Eastern Exposure," Review of *Smoked Glass*, by Alden Nowlan. *Canadian Forum* 57 (March 1978), pp. 30-40.

33. Michael Brian Oliver, p. 41.

34. Ray Fraser, Interview. 19 September, 1999.

35. Alden Nowlan, Letter to League of Canadian Poets. 8 April 1978. Alden Nowlan Papers #40.16.26.13. University of Calgary Library, Calgary.

36. Ray Fraser, Letter to Louis Cormier. 10 April 1978. Ray Fraser Papers, Harriet Irving Library, University of New Brunswick, Fredericton.

37. Alden Nowlan, Diary entry. 29 October 1977. Alden Nowlan Papers #40.112.8f26. University of Calgary Library, Calgary.

Chapter 11: 1977-1983

1. Alden Nowlan, Letter to Barbara Cooper. 27 September 1979. Alden Nowlan Papers #40.21.5.91. University of Calgary Library, Calgary.

2. Alden Nowlan, Letter to Richard Rand Cooper. 11 September 1978. Alden Nowlan Papers #40.21.2.39. University of Calgary Library, Calgary.

3. Alden Nowlan, Letter to Glenn Murray. 15 January 1971. Alden Nowlan Papers #40.21.3.44. University of Calgary Library, Calgary.

4. Alden Nowlan, Diary entry. 7 July 1972. Alden Nowlan Papers #40.113.1f50. University of Calgary Library, Calgary.

5. Anonymous, Letter to Alden Nowlan. n.d. Alden Nowlan Papers #40.21.5.10. University of Calgary Library, Calgary.

6. Alden Nowlan, Letter to Marie Bragdon Atherton. 29 June 1973. Alden Nowlan Papers #40.21.5.32. University of Calgary Library, Calgary.

7. TNB Production Sold Out Tonight," *Daily Gleaner* (14 January 1978), p. 2.

8. Alden Nowlan, Letter to David Brown. 7 January 1978 [1979]. Alden Nowlan Papers #40.3.31.7. University of Calgary Library, Calgary.

9. Alden Nowlan, Letter to Al Pittman. 18 October 1981. Alden Nowlan Papers #40.25.48.44. University of Calgary Library, Calgary.

10. Ray Fraser, Interview. 19 September 1999.

11. Alden Nowlan, Letter to John Nowlan. 1 May 1979. Alden Nowlan Papers #40.24.3.83. University of Calgary Library, Calgary.

12. Alden Nowlan, Letter to Robert Cockburn. 4 June 1980. Alden Nowlan Papers #40.31.6.66. University of Calgary Library, Calgary.

13. Alden Nowlan, Letter to Robert Cockburn. 11 July 1981. Alden Nowlan Papers #40.31.6.72. University of Calgary Library, Calgary.

14. Alden Nowlan. "Battle of the Blueberries: It's Grunt against Cobbler," *Atlantic Insight* (August 1980), p. 61.

15. Description of Cuba trip from Alden Nowlan, "Cuba Is a Great Place to Visit." *Atlantic Insight* (November 1979), pp. 36-38, and from a series of articles in the *Telegraph-Journal* (28 April-7 May 1979).

16. Alden Nowlan, Letter to David Brown. 7 January 1978. Alden Nowlan Papers #40.3.31.7. University of Calgary Library, Calgary.

17. Alden Nowlan, Letter to John Nowlan. 7 September 1980. Alden Nowlan Papers #40.24.3.102. University of Calgary Library, Calgary.

18. Alden Nowlan, Letter to Walter Learning. 26 November 1981. Alden Nowlan Papers #40.17.2.52. University of Calgary Library, Calgary.

19. Alden Nowlan, Letter to Greg Cook. 22 February 1979. Alden Nowlan Papers #40.9.12.43. University of Calgary Library, Calgary.

20. Alden Nowlan, Letter to Ken Miller. 30 March 1980. Alden Nowlan Papers #40.19.6.8. University of Calgary Library, Calgary.

21. Alden Nowlan, Letter to Ken Miller. 17 April 1980. Alden Nowlan Papers #40.19.6.10. University of Calgary Library, Calgary.

22. Anne Munton, "Going Up and Down the Road: Maritime Poetry Today," *Fiddlehead* 136 (June 1983), p. 89.

23. Anne Morton, Review of *I Might Not Tell Everybody This*, by Alden Nowlan, *Quarry* 31 (Autumn 1982), p. 72.

24. Patrick O'Flaherty, "Rag-and-Bone Shop," *Canadian Forum* 62 (June/ July 1982), p. 37.

25. Alden Nowlan, Letter to Nicholas Catanoy. 17 August 1982. Alden Nowlan Papers #40.6.9.69. University of Calgary Library, Calgary.

26. Alden Nowlan, Letter to John Nowlan. 10 January 1982. Alden Nowlan Papers #40.24.3.113. University of Calgary Library, Calgary.

27. Alden Nowlan, "Belfast: Friendliness Amid the Barbed Wire," *Telegraph-Journal* (6 September 1982), p. 5.

28. Alden Nowlan, "Oh, How Dublin Has Changed!" *Telegraph-Journal* (8 September 1982), p. 7.

29. Alden Nowlan, "Nowlan in Ireland: A Poet's Progress," *Atlantic Insight* (October 1982), p.17.

30. Alden Nowlan, Letter to Rachel (Sylvia Reese) Pride. 5 May 1983. Alden Nowlan Papers #40.26.5.80. University of Calgary Library, Calgary.

31. Alden Nowlan, Letter to Robert Cockburn. 9 June 1983. Alden Nowlan Papers #40.31.6.88. University of Calgary Library, Calgary.

32. Alden Nowlan, "Requiem For a Book Publisher," *Telegraph-Journal* (4 June 1983), p. 9.

33. Alden Nowlan, "Mulroney May Be the Unknown PM, *Telegraph-Journal* (11 June 1983), p. 11.

34. Al Pittman, Interview. 28 November 1999.

35. David Adams Richards, "*Lockhartville* and Kevin O'Brien." *A Lad from Brantford and Other Essays* (Fredericton: Broken Jaw, 1994), p. 42.

36. Michael Brian Oliver, *Canadian Writers and Their Works: Alden Nowlan* (Toronto: ECW Press, 1990), p. 95.

BIBLIOGRAPHY

Books and chapbooks by Alden Nowlan

Between Tears and Laughter. Toronto: Clarke, Irwin, 1967.

Bread, Wine and Salt. Toronto: Clarke, Irwin, 1967.

A Darkness in the Earth. Eureka, California: Hearse, 1959.

Double Exposure. Fredericton: Brunswick, 1978.

Early Poems. Fredericton: Fiddlehead, 1983.

An Exchange of Gifts. Ed. Robert Gibbs. Toronto: Irwin, 1985.

Frankenstein. With Walter Learning. Toronto: Clarke, Irwin, 1976.

Gardens of the Wind. Saskatoon: Thistledown, 1982.

I Might Not Tell Everybody This. Toronto: Clarke, Irwin, 1982.

I'm a Stranger Here Myself. Toronto: Clarke, Irwin, 1974.

Miracle at Indian River. Toronto: Clarke, Irwin, 1968.

The Mysterious Naked Man. Toronto: Clarke, Irwin, 1969.

Playing the Jesus Game. Trumansburg, NY: New Books, 1970.

The Rose and the Puritan. Fredericton: Fiddlehead, 1958.

Smoked Glass. Toronto: Clarke Irwin, 1977.

The Things Which Are. Toronto: Contact, 1962.

Under the Ice. Toronto: Ryerson, 1961.

Various Persons Named Kevin O'Brien. Toronto: Clarke, Irwin, 1973.

The Wanton Troopers. Fredericton: Goose Lane, 1988.

Wind in a Rocky Country. Toronto: Emblem Books, 1960.

Will Ye Let the Mummers In? Toronto: Irwin, 1984.

Other works by Alden Nowlan consulted for this book

"Alden Nowlan's Canada." *Maclean's* (June 1971), pp. 17, 40.

"Alden Nowlan: Autobiographical Sketch." *Yes* 16 (October 1967), p. 19.

Atlantic Advocate. Monthly column. September 1970 - June 1983.

"Battle of the Blueberries: It's Grunt Against Cobbler." *Atlantic Insight* (August 1980), p. 61.

"Cuba Is a Great Place to Visit." *Atlantic Insight* (November 1979), pp. 36-38.

"A Defense of Obscenity," *Delta* 8 (Fall 1959), pp. 27-28.

"Ginsberg: Truth Is a Five-Letter Word." *Telegraph-Journal* (27 March 1967), p. 5.

"Hatfield Country." *Maclean's* (November 1971), pp. 40-42, 76-80.

"I Discovered a Mountain." *Family Herald* (28 July 1955), pp. 24-25.

"The Lodges: Down But Not Out, and Far from Forgotten." *Atlantic Insight* (November 1980), pp. 55-57.

"The New Brunswick Papers: What About the Irvings?" *Canadian Newspapers: The Inside Story*. Ed. Walter Stewart. Edmonton: Hurtig, 1980, pp. 63-72.

"Nowlan in Ireland: A Poet's Progress." *Atlantic Insight* (October 1982), pp. 16-19.

Review of *The Camera Always Lies,* by Hugh Hood. *Canadian Forum* 48 (May 1968), pp. 46-47.

Review of *Death Goes Better with Coca-Cola,* by Dave Godfrey. *Canadian Forum* 47 (March 1968), p. 282.

"Something to Write About." *Canadian Literature* 68-69 (1976), pp. 7-12.

Telegraph-Journal. Weekly column. September 1968 - June 1983.

Major repositories of documents related to Alden Nowlan

Alden Nowlan Papers. University of Calgary Library, Calgary.

Alden Nowlan Papers. Harriet Irving Library, University of New Brunswick, Fredericton.

Fiddlehead Papers. Harriet Irving Library, University of New Brunswick, Fredericton.

Ray Fraser Papers. Harriet Irving Library, University of New Brunswick, Fredericton.

Other works consulted for this book

Acorn, Milton. "Sealed with a Kiss and a Tear." *Cross-Canada Writers' Quarterly* 7.2 (1985), p. 17.

Adachi, Ken. "Poet's Work Aimed at Ordinary People." *Toronto Star* (28 June 1983), p. C1.

Bly, Robert. "For Alden Nowlan, with Admiration." Introduction to *Playing the Jesus Game,* by Alden Nowlan. Trumansburg NY: Crossing, 1970.

Bruce, Harry. "Alden Nowlan: January 25, 1933 + June 27, 1983." *Atlantic Insight* (August 1983), p. 17.

Cameron, Donald. "The Poet from Desolation Creek." *Saturday Night* (May 1973), pp. 28-31.

———. Review of *Miracle at Indian River,* by Alden Nowlan. *Dalhousie Review* 48 (Winter 1968-69), pp. 591, 593.

Cockburn, Robert. Review of *Bread, Wine and Salt*, by Alden Nowlan. *Fiddlehead* 75 (Spring 1968), pp. 74-76.

Cogswell, Fred. "Alden Nowlan as Regional Atavist." *Studies in Canadian Literature* 11 (1986), pp. 206-225.

Colombo, John Robert. Review of *I'm a Stranger Here Myself*, by Alden Nowlan, *Tamarack Review* 66 (June 1975), p. 106.

———. "Wit, Wisdom and Two Chapbooks," *Waterloo Review* 2 (Winter 1960), pp. 78-81.

Cook, Greg. "Alden Nowlan: Something Rare and Beautiful." *New Brunswick Reader* (29 April 1995), pp. 9-12.

———. Interview with Alden Nowlan. *Amethyst* 2 (Summer 1963), pp. 16-25.

———. "One Heart, One Way: A Life of Alden Nowlan in Progress." *Nashwaak Review* 2 (Fall 1996), pp. 173-179.

———. "The Wine of Astonishment." *New Brunswick Reader* (27 June 1998), pp. 5-8.

Cormier, Louis. "Unstuck." *Pottersfield Portfolio* 18 (Fall 1997), pp. 36-39.

Cormier, Michel, and Achille Michaud. *Richard Hatfield: Power and Disobedience*. trans. Daphne Ponder. Fredericton: Goose Lane, 1997.

Costello, Ralph. "Alden Nowlan's Love-in: They Called It a Funeral." *Telegraph-Journal* (2 July 1983), p. 8.

Davies, Gwendolyn. *Studies in Maritime Literary History, 1760-1930*. Fredericton: Acadiensis, 1991.

Donnell, David. Interview with Alden Nowlan. *Books in Canada* 11 (June/July 1982), pp. 26-28.

Donovan, Stewart. "Surviving Shared Worlds: The Parish and the Province: Alden Nowlan and Patrick Kavanagh." *Down East: Critical Essays on Contemporary Maritime Canadian Literature*. Stuttgart: Wissenschaftlicher Verlag Trier, 1996. pp. 197-208.

Doyle, Arthur T. *Front Benches and Back Rooms: A Story of Political Intrigue and Corruption in New Brunswick*. 2nd ed. Fredericton: Omega.

Drew, John. "Eastern Exposure." *Canadian Forum* 57 (March 1978), pp. 39-40.

Ferrari, Leo. "King of Windsor Castle." *New Brunswick Reader* (11 September 1999), pp. 7-11.

Fetherling, Douglas. "A Work in Progress: Remembering Alden Nowlan." *New Brunswick Reader* (17 February 1996), p. 22.

Fraser, Raymond. "Royally Wronged." *Weekend* (17 January 1976), pp. 8-10.

———. "Words," *Pottersfield Portfolio* 18 (Fall 1997), pp. 31-35.

Fraser, Sharon. "Remembering Alden." *Pottersfield Portfolio* 18 (Fall 1997), pp. 40-43.

Gibbs, Robert. Introduction. *An Exchange of Gifts* by Alden Nowlan. Ed. Robert Gibbs. Toronto: Irwin, 1985.

———. "Various Persons Named Alden Nowlan." Introduction. *The Alden Nowlan Papers*. Ed. Apollonia Steele and Jean F. Tener. Calgary: University of Calgary, 1992.

Godfrey, Dave "[Piquefort]." "Bullassin' Lord Brunswick-o." *Canadian Forum* 48 (September 1968), p. 143.

Greer, Anne. *Alienation and Affirmation in the Work of Alden Nowlan*. Diss. Acadia University, 1973.

Hockbruck, Wolfgang. "Centre and Margin: Literature from the Maritimes." *Down East: Critical Essays on Contemporary Maritime Canadian Literature*. Stuttgart: Wissenschaftlicher Verlag Trier, 1996. pp. 9-22.

Hornyansky, Michael. Review of *The Rose and the Puritan*, by Alden Nowlan. *Fiddlehead* 39 (Winter 1959), pp. 43-47.

Ives, Edward D. "Alden Nowlan's Poetry: A Personal Chronicle." *Fiddlehead* 81 (Fall 1969), pp. 61-66.

Keefer, Janice Kulyk. *Under Eastern Eyes: A Critical Reading of Maritime Fiction*. Toronto: University of Toronto, 1987.

Kowalen, Al. Review of *Frankenstein*, by Alden Nowlan and Walter Learning. *Performing Arts Magazine* 13 (Winter 1976), p. 52.

Lauder, Scott. "Decency of Feeling." *Canadian Forum* 55 (April-May 1975), pp. 61-62.

Layton, Irving. "In Memoriam: Alden Nowlan , 1933-1983." *Poetry Canada Review* 5 (Fall 1983), p. 3.

Learning, Walter. "Learning on Nowlan: Final Tribute to a Giant." *UNB Perspectives* (September 1983), p. 5.

Lee, Philip. "'I'll Still Be the Same Old Alden Nowlan.'" *New Brunswick Reader* (21 December 1996), pp. 3-4.

Lemm, Richard. *Milton Acorn: In Love and Anger*. Ottawa: Carleton University, 1999.

Lochhead, Douglas. Review of *Under the Ice*, by Alden Nowlan. *Dalhousie Review* 41 (Autumn 1961), pp. 431, 433.

Lucas, Alec. Review of *Under the Ice*, by Alden Nowlan. *Fiddlehead* 51 (Winter 1962), pp. 59-62.

MacDonald, A.H. *Mount Hope Then and Now*. Halifax: Nova Scotia Hospital, 1996.

Mandel, Eli. "In Memoriam: Alden Nowlan, 1933-1983." *Poetry Canada Review* 5 (Fall 1983), p. 3.

———. "Turning New Leaves." *Canadian Forum* (July 1961), pp. 90-91.

———. "Turning New Leaves." *Canadian Forum* (March 1963), pp. 278-80.

Metcalf, John. Interview with Alden Nowlan. *Canadian Literature* 63 (Winter 1975), pp. 8-17.

———. *Kicking Against the Pricks*. Downsview, ON: ECW, 1982.

Milton, Paul. "*Various Persons Named Kevin O'Brien*: Nowlan's Novel Response to the Critics," *Studies in Canadian Literature* 23 (1998), pp. 36-38.

Morton, Anne. Review of *I Might Not Tell Everybody This*, by Alden Nowlan. *Quarry* 31 (Autumn 1982), pp. 72-75.

Mullaly, Edward. Review of *Frankenstein*, by Alden Nowlan and Walter Learning. *Fiddlehead* 113 (Spring 1977), pp. 150-51.

Munton, Ann. "Going Up and Down the Road: Maritime Poetry Today." *Fiddlehead* 136 (June 1983), pp. 81-90.

O'Flaherty, Patrick. "Rag-and-Bone Shop." *Canadian Forum* 62 (June/July 1982), p. 37.

Oliver, Michael Brian. "Alden Nowlan (1933-1983)." *Canadian Writers and Their Works*. Vol. 7 Poetry Series. Eds. Lecker, David and Quigley. Toronto: ECW, 1990, pp. 76-132.

———. *Poet's Progress: The Development of Alden Nowlan's Poetry*. Fredericton: Fiddlehead, 1978.

Pacey, Desmond. *Creative Writing in Canada*. Toronto: Ryerson, 1961.

Purdy, Al. "Aiming Low." *Tamarack Review* 47 (Spring 1968), pp. 81-97.

———. *Reaching for the Beaufort Sea: An Autobiography*. Madiera Park, BC: Harbour, 1993.

Reid, Mark. "Monarch and the Media." *Telegraph-Journal* (29 August 1998), pp. 1, 10.

Richards, David Adams. "Letter to a Young Maritime Writer." *New Brunswick Reader* (10 July 1999), pp. 6-8.

———. "Lockhartville and Kevin O'Brien." *A Lad from Brantford and Other Essays*. Fredericton: Broken Jaw, 1994, pp. 36-42.

———. "Nowlan." *New Brunswick Reader* (27 June 1998), p. 14.

Roberts, Sir Charles G.D. "Bliss Carman." *Dalhousie Review* 9 (1930), p. 417.

Scott, Virginia. "'Down Shore': Alden Nowlan's Poetry of the Late Sixties." *American Review of Canadian Studies* (Spring 1992), pp. 23-38.

Sherman, Joseph. "Remembering the Big Nowlan." *The Buzz: Arts & Entertainment on PEI.* (June 1998).

Solecki, Sam. Review of *Between Tears and Laughter*, by Alden Nowlan. *Queen's Quarterly* 80 (Summer 1973), pp. 311-313.

Sorfleet, Robert. Interview with Alden Nowlan. *Manna* 4 (1973), pp. 39-49.

Sullivan, Rosemary. *Shadowmaker: The Life of Gwendolyn MacEwan*, Toronto: HarperCollins, 1995.

Sutherland, Fraser. "Nowlan Meant Integrity to a Generation of Writers." *Globe and Mail* (28 June 1983), p. 19.

Tunney, Mark. "The Night Editor." *New Brunswick Reader* (27 June 1998), pp. 3-4.

Tyrwhitt, Janice. "The Man from Desolation Creek." *Reader's Digest* 124 (March 1984), pp. 67-71.

Waddington, Miriam. "Japanese Flowers, Autumn Vistas." *Canadian Literature* 9 (Summer 1961), pp. 70-72.

Whitelaw, Marjory. "In Fredericton, Poetry Is a Major Industry." *Saturday Night* (February 1971), pp. 21-24.

Whiten, Clifton. "In Memoriam: Alden Nowlan — 1933-1983." *Poetry Canada Review* 5 (Fall 1983), p. 3.

Wilson, Milton. "Letters in Canada: 1961: Poetry." *University of Toronto Quarterly* 31 (1962), pp. 432-454.

———. "Letters in Canada: 1962: Poetry." *University of Toronto Quarterly* 32 (July 1963), p. 377.

INDEX

Patrick Toner, a graduate of St. Thomas University and Carleton University, is a teacher and administrator in the English as a Second Language program at the University of New Brunswick, Saint John. *If I Could Turn and Meet Myself* is the first full-length study of Alden Nowlan's life. Toner has used published materials, the Nowlan letters and papers at the University of Calgary, interviews with Nowlan's family (some of whom have never before been approachable), and conversations with a legion of Nowlan's friends and acquaintances to probe the life of this unusual man with understanding, insight, and Nowlan's own love of a good story.